Beginner's Guide to Visual Basic .NET Programming

A practical approach to VB.NET

Serhan Yamacli

Manchester Academic
Publications

Beginner's Guide to Visual Basic.NET Programming – First Edition

© 2019 Serhan Yamacli. All rights reserved.

This book is provided for personal use. Reproduction/distribution in any form is prohibited.

This book is provided for informational purposes only. Author and the publisher do not offer any expressed or implied warranty about the accuracy of information contained in this book. Author and the publisher do not accept any liability for any loss or damage caused from the usage of the information given in this book.

The names of the trademarked/copyrighted software and hardware in this book are for editorial purposes only and to the benefit of the respective trademark/copyright owners. The terms used in this book are not intended as infringement of the trademarks and copyrights.

All product and company names mentioned in this book are trademarks (™) or registered trademarks (®) of their respective holders. Use of them does not imply any affiliation with or endorsement by them. All company, product and service names used in this book are for identification purposes only.

This book is an independent publication and is neither affiliated with, nor authorized, sponsored, or approved by Microsoft Corporation.

Visual Basic, Visual Studio, SQL Server and Access are trademarks of Microsoft Corporation.

This book is dedicated to beginner programmers...

Table of Contents

1. INTRODUCTION 11
2. SETTING UP YOUR DEVELOPMENT ENVIRONMENT 17
   - 2.1. Downloading and Installing Visual Studio 18
   - 2.2. General Options of Visual Studio 21
   - 2.3. Main Panes and Menus of the IDE 22
3. TEST DRIVE: THE HELLO WORLD PROJECT 25
   - 3.1. Creating a New Project 25
   - 3.2. Default Panes of Visual Studio 28
   - 3.3. Files Included in the Project 31
   - 3.4. Adding a Label Control on the Form 32
   - 3.5. Setting Label's Properties 34
   - 3.6. Aligning the Label 36
   - 3.7. Building the Project 38
4. FORM (GUI) ELEMENTS 43
   - 4.1. Form Controls at a Glance 44
   - 4.2. Containers and Menus 46
   - 4.3. Dialogs 48
   - 4.4. Components 49
   - 4.5. Properties of Controls 49
   - 4.6. Events of Controls 55
5. COMMON CONTROLS 59
   - 5.1. Button 59
   - 5.2. CheckBox 63
   - 5.3. CheckedListBox 66
   - 5.4. ComboBox 71
   - 5.5. DateTimePicker 74

5

    5.6. Label 78

    5.7. LinkLabel 80

    5.8. ListBox 82

    5.9. ListView 88

    5.10. MaskedTextBox 92

    5.11. MonthCalendar 96

    5.12. NotifyIcon 99

    5.13. NumericUpDown 105

    5.14. PictureBox 108

    5.15. ProgressBar 113

    5.16. RadioButton 116

    5.17. RichTextBox 119

    5.18. TextBox 121

    5.19. ToolTip 124

    5.20. TreeView 126

    5.21. WebBrowser 131

6. MENUS, DIALOGS AND CONTAINERS 137

    6.1. Menu Type Controls 137

        6.1.1. MenuStrip 137

        6.1.2. ContextMenuStrip 141

        6.1.3. StatusStrip 146

        6.1.4. ToolStrip 148

        6.1.5. ToolStripContainer 150

    6.2. Dialog Type Controls 152

        6.2.1. ColorDialog 152

        6.2.2. Font Dialog 156

        6.2.3. FolderBrowserDialog 158

  6.2.4. OpenFileDialog 162
  6.2.5. SaveFileDialog 167
 6.3. Containers 171
  6.3.1. Panel 171
  6.3.2. GroupBox 174
  6.3.3. TabControl 175
  6.3.4. TableLayoutPanel 180
  6.3.5. SplitContainer 184
  6.3.6. FlowLayoutPanel 187
7. VARIABLES AND CONSTANTS 193
 7.1. Variables 193
  7.1.1. Declaring Variables 193
  7.1.2. Rules about Variable Naming 195
  7.1.3. Variable Types 196
  7.1.4. General Type Conversions 201
  7.1.5. String Conversions 203
 7.2. Constants 208
8. CONDITIONAL STATEMENTS 213
 8.1. Operators 213
  8.1.1. Comparison Operators 213
  8.1.2. Arithmetic Operators 218
  8.1.3. Practical Operators 223
 8.2. If-Else Statement Types 228
  8.2.1. The If Statement 228
  8.2.2. The If-Else Statement 232
  8.2.3. The If-ElseIf-Else Statement 234
 8.3. The Select-Case Statement 237

9. LOOPS 241
9.1. The For-Next Loop 241
9.2. The For Each-Next Loop 244
9.3. The While-End Loop 248
9.4. The Do-Loop Structure 252
9.5. Continue and Exit Keywords 255

10. ARRAYS AND COLLECTIONS 261
10.1. Arrays 261
10.1.1. Declaring Arrays 261
10.1.2. Multidimensional Arrays 266
10.1.3. Array Operations 269
10.2. Collections 275
10.2.1. Hashtable 276
10.2.2. ArrayList 278

11. METHODS 285
11.1. Declaration of Sub Procedures and Functions 285
11.2. Accessibility Modifiers 286
11.3. Function Example 286
11.4. Sub Procedure Example 291
11.5. Passing Parameters to Methods 294
11.5.1. Call by Value 294
11.5.2. Call by Reference 297
11.6. Passing Arrays to Methods 299

12. CLASSES AND OBJECTS 305
12.1. General Information and Template 305
12.2. Declaring Classes in the Same File 306
12.3. Declaring Classes in a New File 311

12.4. Constructor Methods 317
12.5. Property Structures 322
13. FREQUENTLY USED CLASSES IN VB.NET 331
13.1. The String Class 331
13.2. The StringBuilder Class.. 338
13.3. The Math Class... 343
14. HANDLING ERRORS 351
14.1. The Try-Catch Structure... 351
14.2. The Try-Catch-Finally Structure 355
14.3. The Throw Keyword 356
15. DATABASE CONNECTIONS USING ADO.NET 361
15.1. Creating an Access Database.. 362
15.2. Reading Database Entries from our VB.NET Program........... 369
15.3. Adding/Updating/Deleting Database Entries from our VB.NET Program 376
16. DEVELOPING A CAR RACING GAME IN VISUAL BASIC.NET 397
16.1. Creating the Game Project and Preliminary Works 397
16.2. Adding Cars to the Game 405
16.3. Displaying Score 411
16.4. Detecting Collosions and Ending the Game........................... 412
EPILOGUE.. 418
REFERENCES 419

Chapter 1

INTRODUCTION

Welcome to your guide to Visual Basic .NET programming.

This book aims to teach Visual Basic .NET programming in Visual Studio environment. You don't need to have programming experience to learn the concepts and projects presented in this book. I'll assume that you have no knowledge on programming and graphical user interface design. I'll try to explain every bit of Visual Basic .NET programming with plain words and will try to make things easy to get for you. This book will take you as a beginner and at the end of the book; you'll be able to create your very own desktop applications that are ready to run. By the way, I'd like to remind you that a single book cannot make you an expert on a subject. However, this book will teach you a lot and you'll have a solid background to learn more afterwards.

Visual Basic .NET is extensively utilized to create software ranging from desktop applications to dynamic web sites. Visual Basic .NET incorporates various advantages of different programming languages. Since the strong programming structure of Visual Basic .NET and .NET Framework is combined by visual programming in the Visual Studio environment, you can create visually elegant and functional applications easily.

Visual Basic.NET is closely related to a concept called ".NET Framework". .NET Framework is a platform on which various application types can be developed such as desktop applications, mobile apps or dynamic web sites. Let's overview the .NET concept:

In a computer, an operating system such as Windows manages system resources and hardware. Applications running on the computer communicate with the operating system and access the resources of the computer as the operating system directs. In .NET based applications (such as applications written in Visual Basic .NET), .NET Framework provides a communication layer between the application and the operating system. Applications can use hardware and software resources by the help of .NET Framework. .NET Framework also includes an extensive library which makes our lives easier for developing Visual Basic .NET applications. The programs which run on top of .NET framework are also called as "managed applications". In managed applications, the memory management is performed by .NET framework hence the programmer does not need to deal with the memory allocation manually.

.NET Framework is automatically installed in Windows therefore it is ready to be used.

Another term you may hear frequently regarding the .NET Framework is the CLR. It means **C**ommon **L**anguage **R**untime. It is a part of the .NET Framework which is responsible for managing runtime tasks such as memory allocation and error handling.

Apart from CLR, .NET Framework also has two other main components called CLS and CTS. CLS is an acronym for **C**ommon **L**anguage **S**pecification and CTS means **C**ommon **T**ype **S**ystem. CLS is a bunch of rules that enables various applications developed in different languages to be able to run on the same .NET platform. Similarly, CTS enables the compatibility of variable types of different languages which are based on the .NET Framework. The relation of these concepts is shown in Figure 1.1.

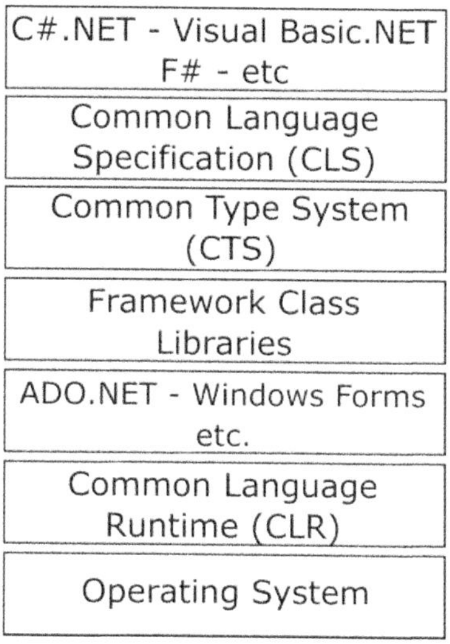

CHAPTER 1. INTRODUCTION

C#.NET - Visual Basic.NET F# - etc
Common Language Specification (CLS)
Common Type System (CTS)
Framework Class Libraries
ADO.NET - Windows Forms etc.
Common Language Runtime (CLR)
Operating System

Figure 1.1. Various software layers used in .NET applications

As we have stated before, .NET Framework also includes loads of libraries. A software library is a group of ready-made code. For example, there is class library called Math which contains functions for performing mathematical operations. The Math library has hundreds of mathematical functions. When we need to perform the operation 2^x in our program, we don't need to develop and implement an algoritm for this. We can just use the following code:

```
Math.Pow(2, x)
```
Code 1.1

By this code, we tell that we want to use the Pow (power) function of the Math library. And we want to perform the operation Pow(2, x) which means 2^x.

After a Visual Basic .NET program code is written, it should be compiled before running. In .NET platform, when a Visual Basic .NET code is compiled, it is converted to a format called Microsoft Intermediate Language (IL). An executable file (machine code) is then generated from this file and executed by CLR. This process is summarized in Figure 1.2.

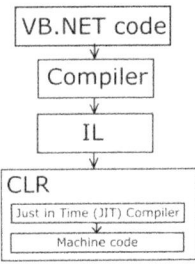

Figure 1.2. Compilation of a Visual Basic .NET source code to executable machine code

Fortunately, Visual Studio does all the compilation process automatically. After designing the visual interface of our program and writing the associated Visual Basic .NET code in our project, we compile and build it with a single click and then viola! Visual Studio generates an executable file (a file with .exe extension). When we double click the exe file, it runs as usual.

In this book, I'll teach Visual Basic.NET language completely from a visual point of view. In other words, you'll learn both the design of Windows forms (the visual part of desktop applications) and writing the associated Visual Basic.NET code at the same time. Therefore, you'll be ready for developing complete desktop applications after you finish this book.

The outline of this book is as follows: Firstly, I'll explain the steps required for installing Visual studio – the development environment used for developing Visual Basic.NET applications. Then, I'll show the usage of common Windows form controls: progress bars, buttons, file menus, etc. that we frequently use in everyday desktop applications. In the following chapters, you'll learn Visual Basic.NET coding concepts such as variables, conditional statements, loops, methods and classes. I'll show a lot of program examples in each of these subjects so that you'll establish a solid Visual Basic.NET programming background. Then, you'll learn how you can connect your applications to Access databases for permanent data storage, again with several program examples. Finally, we'll develop a simple game in Visual Basic.NET where we'll use various programming concepts together.

I'll not introduce complicated subjects until I'm sure that you understand the basics because it is very easy to get lost while learning a new programming language. You'll not be in such a situation with this book. I'll try to teach new concepts in the simplest way possible. Please don't forget that learning a programming language is a non-stop process, it never ends and this book will help you get started easily.

Now, you know the aims and the method of this book. We will continue with installation of Visual Studio integrated development environment on our PC in the following chapter.

Note 1: We will abbreviate Visual Basic .NET as **VB.NET** in this book.

Note 2: You can download complete project files and colour figures contained in this book from the book's website at www.yamaclis.com/vbnet.

Chapter 2

SETTING UP YOUR DEVELOPMENT ENVIRONMENT

In this chapter, we'll set up the development environment: Visual Studio.

Visual Studio is an integrated development environment (IDE), meaning that it has all the components to develop applications from start to finish. Visual Studio supports several programming languages including VB.NET, C# and C++, which means that we can utilize Visual Studio to develop applications by writing code in one of these languages. Furthermore, Visual Studio is not only used for developing desktop applications but also for building mobile apps and dynamic websites.

The latest version of Visual Studio is Visual Studio 2019. There are several versions of Visual Studio including **Visual Studio Community, Visual Studio Professional, Visual Studio Enterprise and Visual Studio Code.**

Visual Studio Community is the free and fully-featured IDE for students and individual developers whereas Visual Studio Professional includes the professional development tools and services which is suitable for small software development teams. On the other hand, Visual Studio Enterprise is generally used by development teams of all sizes. In addition to these visual IDEs, there is another version called Visual Studio Code, a free code editing environment which runs on several operating systems. Among these versions, the Visual Studio Community edition is the one we need for starting our VB.NET programming journey since it's free and suitable for individuals. Let's see how we'll download and install it.

2.1. Downloading and Installing Visual Studio

Please navigate to https://visualstudio.microsoft.com/ in your web browser. You'll see the download page shown in Figure 2.1.

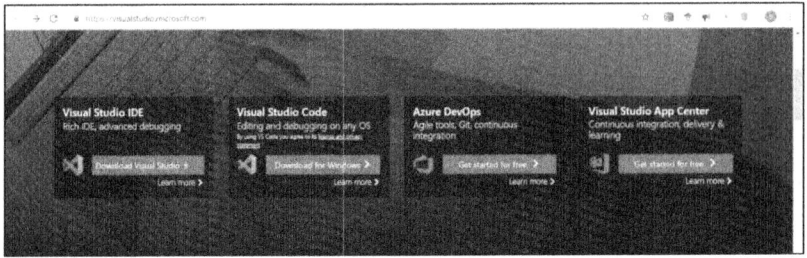

Figure 2.1. Visual Studio download options

Click on the **Download Visual Studio** button of the Visual Studio IDE section and then select **Community 2019** from the drop down menu. This will initiate the download of the online installer having the size of a few megabytes. Double click on the downloaded file and then you'll get the following message:

Figure 2.2. Visual Studio installation – first message

Please click Continue in this message if you agree to the terms so that the installer will start preparing the installation:

Figure 2.3. Visual Studio installation – second message

CHAPTER 2. SETTING UP YOUR DEVELOPMENT ENVIRONMENT

Visual Studio installation options window will appear in a few minutes as follows:

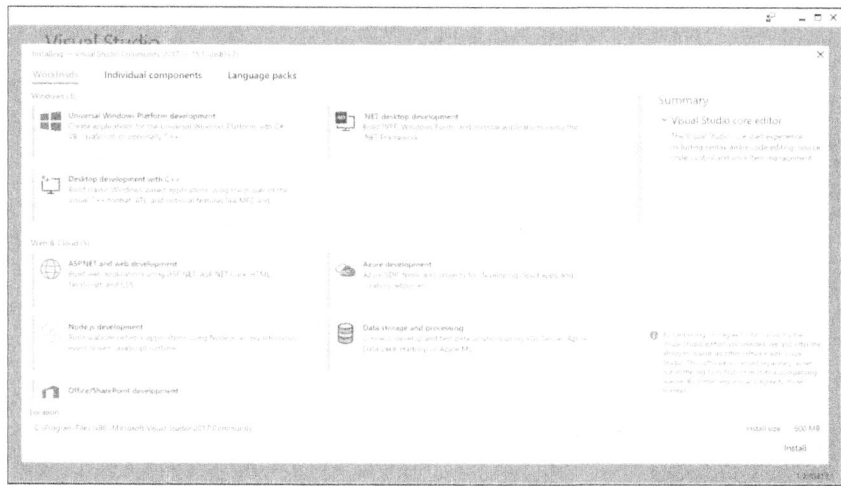

Figure 2.4. Visual Studio installation options

We'll develop VB.NET desktop applications therefore we need to select **.NET desktop development** options. You can of course install other development tools also if you're interested but we'll only cover visual VB.NET in this book and installing .NET desktop development option is enough for this as indicated by the arrows in Figure 2.5.

I didn't change the default installation location shown inside the rectangular box in the bottom left this figure. In the bottom right, the installation informs us that this installation will take around 8GB of hard disk space. If you're OK with these settings, please click the **Install** button at the bottom right corner and then Visual Studio installation will begin. Please note that this is an online installer therefore it will download the actual installation files and install them. This will take some time depending on your Internet connection speed (around 5 minutes with a fiber connection). The installation window shown in Figure 2.6 will appear during this process.

19

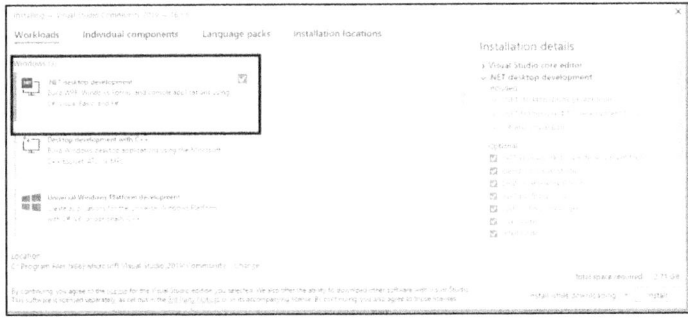

Figure 2.5. Selecting the required components during installation

Figure 2.6. Visual Studio online installer – installation window

After the installer finishes, Visual Studio will be indicated as **Installed** as given in Figure 2.7. You can now click on the **Launch** button here or find Visual Studio 2019 from the Start Menu → All Programs as shown in Figure 2.8.

When we start Visual Studio for the first time, it will ask if we'd like to sign in using our Microsoft account as in Figure 2.9. Signing in to Visual Studio has several benefits like synchronizing your work among different computers. It's up to you to sign in or not at this stage.

CHAPTER 2. SETTING UP YOUR DEVELOPMENT ENVIRONMENT

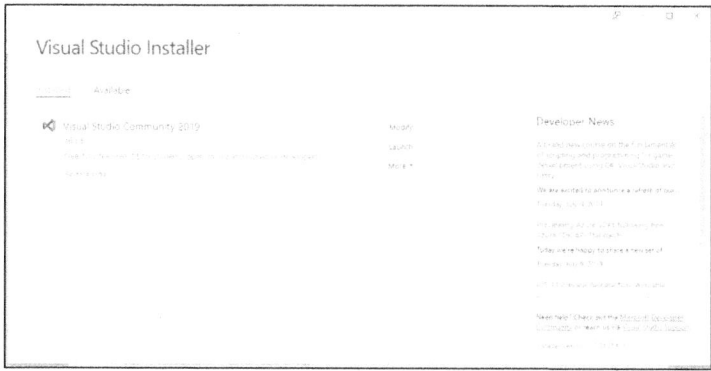

Figure 2.7. Installation complete window

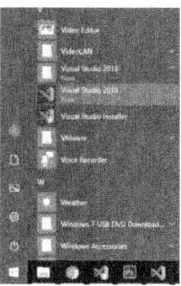

Figure 2.8. Launching Visual Studio from the Start Menu

Figure 2.9. Visual Studio sign in screen

2.2. General Options of Visual Studio

After you sign-in or click **Not now, maybe later** button, the following options window will appear:

Figure 2.10. Options window of Visual Studio

Let's start with the General Development Settings (as selected in the figure above) so that we can overview the general structure of Visual Studio. You can select the colour theme as you wish. Please click the **Start Visual Studio** button at the bottom right of this window. The **Start Page** will then appear as shown in Figure 2.11.

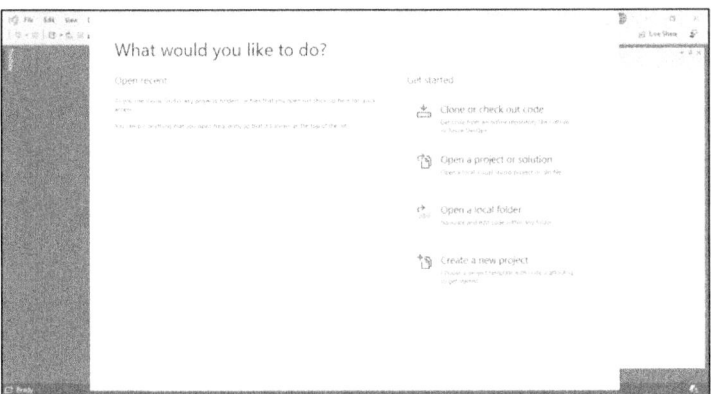

Figure 2.11. Start Page of Visual Studio

2.3. Main Panes and Menus of the IDE

The main sections of this window are: **Open recent, Clone or check out a code, Open a project or solution, Open a local folder** and the **Create a new project**. We can access recently created projects of Visual Studio from the **Open recent** section. **Create a new project** part is for creating new files or projects and this is the thing we will use frequently.

The important menus existing at the top menu bar can also be summarized as follows:

- In the **File** menu, there are items related to creating a new project, opening existing projects and printing.
- The **Edit** menu contains operations like Undo, Redo, Delete, etc. We use these operations when we're writing code and designing user interfaces.
- **View** menu lets us to open/close the panes of Visual Studio.
- The **Project** menu contains buttons to add new items to our project such as a new form or a class file.
- **Debug** menu has the tools for debugging the project, i.e. tools for catching the problematic code lines.
- The **Team** menu lets us to manage connections with the members of our software development team (if any).
- **Tools** menu lets us to add packages and databases to our project and to adjust Visual Studio settings.
- **Test** menu lets us to apply tests to our project.
- The **Analyse** menu has advanced tools for analysing our project, such as tools for performance measurement.
- **Window** menu has the options for rearranging the windows/panes of Visual Studio and also resetting window preferences.
- The **Help** menu has the usual help menu structure together with buttons to send feedback to Microsoft.

Please note that these menus include many more functions than these and we'll use them as we develop projects in the following chapters.

In the next chapter, we'll develop our first Visual Studio project (the Hello World project) which will let us to test if our programming environment is working properly and also give an idea on the general steps of developing VB.NET applications.

Chapter 3

TEST DRIVE: THE HELLO WORLD PROJECT

A good convention to start learning a programming language and a development environment is to try a Hello World example. It is just displaying the "Hello World" expression on the screen. OK, I know it is not a program that you'd be proud of showing to your family or friends but its usefulness stems from testing whether your programming environment is working normally and to see if you're ready to go for real projects. In our very first VB.NET project, we will write **Hello, World!** text in the middle of the program window in any colour and font we like.

3.1. Creating a New Project

When Visual Studio is running, please select **File → New → Project** as shown below:

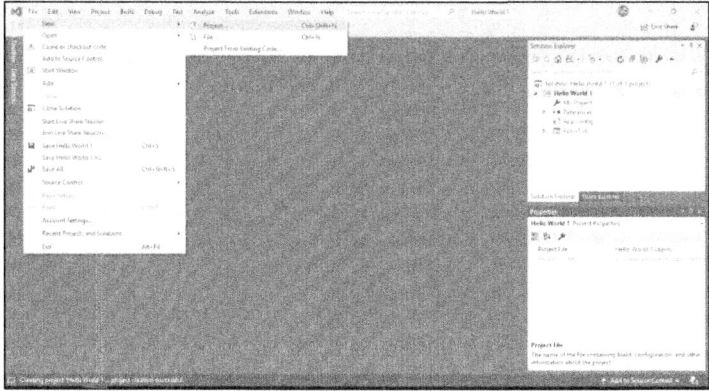

Figure 3.1. Creating a new project

A window showing the possible project types will appear. First of all, select **Visual Basic** from the Language selection box at the top:

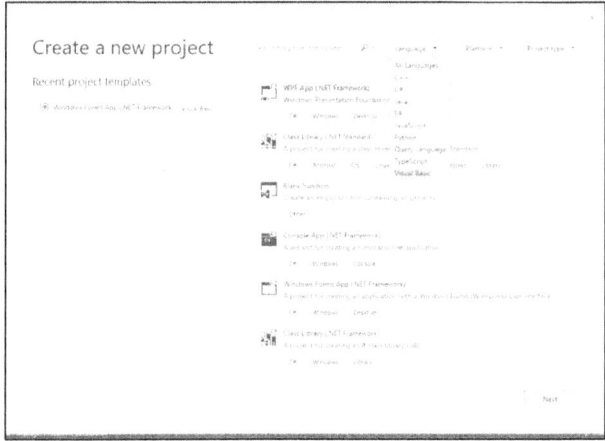

Figure 3.2. Selecting Visual Basic language

Then, various Visual Basic project types will appear in the middle pane:

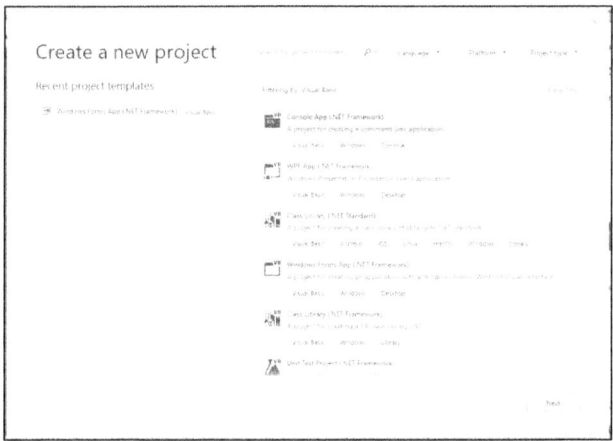

Figure 3.3. Visual Basic project types in Visual Studio

The widely used Visual Basic project types are summarized below:

- **WPF App:** This is a project type which is built upon **W**indows **P**resentation **F**oundation (WPF), an advanced graphical platform for desktop application development.

- **Windows Forms App:** The project type which contains Windows Forms graphical interface.
- **Console App:** This is used for creating console applications, i.e. applications which run in command line without any graphical interface.
- **Class Library:** This option is used for developing classes in .dll files which can be shared among projects.

We will develop our applications in Windows Forms through this book due to their wide usage and maturity. Therefore, select this project type for our Hello World project and then click Next:

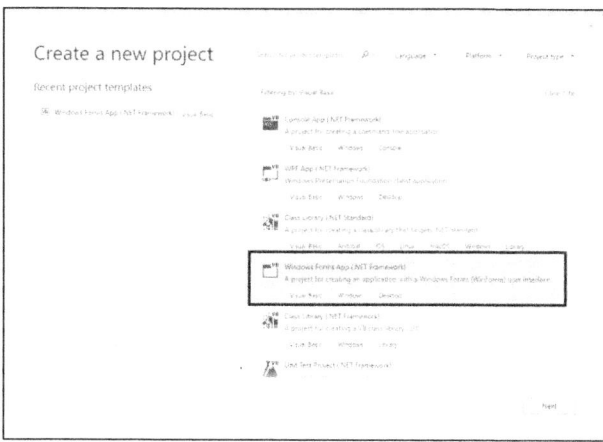

Figure 3.4. Selecting the project type and saving options

Then, the following dialog will appear in which we can enter the project name, location for the project files, etc. I have named the project as **Hello World** and then selected a folder on my computer. We can leave the other options as they are for now and then click Create to create and open our very first VB.NET project:

BEGINNER'S GUIDE TO VISUAL BASIC.NET PROGRAMMING

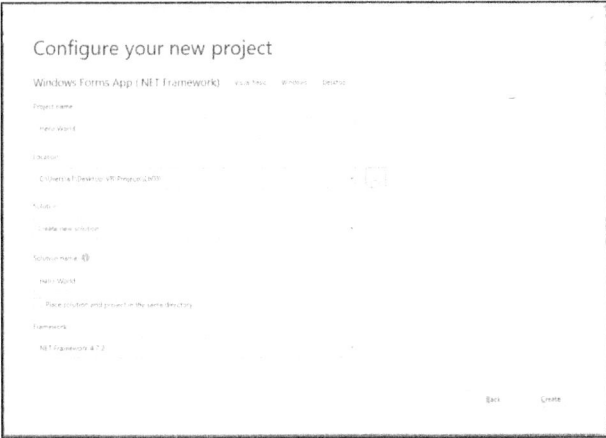

Figure 3.5. Project settings

After clicking the **Create** button, Visual Studio will create the project and show the default Windows Form named **Form1** as shown below:

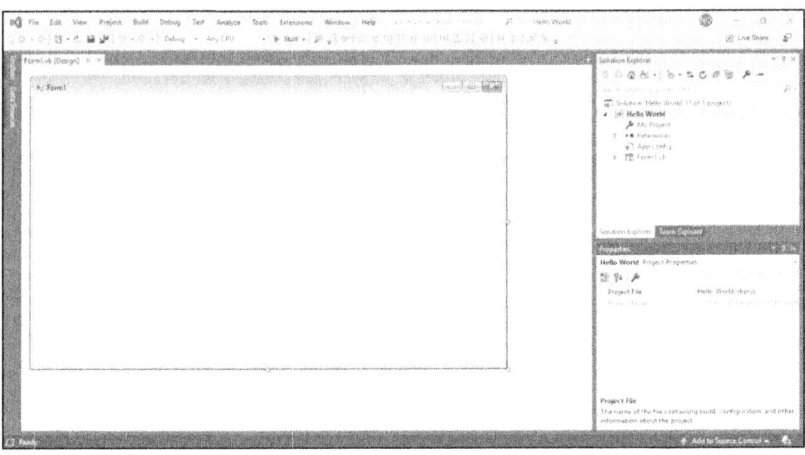

Figure 3.6. Visual Studio window just after creating our project

3.2. Default Panes of Visual Studio

Visual Studio automatically opens the **Form1.cs [Design]**, which is added to Windows Forms projects by default.

Let's now overview the default panes of of Visual Studio (please refer to Figure 3.6):

CHAPTER 3. TEST DRIVE: THE HELLO WORLD PROJECT

- At the top right, the pane called **Solution Explorer** is displayed. We can view the forms and other related files included in our project from here. We can double-click to open them in the middle pane for editing.
- There is the **Properties** window just below the Solution Explorer. We can change the properties of graphical user interface (GUI) elements from here. Currently, Form1 is opened in the [Design] mode therefore the properties pane shows the properties of Form1. Most form elements have dozens of properties. Because of this, the **Properties** window has different modes for displaying these properties as shown below:

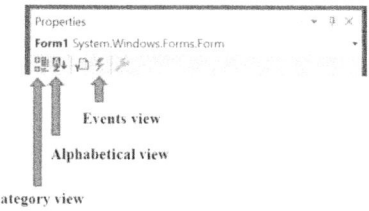

Figure 3.7. Various modes of the Properties window

Alphabetical view lists the properties in an alphabetical order from A to Z. Categorized view shows the related properties together. Another view is the **Events** view which shows the events related to the selected form component. Events are the actions related to a form component such as clicking on a button.

There are also three more windows which are currently hidden at the top left side as shown by the arrow in Figure 3.7. These are Toolbox and Data Source windows.

- **Data Sources** window is the section that displays the details of the data sources in our projects. For example, it shows the details of the databases included in our project.
- The **Toolbox** window is the place that contains the form controls and components we can use on the forms. These will be explained in detail in the next chapter.

29

BEGINNER'S GUIDE TO VISUAL BASIC.NET PROGRAMMING

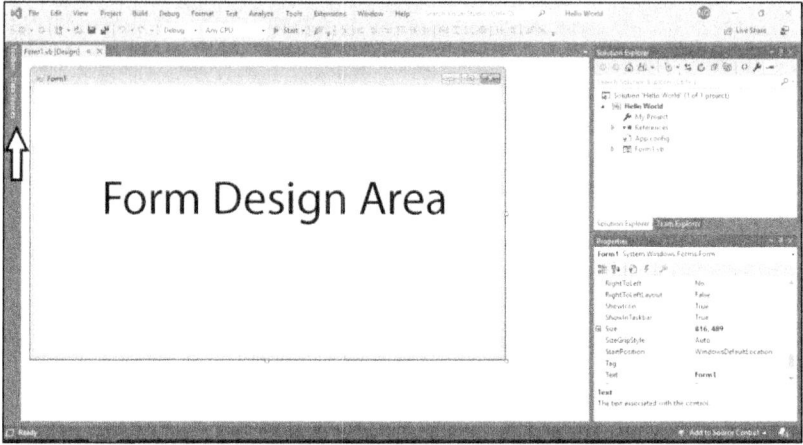

Figure 3.8. Hidden windows at the left hand side

The default views of these windows are shown in the following figures:

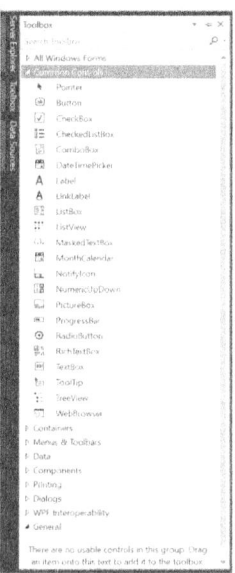

Figure 3.9. The Toolbox window

30

CHAPTER 3. TEST DRIVE: THE HELLO WORLD PROJECT

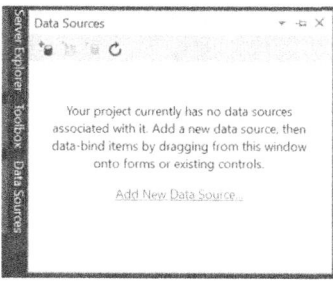

Figure 3.10. The Data Sources window
(empty, since we didn't add any databases yet)

In our Hello World project, Form1.vb was opened in the [Design] mode as shown in Figure 3.8. This file contains both the graphical components and the VB.NET code we write for Form1. You can view the project hierarchy and files from the **Solution Explorer** window.

3.3. Files Included in the Project

Let's also overview our project files in the Windows Explorer. Please navigate to the folder you created for your project and open it in Windows to see the contents as below:

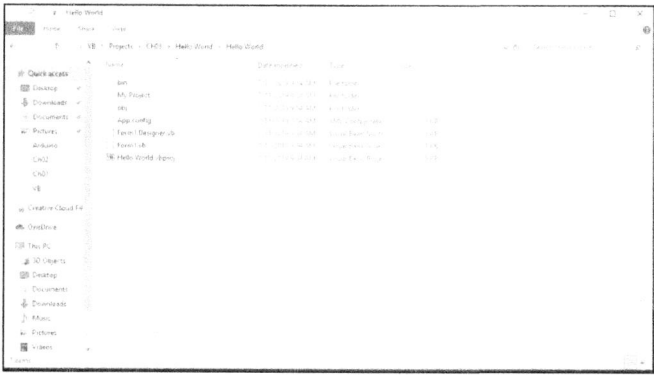

Figure 3.11. Files and folders in the project directory

As you can see, there are several files and folders in our project directory. The widely used file extensions and associated file properties can be summarized as follows:

31

- **.vb files:** These are the source code files for VB.NET projects. vb is an abbreviation for visual basic.
- **.sln files:** These are **solution** files. They may contain one or more projects.
- **.vbproj:** These are VB.NET project files and contain the whole project information such as the .NET framework version, target CPU and files included in the project.

3.4. Adding a Label Control on the Form

Our aim was to display the "Hello, World!" text in our application. Therefore, we need to add a **form control** on the form that can display text on the form.

> Form elements that are visible to the user are called as **form controls** (or shortly **controls**) in Visual Studio.

There are several controls that can display text on the form but the most appropriate one is the **Label** for our simple example. Labels display static text on the form that cannot be edited by the user but can be changed programmatically. In order to add a Label on the form, open the **Toolbox** window from the left side and select **Common Controls** to view the frequently used controls as shown by numbers 1 and 2 in the following figure:

CHAPTER 3. TEST DRIVE: THE HELLO WORLD PROJECT

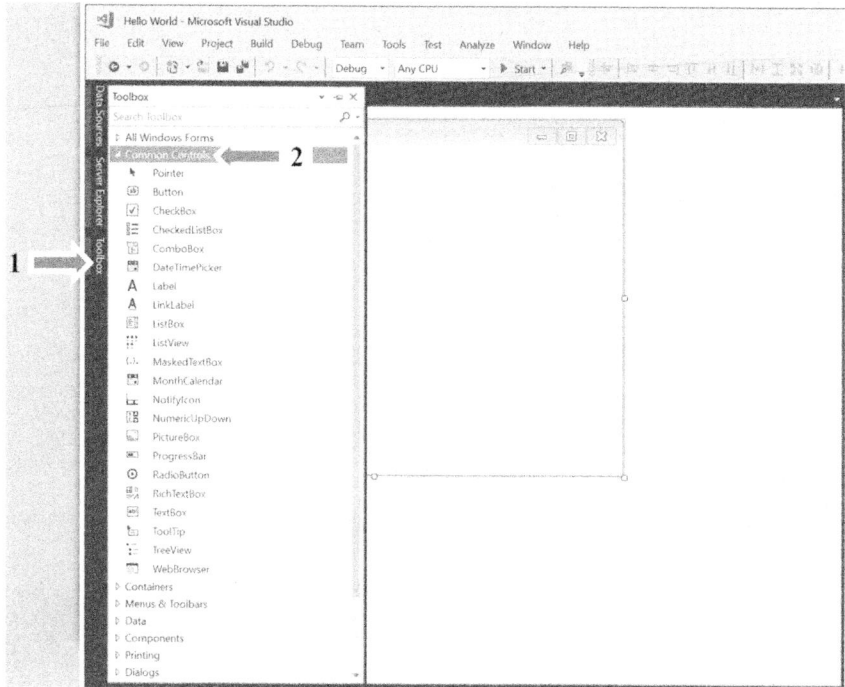

Figure 3.12. Opening the Common Controls list

Please note that the Toolbox window overlaps with Form1 leading Form1 not to be shown properly. In order to overcome this, let's pin the Toolbox since we'll use it frequently anyway. For this, click the **Dock** option from the small drop-down menu as shown in the following figure:

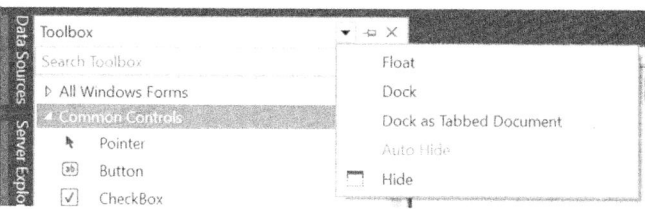

Figure 3.13. Docking the Toolbox

We're now ready to place the Label control on Form1. Please select Label from Toolbox then drag and drop it somewhere in the middle of the form as shown below:

33

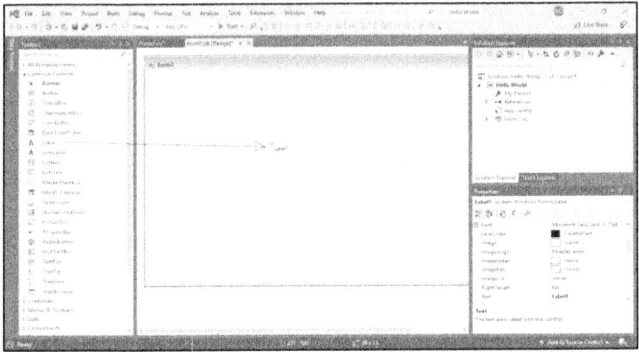

Figure 3.14. Adding a Label control on the form

3.5. Setting Label's Properties

When this control is added, it will be selected by default. Therefore, the properties window will display the editable properties of the Label. The Label is supposed to display the text "Hello, World!", so we need to change its **Text** property from **label1** to **Hello, World!** Please find its Text property and then change it as shown in Figure 3.15.

We now have the Hello, World! Text on the Label. Great. However, this text might seem small and thin especially in high-resolution displays. Therefore, it is better to change the Font properties of the Label. For this, please find the **Font** property in the properties window and then click on the ellipsis just at its right as shown in Figure 3.16.

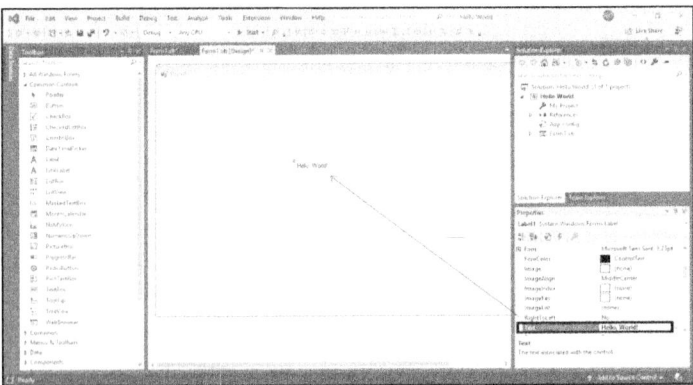

Figure 3.15. Changing the Text property of the Label

CHAPTER 3. TEST DRIVE: THE HELLO WORLD PROJECT

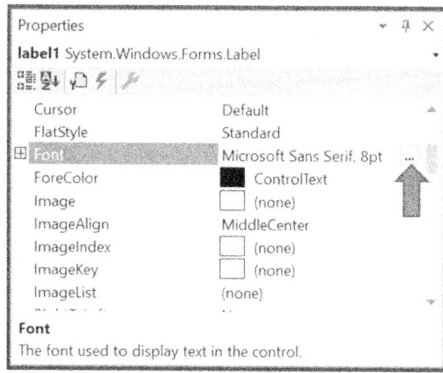

Figure 3.16. Opening the Font options of the Label

Figure 3.17. Editing the Font properties of the Label

I've changed the Font as shown in the figure above. You can also change the text or background colour from the **ForeColor** and **BackColor** properties if you wish.

Let's check Form1 now after these changes:

Figure 3.18. Layout of Form1

35

3.6. Aligning the Label

As you can see from this figure, it is not always easy to place a Label in the middle of the form. However, Visual Studio offers easy to use tools for aligning controls. In order to align the Label control in the middle of the form, please select the Label, then open the **Format** menu and then select **Center in Form → Horizontally** as shown in Figure 3.19. Please repeat this process again but now, select **Center in Form → Vertically**. These are shown by the arrows in the figure. After these steps, the Label will be centred on the form both horizontally and vertically meaning that the Label will be aligned in the middle of the form.

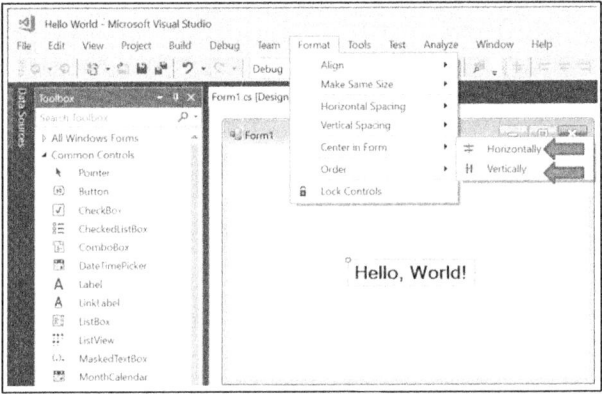

Figure 3.19. Centring the Label on the form

After these steps, the Form looks like below:

Figure 3.20. Centred Label on the Form

Our GUI design is complete now. Since we don't want our Hello World application to do something interactive, we don't need to write a single line of code in this project. However, I want to show you the file on which we'll do actual coding in the following chapters. As I stated earlier, the Form1.cs file in fact consists of a Design mode and a Code mode. We dealt with the Design mode here. In order to view it in the Code mode, right-click somewhere empty on the Form and then select **View Code** as shown in the following figure:

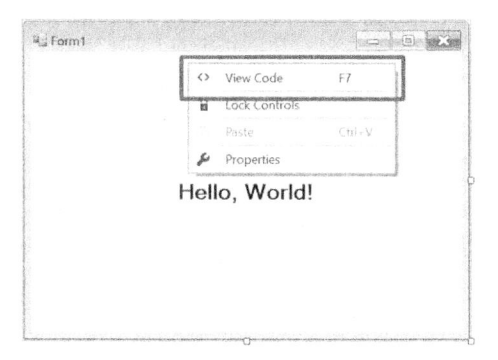

Figure 3.21. Viewing the coding part of the Form1.cs file

The following code editor will then appear in the middle pane showing the default code listing of Form1.cs file:

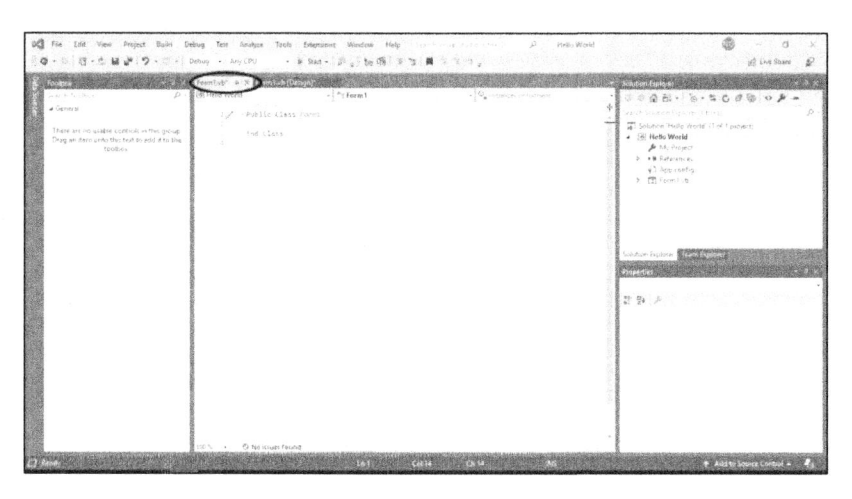

Figure 3.22. The default code of Form1

Note that these are the default code lines generated automatically by Visual Studio. I know these lines may not mean a lot for now. However, we'll cover these in detail and you'll see that they are not actually complicated.

3.7. Building the Project

Let's now build our project and run the resulting executable file. The easy way of doing this is to click on the **Start** button in the menu bar as shown by the arrow in Figure 3.23.

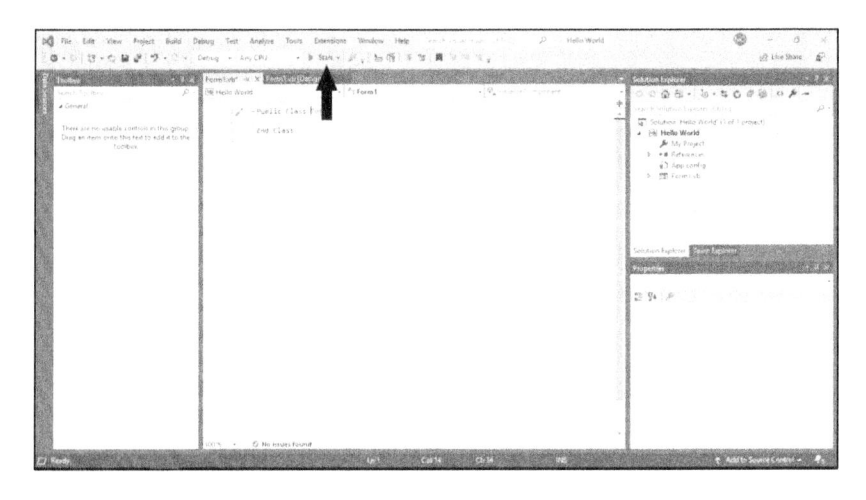

Figure 3.23. Building the project with the Start button

Visual Studio will generate the executable file with .exe extension and run it as below:

Figure 3.24. Our Hello World program

CHAPTER 3. TEST DRIVE: THE HELLO WORLD PROJECT

In order to stop the program and return to the editor view in Visual Studio, you can just close the program as usual (click the cross button at the top right corner of the program) or click the **Stop** button in Visual Studio as indicated by the arrow in Figure 3.25.

You may wonder where your executable file is. It is under the **/bin/debug** folder in the project folder as shown in Figure 3.26. You can run your Hello World program also by double-clicking this file here.

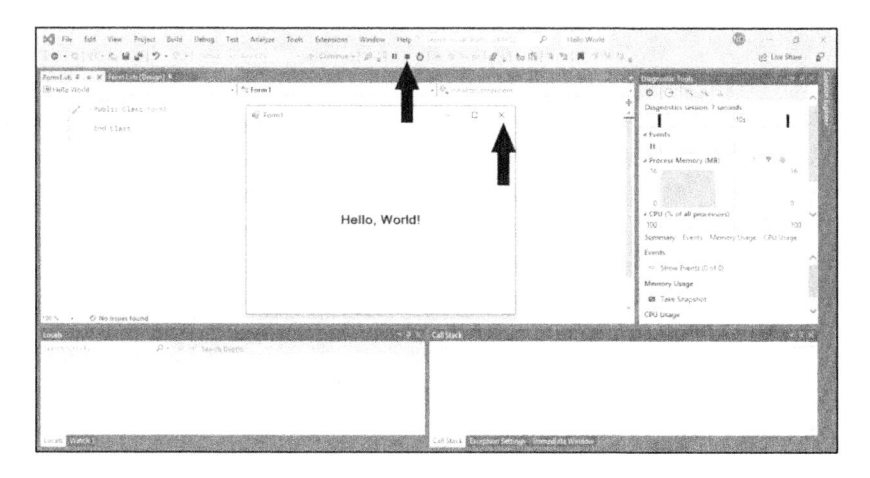

Figure 3.25. Options for stopping the running program

Figure 3.26. The product of our Hello World project: Hello World.exe file

BEGINNER'S GUIDE TO VISUAL BASIC.NET PROGRAMMING

If you want to open this project again later, you can either find it in the Recent section of the Visual Studio Start Page as in Figure 3.27 or use **File → Open → Project/Solution** and double-click the Hello World.sln file as shown in Figure 3.28 and Figure 3.29.

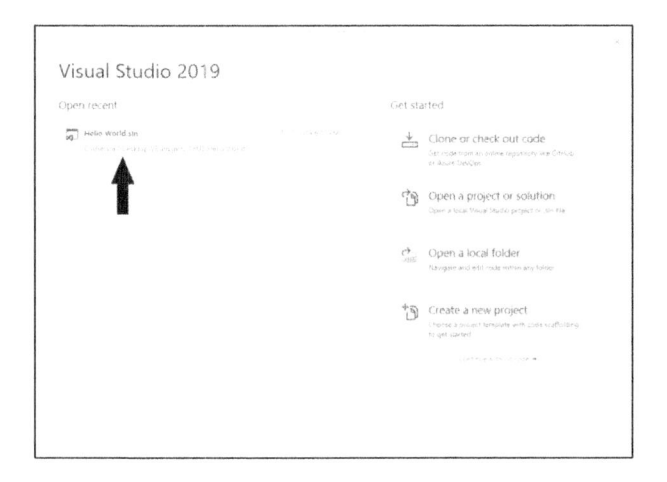

Figure 3.27. Opening the project from the Recents projects section

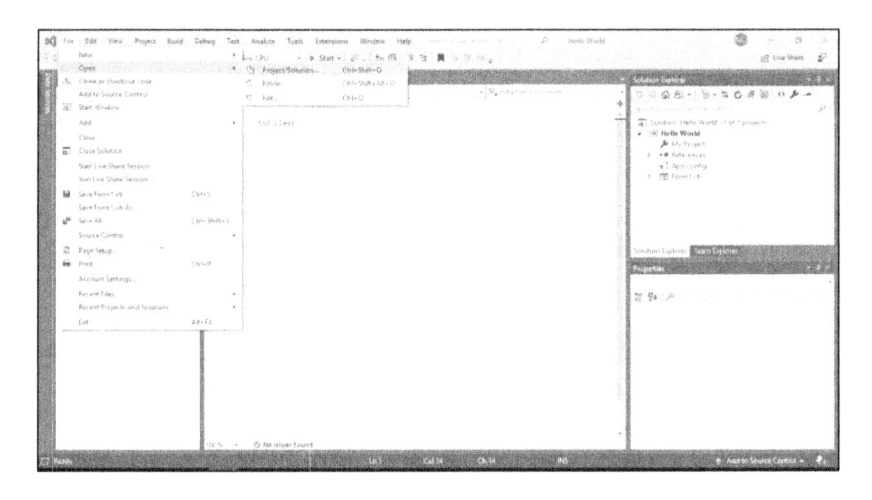

Figure 3.28. Opening a project from the File menu

CHAPTER 3. TEST DRIVE: THE HELLO WORLD PROJECT

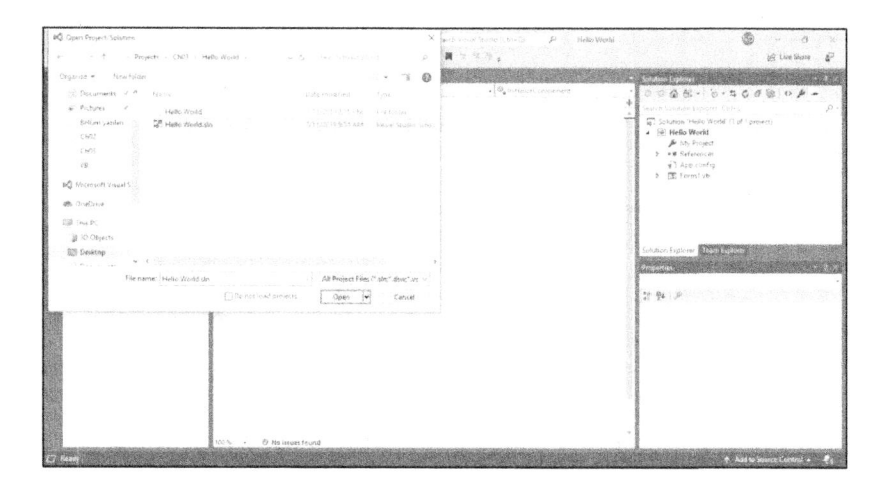

Figure 3.29. Opening the solution file Hello World.sln

That's all for this chapter. We have learned how to create a new project, place a Label control on the form, setting basic properties of the Label visually and aligning it in the middle. And then we built the project and created the executable file.

As you may have noticed from the Toolbox, there are a lot of controls that can be used on Windows forms. Since our aim is to learn both GUI design and VB.NET coding, it is required to know how we can use other control types like a Button or a TextBox. In the next two chapters, we'll learn working with commonly used form controls together with the associated basic VB.NET coding before moving on to actual coding lectures in the following chapters.

Chapter 4

FORM (GUI) ELEMENTS

We'll overview the elements used in designing graphical user interface (GUI) of our VB.NET programs in this chapter. These elements consist of controls and components. Controls are visible elements of the form while components act in the background.

There are several types of form controls in Visual Studio for use on forms. These controls enable our VB.NET code to communicate with the user. Buttons and file opening dialogs are typical examples of form controls.

From a functional viewpoint, controls have two groups of actions: initiating an **event** or performing **input/output**. Some controls are famous for their events and others for their input/output capabilities.

An event example: When we click a button in an application, we trigger something to happen. Therefore, **clicking is an event** for the button. When an event occurs, the program does something depending on the VB.NET code we attach to the event of the control.

An input/output example: When we pull data from a database, we may want to display it in a grid-like fashion on the form. This is an output example.

The appearances of controls are set via their properties. In the previous chapter, we did set the properties of a Label, as you may remember and these settings affected the appearance of the Label.

It is worth noting that some properties and events are common among controls. For example, many controls have the **BackColor** property. Similarly, several controls have the **MouseClick** event. Therefore, I will explain these common properties and events only once in order to avoid unnecessary repetitions in this chapter.

4.1. Form Controls at a Glance

It is useful to overview commonly used controls and then use them in sample projects with the associated VB.NET code.

The **commonly used form controls** are shown in the following table:

Reference number	Name	Image	Information
1	Button	Button	When clicked, raises an event.
2	CheckBox	CheckBox	User can select the option associated with the CheckBox
3	CheckedListBox	CheckedListBox	Items list with a checkbox for each
4	ComboBox	ComboBox	Editable text box with a drop-down list
5	DateTimePicker	DateTimePicker	User can select date and time information
6	Label	Label	Displays static text on the form
7	LinkLabel	LinkLabel	Label with hyperlink functionality
8	ListBox	ListBox	Listed items in a box
9	ListView	ListView	Listed items displayed in various formats

CHAPTER 4. FORM (GUI) ELEMENTS

Reference number	Name	Image	Information
10	MaskedTextBox	(.)- MaskedTextBox	Text box that forces to enter text in a specified format
11	MonthCalendar	MonthCalendar	A calendar control from which a date can be selected
12	NotifyIcon	NotifyIcon	An icon element in the notification area
13	NumericUpDown	NumericUpDown	Provides a numeric value which can be changed by arrow clicks
14	PictureBox	PictureBox	Used for displaying an image
15	ProgressBar	ProgressBar	Shows the progress of an operation
16	RadioButton	RadioButton	Enables to select only one of several options
17	RichTextBox	RichTextBox	Advanced text box with paragraph formatting, etc.
18	TextBox	TextBox	Enables the user to input text
19	ToolTip	ToolTip	Displays short info when mouse is over
20	TreeView	TreeView	Displays hierarchical items
21	WebBrowser	WebBrowser	Displays web pages on the form

Table 4.1. Common controls (cont'd)

45

You can find these controls in the Common Controls section of the Toolbox as shown below:

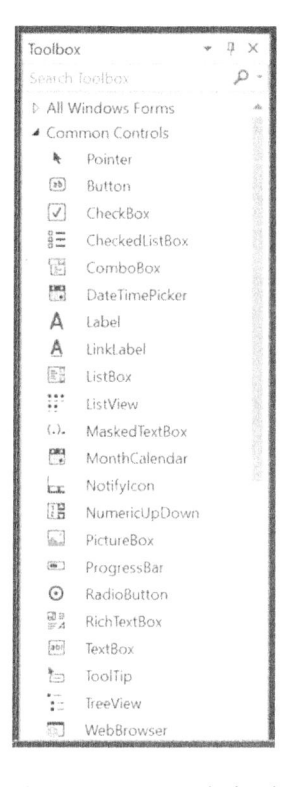

Figure 4.1. Common controls in the Toolbox

4.2. Containers and Menus

Containers are the controls that are used to group other form elements. Container types provided in Visual Studio are as follows:

Reference number	Name	Image	Information
1	FlowLayoutPanel	FlowLayoutPanel	Provides a liquid layout
2	GroupBox	GroupBox	Groups and draws a frame around its elements
3	Panel	Panel	Simply groups its elements

CHAPTER 4. FORM (GUI) ELEMENTS

Reference number	Name	Image	Information
4	SplitContainer	SplitContainer	Provides a two vertical resizable areas for a container
5	TabControl	TabControl	Provides tabbed areas to place elements
6	TableLayoutPanel	TableLayoutPanel	Table shaped container

Table 4.2. Containers used for grouping controls (cont'd)

Containers are listed in the Toolbox as shown below:

▲ Containers
　Pointer
　FlowLayoutPanel
　GroupBox
　Panel
　SplitContainer
　TabControl
　TableLayoutPanel

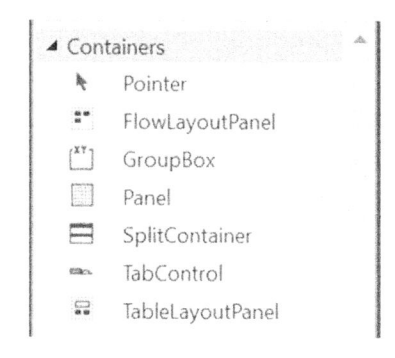

Figure 4.2. Containers in the Toolbox

On the other hand, menus and toolbars are special types of controls that provide easy access to commands on a form. Widely used examples include the File menu at the top of the form and the right-click menu for copy, paste, etc. commands. Visual Studio has the following menu and toolbar options:

Reference number	Name	Image	Information
1	ContextMenuStrip	ContextMenuStrip	The right-click menu
2	MenuStrip	MenuStrip	Groups commands by functionality like the File menu

47

Reference number	Name	Image	Information
3	StatusStrip	StatusStrip	Displays info at the status bar (which is at the left bottom of the form)
4	ToolStrip	ToolStrip	A toolbar that may contain various control types, not just text
5	ToolStripContainer	ToolStripContainer	Used for placing toolbars on each side of the form

Table 4.3. Menus and toolbars (cont'd)

MenuStrip and ContextMenuStrip are the widely used menu type controls. On the other hand, StatusStrip and ToolStrip are also sometimes used to display information to the user.

4.3. Dialogs

Dialogs are the controls that are triggered for gathering information from the user. Examples include the dialogs for selecting a file to open or the dialog for selecting the font properties. Available dialog controls are summarized as follows:

Reference number	Name	Image	Information
1	ColorDialog	ColorDialog	Enables the user to select colour
2	FolderBrowserDialog	FolderBrowserDialog	Used for selecting a folder
3	FontDialog	FontDialog	Used for setting font properties

CHAPTER 4. FORM (GUI) ELEMENTS

Reference number	Name	Image	Information
4	OpenFileDialog	OpenFileDialog	Used for selecting a file to open
5	SaveFileDialog	SaveFileDialog	Used for setting the filename for saving

Table 4.4. Dialog types (cont'd)

4.4. Components

Components are form elements that are not visible to the user and do background tasks. A typical example is the Timer component which is used for triggering an event at regular time intervals in the background.

Visual Studio provides many other controls and components. We'll explain and use them in our projects when required in the following chapters.

Now, we got a glimpse of the frequently used form controls. Let's move on to the common properties of these controls.

4.5. Properties of Controls

As it was stated before, most controls share same properties. Let's study these common properties which we will frequently use during form design.

Let's create a new VB.NET project in Visual Studio and place a Button on the form by drag&drop operation as shown in Figure 4.3. In this figure, the dashed line arrow shows the properties pane for the Button since it is the selected element on the form. Just below the **Properties** title, the name of the Button is shown as **button1**. Next to this name is the class to which this control belongs is shown: **System.Windows.Forms.Button**. This is a typical class structure, meaning that the **Button** class is derived from **Forms** class of the **Windows** class that is under the **System** class. This may be confusing for now; you can just remember that the class of the control is shown here; therefore it will be different for a Label or a ProgressBar control.

49

BEGINNER'S GUIDE TO VISUAL BASIC.NET PROGRAMMING

The properties of button1 under the properties window are sorted by category in this figure. If yours is not sorted in this way, just click on the sorting button to sort by category. We will study the commonly used properties of this control now.

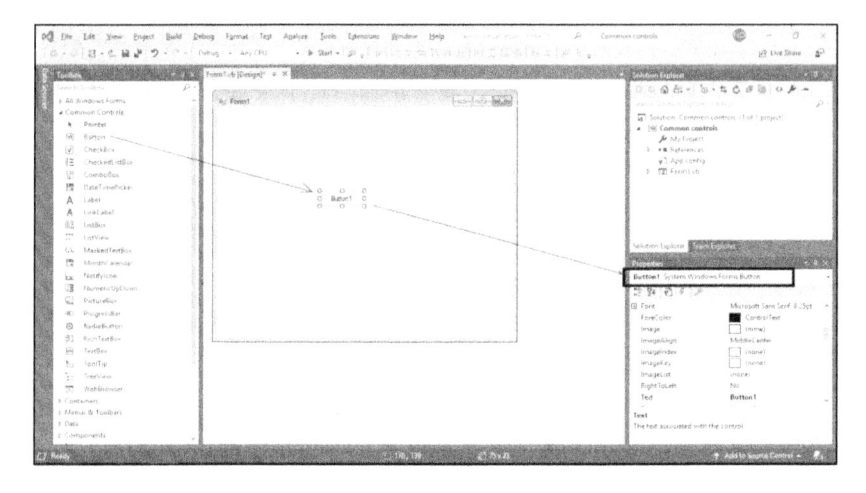

Figure 4.3. Properties of the Button control

The first category lists the properties related to Accessibility as summarized below, these are used by text to speech programs to make your program accessible to people who need assistive technology:

> You don't need to memorize these; just try to get the general idea and then you will learn them easily as you use them in your projects.

1. **AccessibleDescription**: This gives a text description of a control's appearance.

2. **AccessibleName**: This is a label giving the description of the control.

3. **AccessibleProperty:** This property gives information the text-to-speech programs about the type of this control.

The second category shows the properties related to the appearance of the control such as:

4. **BackColor:** Sets the background colour of the control.

CHAPTER 4. FORM (GUI) ELEMENTS

5. **BackgroundImage:** We can set a background image to the control with this property.

6. **BackgroundImageLayout:** Sets the layout of the background image (if any). The options include **None**, **Tile**, **Stretch**, **Center** and **Zoom**. We can select one of these options by clicking the arrow just at the right of this property as shown below:

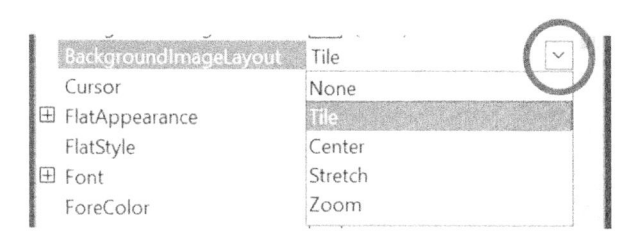

Figure 4.4. Opening the options of the **BackgroundImageLayout** property

7. **Cursor**: Determines the shape of the mouse pointer when it's on the control.

8. **Font**: Sets the font of the text property of the control. We can open the font dialog by clicking the ellipsis at its right as in Figure 4.5.

9. **ForeColor**: Sets the colour of the text of the control.

10. **Image**: Sets a foreground image for the control.

11. **Text**: Sets the text of the control.

12. **TextAlign**: Sets the alignment of the text on the control. Shows several options for the text location when the arrow at its right is clicked as indicated in Figure 4.6.

Under the **Behavior** category of the Properties pane, the widely used properties are the **ContextMenuStrip** and **Visible**.

13. **ContextMenuStrip**: Sets the menu which will appear when the control is right-clicked.

51

BEGINNER'S GUIDE TO VISUAL BASIC.NET PROGRAMMING

14. **Visible**: Sets if the control will be visible to the user. Controls are sometimes hidden/unhidden depending on the user input or a computation result.

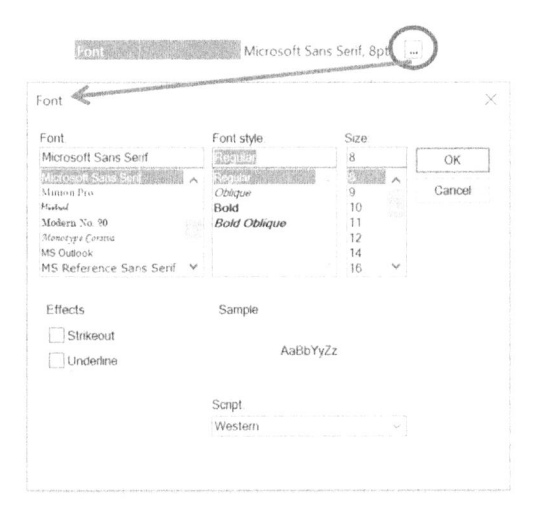

Figure 4.5. Opening the font properties dialog

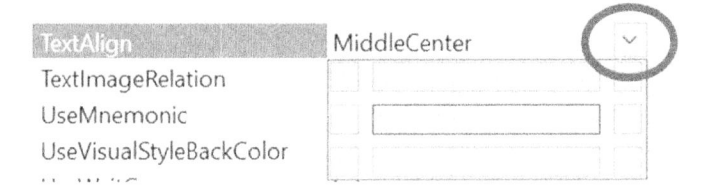

Figure 4.6. Setting the TextAlign property

In the **Design** category, the **Name** is one of the most important properties.

15. **Name:** This is the name of the control. We access the control via this name in the VB.NET code therefore it is very important. It is a good practice to give a meaningful name to controls during form development. The general rule is the camel type naming in VB.NET. For example, if the button will connect to a database, it is convenient to name it as connect**D**atabase**B**utton. This is called camel type naming since the capital letters in the middle of the name is thought to be similar to the humps of a camel.

Finally, in the **Layout** category, the following properties are common to most controls therefore widely used:

16. **Anchor**: This is also an important property. It sets which edges of the control will have a fixed distance from the edges of the form. Its default value is **Top, Left** meaning that when the form is resized, the control will stay at a fixed distance from the top and left edges of the form. For example, consider our form given in Figure 4.3. When we pull the right edge of the form to resize (drag&drop the small point in the middle of the right edge), the button will stay at its place as follows:

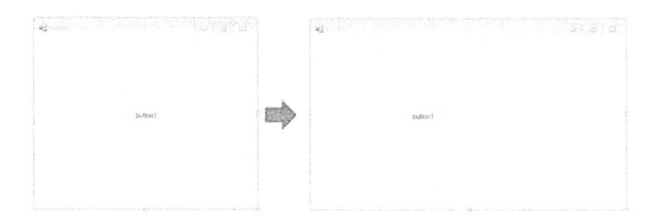

Figure 4.7. Button stays fixed at its place with the Anchor property of **Top, Left**

However, if we change the **Anchor** property to **Top, Left, Right** by activating the right **Anchor** as in Figure 4.8, the Button will stretch when we resize the form as shown in Figure 4.9.

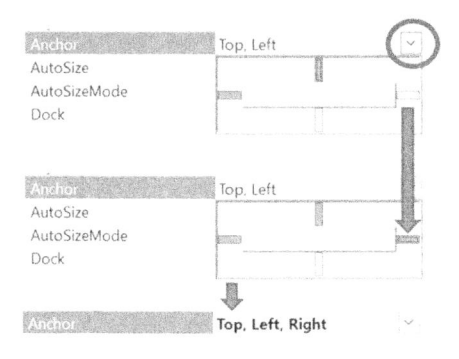

Figure 4.8: Changing the Anchor properties

53

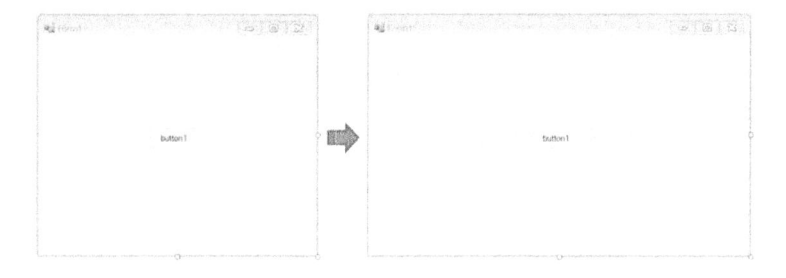

Figure 4.9. Button stretches when its Anchor properties are updated as **Top, Left, Right**

17. **Dock**: Used for docking the control in one of five areas on the form. The docking options are shown in the figure below. Note that its options box is opened by clicking the arrow at the right as we did for other properties.

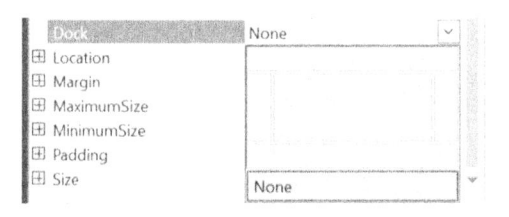

Figure 4.10. Docking options (**None** is selected by default)

18. **Location**: This property defines the location of the control on the form relative to the top left of the form.

19. **MaximumSize**: This property sets the maximum allowed size of the control. Used for forms rather than controls in practice.

20. **MinimumSize**: This sets the minimum allowed size of the control.

21. **Size**: Sets the dimensions of the control in pixels.

Short explanations of properties appear at the bottom space of the properties window once a property is selected as shown in Figure 4.11.

CHAPTER 4. FORM (GUI) ELEMENTS

Properties of controls and other form elements can also be changed programmatically in real time during runtime.

Figure 4.11. Short explanation for the selected property appears at the bottom of the properties window

4.6. Events of Controls

Events take care of the things happening on the form. Clicking a button or selecting an option from a drop-down box are examples of events. The code that will be executed when an event happens are written in the .vb file of the project.

Each control type has a default event that can be created in the code just by double-clicking the control. For example, let's place a **CheckBox** on the form by drag&drop as in Figure 4.12. Form1 is in [Design] mode as it is shown inside the ellipse. When we double-click checkBox1 on this form, code view of Form1 opens in the editor as shown in Figure 4.13.

The default event for a CheckBox is the **CheckChanged** event which fires (executes) when the check of the CheckBox changes, i.e. when it is checked or unchecked. This default event handling method named checkBox1_CheckChanged(...) is created when checkBox1 is double clicked on the form as shown inside the rectangle in Figure 4.13.

55

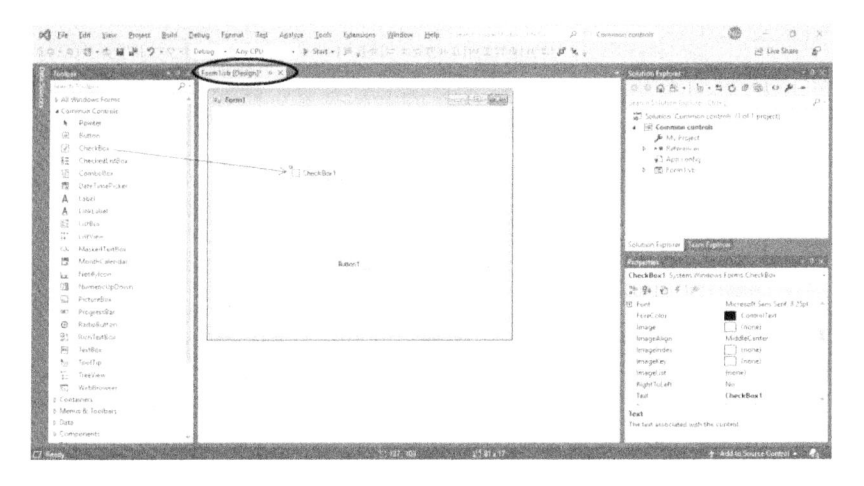

BEGINNER'S GUIDE TO VISUAL BASIC.NET PROGRAMMING

Figure 4.12. Placing a CheckBox on the form

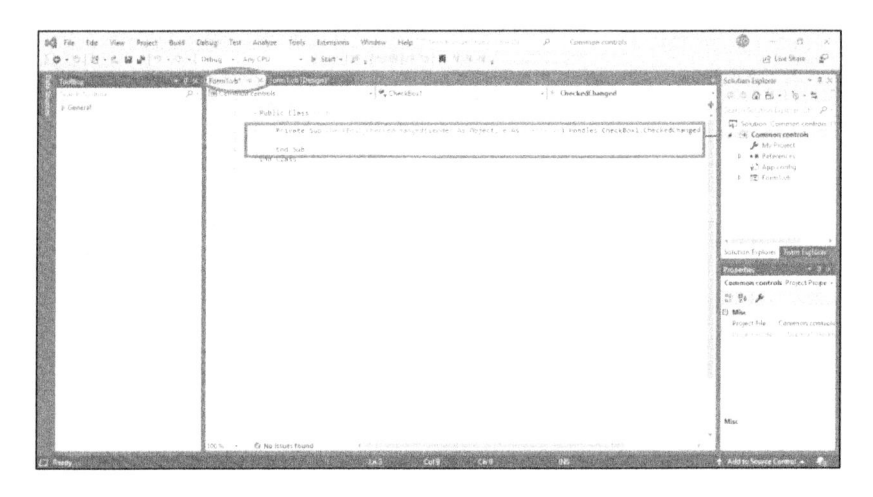

Figure 4.13. The event handler code created by double-clicking checkbox1

The following method is automatically created for handling the CheckChanged event in the Form1.vb file:

```
Private Sub CheckBox1_CheckedChanged(sender As Object, e As EventArgs) Handles CheckBox1.CheckedChanged
    'VB.NET code goes here
End Sub
```
Code 4.1

When the check of checkBox1 is changed, `checkBox1_CheckedChanged` will be triggered and the code inside the curly brackets indicated by the **'VB.NET code goes here** will be executed. Don't worry about the VB.NET code lines here. We'll study them in detail.

Each control has a default event. As we have seen above, the default event of a CheckBox is the CheckChanged event. Similarly, the default event for a Button is the Click event that is triggered when the button is clicked. Apart from the default ones, controls also have several other events which are triggered by different actions. We can view all the events of a control from the Properties window. When we click the lightning symbol ⚡ in the Properties window, all events of a control is displayed as shown in Figure 4.14.

There are dozens of events and a small portion of them are frequently used. Just like common properties, most controls share frequently used events. These events and short information on the actions triggering them are summarized in Table 4.5.

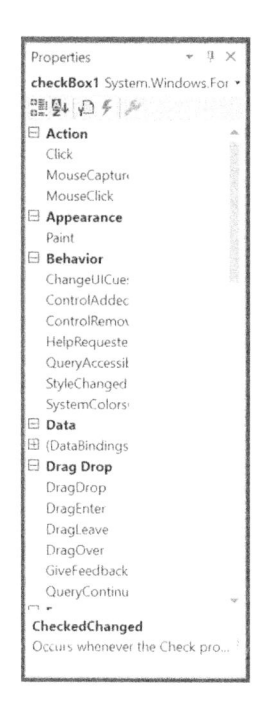

Figure 4.14. All events of a CheckBox control listed in categories

Reference number	Name	Triggered when...	Method format
1	BackColorChanged	the background color is changed	ControlName_BackColorChanged(...)
2	BackgroundImageChanged	the background image is changed	ControlName_BackgroundImageChanged(...)
3	CursorChanged	the cursor type is changed	ControlName_CursorChanged(...)
4	KeyPressed	a key on the keyboard is pressed when the control is active	ControlName_KeyPressed(...)
5	Load	the form is loaded (at the beginning of the execution of the program)	FormName_Load(...)
	MouseClick	the control is clicked with mouse	ControlName_MouseClicked(...)
7	MouseDoubleClick	the control is double-clicked with mouse	ControlName_MouseDoubleClicked(...)
8	Move	the control is moved	ControlName_Move(...)
9	Resize	the control is resized	ControlName_Resize(...)
10	TextChanged	the text of the control is changed	ControlName_TextChanged(...)

Table 4.5. Commonly used events

The Load event of the form and the Click event of buttons are used almost in most projects.

In the next chapter, we will use commonly used controls in small projects where we'll learn the utilization of these controls and their events in detail.

Chapter 5

COMMON CONTROLS

In this chapter, we will study commonly used controls in detail because they are the backbones of GUI (form) design. We will use them in small projects where their properties and events will be programmed. This will be a gentle beginning of our VB.NET coding journey.

5.1. Button

Buttons are used for triggering actions.

Figure 5.1. A button

Buttons have the following properties:

- **Image**: The foreground image of the button.
- **TextAlign**: The alignment of the text on the button.
- **FlatStyle**: Sets the appearance of the button.

Please note that the properties discussed here are the ones additional to the common properties discussed in the previous chapter.

A simple Button example: Let's create a small project incorporating a Button step-by step:

1. Create a new VB.NET project in Visual Studio.
2. Place a Button on the form.
3. Set the Text property of the Button as **Change**.
4. Set the Name property of the Button as **changeButton**.

59

5. Set the FontSize property of the Button to 12 points.

Our form will appear as follows after these steps:

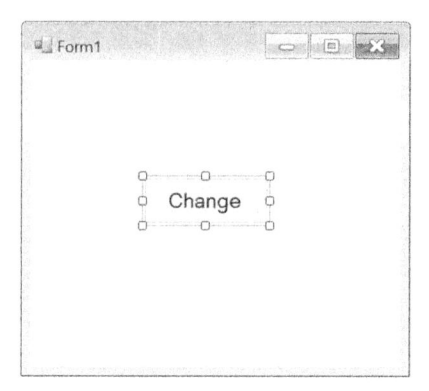

Figure 5.2. Button on the form

6. Double-click on the Button to create its default **Click** event method. The code editor will appear in Visual Studio:

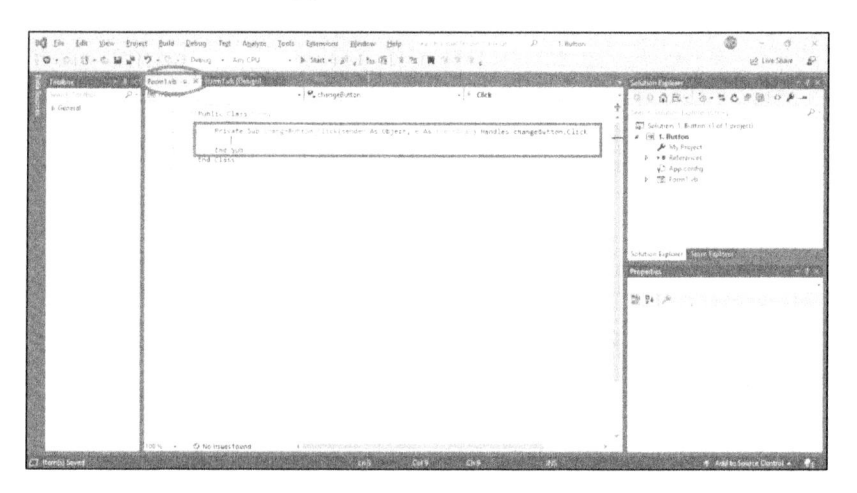

Figure 5.3. Button's Click event method in the code file

As you can see, the editor already has several lines of VB.NET code. We'll explain each of them gradually. But for now let's focus on the button's event handler method shown inside the rectangle. This method is automatically created when we double-clicked the button on the form. We can write any VB.NET code inside this method before the **End Sub**

CHAPTER 5. COMMON CONTROLS

statement which will be executed when the user clicks the button (i.e. when the button's Click event is called).

7. Let's add the following code lines inside the ChangeButton_Click(...) method:

```
changeButton.Text = "Clicked!"
changeButton.BackColor = Color.White
```
Code 5.1

First of all, you'll notice that when you're typing these lines, Visual Studio will try to understand what you're trying to write and complete it as shown below. You can press the **Tab** button on your keyboard to let the Visual Studio complete your code line. This is called as the "IntelliSense technology".

Figure 5.4. Code completion in Visual Studio code editor

Let's now try to understand what these code lines mean. The first line changeButton.Text = "Clicked!" means "Set the Text property of the control named changeButton to "Clicked!" ". You can see that the texts are written inside double quotes in VB.NET. These are important rules.

The second line, changeButton.BackColor = Color.White means that "Set the background colour of changeButton to white." Therefore, these two lines will change the text of the button to "Clicked!" and the

61

background colour of the form to white **when the button's Click event happens**.

The complete Form1.vb code is also given below for your convenience:

```
Public Class Form1
    Private Sub ChangeButton_Click(sender As Object, e As EventArgs) Handles changeButton.Click
        changeButton.Text = "Clicked!"
        changeButton.BackColor = Color.White
    End Sub
End Class
```
Code 5.2

We'll now build and run the project as we did in Chapter 3. Just click the Start button in Visual Studio and our project will be built and run as in Figure 5.5.

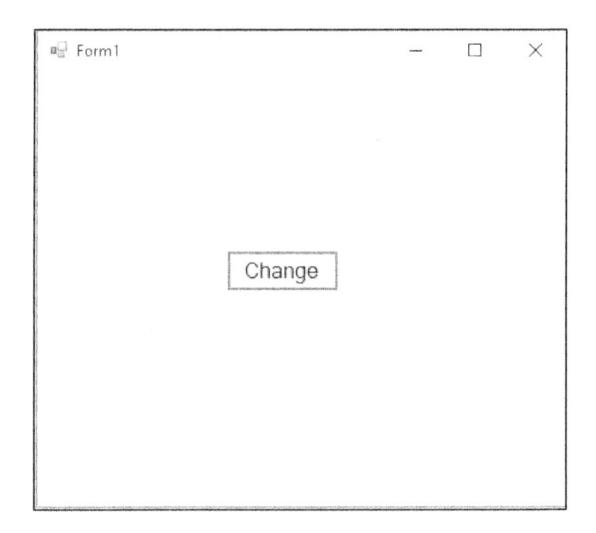

Figure 5.5. Our program at the start

Now, let's click the Change button and this will trigger the button's Click event. Then the code we've written inside this Click method will be executed. The button's text and the background colour of the form will be changed as shown below:

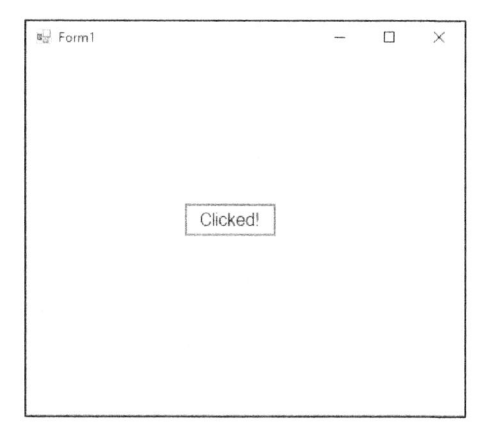

Figure 5.6. Our program after the button is clicked

You now learned how make a program to do something by clicking a button. We will learn using the CheckBox control in our next example.

5.2. CheckBox

CheckBoxes are the controls in which the user checks or unchecks its box. We can think them as Yes/No questions because there are only two possibilities for a CheckBox: checked *or* unchecked.

CheckBoxes have the following frequently used properties:

- **CheckAlign**: Sets the position of the box relative to the text of the CheckBox.
- **Checked**: Sets the checked status of the CheckBox programmatically.
- **TextAlign**: Aligns the text of the CheckBox.

Let's see a CheckBox in action by an example:

1. Create a new VB.NET project in Visual Studio.
2. Place a CheckBox from the Common Controls tab to the middle of the form.
3. Set the Text property of the CheckBox as **Change the background?**
4. Set the Name of the CheckBox as **changeBackColourCheckBox**.
5. Set the font size of the CheckBox Text (via Font property of the CheckBox) to 12 points.

These initial steps and our form are shown below:

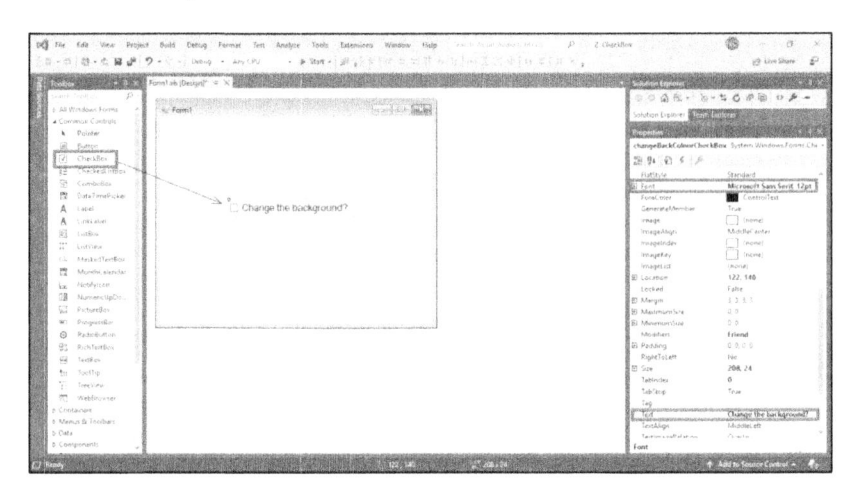

Figure 5.7. Placing a CheckBox on the form and setting its Text and Font Size properties

6. Let's now double-click the CheckBox on the form to create its default event handler, **CheckedChanged**, which is fired when the CheckBox is checked or unchecked:

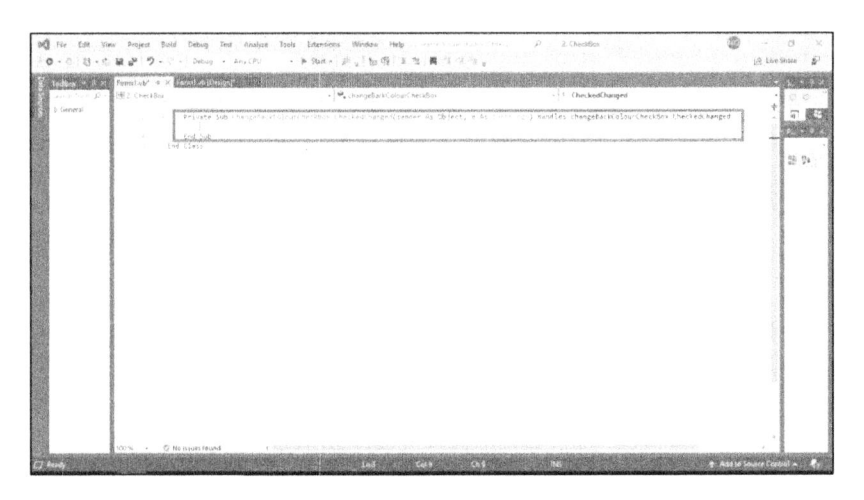

Figure 5.8. The CheckChanged event handler method created in the Form1.cs file

Just as we did for the Button example, we'll write the code inside the curly brackets. Let's add the line Me.BackColor = Color.White so that the changeBackColourCheckBox_CheckChanged(...) event handler method will be as follows:

```
Private Sub ChangeBackColourCheckBox_CheckedChanged(sender 
As Object, e As EventArgs) Handles 
changeBackColourCheckBox.CheckedChanged

        Me.BackColor = Color.White

    End Sub
```
Code 5.3

In this code line, Me keyword refers to the form itself therefore Me.BackColor means the background colour of the form itself. After adding our code, we can build and run the project. When we check the CheckBox, the background colour of the form will change to white as shown in Figures 5.9 and 5.10.

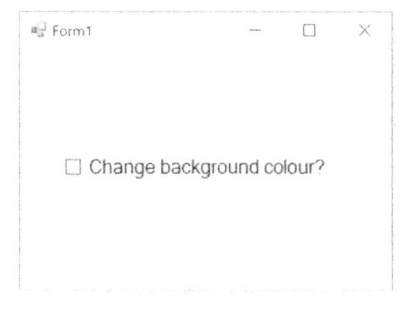

Figure 5.9. The program before checking the CheckBox

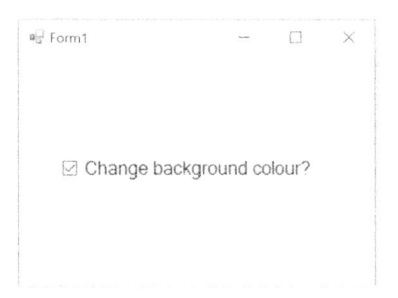

Figure 5.10. Background colour changed after checking the CheckBox

In this example, the code line Me.BackColor = Color.White executes independent of the state of the CheckBox. In other words, we couldn't check if the CheckBox is checked or unchecked; Me.BackColor = Color.White will execute in either case. In order to make this distinction, we need to employ conditional statements in VB.NET therefore; we'll do that in the upcoming chapters after learning conditional statements.

> It is worth noting that a form may contain multiple CheckBoxes that can be selected independently, i.e. more than one CheckBox can be selected at the same time.

5.3. CheckedListBox

This is a list that contains multiple items which can be checked/unchecked independently. Items in a CheckedListBox can be added during development or during runtime programmatically.

Let's create our CheckedListBox example in Visual Studio as usual:

1. Create a new VB.NET project in Visual Studio.
2. Place a CheckedListBox in middle of the form.
3. Set the Name property of this control as pcCheckedListBox (*pc* is for *programming concepts* here).
4. When a CheckedListBox is placed, it doesn't have any items by default. In order to add items, please click on the small arrowhead located at the top of the CheckedListBox as indicated inside the circle below:

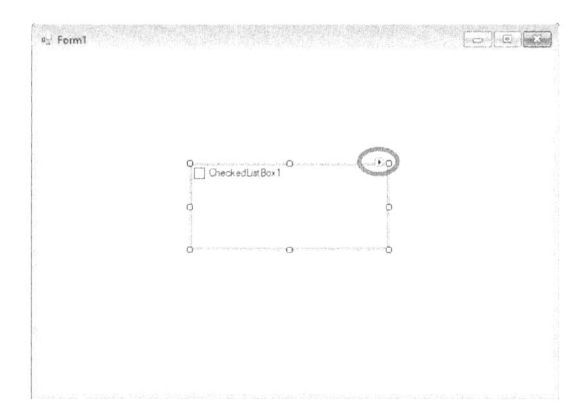

Figure 5.11. Arrowhead for adding items to the CheckedListBox

CHAPTER 5. COMMON CONTROLS

5. When that small arrow is clicked, a small menu will appear as in Figure 5.12. Click on the **Edit Items** there to open a window where we'll add items.
6. In the opened String Collection Editor, we need to enter one string per line. Each string will correspond to a new item inside the CheckedListBox. I entered the strings shown in Figure 5.13 but you may enter any string as you wish.
7. After clicking the OK button, we'll have our CheckedListBox populated with these items as shown in Figure 5.14.

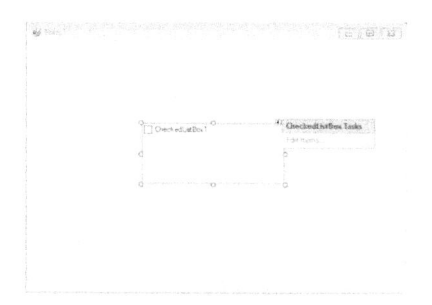

Figure 5.12. The tasks menu of CheckedListBox

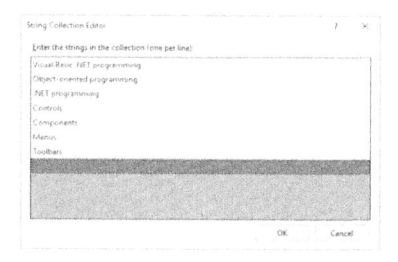

Figure 5.13. Adding items to CheckedListBox

Figure 5.14. CheckedListBox with items we entered

BEGINNER'S GUIDE TO VISUAL BASIC.NET PROGRAMMING

8. Double-click the CheckedListBox to create its default event handler method **SelectedIndexChanged**. This event occurs when the selected item is changed.

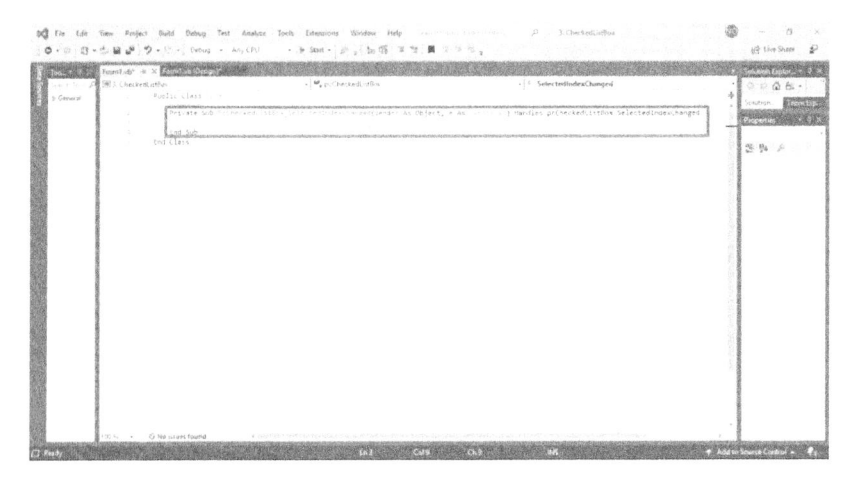

Figure 5.15. The automatically generated SelectedIndexChanged event handler method

9. Let's write a code line that takes the text of the selected item and shows it in a message box. For this, we'll place the code MessageBox.Show(pcCheckedListBox.SelectedItem.ToString()) inside the SelectedIndexChanged event handler method as follows:

```
Private Sub PcCheckedListBox_SelectedIndexChanged(sender As
Object, e As EventArgs) Handles
pcCheckedListBox.SelectedIndexChanged

    MessageBox.Show(pcCheckedListBox.SelectedItem.ToString())

End Sub
```
Code 5.4

The MessageBox.Show(...) method displays a message box with the argument (the string inside the parentheses) written on it. We need to pass an argument which is of string type, i.e. a single line text. We take the Text property of the selected item in the CheckedListBox by the expression pcCheckedListBox.SelectedItem.ToString() which means "get the Text of the selected item of the pcCheckedListBox control and

68

CHAPTER 5. COMMON CONTROLS

convert it to string format". Therefore, when we select an item from the CheckedListBox, its text will be displayed in the message box.

We can now build and execute our program. It will appear as follows:

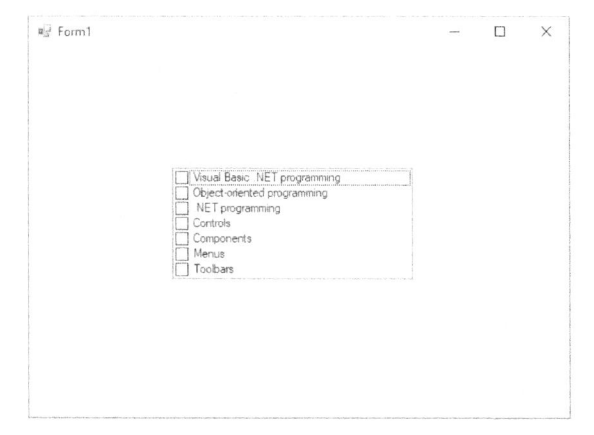

Figure 5.16. Our sample program for demonstrating CheckedListBox

When we click on one of the items, for example on the **Visual Basic.NET programming** item, a message box will appear as follows:

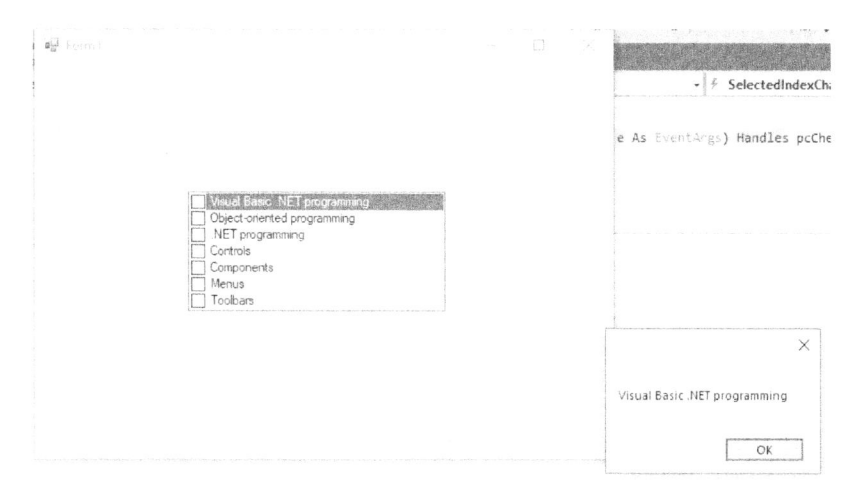

Figure 5.17. Message box showing the item we clicked on the CheckedListBox

69

The message box only has an OK button and disappears when we click this button. Message box is a type of **Dialog** which will be studied in more detail later.

You may have noticed that the item isn't checked when you clicked on. It is because the **CheckOnClick** property is False by default for a CheckedListBox. We can set this property as True as shown below:

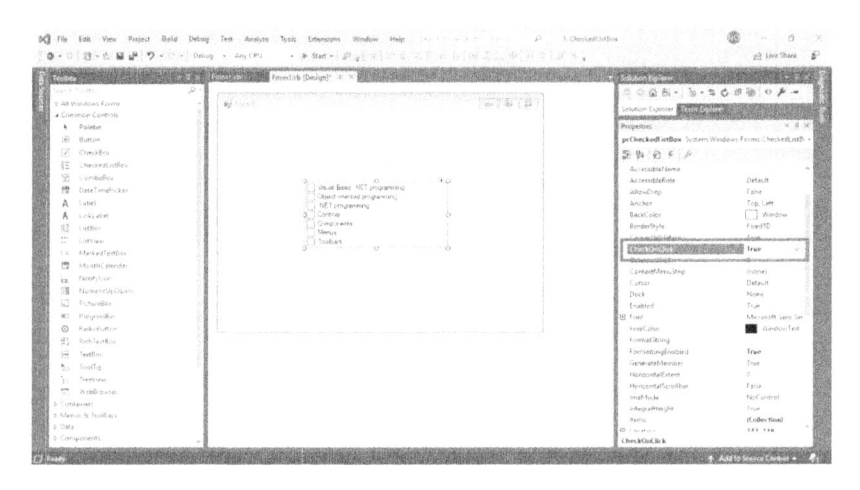

Figure 5.18. Setting the CheckOnClick property as True

If we build and run our program again, the items will be checked when we click on them together with the popping up message box as shown in Figure 5.19.

As in the case with CheckBoxes, a form may contain multiple CheckedListBoxes which can be selected independently.

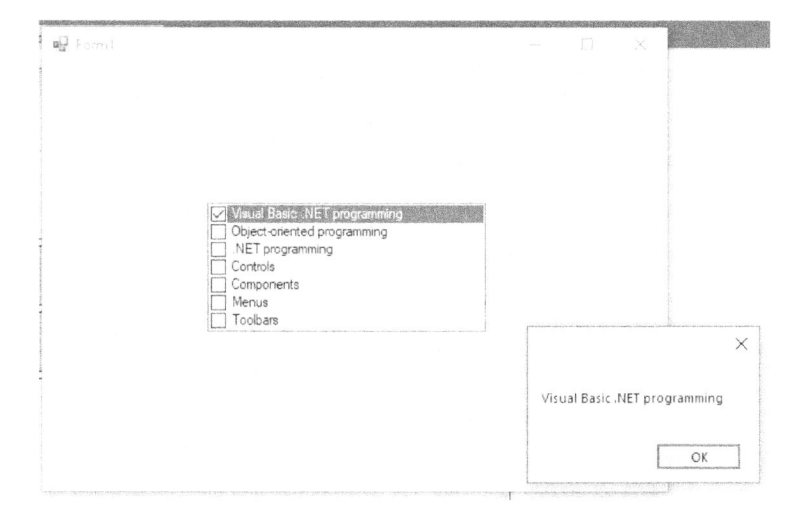

Figure 5.19. The CheckedListBox with its CheckOnClick property set as True

5.4. ComboBox

ComboBox provides a drop-down list of items for selection. Frequently used properties of ComboBox are as follows:

- **DropDownStyle**: Sets the appearance and possibility of adding new elements to the ComboBox.
- **MaxDropDownItems**: Specifies the maximum number of items which will be shown in the list.

A simple ComboBox example: Here's a small project using a ComboBox:

1. Let's create a new VB.NET project in Visual Studio.
2. Place a ComboBox on the form.
3. Set the Name property of the ComboBox as **genderComboBox**.
4. As we did in the CheckedListBox example, click the small arrowhead at the top of the ComboBox to open Edit Items window as in Figure 5.20 and 5.21.
5. Let's enter the items as "Female" and "Male" as shown in Figure 5.22.

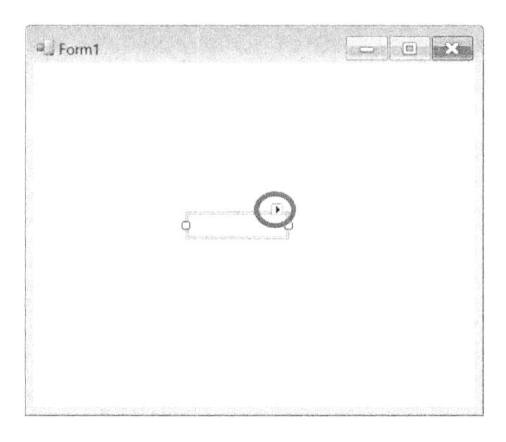

BEGINNER'S GUIDE TO VISUAL BASIC.NET PROGRAMMING

Figure 5.20. Opening the small menu of the ComboBox

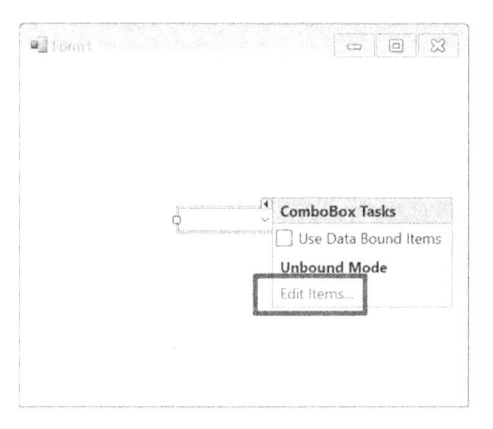

Figure 5.21. Opening the Edit Items menu for the ComboBox

Figure 5.22. Adding items for a ComboBox

72

CHAPTER 5. COMMON CONTROLS

6. Double-click the ComboBox control to create its default event handler SelectedIndexChanged() which is executed when the user changes the selected item.
7. Add the following code to the body (the part between the curly brackets) of the genderComboBox_SelectedIndexChanged() method which will display a message box: MessageBox.Show(genderComboBox.SelectedItem.ToString()); as follows:

```
Public Class Form1
    Private Sub GenderComboBox_SelectedIndexChanged(sender As Object, e As EventArgs) Handles genderComboBox.SelectedIndexChanged

MessageBox.Show(genderComboBox.SelectedItem.ToString())

    End Sub
End Class
```

Code 5.5

8. We can now build and run the project:

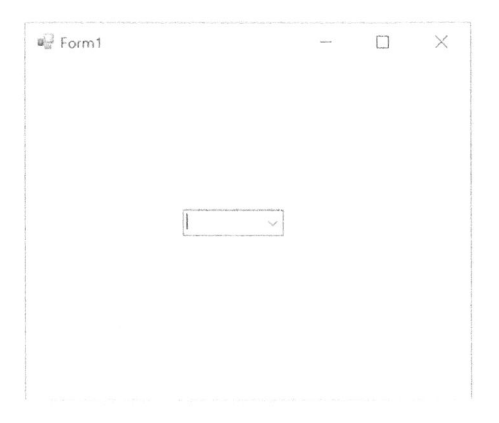

Figure 5.23. The ComboBox example

When we select a value from the ComboBox, it will be shown in a message box as in Figure 5.24.

73

We can set if the user can enter new values to the ComboBox by its DropDownStyle property. If this property is set as **Simple**, it will allow for entering extra values to the ComboBox. Moreover, we can programmatically add or delete items from the ComboBox by `Add()` and `Remove()` methods.

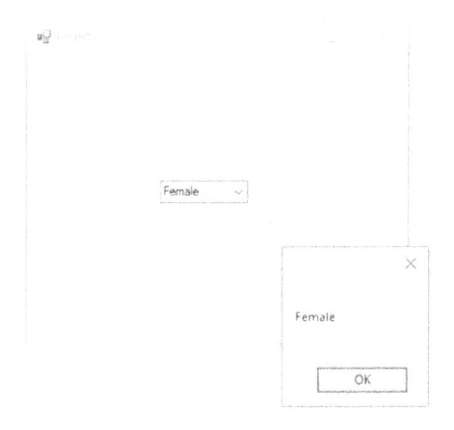

Figure 5.24. Message box displaying the selected item

5.5. DateTimePicker

This control enables the user to select date and time values. It has three main properties:

- **MinDate**: The minimum date shown for selection.
- **MaxDate**: The maximum date available for selection.
- **Format**: The format of the date and time shown in the control.

Let's see how we can use DateTimePicker and get the date and time values from it in a simple project:

1. Please create a new VB.NET project in Visual Studio.
2. Place a DateTimePicker and a Button on the form as shown below:

CHAPTER 5. COMMON CONTROLS

Figure 5.25. Layout of the form

3. For the Button: set its Text property as **Show Selected Date** and its Name as **showDateButton**.
4. Leave the Format property of the DateTimePicker as is (**Long**).

The form should look like below:

Figure 5.26. Current state of the form

5. When the user clicks the button, a message box will show the selected date. For this, double-click the button to create its default event handler **Click** as we learned in Subsection 5.1:

75

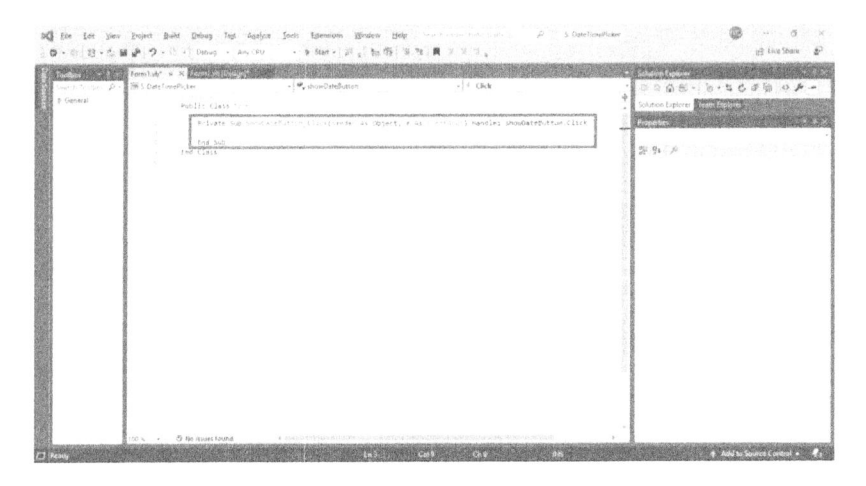

Figure 5.27. The default event handler of the button

6. In order to show the selected date in a message box, we'll take the **Value** property of the DateTimePicker inside the event handler of the button as follows:

```
Public Class Form1
    Private Sub ShowDateButton_Click(sender As Object, e As EventArgs) Handles showDateButton.Click

MessageBox.Show(DateTimePicker1.Value.ToLongDateString())

    End Sub
End Class
```
Code 5.6

Since the Name property of the DateTimePicker control is DateTimePicker1 by default, we take its Value property and convert it to a string using the method toLongDateString() for being able to show in the message box.

7. Now, build and run the project:

CHAPTER 5. COMMON CONTROLS

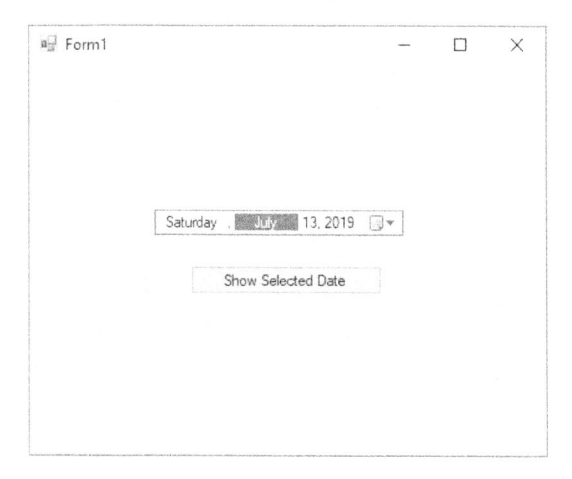

Figure 5.28. The DateTimePicker example

Current date is shown in the DateTimePicker by default. We can select another date from the list by clicking the arrowhead to the right of the DateTimePicker as in Figure 5.29.

We may now click the **Show Selected Date** button to shown the picked date in a message box as shown in Figure 5.30.

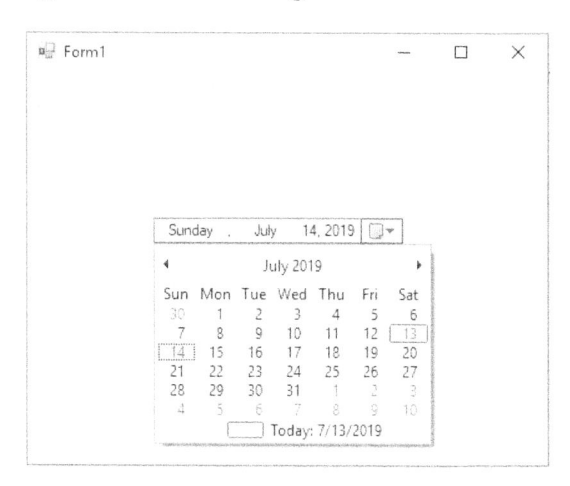

Figure 5.29. Picking a different date

77

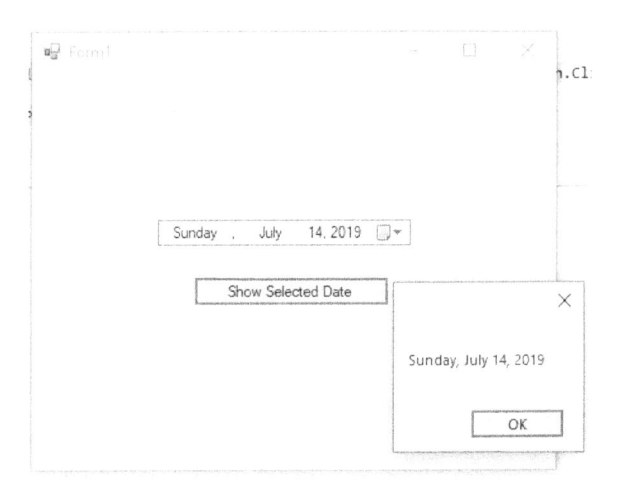

Figure 5.30. Displaying the selected date in the message box

5.6. Label

Labels are just static texts on the form. Labels cannot be edited by the user but can be added, removed or changed programmatically. The important properties of Labels are as follows:

- **Text**: The text written on the label.
- **AutoSize**: Resizes the Label proportional to its text length.
- **TextAlign**: Aligns the text on the left, centre or right side of the Label.

A simple Label example: We will use a Label, a Button and a CheckBox together in this example.

1. Create a new VB.NET project in Visual Studio.
2. Place a Label, a Button and a CheckBox on the form as shown in Figure 5.31.
3. Change the button's Name as **changeLabelButton** and Text as **Change the Label**.
4. Similarly, set the Name and the Text properties of the CheckBox as **changeLabelCheckBox** and **Change the Label**.
5. Set the Name and the Text of the Label as **changingLabel** and **Default**.

CHAPTER 5. COMMON CONTROLS

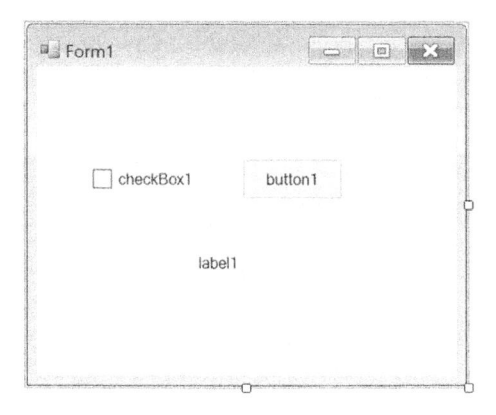

Figure 5.31. The layout of the form

After these changes, the form should look as follows:

Figure 5.32. The appearance of the form after changes

6. We'll now create event handlers for both the CheckBox and the Button which will change the Text property of the Label. For this, double-click the Button and add the code line `changingLabel.Text = "Button clicked"` which will set the Text of the Label as **Button clicked**.
7. Now, double-click the CheckBox to create its default event handler method and add `changingLabel.Text = "Checkbox checked/unchecked";` to the body of this method. After these changes, these event handlers will be as follows:

79

```
Public Class Form1
    Private Sub ChangeLabelButton_Click(sender As Object, e
As EventArgs) Handles changeLabelButton.Click

        changingLabel.Text = "Button clicked"

    End Sub

    Private Sub ChangeLabelCheckBox_CheckedChanged(sender
As Object, e As EventArgs) Handles
changeLabelCheckBox.CheckedChanged

        changingLabel.Text = "Checkbox checked/unchecked"

    End Sub
End Class
```
Code 5.7

8. When we build and run the project, the Label will show **Default**, and then it will be changed as we click the Button or check the CheckBox as shown below:

Figure 5.33. The Label example

5.7. LinkLabel

LinkLabels are Label like controls with the hyperlink functionality, i.e. the user may click on the LinkLabel to open a location (generally a web page).

The main properties of LinkLabels are as follows:

- **LinkColor**: Sets the text colour of the LinkLabel.
- **VisitedLinkColor**: The colour of the LinkLabel after the link is visited by the user.
- **LinkBehavior**: Sets if the link will be underlined or not.

A LinkLabel example:

1. Create a new VB.NET project in Visual Studio.
2. Place a LinkLabel on the form as shown below:

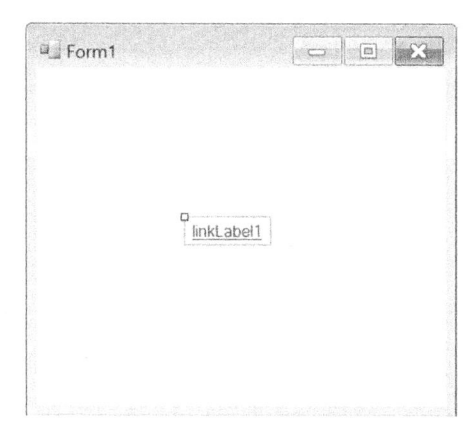

Figure 5.34. A LinkLabel on the form

3. Set the Text property of the LinkLabel as **Visit the homepage.**
4. Change the Name property of the LinkLabel from linkLabel1 to **visitHomepageLinkLabel**. The form should look as in Figure 5.35.
5. Now, double-click on the LinkLabel to create its default event **LinkClicked**.
6. Insert the following code inside the body of the event handler method: System.Diagnostics.Process.Start("www.msdn.com") This code line is used to open the link given inside the parantheses. When the user clicks the LinkLabel, the web browser will open the Microsoft Developer Network (MSDN) website. The event handling method VisitHomepageLinkLabel_LinkClicked() will be as shown below:

```
Private Sub VisitHomepageLinkLabel_LinkClicked(sender As
Object, e As LinkLabelLinkClickedEventArgs) Handles
visitHomepageLinkLabel.LinkClicked

    System.Diagnostics.Process.Start("www.msdn.com")

End Sub
```
Code 5.8

Figure 5.35. The form after the changes

7. Build and run the project. When the Visit the homepage text is clicked, the default web browser will be launched and navigate to the website automatically as shown in the following figure:

Figure 5.36. The LinkLabel opens the specified web page

5.8. ListBox

ListBox displays a list of items. It is used to display items to the user and let the user to select items from. Items can be added to the ListBox visually during the development or programmatically during runtime.

Commonly used properties and methods of ListBoxes are as follows:

CHAPTER 5. COMMON CONTROLS

We have mentioned **methods** several times until this point. As you may have noticed, they are used to perform a function. Please note that methods are used with parentheses next to them as shown below.

- **Items**: Used for accessing the items in a ListBox.
- **Add()**: Used for adding new items.
- **Remove()**: Removes an item.
- **SelectedItem**: Returns the name of the selected item.
- **SelectedIndex**: Returns the index of the selected item.
- **Count**: Returns the number of the items in the ListBox.
- **Clear()**: Removes all items from the ListBox.

Let's develop a project that includes a ListBox. We'll use Buttons to add/remove items to the ListBox and to show the user-selected item in a message box.

1. Create a new VB.NET project in Visual Studio.
2. Place a ListBox and three Buttons on the form as shown in Figure 5.37.

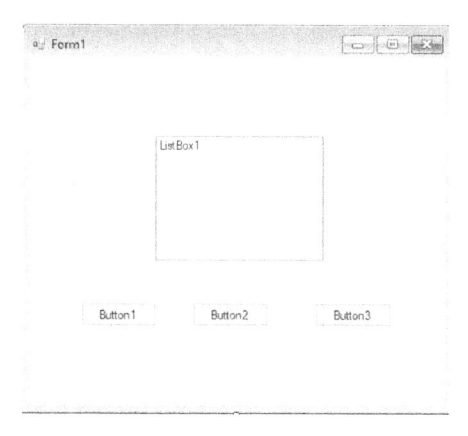

Figure 5.37. Layout of the form

3. Set the Text properties of button1, button2 and button3 as **Add random**, **Remove selected** and **Show item count**, respectively.
4. Change the Name properties of button1, button2 and button3 as **addRandomButton**, **removeSelectedButton** and **ItemCountButton**, respectively.

83

5. After these changes, the form should look as shown in Figure 5.38.

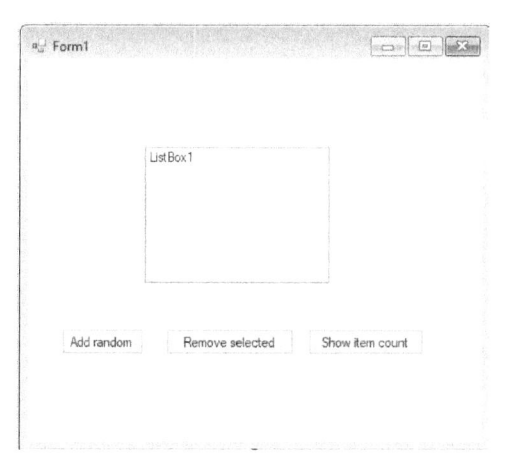

Figure 5.38. The form after the changes

6. When the user clicks the **Add random** button, a random number between 1 and 10000 will be generated and added to the ListBox. For this, double-click the Add random button to create its Click event handler. Add the following random number generating code inside the body of this event handling method:

```
Private Sub AddRandomButton_Click(sender As Object, e As
EventArgs) Handles addRandomButton.Click

        Dim rnd As New Random()
        ListBox1.Items.Add(rnd.Next(1, 10000).ToString())

End Sub
```
Code 5.9

In this code, firstly a random number generator object is created by the expression `Dim rnd As New Random()`. Then in the next line, a random number between 1 and 10000 is generated by the expression `rnd.Next(1, 10000)` and then converted to String for adding to the ListBox using the `Add()` method. This code will execute each time the user clicks the **Add random** button therefore, will add a different random number to the ListBox.

7. Similarly, double-click the **Remove selected** button to create its event handler and add the necessary code to remove the selected item with the following code:

```
Private Sub RemoveSelectedButton_Click(sender As Object, e As EventArgs) Handles removeSelectedButton.Click

    ListBox1.Items.Remove(ListBox1.SelectedItem)

End Sub
```
Code 5.10

The Remove() method removes the item written inside the parentheses. In this code, we have passed the selected item inside the method as Remove(ListBox1.SelectedItem) so that the user-selected item will be removed by this method.

8. Finally, double-click the **Show item count** button to generate its event handler and place the following code inside it so that a message box will show the number of items in the ListBox:

```
Private Sub ItemCountButton_Click(sender As Object, e As EventArgs) Handles ItemCountButton.Click

    MessageBox.Show("Number of items: " + ListBox1.Items.Count.ToString())

End Sub
```
Code 5.11

In this code, ListBox1.Items.Count.ToString() returns (gives) the number of items of the ListBox as a text. Instead of showing just a number in the message box, we have **merged** it with the text "Number of items: " using the + operator. Therefore, if the number of items in the ListBox is 5, the message box will show: **The number of items: 5**.

9. After we build and run the project, the ListBox will be empty as in Figure 5.39. After clicking the **Add random** button several times, the ListBox will be populated with random numbers as in Figure 5.40.

85

Figure 5.39. The program at its initial state

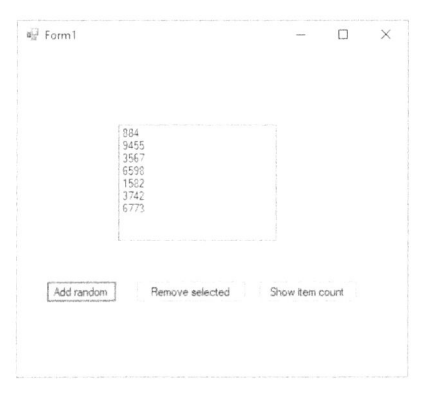

Figure 5.40. The populated ListBox

10. We can now select an item from the ListBox by single-clicking on it. Then, we may click the **Remove Selected** button to remove the selected item as shown in Figure 5.41. The item will be removed as in Figure 5.42. Please note that if the same item appears more than once in the ListBox and it is selected for removal, the item is removed from top to bottom one by one.
11. Finally, when the user clicks the **Show item count** button, a message box will appear to show the number of items as shown in Figure 5.43.

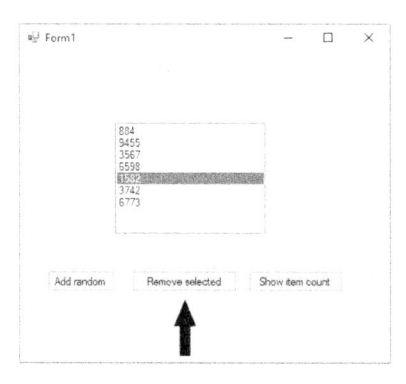

Figure 5.41. An item is selected from the ListBox

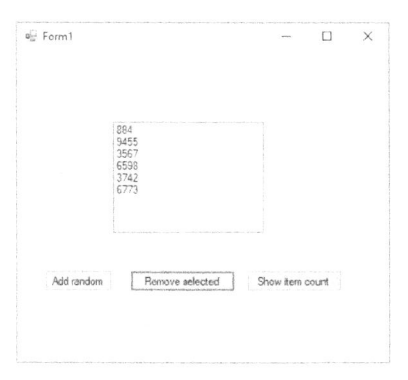

Figure 5.42. The selected item has been removed from the ListBox

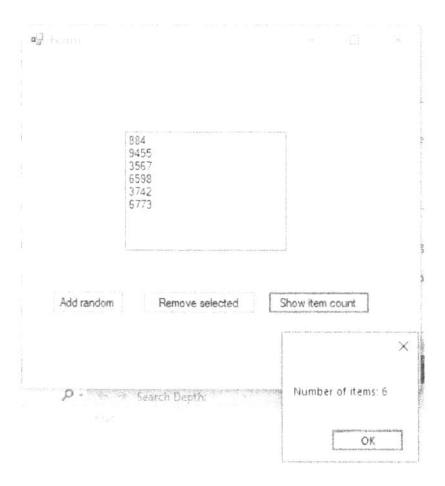

Figure 5.43. The item count is shown in a message box

87

5.9. ListView

ListView is used to display items in various ways. Let's see how we can display items in a ListView by an example:

1. Create a new VB.NET project in Visual Studio.
2. Place a ListView in the middle of the form.
3. Click the arrowhead located at the top of the ListView to open the menu:

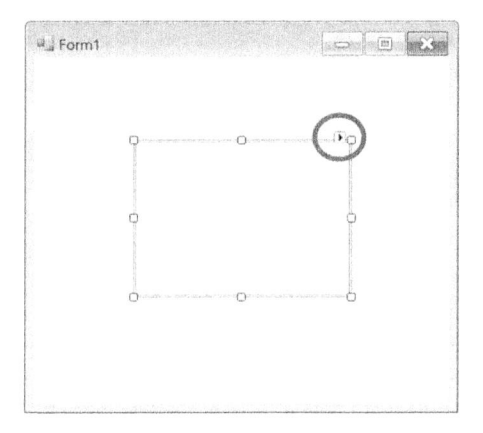

Figure 5.44. Opening the menu of the ListView

4. Click the **Edit Columns** for editing the columns of the ListView:

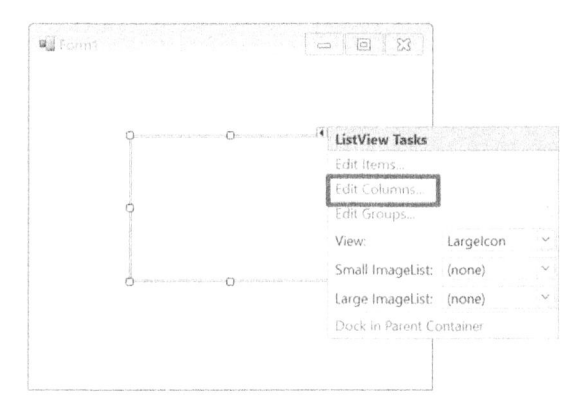

Figure 5.45. Opening the column menu

5. Add a new column and set its Name property as **Name**:

CHAPTER 5. COMMON CONTROLS

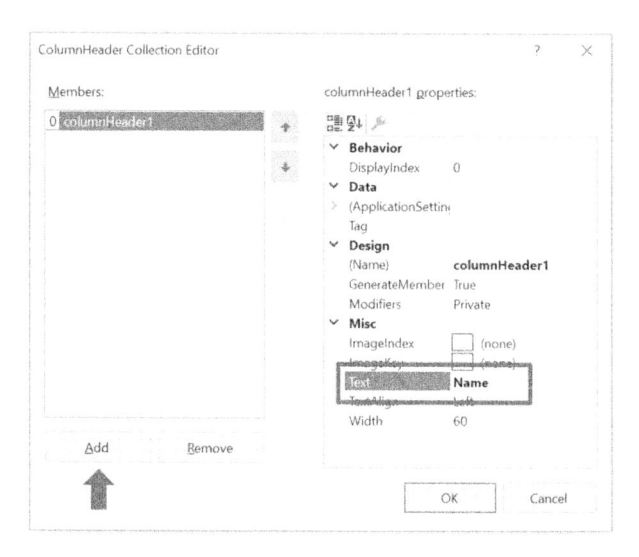

Figure 5.46. Adding a new column

Add two more columns and set their Name properties as **Surname** and **Age**, respectively.

6. These columns will not yet be visible since the ListView is in the **LargeIcon** view. We need to switch this property as **Details** as shown below:

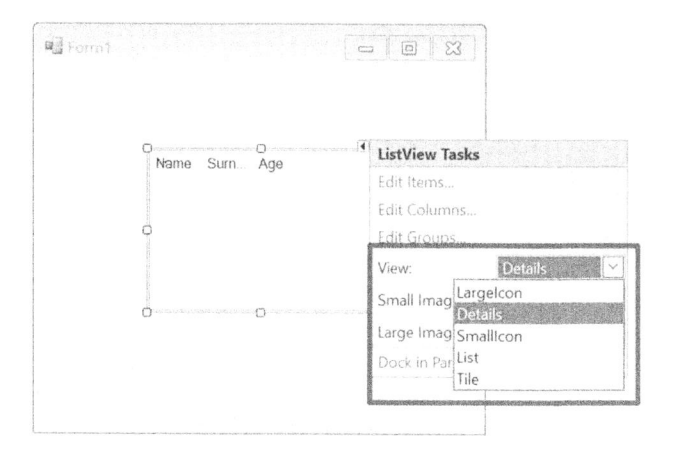

Figure 5.47. Setting the View property

89

The columns will be visible now. However, still not aligned properly. We can drag the columns to fit them properly in the ListView control as follows:

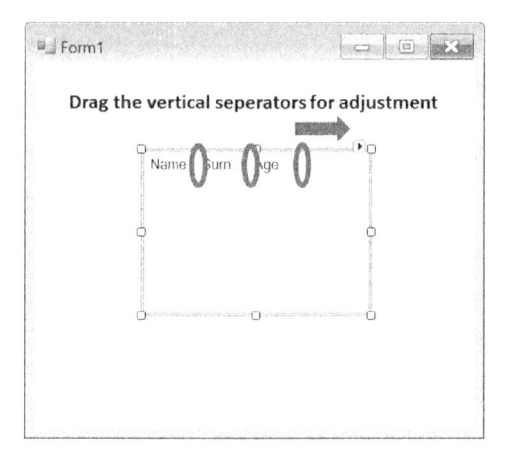

Figure 5.48. Adjusting the widths of columns

After this operation, columns will fit inside as shown in Figure 5.49.

Moreover, the gridlines of the ListView control can be made visible by setting its **GridLines** property as **True** as shown in Figure 5.50.

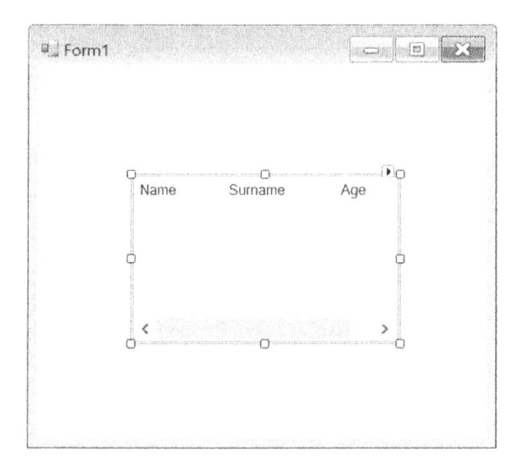

Figure 5.49. Columns fitted inside the ListView

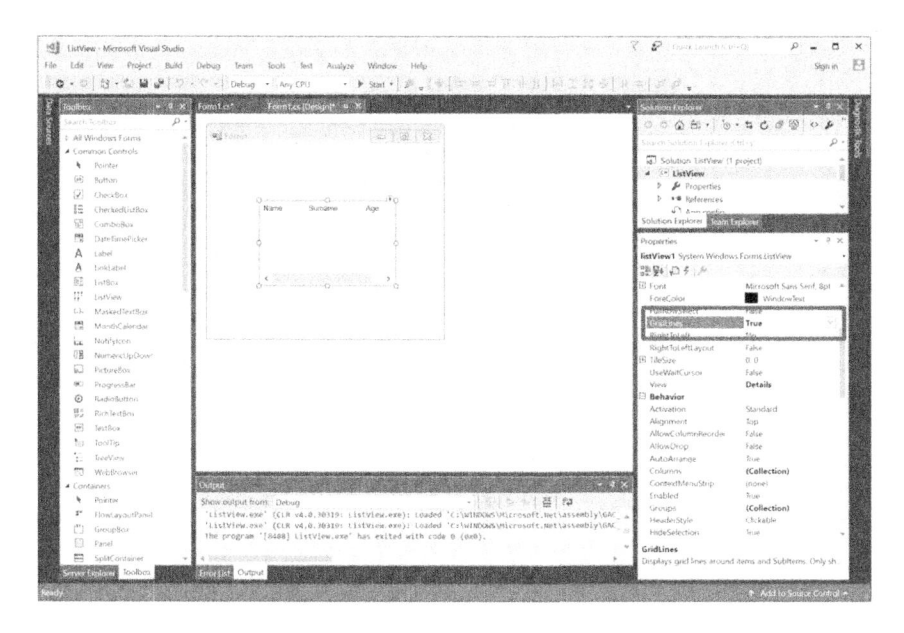

Figure 5.50. Displaying the gridlines

7. Adding items to a ListView is not like assigning a property. Instead, we need to create an **object** to hold data we'll pass to the ListView. The following code snippet creates a ListViewItem object that will temporarily hold the data we'll write to the ListView:

```
Dim listvi = New ListViewItem("John")
listvi.SubItems.Add("Cardle")
listvi.SubItems.Add("35")
```
Code 5.12

We'll then add the contents of listvi item to the ListView control as follows:

```
ListView1.Items.Add(listvi)
```
Code 5.13

These code lines will not be executed automatically, we need to insert them inside an event method. We can write them in the Load method of the form, Form1, so that these code lines will be executed when the form loads (i.e. when the program starts running). For this, double-click somewhere empty on the form to create its Load method and then write the code lines inside its body as follows:

```
Private Sub Form1_Load(sender As Object, e As EventArgs) Handles MyBase.Load

        Dim listvi = New ListViewItem("John")
        listvi.SubItems.Add("Cardle")
        listvi.SubItems.Add("35")
        ListView1.Items.Add(listvi)

    End Sub
```
Code 5.14

8. When we build and run the project, these code lines will run as soon as the form is loaded and the ListView will be populated as follows:

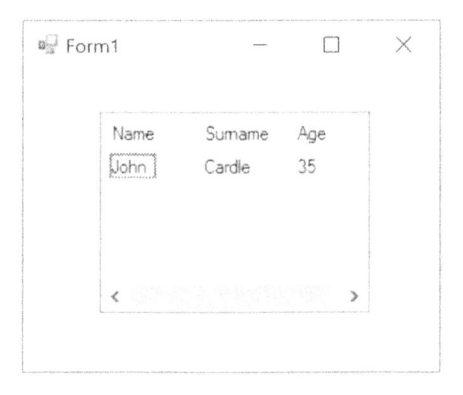

Figure 5.51. The populated ListView

5.10. MaskedTextBox

MaskedTextBoxes are used for entering text (string) in a specified format. For example, if the user will enter the phone number in a program, it can only be of the form (_ _ _) _ _ _-_ _ _ _. For this task, we can use a MaskedTextBox where we set its mask as a phone number.

Frequently used properties of MaskedTextBoxes are as follows:

- **BorderStyle**: Sets the borders of the MaskedTextBox.
- **TextAlign**: Alignes the text inside the MaskedTextBox.
- **BeepOnError**: Beeps if the user tries to enter a disallowed input.

CHAPTER 5. COMMON CONTROLS

A **MaskedTextBox example**: Let's see the MaskedTextBox in action. We'll take phone numbers from a MaskedTextBox and add them to a ListBox in this example.

1. Create a new VB.NET project in Visual Studio.
2. Place a MaskedTextBox on the form.
3. Place a button next to the MaskedTextBox.
4. Finally, place a ListBox below them. The form will look as follows:

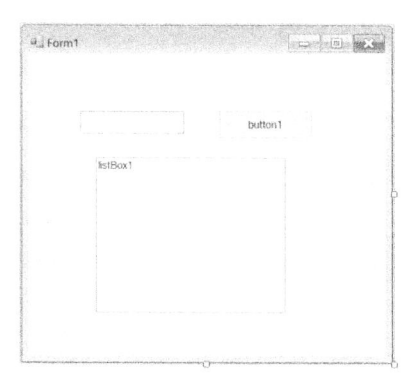

Figure 5.52. Layout of the form

5. Set the Name of the Button as **addButton** and its Text as **Add**.
6. Similarly, set the Name of the ListBox as **numbersListbox**.
7. Finally, set the Name of the MaskedTextBox as **numbersMaskedTextBox**. The form will be as follows after these changes:

Figure 5.53. Current state of the form

93

8. In order to specify the input format of the MaskedTextBox, we should set a mask. For this, click the arrowhead at the top of the MaskedTextBox and select **Set Mask** as shown in Figures 5.54 and 5.55:

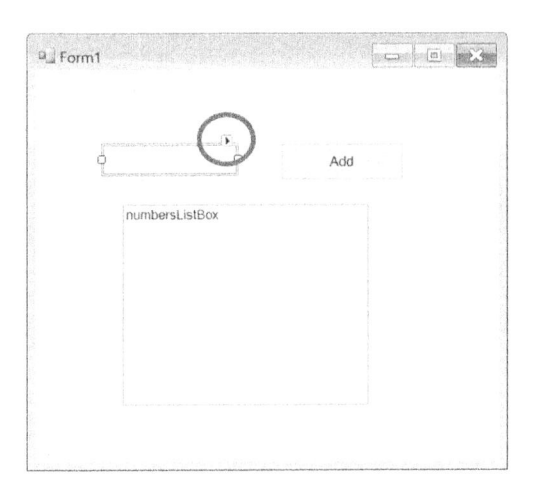

Figure 5.54. Opening the MaskedTextBox menu

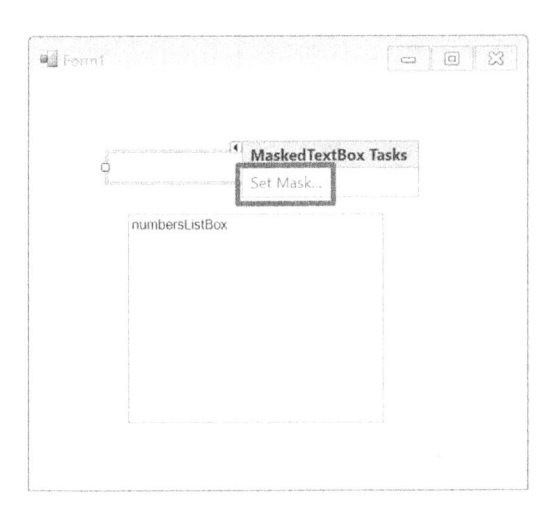

Figure 5.55. Setting the mask for the MaskedTextBox

In the Set Mask menu, we can select among various specifications. For this example, we will select **Phone number** mask as in Figure 5.56.

CHAPTER 5. COMMON CONTROLS

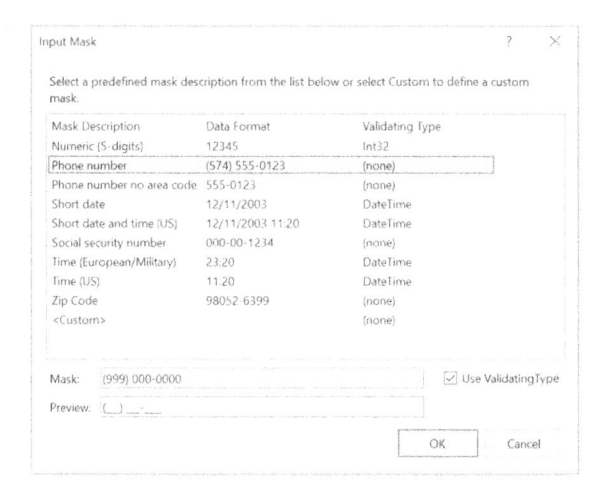

Figure 5.56. Setting the Phone number mask

9. We'll take the phone numbers and list them in the ListBox when the Button is clicked. For this, we need to create the Button's default event handler method: Click. Just double-click the Button to create this method as usual. We need to **get the Text of the MaskedTextBox** and **add this Text to the ListBox**. We can use the following code line for this:

```
numbersListBox.Items.Add(numbersMaskedTextBox.Text)
```
Code 5.15

After adding this line, the click handler method will be as follows:

```
Private Sub AddButton_Click(sender As Object, e As
EventArgs) Handles addButton.Click

    numbersListBox.Items.Add(numbersMaskedTextBox.Text)

End Sub
```
Code 5.16

10. Finally, when we build and run the project, we get the following program window:

95

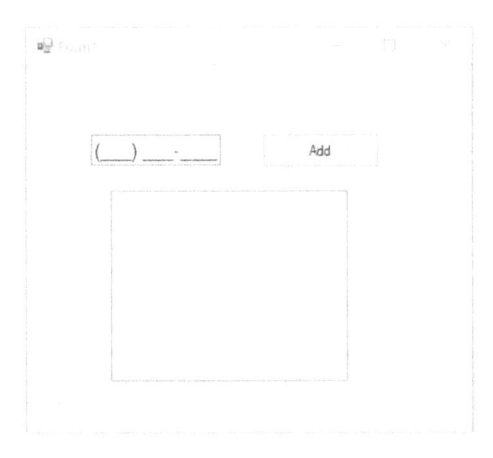

Figure 5.57. Initial view of the program

We may only enter phone numbers inside the MaskedTextBox. When we click the Add button, the phone number will be added to the ListBox as follows:

Figure 5.58. The program after two phone numbers were added

5.11. MonthCalendar

This control shows calendar in month format so that the user can pick a date from it. MonthCalendar is similar to DateTimePicker. Their difference is that MonthCalendar's calendar view is always open for selecting a date, while the user needs to click on the DateTimePicker to open the view to select date.

The properties of MonthCalendar are as follows:

- **MinDate**: The minimum date the MonthCalendar will show.
- **MaxDate**: Maximum date the MonthCalendar will show.
- **BoldedDates**: Used for showing special dates in bold.
- **ShowToday**: Sets if today's date will be shown at the bottom of the calendar or not.
- **SelectionStart**: Holds the selected starting date.
- **SelectionEnds**: Holds the selected ending date.
- **SelectionRange**: Holds the range of days between the selected starting date and ending date.

A MonthCalendar Example: Let's show the range of days between the selected starting and ending dates of a MonthCalendar on a Label in this example.

1. Create a new VB.NET project in Visual Studio.
2. Place a MonthCalendar and a Label on the form as follows:

Figure 5.59. Layout of the form

3. Set the Name of the Label as **rangeLabel** and its Text as **SelectionRange:**.
4. Set the Name of the MonthCalendar as **selectDates**.
5. The default event for the MonthCalendar is the **DateChanged** event, which fires when the selected date(s) change. Therefore, double-click

the MonthCalendar to create its default event handler method SelectDates_DateChanged(...).

6. Add the following code line to display the SelectionRange when the user selects date range on the calendar: rangeLabel.Text = selectDates.SelectionRange.ToString(). After this addition, the default event handler method will be as follows:

```
Private Sub SelectDays_DateChanged(sender As Object, e As
DateRangeEventArgs) Handles selectDays.DateChanged

    rangeLabel.Text = selectDates.SelectionRange.ToString()

End Sub
```
Code 5.17

7. Let's build and run the project. Today's date will be automatically selected on the MonthCalendar control by default and the Label will display its default text:

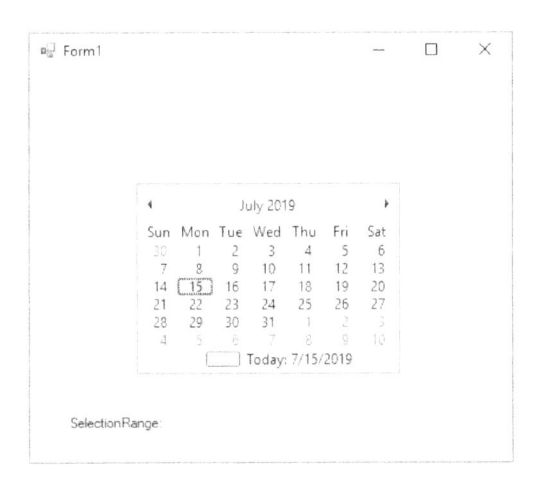

Figure 5.60. The initial view of the program

We can now select dates from the calendar. For this, click on a starting date, hold down the mouse button, and drag the mouse pointer to the ending date. The selected dates will then be shown by a grey background while the Label will display the selection range as in Figure 5.61.

It is worth noting that the maximum selection range is 7 days by default. You can change it by setting the **MaxSelectionCount** property of the MonthCalendar control.

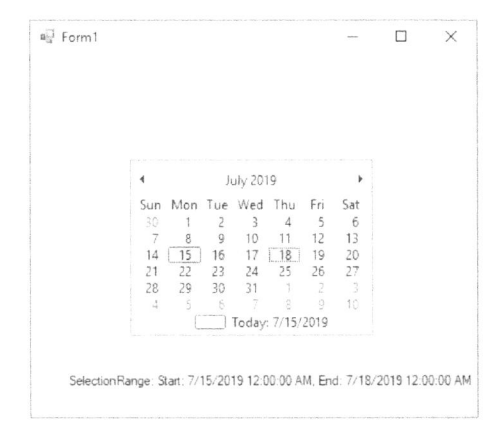

Figure 5.61. Label showing the selected range

5.12. NotifyIcon

This control is used for displaying an icon in the notification area of Windows. Notification area is at the right of the taskbar as shown below:

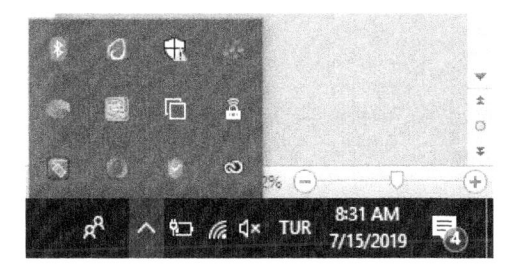

Figure 5.62. The notification area

The important properties of the NotifyIcon are as follows:

- **Icon**: The Icon property of the NotifyIcon specifies which icon file (*ico) is to be used as the application icon in the notification area.
- **ContextMenuStrip**: Specifies the right-click menu of the NotifyIcon.

ContextMenuStrip is a menu component which is used for specifying a menu for the right-click as mentioned in the previous chapter.

NotifyIcon control is generally used together with the ContextMenuStrip.

Let's see how we can use NotifyIcon in conjunction with the ContextMenuStrip in an example:

1. Create a new VB.NET project in Visual Studio.
2. Place a NotifyIcon and a ContextMenuStrip on the form. As you drag&drop these elements on the form, you will see that **they do not appear on the form**. It is because these elements operate in the background and not displayed to the user. After drag&drop operations, you will see these elements below the form design pane:

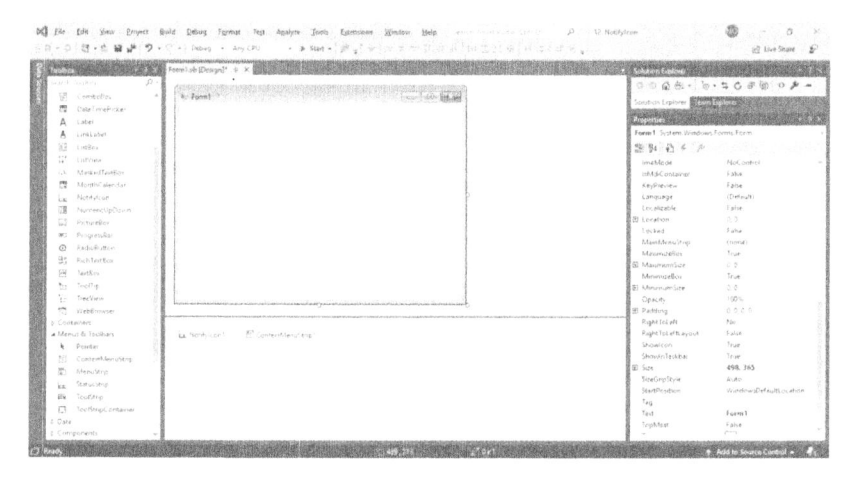

Figure 5.63. NotifyIcon and ContextMenuStrip elements of the form

3. Click on the contextMenuStrip1 menu (as shown in Figure 5.63) and then it will temporarily appear on the form for entering a right-click menu as in Figure 5.64. Let's insert an **Exit** item for this example as shown in Figure 5.65.
4. We will now set the action the **Exit** menu will perform. For this, double-click on the **Exit** item so that its event handler method `ExitToolStripMenuItem_Click(...)` will be created in the editor as shown in Figure 5.66.
5. Add the code line `Application.Exit()` inside this event handler, which will cause the application to quit when executed:

```
Private Sub ExitToolStripMenuItem_Click(sender As Object, e
As EventArgs) Handles ExitToolStripMenuItem.Click

    Application.Exit()

End Sub
```
Code 5.18

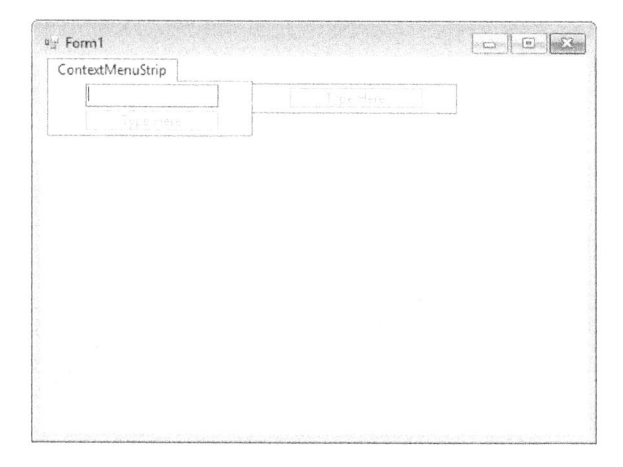

Figure 5.64. ContextMenuStrip appearing on the form for entering menu items

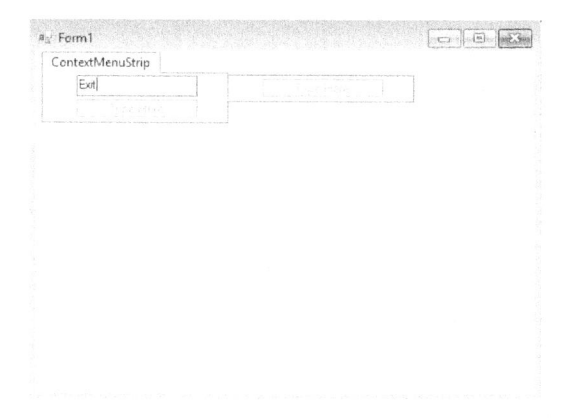

Figure 5.65. Adding the Exit item to the ContextMenuStrip

ContextMenuStrip is set for now. We now need to assign this menu to the NotifyIcon control. Click the notifyIcon1 in the form designer and navigate to its properties. In the properties pane, set the

ContextMenuStrip property as contextMenuStrip1 as shown in Figure 5.67.

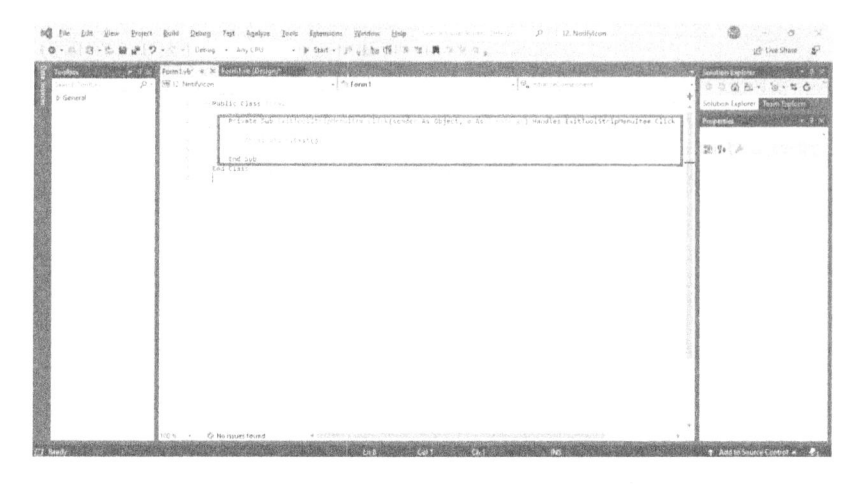

Figure 5.66. The event handler for the **Exit** item shown in the editor

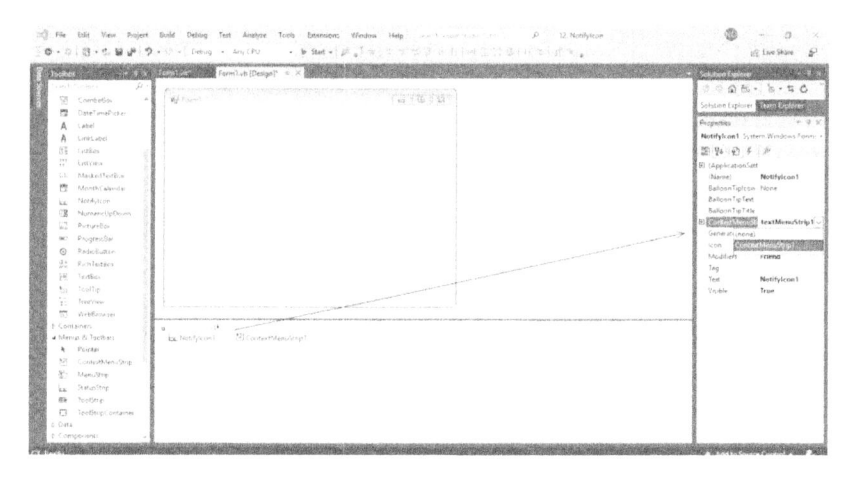

Figure 5.67. Setting the ContextMenuStrip as contextMenuStrip1 for the notifyIcon1

6. We now need to assign an icon for the NotifyIcon so that it will appear in the notifications area. Again in the properties window, click the ellipsis at the Icon property as shown below:

CHAPTER 5. COMMON CONTROLS

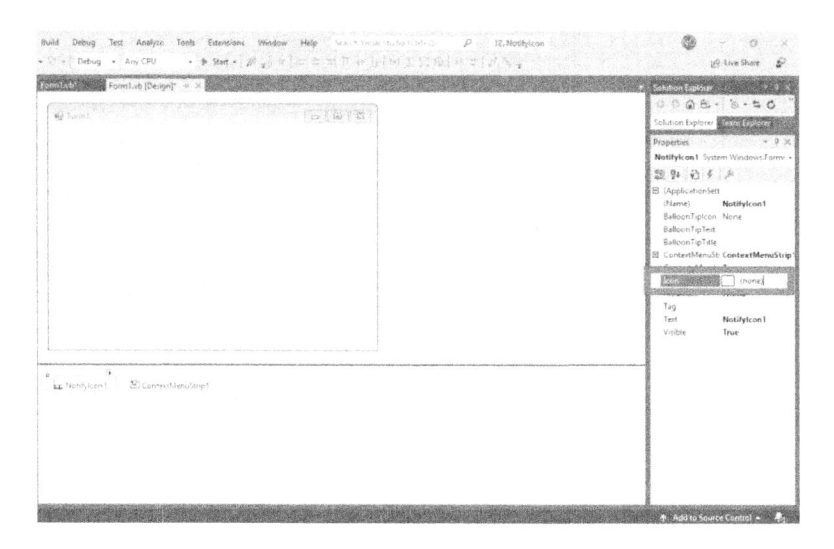

Figure 5.68. Adding an icon for the NotifyIcon

This will open a file dialog so that you can select an icon file for the NotifyIcon. Please note that only .ico files are accepted. You can find one from the Internet or use the file you downloaded from this book's accompanying website. After selecting the .ico file, it will be shown at the properties pane as in Figure 5.69.

7. We can now build and run the project. Since we didn't place any visible controls on the form, the application window will be empty as in Figure 5.70. However, its NotifyIcon will be in the notifications area as shown in Figure 5.71. Please note that if you used a different icon file, it will be shown in the notification area.
8. When we right-click on the notification icon, the ContextMenuStrip will be shown. We only added an Exit item therefore; it will be as in Figure 5.72.
9. When we click on the Exit item, the method given in Code 5.18 will be executed which will quit the application. Note that we can add as many items as we like in the right-click menu.

103

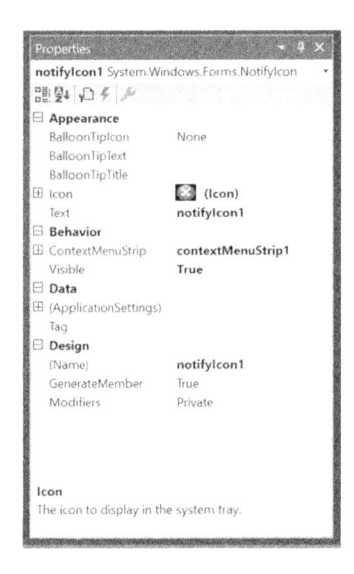

Figure 5.69. The icon of the NotifyIcon is assigned

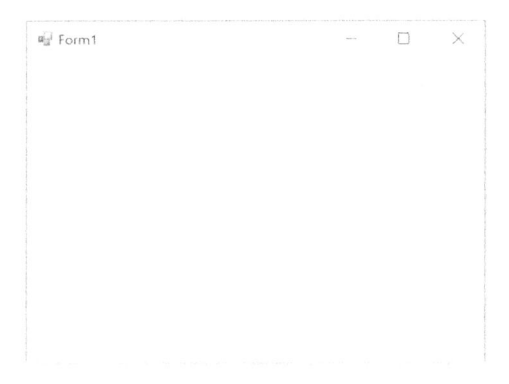

Figure 5.70. Empty application window

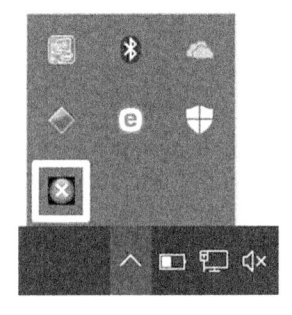

Figure 5.71. Notification icon of the application

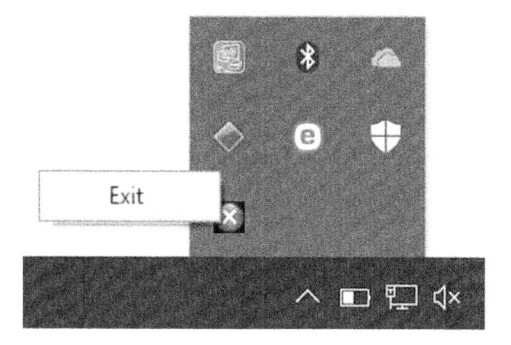

Figure 5.72. Right-click menu connected to the notification icon

5.13. NumericUpDown

NumericUpDown displays numeric data which can be incremented and decremented using its up and down arrows. Its numeric value can be set or read programmatically.

The main properties of NumericUpDown control are as follows:

- **Value**: The number displayed in the NumericUpDown.
- **Minimum**: Minimum value of the NumericUpDown.
- **Maximum**: Maximum value of the NumericUpDown.
- **Increment**: Sets the increment/decrement step of the NumericUpDown.

Let's use the NumericUpDown in a simple example:

1. Create a new VB.NET project in Visual Studio.
2. Place a NumericUpDown and a ListBox on the form as in Figure 5.73. In this example, as the value of the NumericUpDown is changed, it will be added to the ListBox.

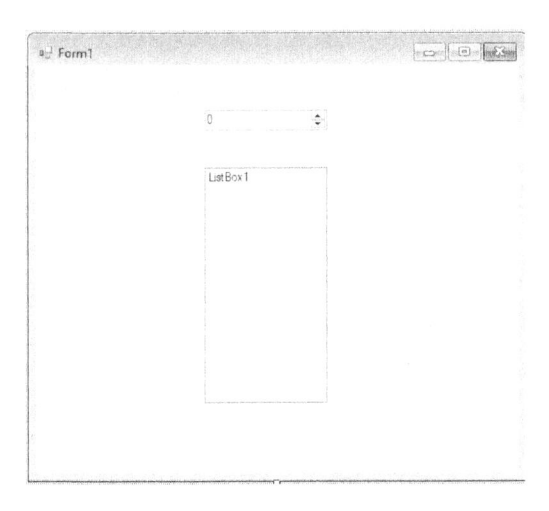

Figure 5.73. Layout of the form

3. Set the FontSize properties of both NumericUpDown and the ListBox as 12 units so that the numbers will be displayed bigger (the default Font Size is 8 units).
4. Set the Name of the NumericUpDown control as **evenNumericUpDown**.
5. Set the Name of the ListBox as **numbersListBox**.
6. Double-click somewhere empty on the form to create Form1's default event handler Form1_Load(...) as we used before. Add the following code lines inside so that the NumericUpDown will be configured as soon as the application starts running:

```
Private Sub Form1_Load(sender As Object, e As EventArgs) Handles MyBase.Load

        evenNumericUpDown.Minimum = 0
        evenNumericUpDown.Maximum = 200
        evenNumericUpDown.Increment = 2

End Sub
```
Code 5.19

In this method, the limits of the value of NumericUpDown is set as 0 and 200, the display value will not go below or above these values. In the third code line, the increment step is set as 2. Since the starting value of

CHAPTER 5. COMMON CONTROLS

the NumericUpDown is 0, its value will increase like 2, 4, 8, etc. Therefore, this NumericUpDown will display only even numbers.

7. Similarly, double-click on the NumericUpDown control so that its default event handler evenNumericUpDown_ValueChanged(...) will be created. This method will be called when the value of the NumericUpDown is changed:

```
Private Sub EvenNumericUpDown_ValueChanged(sender As Object,
e As EventArgs) Handles evenNumericUpDown.ValueChanged

numbersListBox.Items.Add(evenNumericUpDown.Value.ToString())

End Sub
```
Code 5.20

In this code line, the Value of the evenNumericUpDown control is read and converted to string. This string representation is then passed to the Add() method of the numbersListBox.Items so that the value displayed in the evenNumericUpDown is added to the numbersListBox each time the value of the evenNumericUpDown is changed.

8. We can now build and run the project. The program will appear as follows:

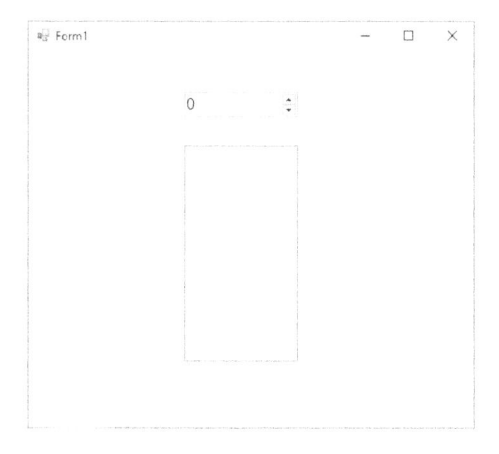

Figure 5.74. The program when it first starts

107

As we increase/decrease the value of the NumericUpDown control, its value will be added to the ListBox as shown in Figure 5.75.

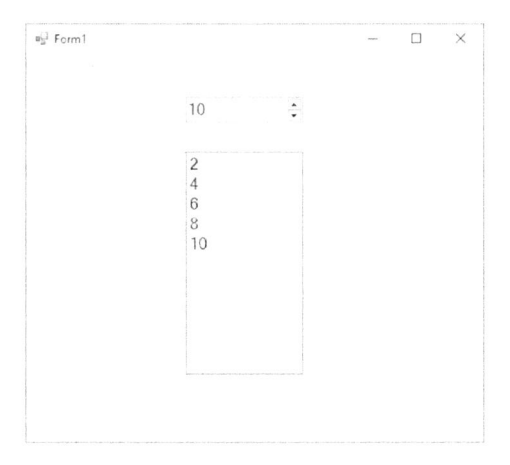

Figure 5.75. The ListBox is populated by even numbers after successive changes in the NumericUpDown's value

5.14. PictureBox

PictureBox is used for displaying images. The image to be shown in a PictureBox is either set during the development or programmatically at runtime. The main properties of a PictureBox are as follows:

- **Image**: Used for setting the image to be displayed.
- **SizeMode**: Sets how the image will be inserted inside of the PictureBox. It has three frequently used options: **Normal**, **Stretch** or **CenterImage**.

Let's develop a simple example in which the SizeMode of an image is set by clicking the respective buttons:

1. Create a new VB.NET project in Visual Studio.
2. Place a PictureBox and three Buttons on the form as follows:

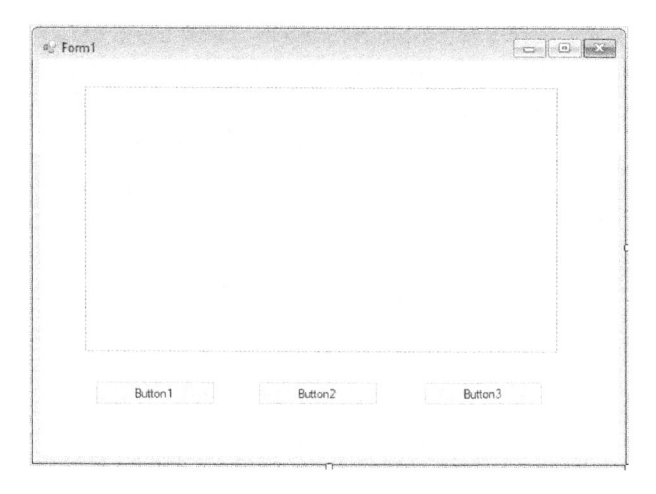

Figure 5.76. Layout of the form

3. Set the Name properties of the Buttons as **normalButton**, **stretchButton** and **centerButton**, respectively.
4. Set the Text properties of the Buttons as **Normal**, **Stretch** and **Center**, respectively.
5. Set the Name property of the PictureBox as **resizePictureBox**.
6. Click the arrowhead located at the top of the PictureBox as shown below:

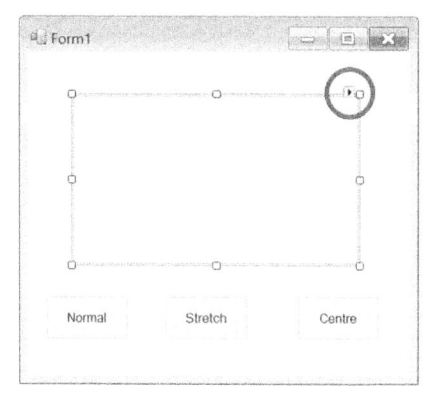

Figure 5.77. Opening the Tasks menu of the PictureBox

7. Click the **Choose Image** item:

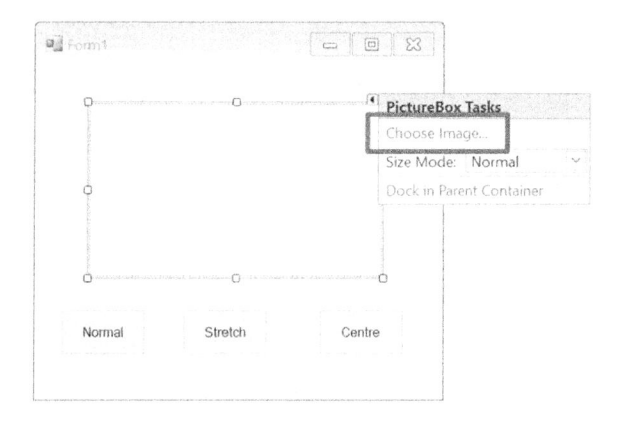

Figure 5.78. Choosing an image for the PictureBox

8. It is better to choose an image from your computer and import it into the project for portability as shown in Figure 5.79. For this, select the **Local resource** and the **Import** button to select an image from your computer. You can use the image provided in the books's accompanying website for this example (seaview.jpg).

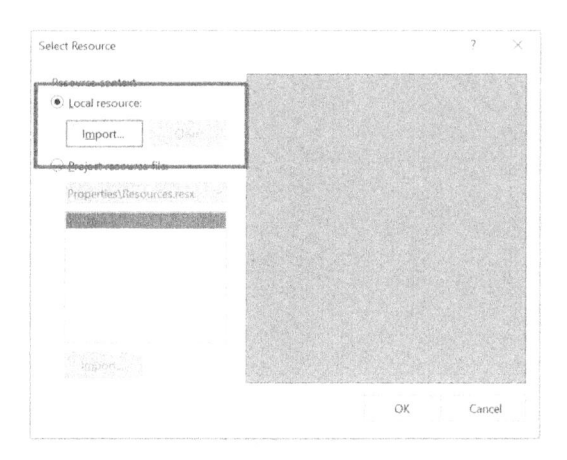

Figure 5.79. Importing an image into the project

9. When we choose the image, it will be previewed as follows:

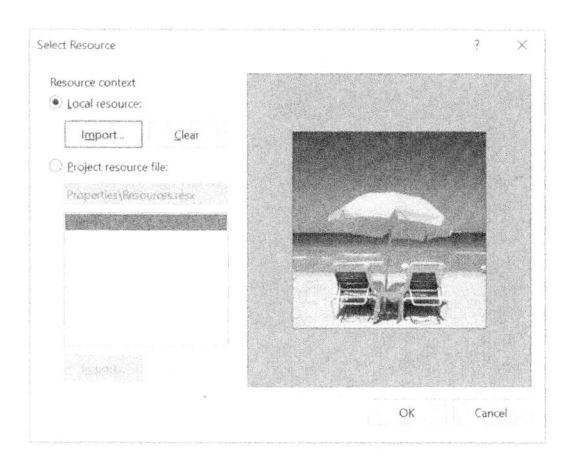

Figure 5.80. Previewing the imported image

After we click OK, the image will be available on the form.

10. We can now set the actions for the Buttons which will resize the image accordingly. Double-click the Buttons to create their default Click events. Then, add the following code lines to the **normalButton**, **stretchButton** and **centerButton**, respectively.

```
Private Sub NormalButton_Click(sender As Object, e As EventArgs) Handles normalButton.Click

    resizePictureBox.SizeMode = PictureBoxSizeMode.Normal

End Sub

Private Sub StretchButton_Click(sender As Object, e As EventArgs) Handles stretchButton.Click

    resizePictureBox.SizeMode = PictureBoxSizeMode.StretchImage

End Sub

Private Sub CenterButton_Click(sender As Object, e As EventArgs) Handles centerButton.Click

    resizePictureBox.SizeMode = PictureBoxSizeMode.CenterImage

End Sub
```
Code 5.21

The image is resized to normal, stretched and centred modes, respectively, inside these methods.

11. We can now build and run the project. By default, the image will appear in the Normal mode as follows:

Figure 5.81. Image in the Normal mode initially

When the **Stretch** button is clicked, image will be stretched inside the PictureBox:

Figure 5.82. Image in the Stretch mode

Finally, image will be centred inside the PictureBox when the Centre button is clicked:

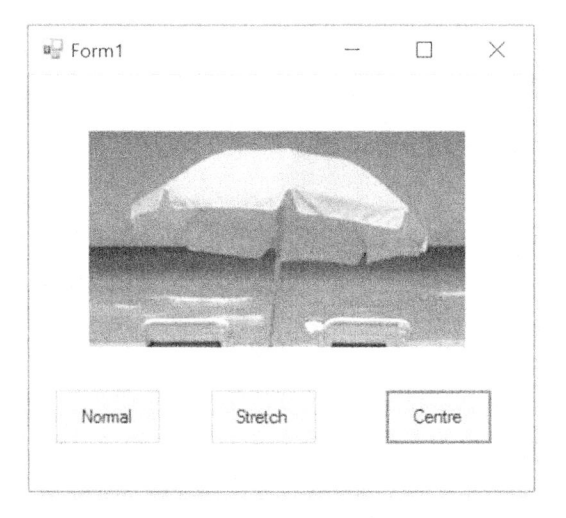

Figure 5.83. Image in the Centre mode

5.15. ProgressBar

ProgressBar is used for displaying the progress during an operation. It has the following commonly used properties:

- **Minimum**: Minimum value of the ProgressBar.
- **Maximum**: Maximum value of the ProgressBar.
- **Step**: Incremental value of the ProgressBar.

Let's see a ProgressBar in action in a simple example:

1. Create a new VB.NET project in Visual Studio.
2. Place a ProgressBar, a Button and a ListBox on the form as follows:

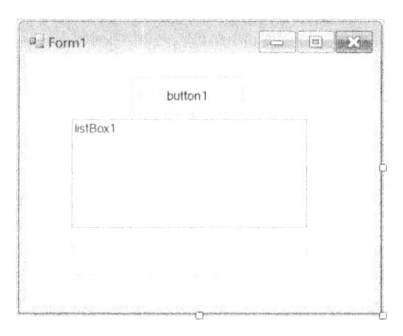

Figure 5.84. Layout of the form

3. Set the Name and the Text of the Button as **incrementButton** and **Increment**, respectively.
4. Set the Name of the ProgressBar as **incrementProgressBar**.
5. Set the Name of the ListBox as **currentValueListBox**.
6. As we click the button, the value of the ProgressBar will increase and the current value of the ProgressBar will be added to the ListBox. Before the actual code, let's set the Minimum, Maximum and Step properties of the ProgressBar as 0, 100 and 1, respectively. In this case, the value of the ProgressBar will start from 0 and increase by 1 until 100. ProgressBar will display this progess visually. We will set these properties of the ProgressBar inside Form1's Load method so that they will be set at the start of the program. For this, double-click the empty space of the form to create its default Load method. Then add the following code lines:

```
Private Sub Form1_Load(sender As Object, e As EventArgs) Handles MyBase.Load

        incrementProgressBar.Minimum = 0
        incrementProgressBar.Maximum = 100
        incrementProgressBar.Step = 1

End Sub
```
Code 5.22

7. Double-click the Button and create its Click event handling method. Each time the user clicks the button, the value of the ProgressBar will increase by 1. The current value will also be added to the items of the ListBox. The following code does this job:

CHAPTER 5. COMMON CONTROLS

```
Private Sub IncrementButton_Click(sender As Object, e As
EventArgs) Handles incrementButton.Click

    incrementProgressBar.Value += 1
    currentValueListBox.Items.Add(incrementProgressBar.Value)

End Sub
```
Code 5.23

The code line `incrementProgressBar.Value += 1` adds 1 to the `Value` property of the `incrementProgressBar`. The next line gets the `Value` of the `ProgressBar` and passes it to the `Add()` method which adds this `Value` to the ListBox.

8. Let's build and run the project. Initially, our program will appear as follows:

Figure 5.85. The program before the Increment button is clicked

After clicking the button several times, the ProgressBar will be filled and its values will be written to the ListBox as shown below:

115

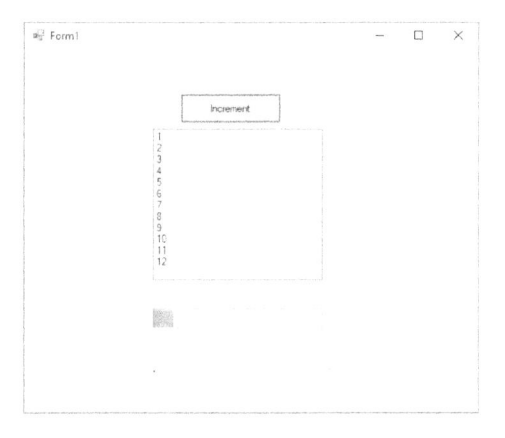

Figure 5.86. The ProgressBar at 21%

5.16. RadioButton

RadioButtons are used for selecting among different options.

RadioButtons are similar to CheckBoxes however only one RadioButton can be selected in a form or group at a time.

The frequently used properties of RadioButtons are as follows:

- **Checked**: Sets if the RadioButton will be checked initially.
- **AutoCheck**: Sets if the RadioButton will automatically be selected when clicked.
- **Enabled**: Sets if the RadioButton will be available for checking.

The following simple example demonstrates the usage of RadioButtons in a project. The user will select the background colour of the form using RadioButtons. Since it is not possible to set the background colour to multiple colours at the same time, it is meaningful to use RadioButtons for this example.

1. Create a new VB.NET project in Visual Studio.
2. Add five RadioButtons on the form as shown below:

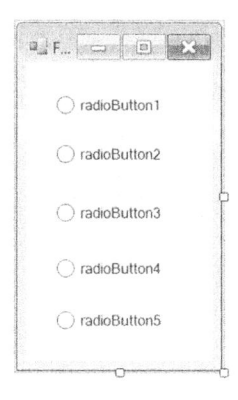

Figure 5.87. Layout of the form

3. Set the Names of these RadioButtons from top to down as **redRadioButton**, **greenRadioButton**, **blueRadioButton**, **whiteRadioButton and brownRadioButton**.
4. Set the Text properties of these RadioButtons from top to down as **Red**, **Green**, **Blue**, **White** and **Brown**.
5. The default event for a RadioButton is **CheckedChanged** which occurs when the RadioButton is checked or unchecked. Double-click the RadioButtons to create their event handler methods. And then add the code lines which will change the background colour of the form accordingly as shown below:

```
Private Sub RedRadioButton_CheckedChanged(sender As Object,
e As EventArgs) Handles redRadioButton.CheckedChanged

    Me.BackColor = Color.Red

End Sub

Private Sub GreenRadioButton_CheckedChanged(sender As
Object, e As EventArgs) Handles
greenRadioButton.CheckedChanged

    Me.BackColor = Color.Green

End Sub

Private Sub BlueRadioButton_CheckedChanged(sender As
Object, e As EventArgs) Handles
```

```
blueRadioButton.CheckedChanged

    Me.BackColor = Color.Blue

End Sub

Private Sub WhiteRadioButton_CheckedChanged(sender As
Object, e As EventArgs) Handles
whiteRadioButton.CheckedChanged

    Me.BackColor = Color.White

End Sub

Private Sub BrownRadioButton_CheckedChanged(sender As
Object, e As EventArgs) Handles
brownRadioButton.CheckedChanged

    Me.BackColor = Color.Brown

End Sub
```

Code 5.24 (cont'd)

As we have seen before, `Me.BackColor` refers to the background colour of the form. Therefore, each RadioButton assigns a different colour to the background of the form in this code snippet.

6. Build and run the project. Since the first RadioButton will be selected by default, the background colour of the form will initially be red as follows:

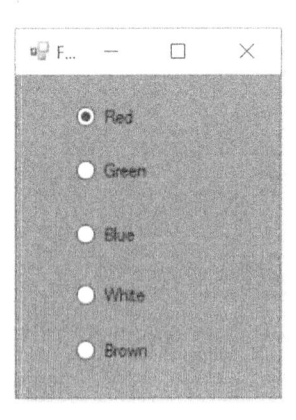

Figure 5.88. The initial state of the program

CHAPTER 5. COMMON CONTROLS

As we check different RadioButtons, the background colour of the form will change accordingly as shown in Figure 5.89.

It is useful to use RadioButtons whenever the selectable options have singular and discrete nature.

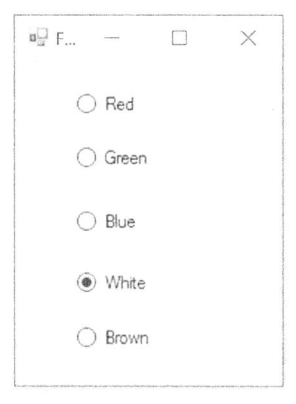

Figure 5.89. The program when the White RadioButton is selected

5.17. RichTextBox

RichTextBox is used for entering text with formatting features such as paragraph and multiline text formatting. The following are important properties of RichTextBoxes:

- **DetectUrls**: Sets if URLs are automatically converted to links.
- **MultiLine**: Sets if multiline text inputs are permitted or not.
- **MaxLength**: The number of characters that can be entered in the RichTextBox.

We'll place a RichTextBox on a form in our example. When we click a button, the text entered in the RichTextBox will be shown in a message box.

1. Create a new VB.NET project in Visual Studio.
2. Place a RichTextBox and a Button on the form as shown in Figure 5.90.
3. Set the Name of the RichTextBox as **inputRichTextBox**.
4. Set the Name and Text of the Button as **showButton** and **Show in MessageBox**.

119

5. Double-click the Button to create its event handler method `showButton_Click()`.
6. Add the code `MessageBox.Show(inputRichTextBox.Text)` into this method.

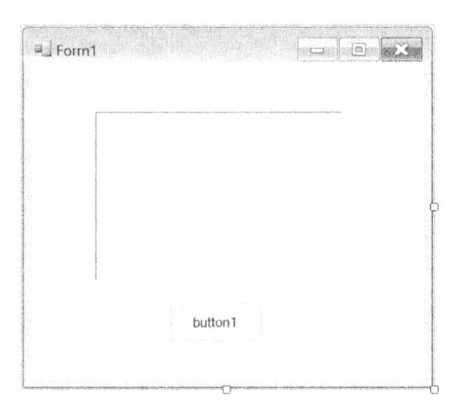

Figure 5.90. Layout of the form

```
Private Sub ShowButton_Click(sender As Object, e As 
EventArgs) Handles showButton.Click

    MessageBox.Show(inputRichTextBox.Text)

End Sub
```
Code 5.24

7. Let's build and run the project. We can enter formatted text inside the RichTextBox. When we click the **Show in MessageBox** button, the text we entered in the RichTextBox will be displayed in a message box. Note that the formatting of the text is preserved when displayed in the message box.

Figure 5.91. Showing the formatted text in a message box

5.18. TextBox

TextBoxes are probably the most frequently used controls after the Button in Windows Forms applications. TextBoxes are simply used to gather text input from the user. It has the following important properties:

- **MultiLine**: Sets if the text input may span multiple lines.
- **WordWrap**: If the text overflows single line, it will automatically be wrapped to the next line.
- **ScrollBars**: Sets if the text scrolling bars will be visible.

In our example, we'll gather text from multiple TextBoxes and merge them before adding to a ListBox.

1. Create a new VB.NET project in Visual Studio.
2. Place three Labels, three TextBoxes, one Button and one ListBox on the form as shown below:

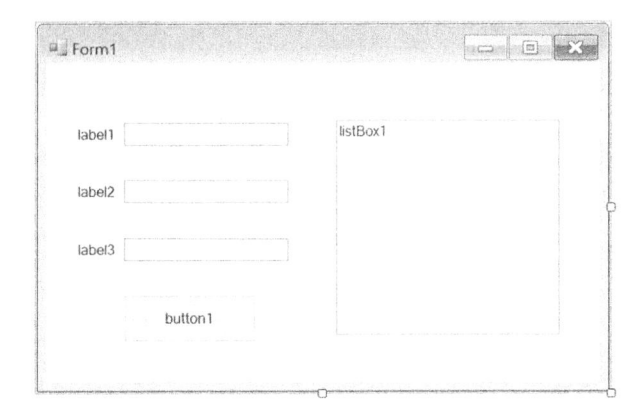

Figure 5.92. Layout of the form

3. Set the Texts of the Labels from top to down as **Name:**, **Lesson:** and **Grade:**.
4. Set the Name properties of the TextBoxes from top to down as **nameTextBox**, **lessonTextBox** and **gradeTextBox**.
5. Set the Text and Name of the Button as **Add Info** and **addInfoButton,** respectively.
6. Set the Name of the ListBox as **infoListBox**. After these changes, the form will look as follows:

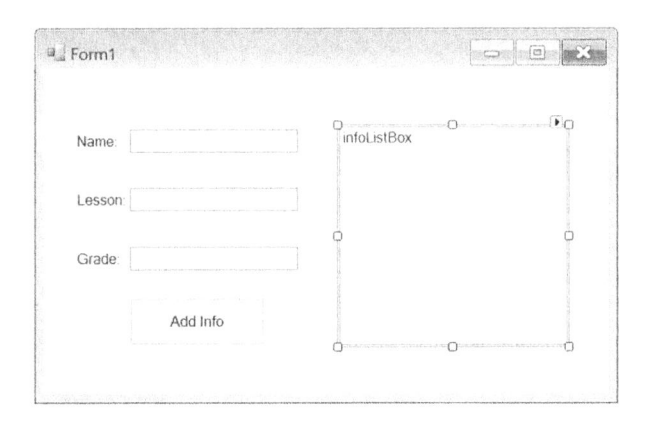

Figure 5.93. Layout of the form after changes

7. When the **Add Info** Button is clicked, the Texts of the TextBoxes will be read, merged and added to the ListBox. For this, create the default

event handler of the button, addInfoButton_Click(...), by double-clicking on it and add the following code:

```
Private Sub AddInfoButton_Click(sender As Object, e As
EventArgs) Handles addInfoButton.Click
        infoListBox.Items.Add(nameTextBox.Text + "-" +
                       lessonTextBox.Text + "-" +
                       "-" + gradeTextBox.Text)
        nameTextBox.Clear()
        lessonTextBox.Clear()
        gradeTextBox.Clear()

End Sub
```
Code 5.26

In the first line, merged texts are passed to the Add() method for performing addition to the ListBox. In this operation, the + operators merge texts. Moreover, hyphens (-) are placed between the texts. It is worth noting that hyphens are written inside double quotes to tell Visual Studio that hyphens should be considered as texts.

After adding merged texts to the ListBox, TextBoxes are cleared by applying the method Clear(). Therefore, all TextBoxes are cleared without user intervention making them ready for entering new inputs.

8. We can now build and run the project. As we input text to the TextBoxes and click the Button, these texts will be merged and added to the ListBox as shown in Figure 5.94.

Please note that the texts written in TextBoxes are considered as texts (strings). Therefore we didn't need to do any conversion when we're writing these inputs in the ListBox.

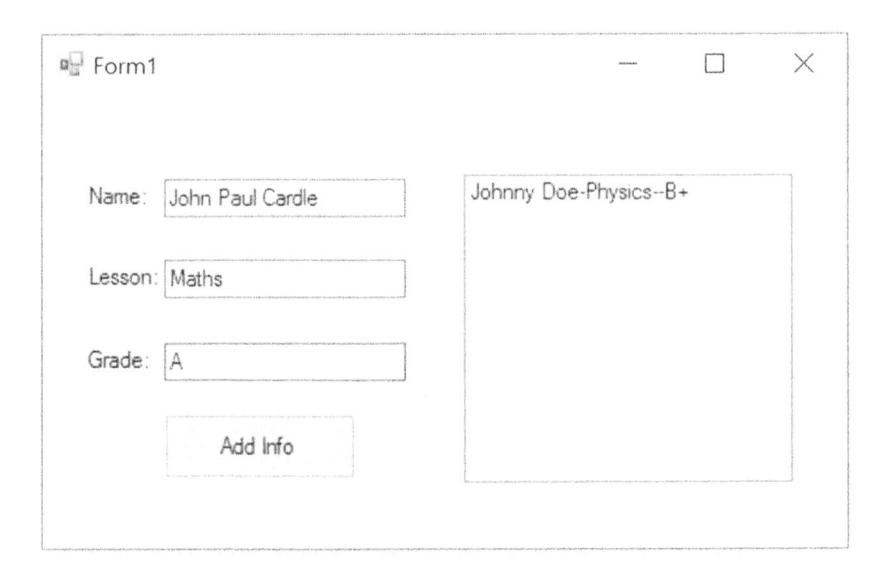

BEGINNER'S GUIDE TO VISUAL BASIC.NET PROGRAMMING

Figure 5.94. Using TextBoxes for text entering (new entries haven't been added to the ListBox yet)

5.19. ToolTip

ToolTips are used for adding tips (small information) about the controls on a form. When the mouse pointer is over the associated control, its ToolTip is activated and displays the related information.

The commonly used properties of ToolTips are as follows:

- **InitialDelay**: The time required for the mouse pointer stay on the control for the ToolTip to show the information.
- **ToolTipIcon**: Specifies the icon that will be shown with the information.
- **IsBalloon**: Sets if the information will be shown inside a balloon.

Let's add a ToolTip to show tips on a simple project.

1. Create a new VB.NET project in Visual Studio.
2. Add a TextBox, a Button and a ToolTip on the form. Note that ToolTip will not be shown on the form but will appear in the pane below:

CHAPTER 5. COMMON CONTROLS

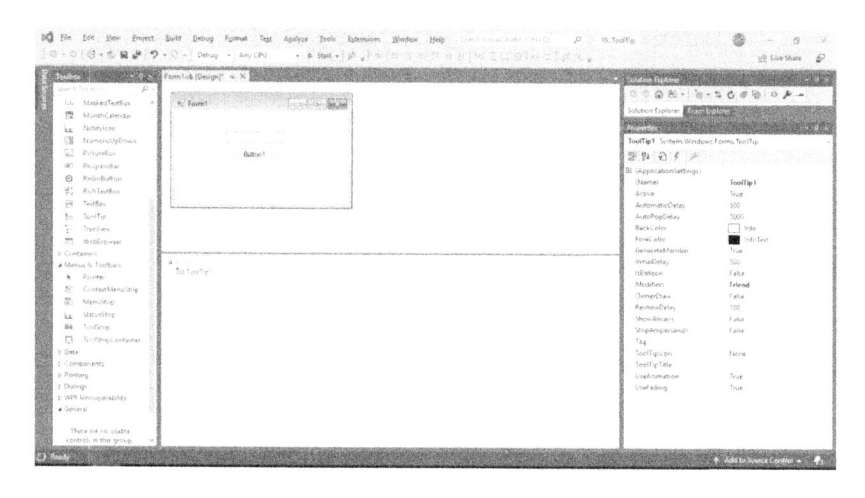

Figure 5.95. ToolTip added on the form appearing at the bottom

3. Set the Text of the Button as **Show**.
4. Set the Name of the ToolTip as **newToolTip**.
5. In order to add a tip to the Button, select it and in the properties pane, navigate to **Misc → Tooltip on newToolTip**. Add the information **Click to display a message box**. as shown in Figure 5.96.
6. We don't need to write code for this example. We can just build and run the project at this stage. When we move the mouse pointer on the Button, the ToolTip message will be displayed as in Figure 5.97.

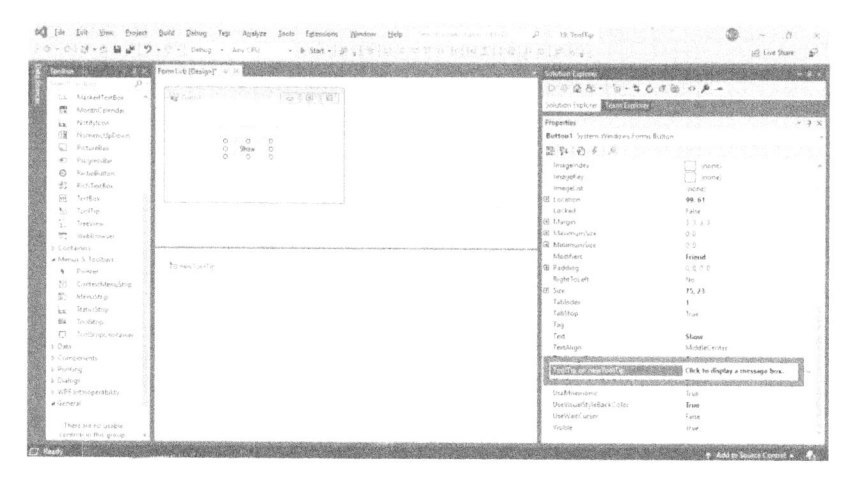

Figure 5.96. Adding a tip for the Button using the ToolTip control

125

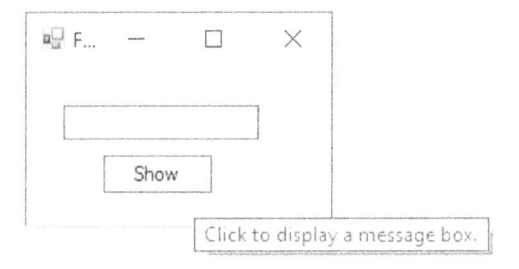

Figure 5.97. Button's tip is displayed when mouse is over it

5.20. TreeView

TreeView control is used for displaying items in a hierarchical manner. TreeView has the following important properties:

- **CheckBoxes**: Sets if checkboxes will appear next to the items for selection.
- **ShowLines**: Sets if a line connecting the nodes will be displayed or not.
- **ShowPlusMinus**: Used for setting if + and − symbols will appear for opening/closing node list.
- **GetNodeCount**: Returns the number of nodes in a TreeView.

In our TreeView example, we'll create two parent nodes in the TreeView and add children to them:

1. Create a new VB.NET project in Visual Studio.
2. Place a TreeView control in the middle of the form as follows (note that you can resize the TreeView as you wish):

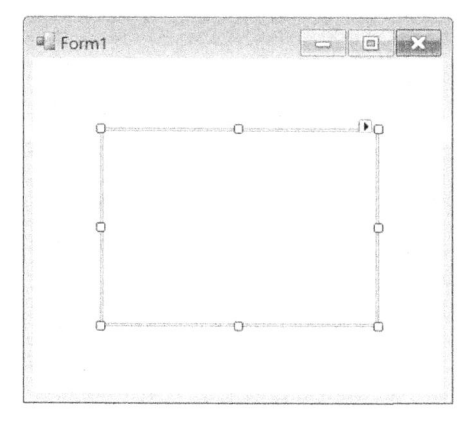

Figure 5.98. TreeView control on the form

3. Click on the arrowhead located at the top of the TreeView:

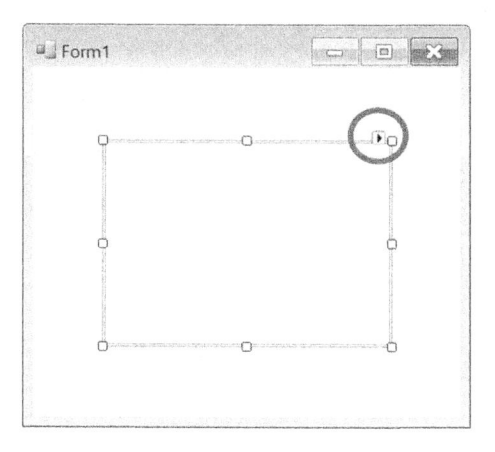

Figure 5.99. Opening the Tasks menu of the TreeView

4. Click on the **Edit Nodes** button in the Tasks menu as follows:

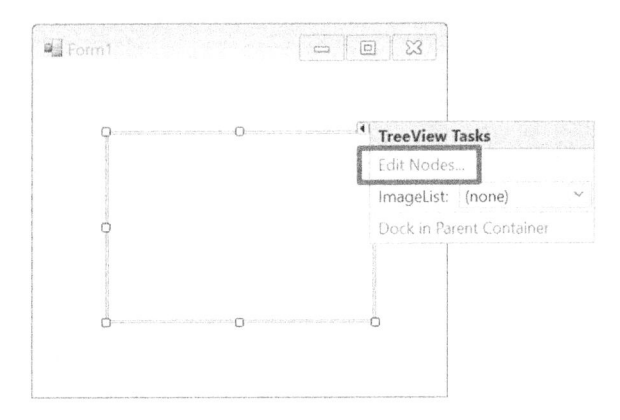

Figure 5.100. Opening the **Edit Nodes** window

5. The TreeNode editor will appear as shown in the following figure. We can edit the items of the TreeView visually from this window. In this window, we need to add a root node by clicking the **Add Root** button:

Figure 5.101. Adding a root node

6. After adding the first root (node), we can edit its properties from the right pane of this window. Let's change its text as **Soups** so that we can list different soups as children of this node later:

CHAPTER 5. COMMON CONTROLS

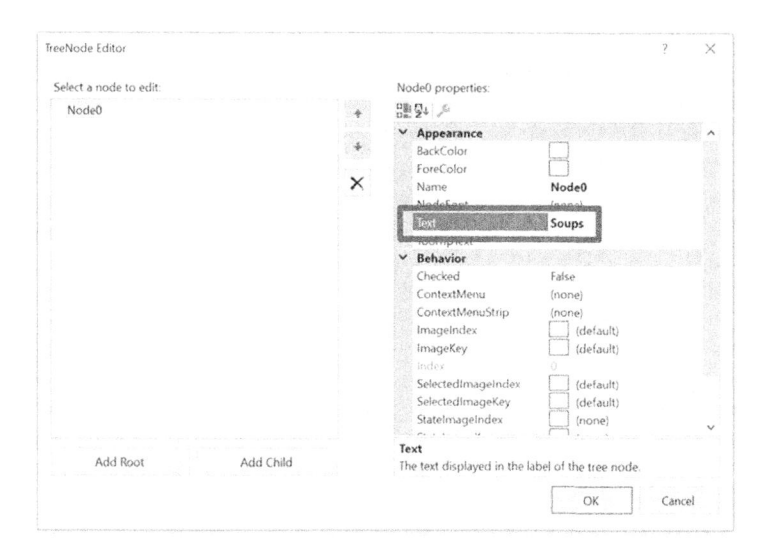

Figure 5.102. Changing the Text property of the newly added node

7. We'll now add child nodes under this parent node. For this, click the **Add Child** button to add child node and then change its Text as **Lentil soup** as shown below:

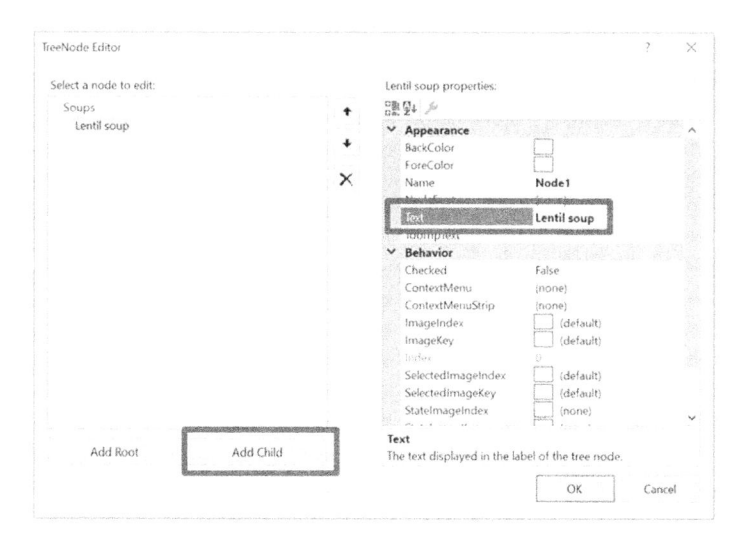

Figure 5.103. Adding a child node and changing its Text property

8. Similarly, let's add two more child nodes and set their Text properties as **Tomato soup** and **Cabbage soup**. Please note that a child node is

129

BEGINNER'S GUIDE TO VISUAL BASIC.NET PROGRAMMING

added under the selected node therefore we need to select the **Soups** node when adding these child nodes.

9. Let's add another parent node named **Pizzas**. Then, add their child nodes as **Margherita**, **Margherita Extra** and **Marinara**. After these additions, the TreeNode editor should look as follows:

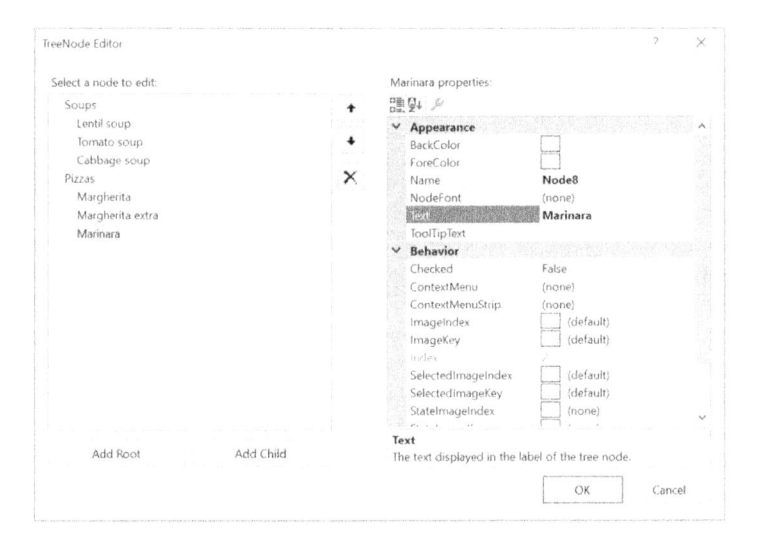

Figure 5.104. TreeNode editor after the entries

10. After entering the data, click **OK** in the TreeView Editor, build and run the project. The TreeView will appear in our program as follows:

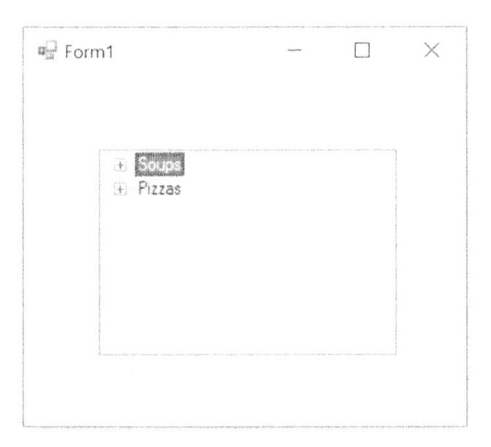

Figure 5.105. The TreeView at runtime

130

We can open the parent nodes to see their child nodes by clicking the + sign as follows:

Figure 5.106. The nodes in the TreeView control

5.21. WebBrowser

WebBrowser control enables to display web pages in an application. It has the following frequently used properties and methods:

- **Url**: Returns the address of the currently displayed web page.
- **ScrollBarsEnabled**: Sets if the scrollbars will be visible by default.
- **GoBack()**: Navigates to the previous web page.
- **GoForward()**: Navigates to the next web page.
- **Navigate()**: Loads the web page at the specified address.
- **Stop()**: Stops loading the webpage.
- **GoHome()**: Navigates to the home page.

Let's see WebBrowser control in action. We'll develop an application in which the user will be able to navigate to web pages and use the basic browser functionality by clicking the buttons.

1. Create a new VB.NET project in Visual Studio.
2. Place a WebBrowser control, a TextBox and four Buttons on the form as follows:

131

Figure 5.107. The layout of the form

3. The user will enter the web address inside the TextBox and click the Button next to it for navigating to this address. Therefore, let's set the Name of the TextBox as **addressTextBox**, Name of the Button next to it as **goButton** and the Text property of this Button as **Go**.

4. Similarly, the middle Buttons will function as the navigation buttons of Back, Forward and Go Home operations. Therefore, we can set their Names as **goBackButton**, **goForwardButton** and **goHomeButton**. Their Texts will be **Back**, **Forward** and **Home**. We can also set the Name of the WebBrowser as **smallWebBrowser**. After these changes, the form will look as shown in Figure 5.108.

5. Double-click the **Go** button to create its default event handler goButton_Click(...). We will write the following code inside this method which will take the Text property of the addressTextBox and pass it to the Navigate() method of the WebBrowser so that the web

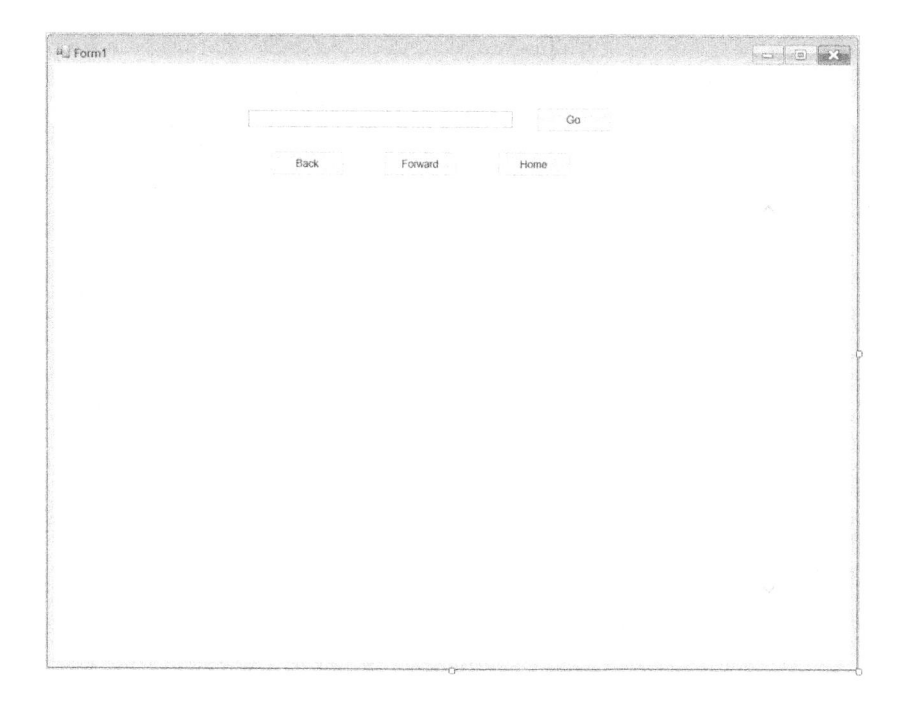

Figure 5.108. Layout of the form after changes

page whose address is written in the TextBox will be displayed in the WebBrowser:

```
Private Sub GoButton_Click(sender As Object, e As
EventArgs) Handles goButton.Click

        smallWebBrowser.Navigate(addressTextBox.Text)

End Sub
```
Code 5.27

6. Similarly, create the event handler methods by double-clicking on the middle Buttons and insert the following code lines for navigating to back, forward and home pages:

```
Private Sub GoBackButton_Click(sender As Object, e As
EventArgs) Handles goBackButton.Click

        smallWebBrowser.GoBack()

End Sub
```

133

```
Private Sub GoForwardButton_Click(sender As Object, e As
EventArgs) Handles goForwardButton.Click

    smallWebBrowser.GoForward()

End Sub

Private Sub GoHomeButton_Click(sender As Object, e As
EventArgs) Handles goHomeButton.Click

    smallWebBrowser.GoHome()

End Sub
```

Code 5.28 (cont'd)

It is worth noting that the goHome() method will navigate to the default home page of the user saved in the Internet Explorer settings.

7. Let's build and run the project. When we enter a web address and click the **Go** button, the web page will be displayed inside the WebBrowser control as follows.

Figure 5.109. The WebBrowser control in charge

If you were calm enough to complete this chapter, congratulations. You now have built the background on the functions of common controls. In the next chapter we'll see the utilization of other form controls such as menus, dialog windows and containers. Don't worry; the next chapter will be shorter than this one ☺.

Chapter 6

MENUS, DIALOGS AND CONTAINERS

In the previous chapter, we have learned common controls. We will study other widely used controls in this chapter: menus, dialogs and containers. Menu type controls enable us to place various menu items on the form like the usual File, Edit menu found in most programs. Dialog type controls are used to open a small dialog box so that the user selects something like a file or a folder. On the other hand, container type controls are used for grouping other controls.

6.1. Menu Type Controls

Menu type controls provide menus on the form with various appearance and positioning possibilities.

6.1.1. MenuStrip

This control is used to add the usual menu which is located at the top of the form by default. Its frequently used properties are as follows:

- **Item**: Enables to access the items of the menu.
- **ShortcutKeys**: Sets the shortcut keys of the menu items.
- **Enables**: Sets if the specific items in the menu will be disabled or enabled.
- **Checked**: Sets if there will be a checkbox next to the menu items.

Let's add a MenuStrip on a form and assign functions to its items in an example:

1. Create a new VB.NET project in Visual Studio.

BEGINNER'S GUIDE TO VISUAL BASIC.NET PROGRAMMING

2. Drag&drop a MenuStrip control from the Toolbox on the form as shown by (1) in Figure 6.1. You will notice that MenuStrip is not shown on the form but below the form as indicated by (2) in this figure.

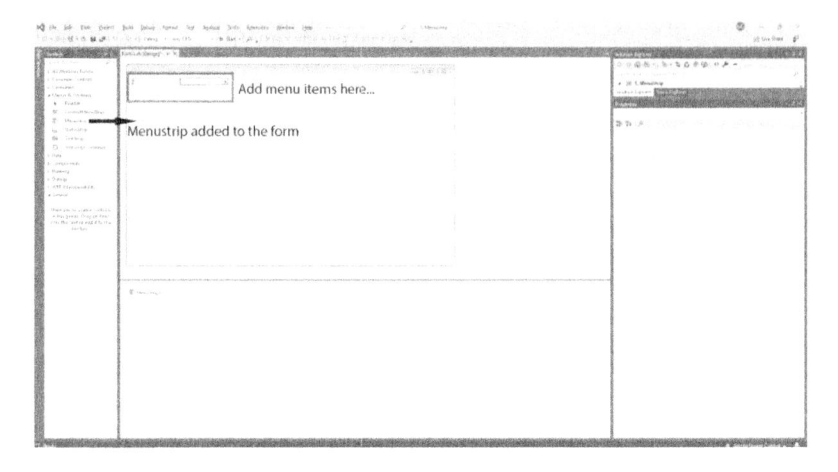

Figure 6.1. Adding a MenuStrip on the form

3. Menu items are entered at the top of the form as indicated by (3). Visual Studio creates new empty items as we create items in this section.
4. For this example, let's firstly name the menu header as **&File** and then add two menu items: one for changing the background colour of the form to white, and another one for quitting the application. We can create these two menu items by typing **&Change colour** and **E&xit** as shown below:

Figure 6.2. Adding menu items

The **Change colour** and **Exit** menu items (buttons) are under the **File** menu as shown above. The reason of inserting **&** symbols in these names is assigning shortcut keys to these items. When the user presses **Alt+(shortcut letter)** on the keyboard, the respective menu item will be activated. In this example, when the user presses **Alt+F**, the File menu will open; and then if **Alt+C** is pressed, the **Change colour** item will be selected, and with the **Alt+X** combination, **Exit** item will be activated. The shortcut letter is shown as underlined as you can see in Figure 6.2. We can assign any letter as the shortcut. Conventionally, the **X** letter is assigned to the Exit item in desktop applications, as we did in this example.

5. After the menu items (buttons) are created, double-click them as usual for creating their default **Click** event handling methods so that we can assign their duties:

```
Private Sub ChangeColorToolStripMenuItem_Click(sender As
Object, e As EventArgs) Handles
ChangeColorToolStripMenuItem.Click

End Sub

Private Sub ExitToolStripMenuItem_Click(sender As Object, e
As EventArgs) Handles ExitToolStripMenuItem.Click

End Sub
```
Code 6.1

Note that the names of the menu items are automatically assigned by Visual Studio.

6. When the user selects the **Change colour** item, the background colour will be set as white. As we have learned before, we can do this by the code line: `Me.BackColor = Color.White`. Similarly, the `Application.Exit()` line is used for terminating the application. We now need to insert these code lines to the event handler methods of the menu items as in Code 6.2.

```
Private Sub ChangeColorToolStripMenuItem_Click(sender As
Object, e As EventArgs) Handles
ChangeColorToolStripMenuItem.Click
        Me.BackColor = Color.White
End Sub

Private Sub ExitToolStripMenuItem_Click(sender As Object, e
As EventArgs) Handles ExitToolStripMenuItem.Click
        Application.Exit()
End Sub
```

Code 6.2

7. We can now build and run the project. The program will appear as follows:

Figure 6.3. The program incorporating a MenuStrip

8. We can use **Alt+F** combination for opening the file menu or use the mouse as usual. When we select the **Change colour** item, the background colour of the form will go white as in Figure 6.4. Similarly, the application will quit if we select the **Exit** item.

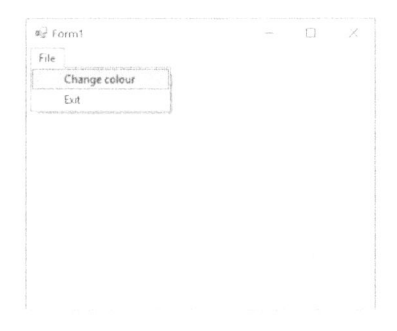

Figure 6.4. The background colour is changed using the menu item

6.1.2. ContextMenuStrip

ContextMenuStrip is used for providing a right-click menu. It can be added on the form itself or on a control. Its properties are similar to those of the MenuStrip.

Let's add a ContextMenuStrip on a RichTextBox with the copy, paste and clear functionalities in a simple example:

1. Create a new VB.NET project in Visual Studio.
2. Add a RichTextBox and a ContextMenuStrip on the form. As in the MenuStrip, ContextMenuStrip will appear below the form as follows:

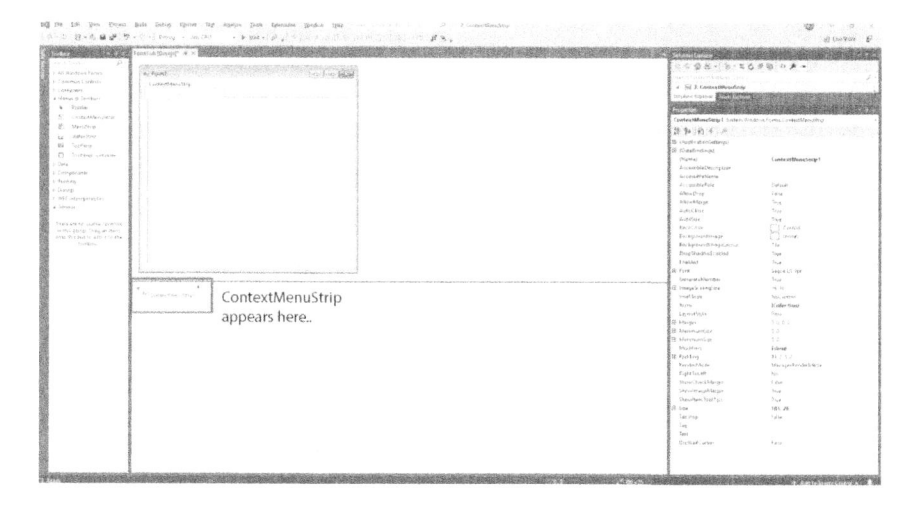

Figure 6.5. ContextMenuStrip added to the form

3. Add the items of **Copy**, **Paste** and **Clear** to the ContextMenuStrip as we did in the MenuStrip example as shown in Figure 6.6.
4. Set the Name of the RichTextBox as **rClickRichTextBox**.
5. We need to create the default Click event handlers of the ContextMenuStrip items. For this, double-click each of them as usual and then the event handling methods shown in Code 6.3 will be generated.

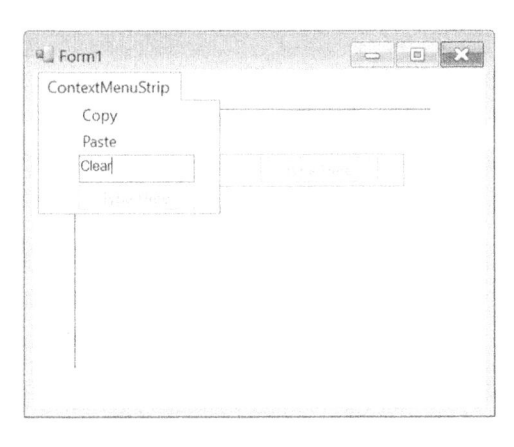

BEGINNER'S GUIDE TO VISUAL BASIC.NET PROGRAMMING

Figure 6.6. Adding items to the ContextMenuStrip

```
Private Sub CopyToolStripMenuItem_Click(sender As Object, e
As EventArgs) Handles CopyToolStripMenuItem.Click

End Sub

Private Sub PasteToolStripMenuItem_Click(sender As Object,
e As EventArgs) Handles PasteToolStripMenuItem.Click

End Sub

Private Sub ClearToolStripMenuItem_Click(sender As Object,
e As EventArgs) Handles ClearToolStripMenuItem.Click

End Sub
```
Code 6.3

6. We will now add the required code lines for the copy, paste and clear functions. The code lines rClickRichTextBox.Copy(); and rClickRichTextBox.Paste(); respectively perform the copy and paste operations. Please note that these lines do not copy and paste the whole content of the RichTextBox but only the selected text. The line rClickRichTextBox.Clear(); clears the RichTextBox as can be seen from the name of the method: Clear(). We insert these code lines to the event handling methods as follows:

CHAPTER 6. MENUS, DIALOGS AND CONTAINERS

```
Private Sub CopyToolStripMenuItem_Click(sender As Object, e
As EventArgs) Handles CopyToolStripMenuItem.Click
    rClickRichTextBox.Copy()
End Sub

Private Sub PasteToolStripMenuItem_Click(sender As Object,
e As EventArgs) Handles PasteToolStripMenuItem.Click
    rClickRichTextBox.Paste()
End Sub

Private Sub ClearToolStripMenuItem_Click(sender As Object,
e As EventArgs) Handles ClearToolStripMenuItem.Click
    rClickRichTextBox.Clear()
End Sub
```

Code 6.4

7. We created the ContextMenuStrip but didn't assign it to any form control. In order to use it in the RichTextBox, we have to set the ContextMenuStrip property of the RichTextBox as the contextMenuStrip1 (the Name of the ContextMenuStrip used in our example) as follows:

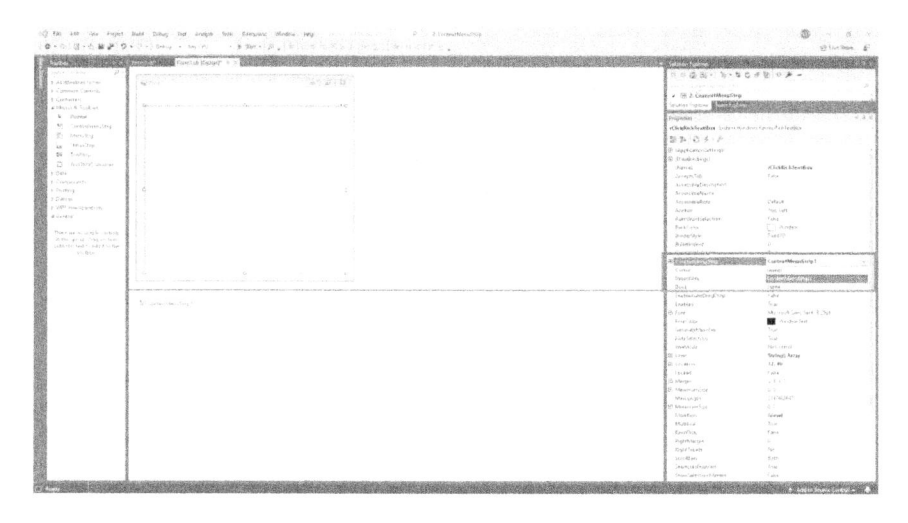

Figure 6.7. Setting the ContextMenuStrip of the RichTextBox

8. We can now build and run the project. The following program window will appear:

143

BEGINNER'S GUIDE TO VISUAL BASIC.NET PROGRAMMING

Figure 6.8. The program window

The right-click menu does not appear on the form as expected. Let's populate the RichTextBox with some text as shown in Figure 6.8. We can now use the copy, paste and clear functions of the right-click menu as shown in Figures 6.9, 6.10 and 6.11, respectively.

Figure 6.9. RichTextBox populated with formatted text

144

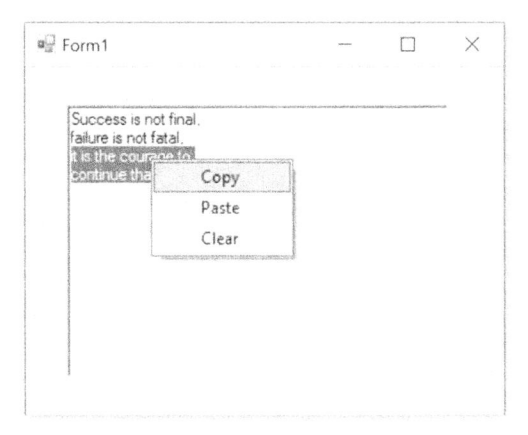

Figure 6.10. Some text selected and copied by the right-click menu

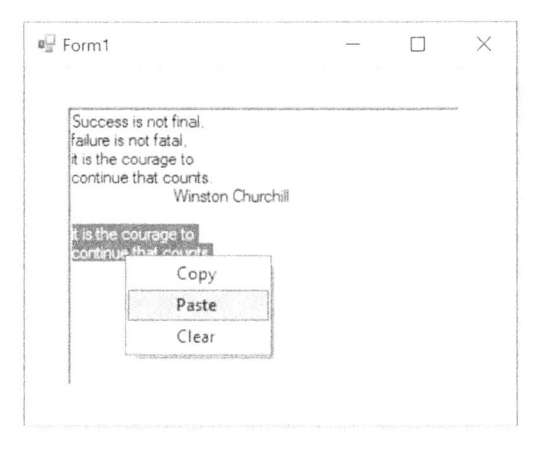

Figure 6.11. Selected text is pasted with the right-click menu

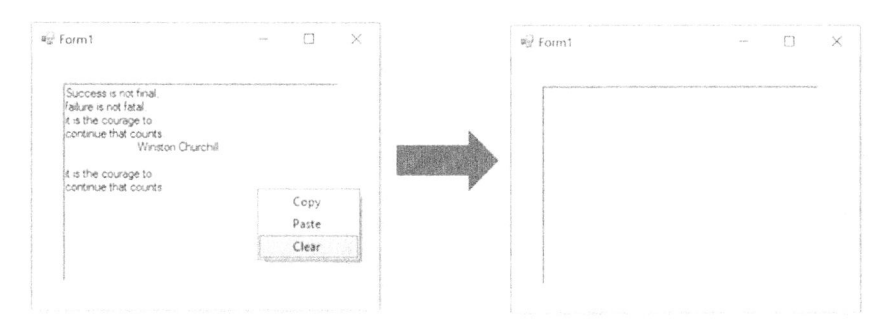

Figure 6.12. RichTextBox cleared with the right-click item: Clear

6.1.3. StatusStrip

StatusStrip is used to give information to the user and generally located at the bottom of the form. StatusStrip may contain various item types such as **StatusLabel**, **ProgressBar** and **DropDownButton**. When we place a StatusStrip on a form, it is positioned at its default location: bottom of the form.

Let's utilize a StatusStrip in a simple example:

1. Create a new VB.NET project in Visual Studio.
2. Add a StatusStrip on the form. It will appear at the bottom of the form by default.
3. We can now add content on the StatusStrip by clicking its arrowhead as shown below:

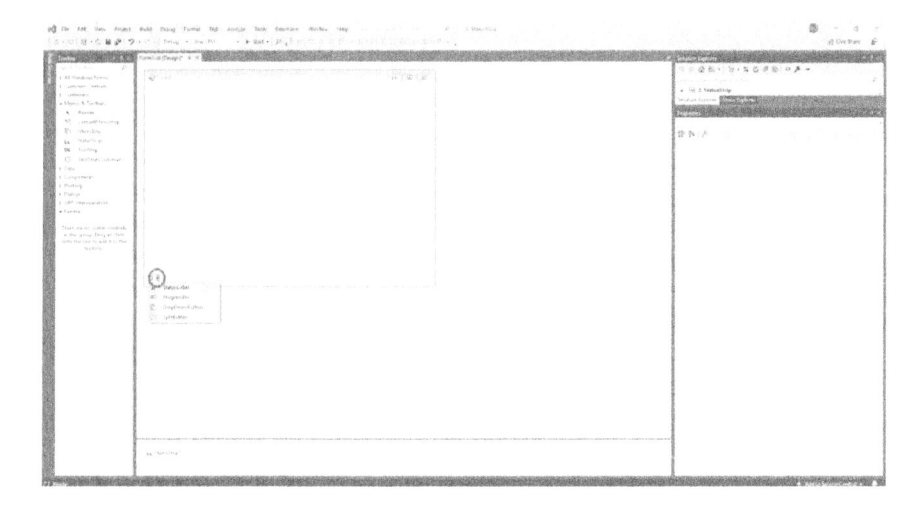

Figure 6.13. Adding a StatusLabel to the StatusStrip

4. When we add a StatusLabel, it appears on the StatusStrip ready to be set as in Figure 6.14.
5. Set the Text property of the StatusStripLabel as **This is a StatusStripLabel** as shown in Figure 6.15.

CHAPTER 6. MENUS, DIALOGS AND CONTAINERS

Figure 6.14. A StatusStripLabel added to the StatusStrip

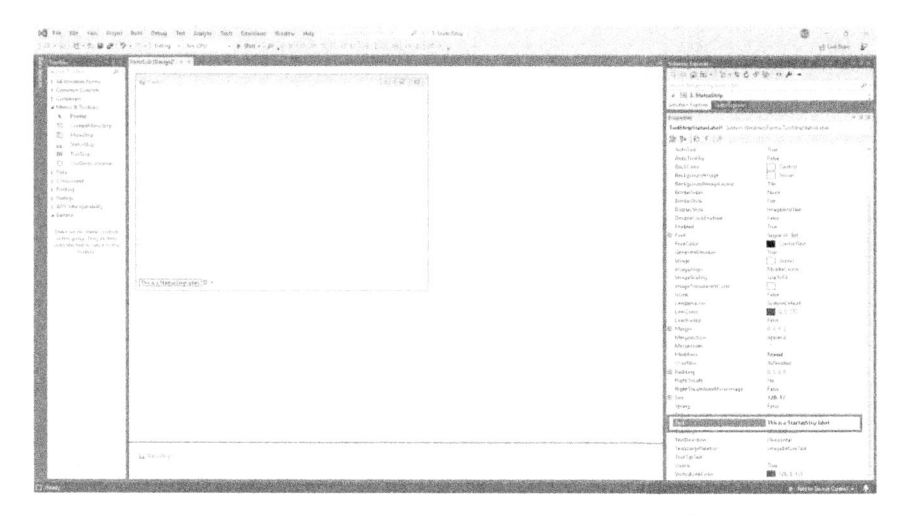

Figure 6.15. Setting the Text of the StatusStripLabel

6. We can now build and run the project. The StatusStrip and its item StatusStripLabel will appear at the status bar of the program as follows:

147

Figure 6.16. StatusStrip and its StatusStripLabel appearing at the bottom of the form

6.1.4. ToolStrip

ToolStrip holds various types of items and generally located at the top of the form below the MenuStrip. ToolStrip is used to create a toolbar on the form. One of its advantages is to be able to change its contents during runtime. The items which can be contained in a ToolStrip include but not limited to **Button, Label, ComboBox, ProgressBar and TextBox**.

Let's use a MenuStrip and a ToolStrip in a sample project:

1. Create a VB.NET project in Visual Studio.
2. Add a MenuStrip and a ToolStrip to the project.
3. As in other menu controls, ToolStrip will not appear on the form but in the below pane:

CHAPTER 6. MENUS, DIALOGS AND CONTAINERS

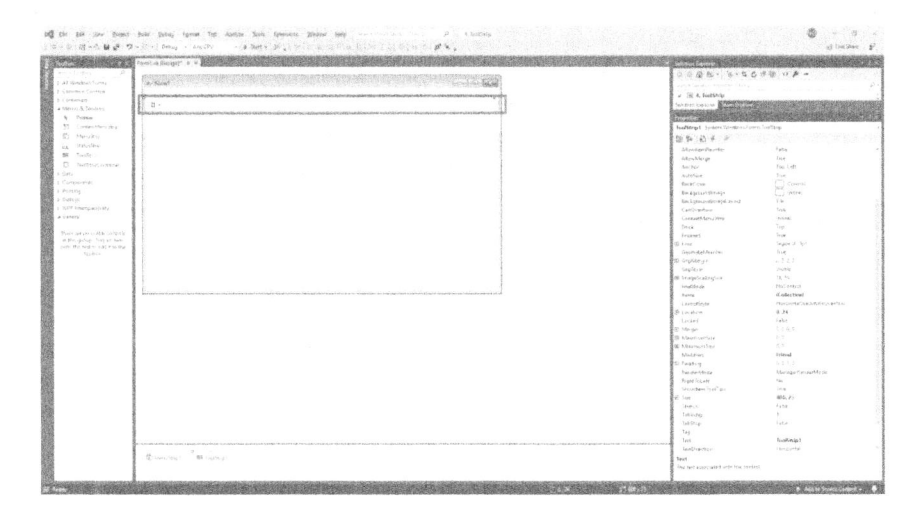

Figure 6.17. ToolStrip location

4. Just as the case for the StatusStrip, we can add items to the ToolStrip by selecting the arrow and then the desired controls to add. I have added a Label and a TextBox to the ToolStrip as shown in Figure 6.18.

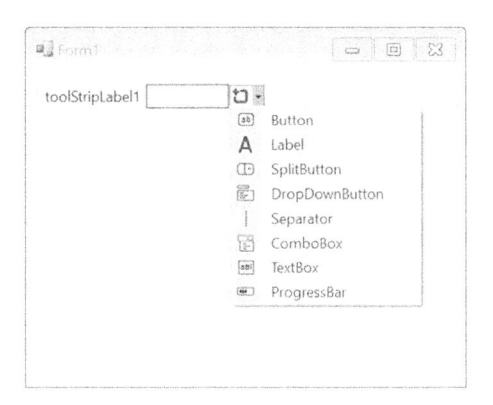

Figure 6.18. Various items added to the ToolStrip

5. Set the Text of the Label to **Here is a ToolStrip Label**.
6. Enter the **File** item to the MenuStrip. This is just for demonstration purposes; we already learned how to use the MenuStrip before.

149

7. Build and run the project. The program should look like below with the ToolStrip below the MenuStrip control:

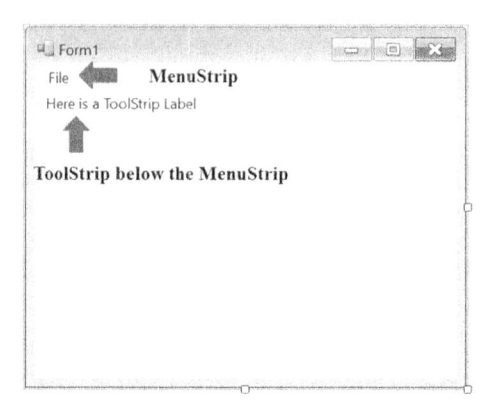

Figure 6.19. MenuStrip and ToolStrip in a sample program

6.1.5. ToolStripContainer

ToolStripContainer provides an area that may contain several ToolStrips. Let's use it in an example:

1. Create a VB.NET project in Visual Studio.
2. Drag&drop a ToolStripContainer to the form, it will be floating by default as shown in Figure 6.20.

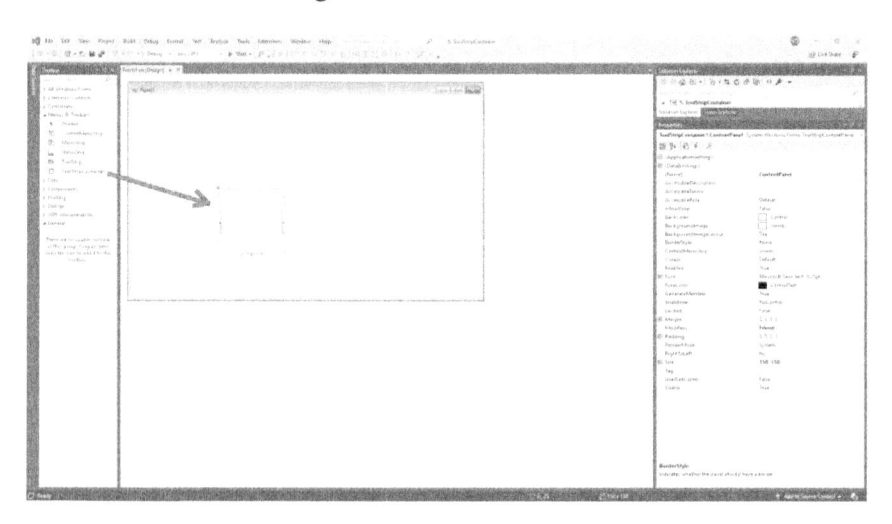

Figure 6.20. Adding a ToolStrip Container to the form

3. We may dock it on the form meaning that it will span the whole form and its middle panel will contain the other controls used in the form. It fills the form by selecting **Dock Fill in Form** from the Tasks menu, which appears by clicking the arrow located at the top of the ToolStrip Container:

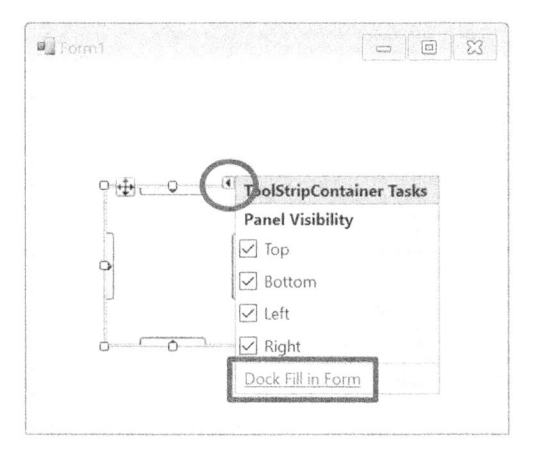

Figure 6.21. Filling the form with the ToolStripContainer

4. We can now insert ToolStrips to the Top, Left, Right or the Bottom sections of the ToolStripContainer by clicking the respective arrows to open the areas which will contain the ToolStrips as shown below:

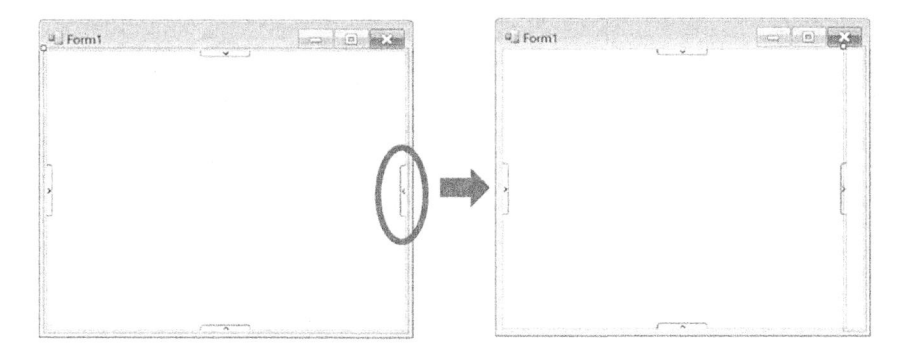

Figure 6.22. Opening the right ToolStrip area on the ToolStripContainer

5. We can now drag&drop a ToolStrip to the opened area and use the ToolStrip as usual:

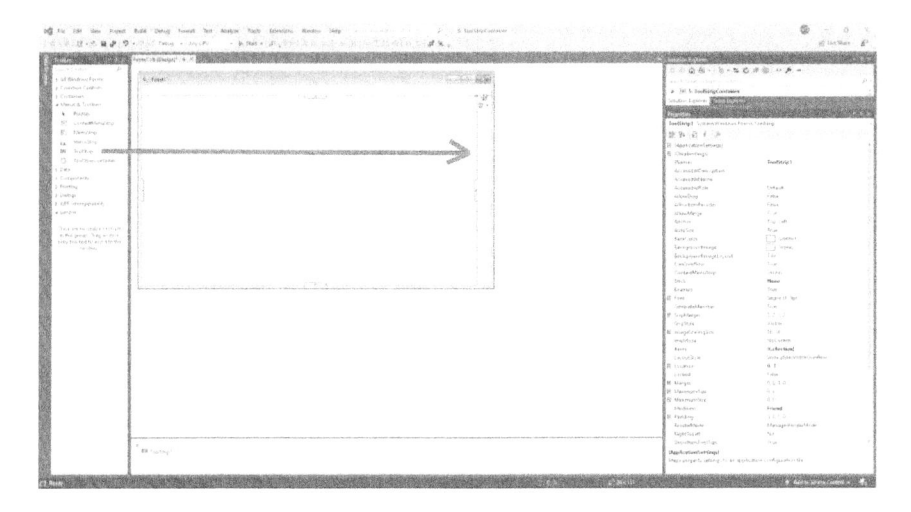

Figure 6.23. Adding a ToolStrip to the opened area

Since it is possible to add images to the buttons in a ToolStrip, it is easy to create professional looking applications with open file, save file, cut, copy, paste, etc. functions having their image buttons in a ToolStrip Container.

6.2. Dialog Type Controls

Dialog type controls provide small dialogs for the user to make a selection.

6.2.1. ColorDialog

ColorDialogs are used for selecting a colour. It has the following important properties:

- **DialogResult**: The type of the returned colour value.
- **ShowDialog**: Used for displaying the dialog window.

Let's use a ColorDialog to set the background colour of the form in an example:

1. Create a VB.NET project in Visual Studio.
2. Drag&drop a ColourDialog to the form. It will appear in the pane below the form. Set its Name property as **selectColourDialog**.

CHAPTER 6. MENUS, DIALOGS AND CONTAINERS

3. Add a Button on the form. Set the Name and the Text properties of the Button as **selectColourButton** and **Select background colour**, respectively. The form should look as follows:

Color dialog appears here.

Figure 6.24. The current state of the form and its controls

4. Double-click the Button to create its default event handler method `selectColourButton_Click()` as shown below:

```
Private Sub SelectColourButton_Click(sender As Object, e As
EventArgs) Handles selectColourButton.Click

End Sub
```
Code 6.5

5. When the user clicks the button, we want the ColorDialog to appear. We use the method ShowDialog() to fire the ColorDialog. We use this method in the following way:

```
Dim colourResult = selectColourDialog.ShowDialog()
```
Code 6.6

In this code line, the dialog box of `selectColourDialog` is opened with the `ShowDialog()` method. When the user selects a colour from the ColorDialog and clicks OK, the `colourResult` object is set to OK. We

153

now need to apply the selected colour to the background colour as we did before:

```
Me.BackColor = selectColourDialog.Color
```
Code 6.7

With this code, the background colour is set to the colour existing in the Color property of the ColorDialog control. We need to insert these code lines to the Button's event handler:

```
Private Sub SelectColourButton_Click(sender As Object, e As EventArgs) Handles selectColourButton.Click

        Dim colourResult = selectColourDialog.ShowDialog()
        Me.BackColor = selectColourDialog.Color

End Sub
```
Code 6.8

6. Build and run the project. The program window shown in Figure 6.25 will appear.

Figure 6.25. The program window

When we click the **Select background colour** button, the ColorDialog will be shown:

CHAPTER 6. MENUS, DIALOGS AND CONTAINERS

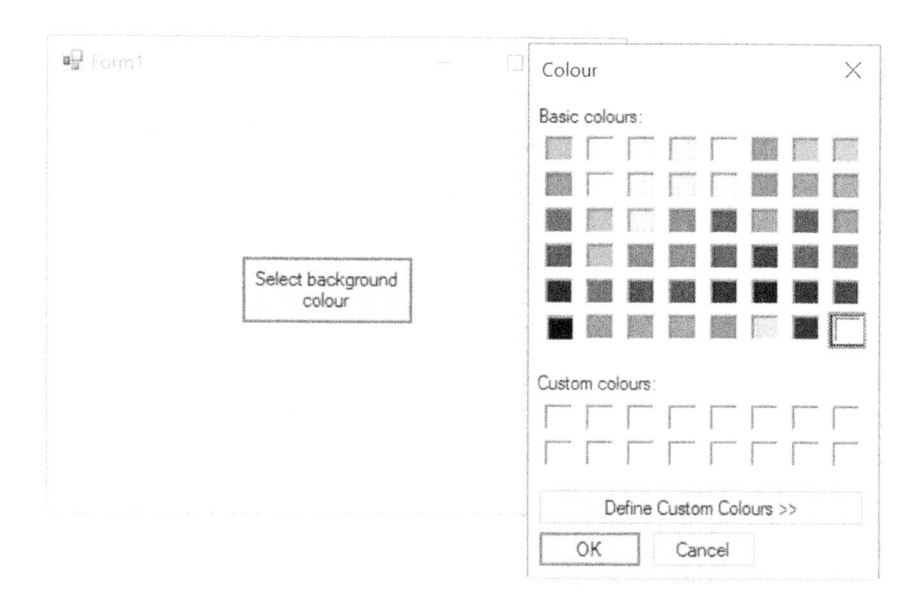

Figure 6.26. The Color Dialog appears

When we select a colour and click the OK button in the ColorDialog, the background colour of the form will take the selected colour. I've selected white as an example and the background colour of the form has changed to white as shown in Figure 6.27.

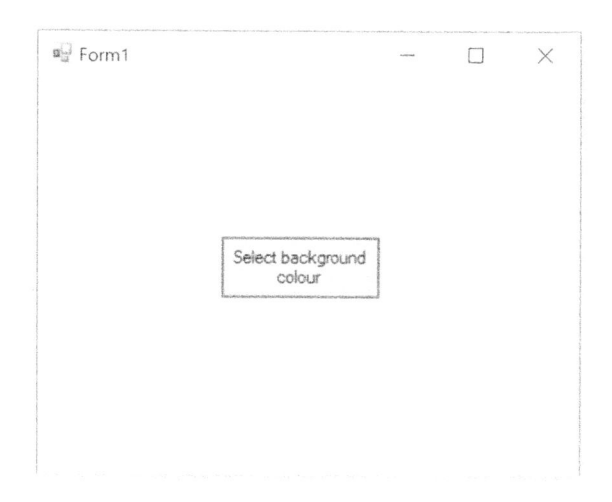

Figure 6.27. The background colour changed to white after selecting white on the ColorDialog

155

6.2.2. Font Dialog

FontDialog works with the same principles of the ColorDialog and used for selecting Font properties from a dialog window. Its properties are similar to those of the ColorDialog.

Let's select the Font properties of a Button's Text using a FontDialog in an example:

1. Create a VB.NET project in Visual Studio.
2. Add a FontDialog to the form. Set the Name property of the FontDialog as **selectFontDialog**.
3. Add a Button in the middle of the form. Set the Name and Text properties of the Button as **fontButton** and **Select font properties**. The form should look as follows:

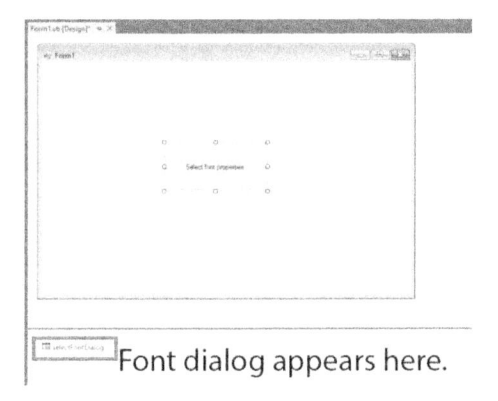

Figure 6.28. FontDialog example

4. We will now create the Click event handler method of the Button. For this, double-click the button and the following method will be created:

```
Private Sub FontButton_Click(sender As Object, e As
EventArgs) Handles fontButton.Click

End Sub
```
Code 6.9

5. As in the ColorDialog, we will use the ShowDialog() method to display the FontDialog as follows:

```
Dim fontResult = selectFontDialog.ShowDialog()
```
Code 6.10

When the user selects the Font properties from the FontDialog and clicks OK, the fontResult object will be set as OK. We'll now set the Button's Text's Font properties to the Font property of the selectFontDialog control:

```
fontButton.Font = selectFontDialog.Font
```
Code 6.11

6. Let's insert these code lines into the button's event handler method:

```
Private Sub FontButton_Click(sender As Object, e As
EventArgs) Handles fontButton.Click

        Dim fontResult = selectFontDialog.ShowDialog()
        fontButton.Font = selectFontDialog.Font

End Sub
```
Code 6.12

7. Build and run the project, the program will appear as in Figure 6.29. Click the **Select font properties** button and the FontDialog will be displayed as shown in Figure 6.30. I've selected bold and underlined in the FontDialog. When the OK button is clicked, this dialog will be closed and the Button's Text will be changed accordingly as in Figure 6.31.

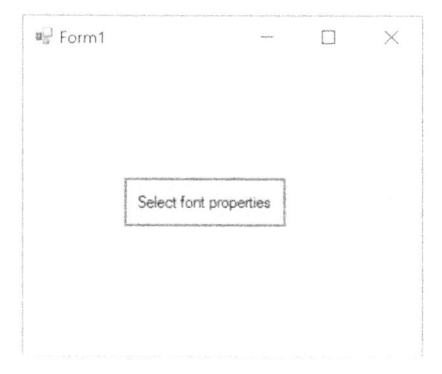

Figure 6.29. The example program with a FontDialog

Figure 6.30. The FontDialog window

Figure 6.31. The Button's font properties set as selected in the FontDialog

6.2.3. FolderBrowserDialog

FolderBrowserDialog is used for displaying and selecting the folders on the computer. It has properties similar to those of the ColorDialog.

We will utilize the FolderBrowserDialog in a simple project. When we select a folder from this dialog, the name of the selected folder will be shown on a Label.

1. Create a VB.NET project in Visual Studio.
2. Add a FolderBrowserDialog to the form. It will appear in the pane below the form. Set the Name property of the FolderBrowserDialog as **selectFolderBrowserDialog**:

CHAPTER 6. MENUS, DIALOGS AND CONTAINERS

Figure 6.32. The sample project with a FolderBrowserDialog

3. Now, add a Button to the form, which will show the FolderBrowserDialog when clicked. Set the Name and the Text properties of this Button as **fbdButton** and **Select a folder**, respectively.
4. Add a label below the Button. We'll set its name to the selected folder's name. But initially, set its Name and Text properties as **selectedFolderLabel** and **Please select a folder...**, respectively. The form should look as follows after these settings:

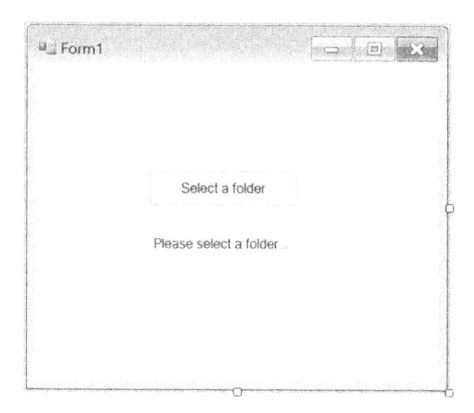

Figure 6.33. The layout of the form

5. Double-click the button to create its Click event handler:
6.

159

```
Private Sub FbdButton_Click(sender As Object, e As
EventArgs) Handles fbdButton.Click

End Sub
```
Code 6.13

7. In order to show the FolderBrowserDialog, we will apply the ShowDialog() to it. The return value will be of the `DialogResult` type as in the previous dialog examples: `Dim fbdResult = FolderBrowserDialog1.ShowDialog()`.
8. We will update the Text of the Label with the selected folder with the following code: `selectedFolderLabel.Text = FolderBrowserDialog1.SelectedPath`. We take the `SelectedPath` property of the FolderBrowserDialog and assign it to the Text property of the Label. We will insert these code lines into the Click event handler method of the button as follows:

```
Private Sub FbdButton_Click(sender As Object, e As
EventArgs) Handles fbdButton.Click

    Dim fbdResult = FolderBrowserDialog1.ShowDialog()
    selectedFolderLabel.Text =
    FolderBrowserDialog1.SelectedPath

End Sub
```
Code 6.14

9. Build and run the project. The following program will appear:

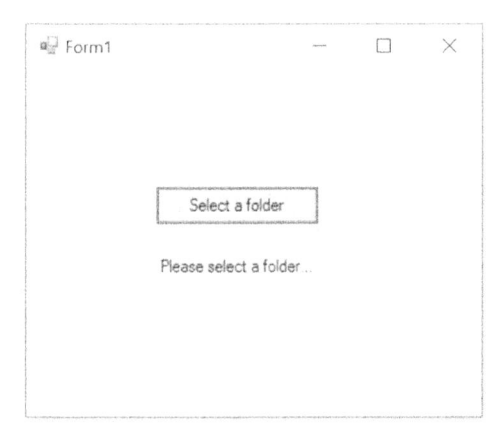

CHAPTER 6. MENUS, DIALOGS AND CONTAINERS

Figure 6.34. The program window

Click the **Select a folder** button and the FolderBrowserDialog will be launched:

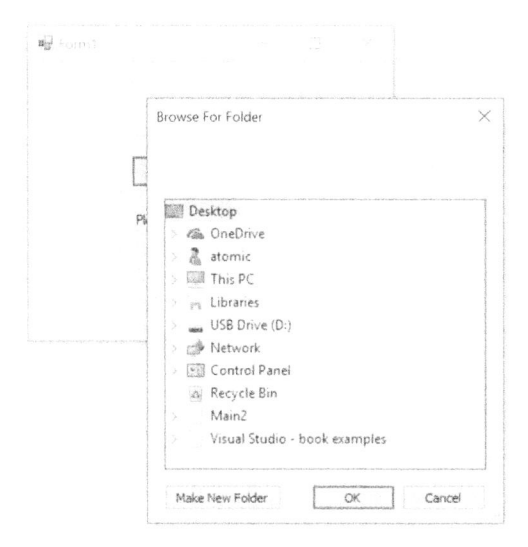

Figure 6.35. The FolderBrowserDialog waiting for a folder selection

When we select a folder from the dialog and click OK button, the full path to the selected folder will be shown in the Label as shown in Figure 6.36.

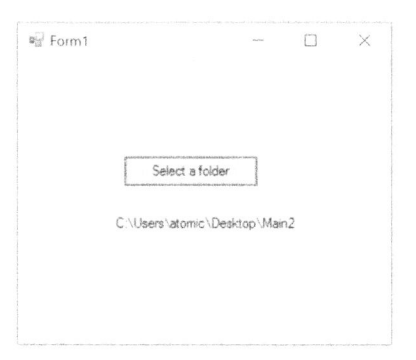

Figure 6.36. Label showing the path to the selected folder Main2

161

6.2.4. OpenFileDialog

This dialog type control provides an interface for opening and reading a file on the computer. It has standard properties as in the previous dialog controls.

We'll open a text file and display its contents using the OpenFileDialog in our example:

1. Create a VB.NET project in Visual Studio.
2. Add an OpenFileDialog on the form. It will appear in the pane below the form. Set the Name property of the OpenFileDialog as **textFileOpenFileDialog** as shown below:

Figure 6.37. OpenFileDialog added to the form

3. Add a Button on the form which will initiate the OpenFileDialog. Set the Name and Text properties of the Button as **openFileButton** and **Click to open a text file**, respectively.
4. Add a RichTextBox on the form below the Button. We will display the contents of the selected text file in this control. Set its Name as **fileRichTextBox**. The form will look as follows after these steps:

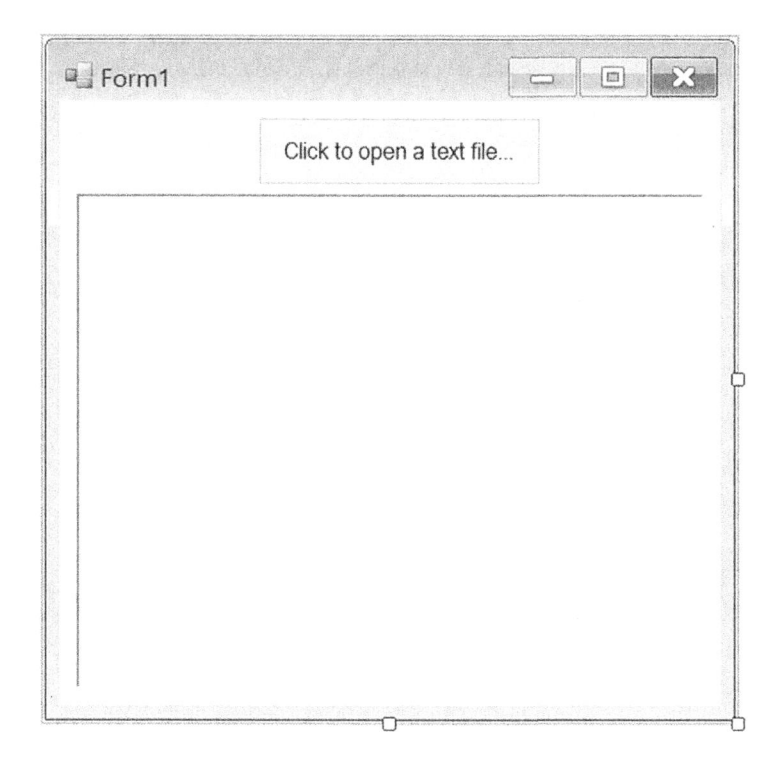

Figure 6.38. Layout of the form

5. We want to open text files only because, the contents of most of other file types (such as images, videos and formatted text files) cannot be displayed in a RichTextBox. We need to set a filter to the OpenFileDialog to open files with .txt extension only. For this, select the textFileOpenFileDialog and set its Filter property as **Text Files | *.txt** as shown in Figure 6.39.
6. When the Button's clicked, the OpenFileDialog window will appear. Therefore, double-click the Button on the form to generate its default event handler method as in Code 6.15.

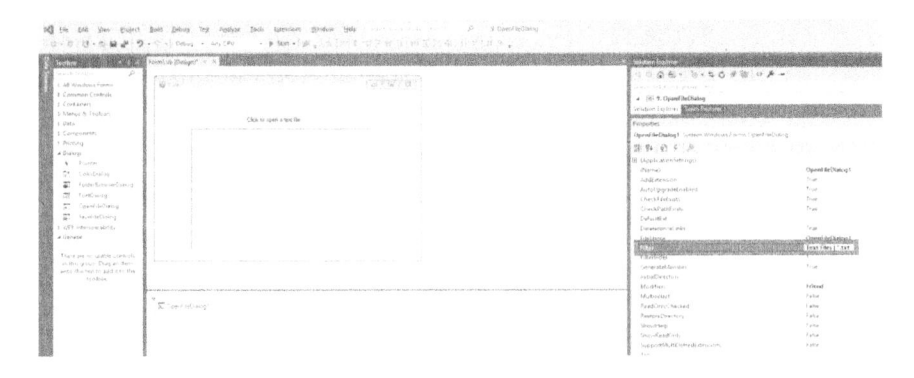

Figure 6.39. Setting the Filter property of the OpenFileDialog

```
Private Sub OpenFileButton_Click(sender As Object, e As
EventArgs) Handles openFileButton.Click

End Sub
```
Code 6.15

7. Firstly, we will add the code line `Dim openFileResult = textFileOpenFileDialog.ShowDialog()` which will launch the file opening dialog box.
8. When the user selects a text file and clicks OK in the file opening dialog, the `FileName` property of the OpenFileDialog will be assigned to the selected filename. We will take this `FileName` and assign it to a new string with the code line `Dim fileName = textFileOpenFileDialog.FileName`. The variable `fileName` will then contain the selected file's name.
9. Then, we will use a special method `ReadAllText()` to read the contents of the text file. This method reads a text file and assigns the contents of the text file to a string variable. The code line `Dim Text = File.ReadAllText(fileName)` will do this job. Note that the method `ReadAllText()` is not included in the default libraries existing in the Form1.vb file. Therefore we need to add the library containing this method to the top of our source code with the line: `Imports System.IO`
10. Finally, we will set the Text of the RichTextBox to the text read from the file with the code line: `fileRichTextBox.Text = Text` After these steps, the Form1.vb file will be as follows:

```
Imports System.IO

Public Class Form1

    Private Sub OpenFileButton_Click(sender As Object, e As
    EventArgs) Handles openFileButton.Click

        Dim openFileResult = textFileOpenFileDialog.ShowDialog()
        Dim fileName = textFileOpenFileDialog.FileName
        Dim Text = File.ReadAllText(fileName)
        fileRichTextBox.Text = Text

    End Sub

End Class
```

Code 6.16

11. Build and run the project. The program window shown in Figure 6.40 will be launched. We need a text file to read from. For this aim, you can use a text file existing on your computer. I created a new text file, **test.txt**, in Notepad for this example. When **Click to open a text file...** button is clicked, it will display Text files as shown in Figure 6.41.

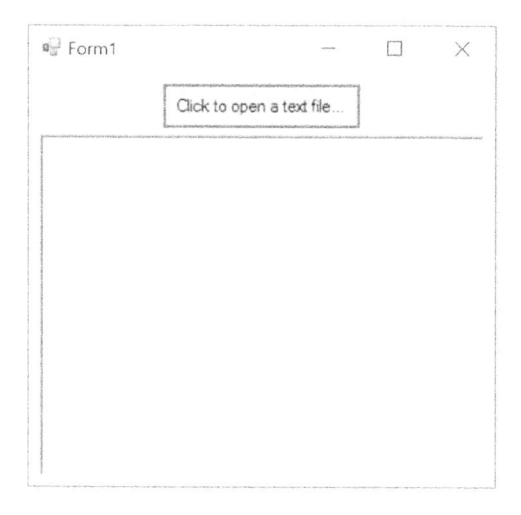

Figure 6.40. The program window

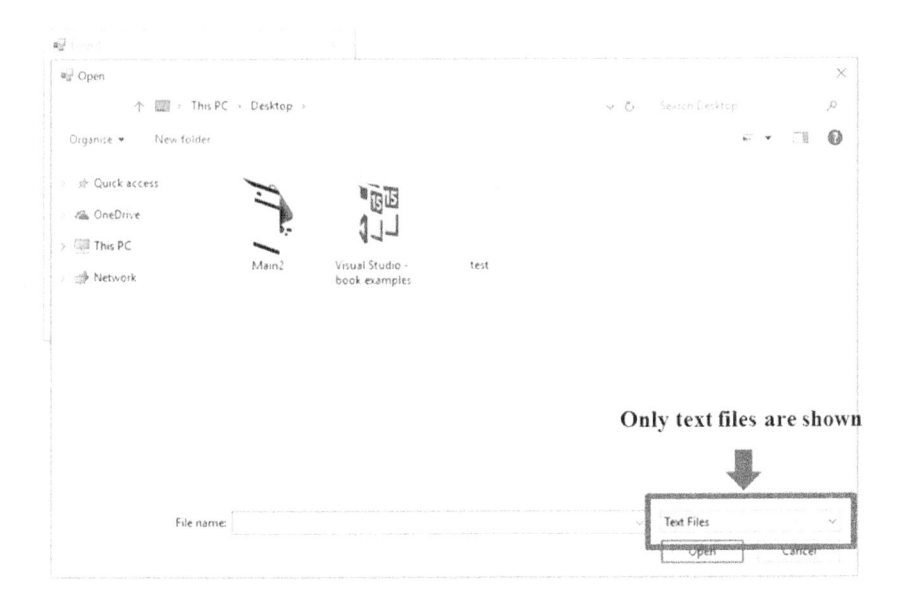

Figure 6.41. OpenFileDialog showing text files only

When the file test.txt is shown in the OpenFileDialog and then OK is clicked, this file is read in our program and its contents are displayed inside the RichTextBox as shown in Figure 6.42.

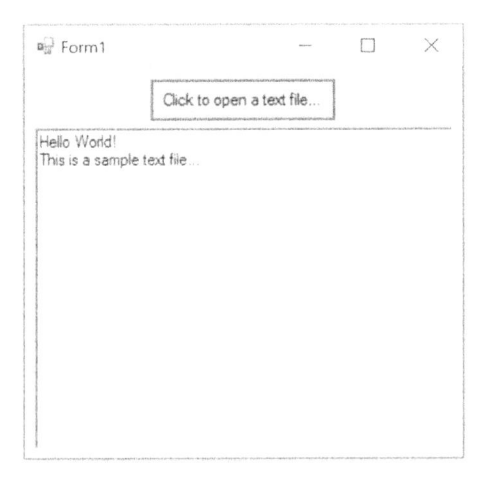

Figure 6.42. The contents of test.txt file read and displayed in our program

It is worth noting that we can read all file types with OpenFileDialog using various file reading methods as we will see in the following chapters after learning more about VB.NET programming.

6.2.5. SaveFileDialog

SaveFileDialog works similar to the OpenFileDialog but doing the opposite job: saving data to a file. Let's use a SaveFileDialog in a project and save the text entered in a RichTextBox to a file:

1. Create a VB.NET project in Visual Studio.
2. Add a SaveFileDialog on the form. It will appear in the pane below the form. Set the Name property of the SaveFileDialog as **textSaveFileDialog** as shown in Figure 6.43.
3. Add a Button and a TextBox to the project as in Figure 6.43.
4. Set the Name and Text of the Button as **saveButton** and **Click to save to a file...**.
5. Set the Name of the RichTextBox as **inputRichTextBox**. After these settings, the form should look as shown in Figure 6.44.
6. When the Button's clicked, the SaveFileDialog window will appear. Therefore, double-click the Button on the form to generate its default event handler method as in Code 6.16.

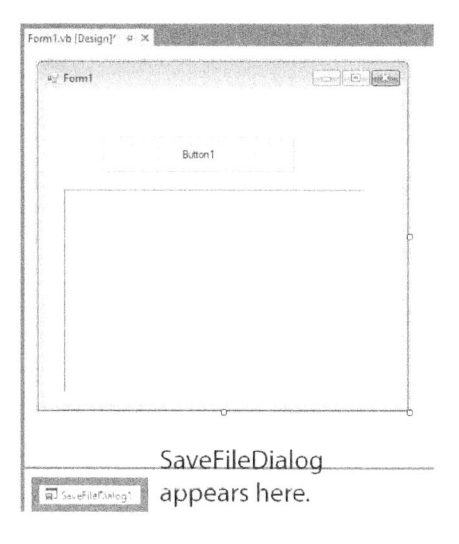

Figure 6.43. Project with a SaveFileDialog

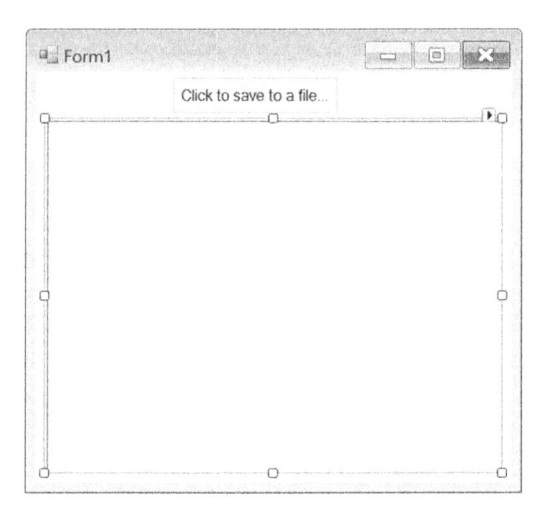

Figure 6.44. The layout of the form

```
Private Sub SaveButton_Click(sender As Object, e As
EventArgs) Handles saveButton.Click

End Sub
```
Code 6.16

7. We'll use the ShowDialog() method to show the dialog. The code line: Dim sfDialog = textSaveFileDialog.ShowDialog() will show the dialog and let the user to select a filename and path to save entered text.
8. We have created and used a random number generator object before. Similarly, we will define a StreamWriter object that has the ability to save data to a file. We define this object with the code line: Dim save = New StreamWriter(textSaveFileDialog.FileName). In this code, the expression in parentheses, textSaveFileDialog.FileName is the filename selected by the user in the file saving dialog box. Note that we have to include the System.IO library with the code line Imports System.IO for being able to use the StreamWriter class as we did for the OpenFileDialog.
9. Actual file writing will be performed by the line: save.Write(inputRichTextBox.Text) which has the Write() method applied on the StreamWriter type object save that was

created in the previous code line. This code line writes the contents of the inputRichTextBox to the specified file.

10. Finally, we need to close the file after writing so that other applications will be able to access the saved file. We do this by the code line: save.Close(). The whole Form1.cs file will be as follows:

```
Imports System.IO

Public Class Form1

Private Sub SaveButton_Click(sender As Object, e As
EventArgs) Handles saveButton.Click

    Dim sfDialog = textSaveFileDialog.ShowDialog()
    Dim save = New StreamWriter(textSaveFileDialog.FileName)
    save.Write(inputRichTextBox.Text)
    save.Close()

End Sub
End Class
```

Code 6.17 (cont'd)

11. We are ready to build and run the project. The program will be as follows:

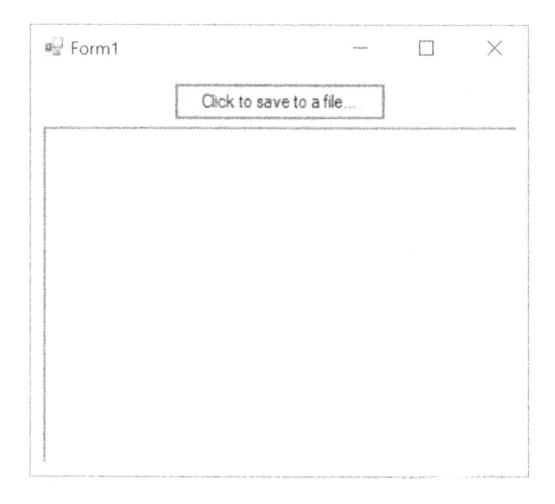

Figure 6.45. The file saving program

BEGINNER'S GUIDE TO VISUAL BASIC.NET PROGRAMMING

We may now input text to the RichTextBox. And then when we click the **Click to save to a file** button, the SaveFileDialog will appear as in Figure 6.46. I've set the file name as test2.txt and selected the Desktop as the folder. When the OK button is clicked in the file saving dialog, the text we entered will be saved to the specified file as shown in Figure 6.47. Note that the formatting of the text is lost when writing to the file using the `Write()` method.

Figure 6.46. SaveFileDialog launched, the filename is chosen as test2.txt

CHAPTER 6. MENUS, DIALOGS AND CONTAINERS

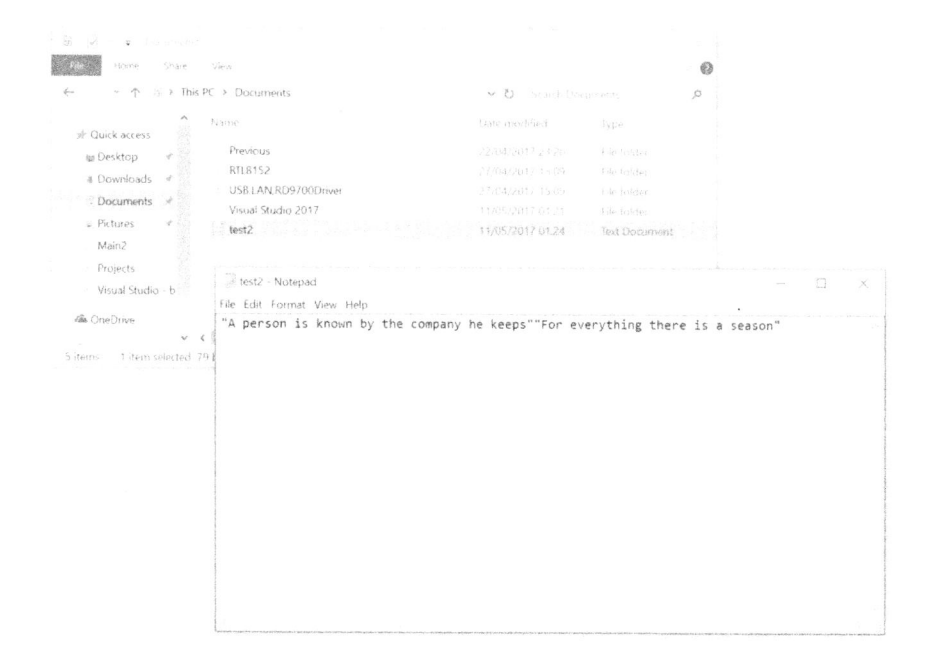

Figure 6.47. Saved file opened in Notepad

6.3. Containers

Containers are used for grouping other controls and laying out the form in a robust and nicer way. It has six types as will be studied in this subsection.

6.3.1. Panel

Panel control is used for grouping and editing other controls. The controls included in a Panel can be moved to another location on the form together without changing their relative positions. Furthermore, common properties of these controls can be edited together. Panels are also used for grouping RadioButtons. Therefore we can use Panels to group RadioButtons on a form where we can select one RadioButton from each Panel.

Let's add three Panels on a form each of them containing three RadioButtons in our example:

1. Create a VB.NET project.

171

BEGINNER'S GUIDE TO VISUAL BASIC.NET PROGRAMMING

2. Add three Panels on the form and divide the form among these Panels vertically as follows:

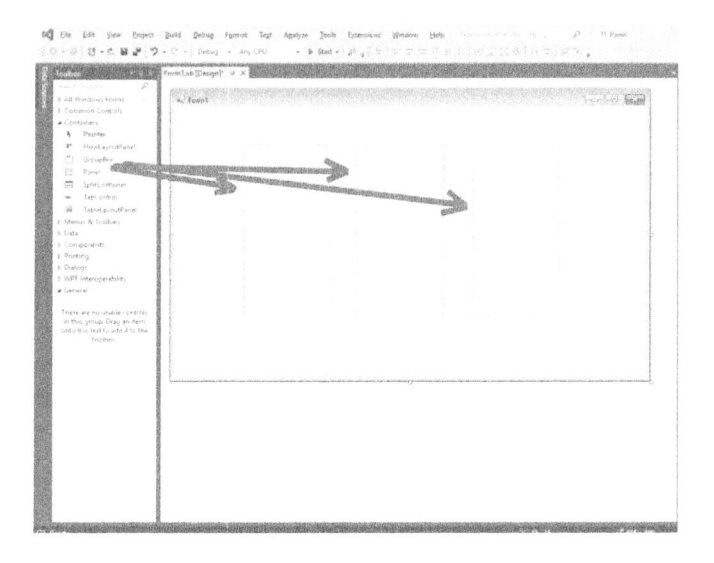

Figure 6.48. Adding three Panels on the form

3. Add three RadioButtons to each of these Panels. Set their Text properties as **Rbutton1-1**, **Rbutton1-2**, **Rbutton1-3**, **Rbutton2-1**, **Rbutton2-2**, **Rbutton2-3**, **Rbutton3-1**, **Rbutton3-2**, **Rbutton3-3**, for each of these Panels:

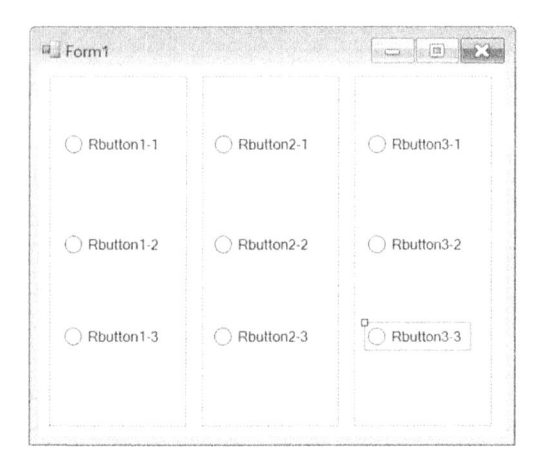

Figure 6.49. Adding RadioButtons to the Panels

4. Build and run the project. As it can be seen from the figure below, the RadioButtons of each Panel can be selected independently. But still, only one RadioButton can be selected in a Panel:

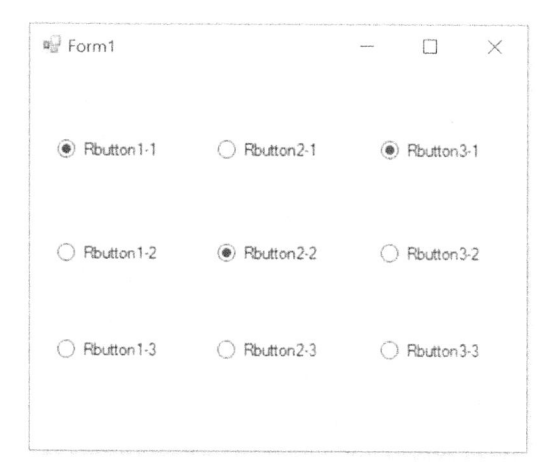

Figure 6.50. The sample program where one RadioButton can be selected in each Panel

Please note that Panel controls do not have borders by default. We can change this by setting their **BorderStyle** properties from **None** to **FixedSingle** or **Fixed3D**. I have changed the BorderStyle properties of the Panels of our example to **FixedSingle** and the appearance of the program window has changed as follows:

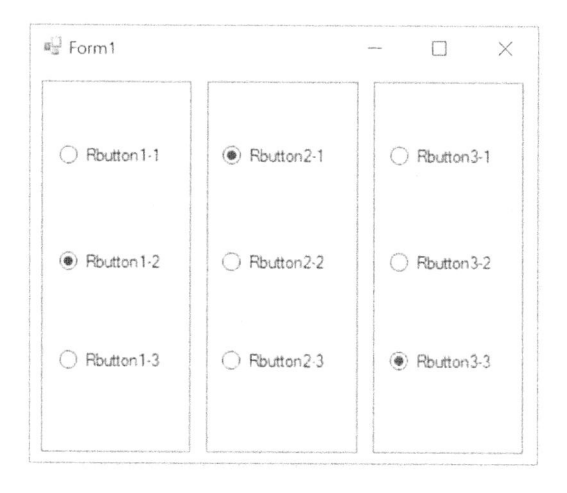

173

Figure 6.51. BorderStyle of Panels set as FixedSingle

Similarly, the **Fixed3D** option for the BorderStyle property also shows borders but with 3D effect as follows:

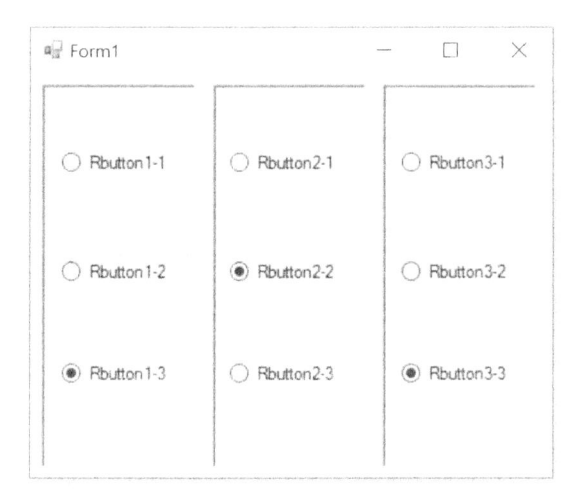

Figure 6.52. BorderStyle of Panels set as Fixed3D

6.3.2. GroupBox

GroupBox has the same functionality as the Panel control. Their difference is that GroupBox control has its name written at the left top.

We will use GroupBoxes to group Dessert and Drink selections in our example:

1. Create a VB.NET project.
2. Add two GroupBoxes and add three CheckBoxes to each of these GroupBoxes. Set the Text properties of these GroupBoxes as **Desserts** and **Drinks**.
3. Set the Text properties of the CheckBoxes of the Desserts GroupBox as **Ice cream**, **Cupcake** and **Cookies**.
4. Similarly, set the Text properties of the CheckBoxes of the Drinks GroupBox as **Soda water**, **Orange juice** and **Strawberry mojito**.
5. Build and run the project. The program window will appear as follows:

Figure 6.53. A program utilizing GroupBoxes

Please note that we can use any control type inside the Panel and GroupBox controls as we need.

6.3.3. TabControl

TabControl provides a tabbed layout similar to the tabs we use in Internet browsers. The advantage of the TabControl is that we can use the form area effectively, he same area is used multiple times. Furthermore, the user may switch different tabs easier compared to opening and closing different forms in an application. Commonly used properties of the TabControl are as follows:

- **SizeMode**: Sets the sizing of tabs. It may take the following values: **Normal**, **FillToRight** and **Fixed**.
- **MultiLine**: Sets if more than one row of tabs are permitted or not.
- **TabPages**: Sets the Names of the tabs.

Let's use TabControl in a simple example. We'll enter text in a TextBox in the first tab and this text will be displayed in all capitals on a Label in the second tab.

1. Create a VB.NET project.

BEGINNER'S GUIDE TO VISUAL BASIC.NET PROGRAMMING

2. Add a TabControl to the form. Click the ellipsis at the **TabPages** property of the TabControl to edit the tabs as indicated below:

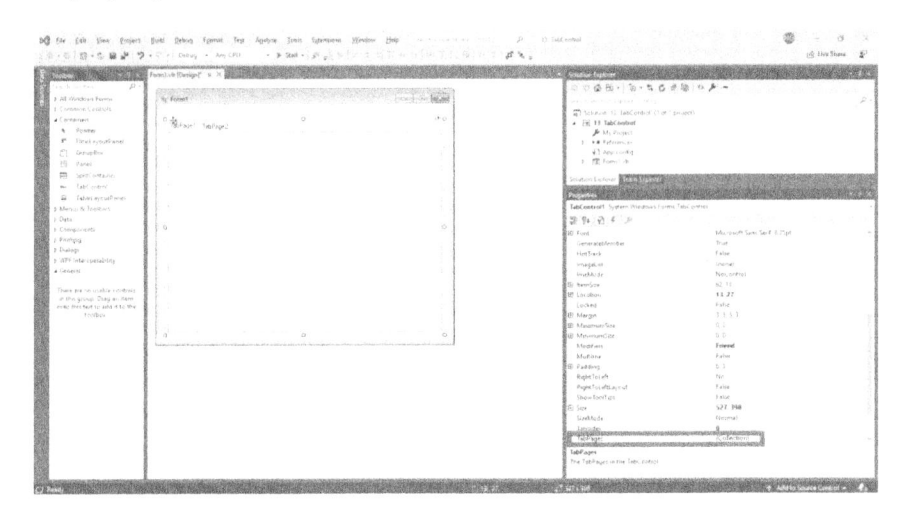

Figure 6.54. Opening the TabPages dialog

3. Set the Text properties of the tabs as **Input** and **Output** in the TabPage Collection Editor:

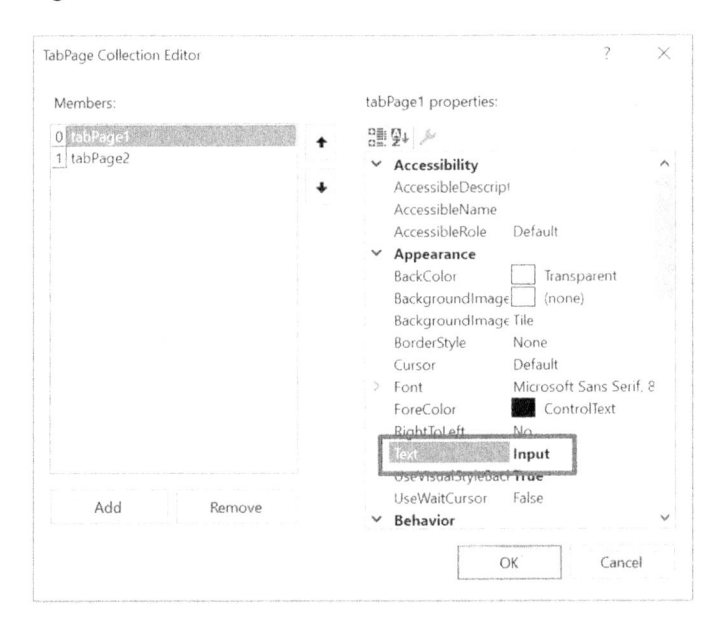

Figure 6.55. Setting the Text property of the first tab

CHAPTER 6. MENUS, DIALOGS AND CONTAINERS

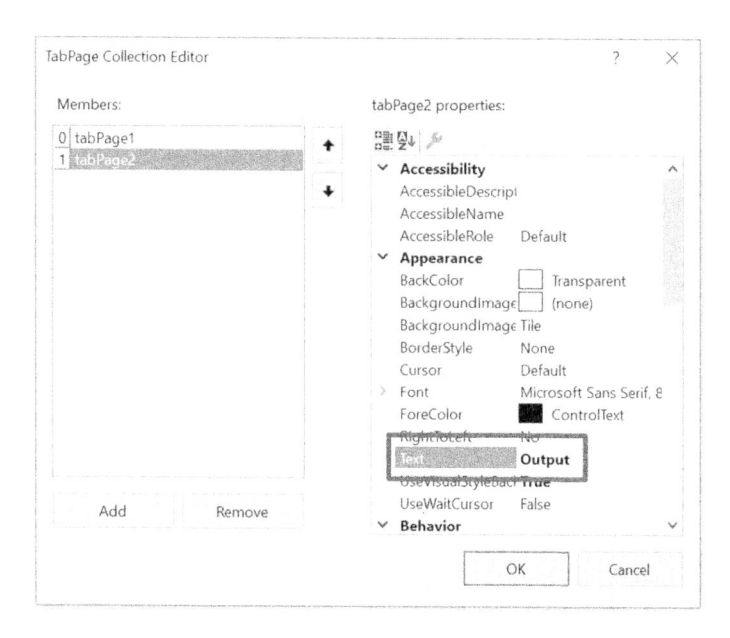

Figure 6.56. Setting the Text property of the second tab

4. Add a TextBox to the first tab. Set the Name of the TextBox as **inputTextBox**.
5. Add a Label to the second tab. Set the Name of the Label as **outputLabel**.
6. We will trigger updating the Label with the converted text whenever the Text of the inputTextBox changes. We will use the event called **TextChanged** for this aim. Select the TextBox and navigate check its events in the bottom right pane by clicking the events (⚡) button as shown below:

BEGINNER'S GUIDE TO VISUAL BASIC.NET PROGRAMMING

Figure 6.57. Selecting the events of the TextBox

7. Double-click the **TextChanged** event as shown in the figure above. The TextChanged event handler will be generated in the Form1.cs file as shown below:

```
Private Sub InputTextBox_TextChanged(sender As Object, e As
EventArgs) Handles inputTextBox.TextChanged


End Sub
```
Code 6.17

8. The Text of the **outputLabel** will be updated when the Text of the **inputTextBox** is changed. The code line outputLabel.Text = inputTextBox.Text.ToUpper() does the required job. It takes the Text of the **inputTextBox**, converts it to all-capitals by the method ToUpper() and then assigns the result to the Text of **outputLabel**. We'll write this code line inside the inputTextBox_TextChanged() method as follows:

```
Private Sub InputTextBox_TextChanged(sender As Object, e As
EventArgs) Handles inputTextBox.TextChanged

    outputLabel.Text = inputTextBox.Text.ToUpper()

End Sub
```
Code 6.18

CHAPTER 6. MENUS, DIALOGS AND CONTAINERS

9. Build and run the project. The following program window with tabs will appear:

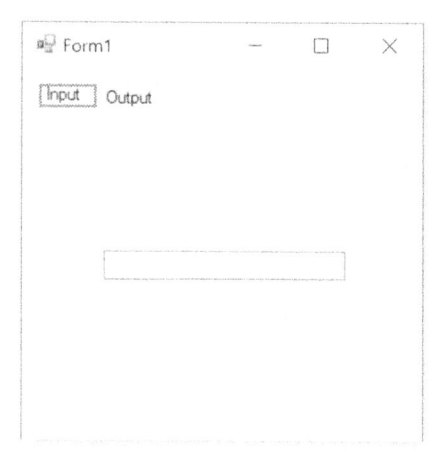

Figure 6.58. The program with TabControl

When we enter a text in the TextBox of the Input tab, this text will be converted to upper case and then written on the Label of the Output Tab as shown in Figures 6.59 and 6.60, respectively. Please note that we didn't need to place a Button to fire the conversion process because the inputTextBox_TextChanged() method automatically executes whenever we change the text of the **inputTextBox**.

Figure 6.59. A text entered in the inputTextBox in the Input tab

179

Figure 6.60. The all-capitals text displayed on the outputLabel of the Output tab

6.3.4. TableLayoutPanel

TableLayoutPanel enables us to design forms in which the controls are aligned in a table layout automatically. We can edit the rows or columns of the TableLayoutPanel per our need.

Let's see how we may utilize a TableLayoutPanel to align the controls in a table-like layout in simple project:

1. Create a VB.NET project.
2. Add a TableLayoutPanel on the form. The TableLayoutPanel has two rows and two columns by default.
3. Click the arrow at the top of the TableLayoutPanel to open the Tasks window where we can add/remove rows and columns as shown below:

CHAPTER 6. MENUS, DIALOGS AND CONTAINERS

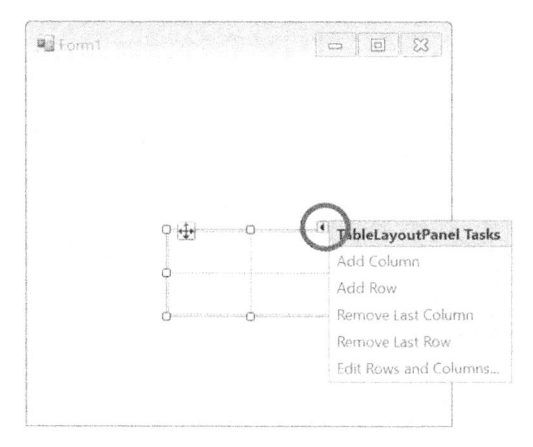

Figure 6.61. The TableLayoutPanel tasks window

4. Click the **Add Column** and **Add Row** buttons once so that our TableLayoutPanel will have 3 rows and 3 columns. After these operations, the TableLayoutPanel will have asymmetric rows and columns:

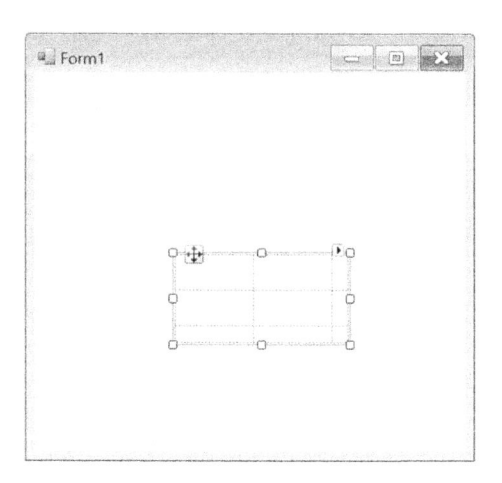

Figure 6.62. TableLayoutPanel with asymmetric cells

5. Open the Tasks dialog of the TableLayoutPanel and select **Edit Rows and Columns...** as follows:

181

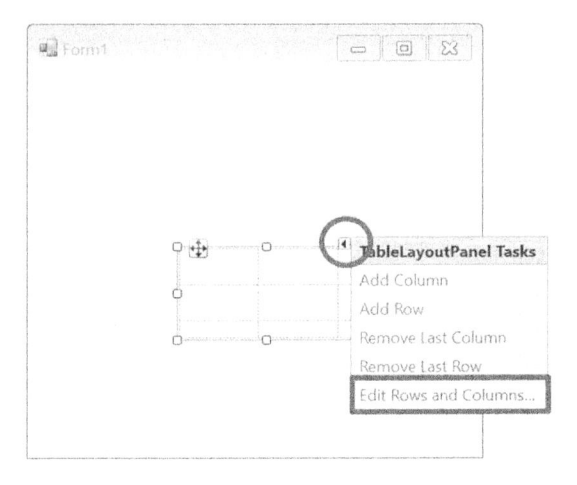

Figure 6.63. Opening the Edit Rows and Columns dialog

6. When the **Columns** is selected, set the Size Types of Column1, Column2 and Column3 as Per cent and set their percentages as 33%, 33% and 34%, respectively as shown in Figure 6.64 so that we will divide them almost equally.

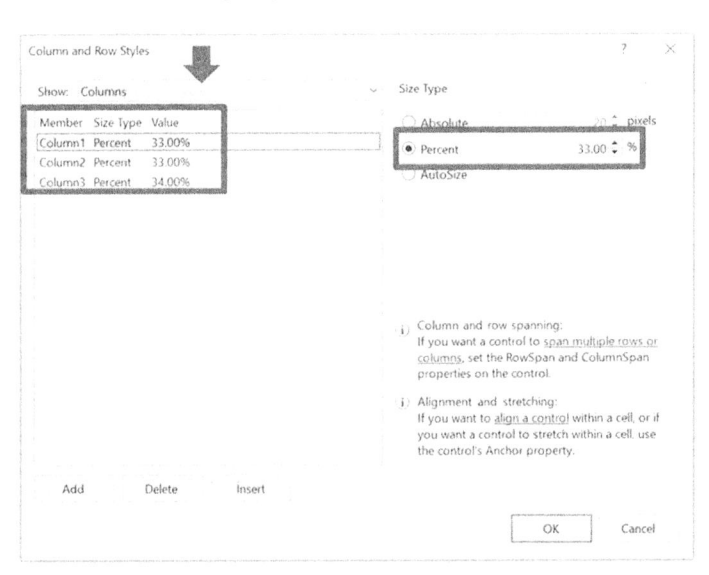

Figure 6.64. Setting column sizes

7. Similarly, select the **Rows** and then set the sizes of Row1, Row2 and Row3 as 33%, 33% and 34% as in Figure 6.65.

CHAPTER 6. MENUS, DIALOGS AND CONTAINERS

8. We can now resize the TableLayoutPanel on the form and the column and row size percentages will be kept as in Figure 6.66.

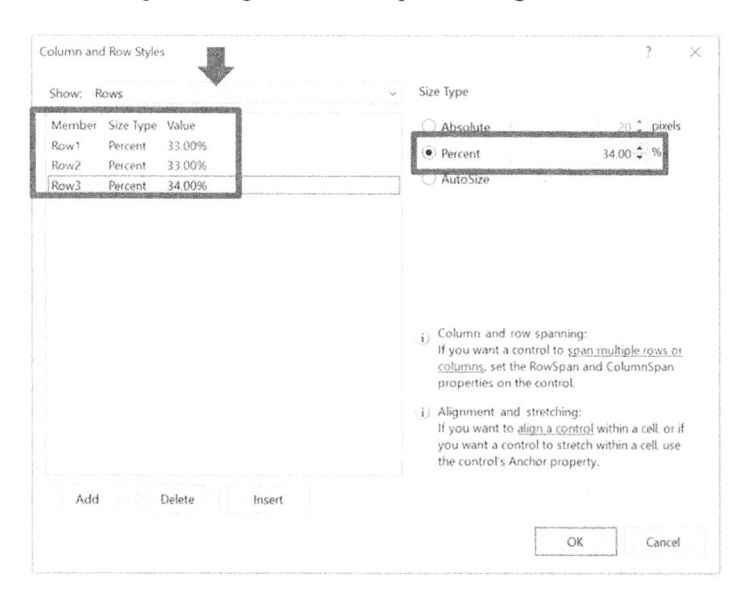

Figure 6.65. Setting row sizes

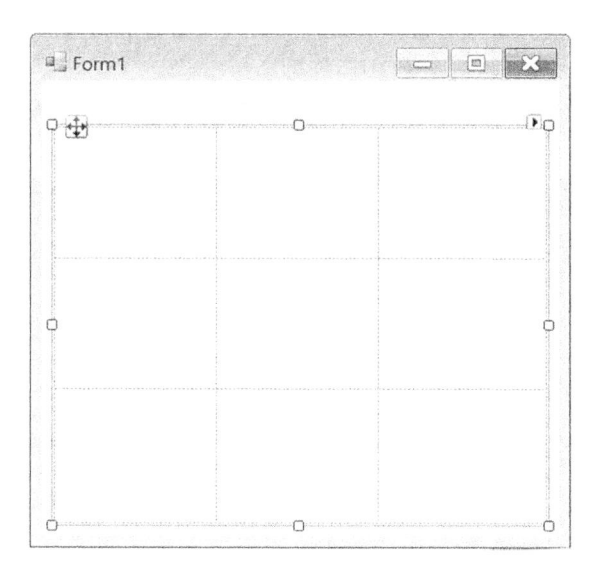

Figure 6.66. Resized TableLayoutPanel

9. Let's build and run the project. The program will appear as follows:

183

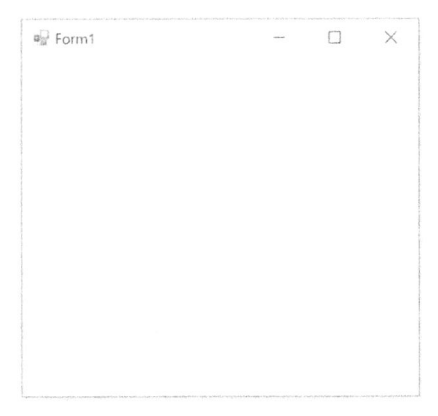

Figure 6.67. TableLayoutPanel not visible by default

As we can see from this window, the TableLayoutWindow does not have a border by default. Since we haven't added any control inside the TableLayoutPanel, the whole form seems empty. We can change the border style of the TableLayoutPanel via its **CellBorderStyle** property. For example, if we set this property as **Single**, borders will be shown as single lines as shown below:

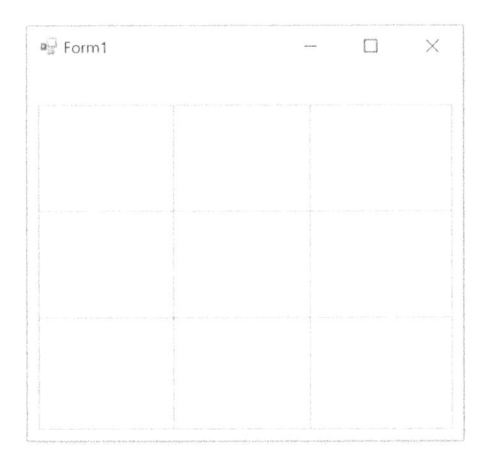

Figure 6.68. The TableLayoutPanel after the **CellBorderStyle** is set as
Single

6.3.5. SplitContainer
SplitContainer is used to divide the form in two vertical or horizontal panels. The sizes of these dividing panels are resizable.

CHAPTER 6. MENUS, DIALOGS AND CONTAINERS

Let's use a SplitContainer to divide a form in an example:

1. Create a VB.NET project.
2. Add a SplitContainer to the form. The SplitContainer will divide the form in two panels as follows:

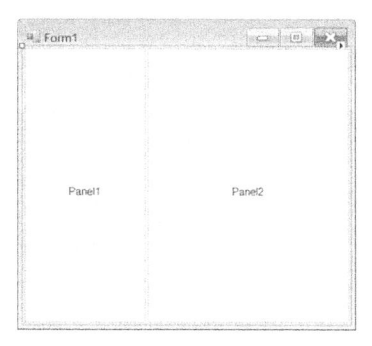

Figure 6.69. SplitContainer divides the form to two vertical panels by default

3. The SplitContainer divides the whole form to two vertical panels by default. We can change these settings from the SplitContainer Tasks dialog which is opened by clicking the arrow on the SplitContainer as follows:

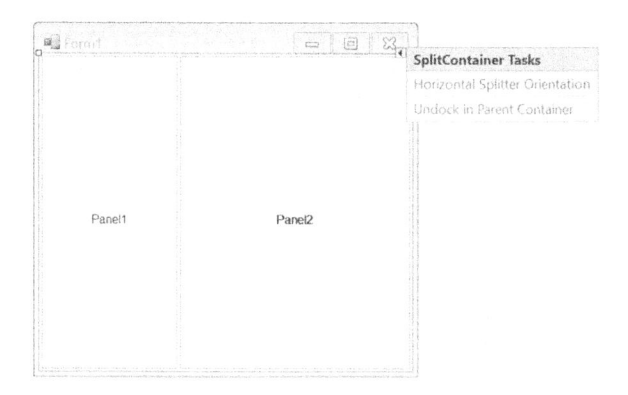

Figure 6.70. The Tasks dialog of the SplitContainer

4. When we click the **Horizontal Splitter Orientation**, the SplitContainer will divide the form horizontally:

185

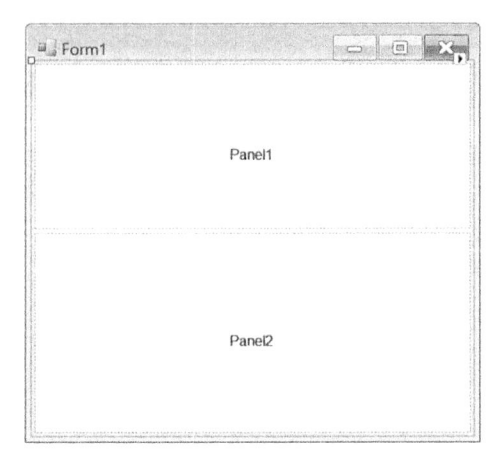

Figure 6.71. SplitContainer dividing the form horizontally

5. Furthermore, we may **undock** the SplitContainer meaning that it may not cover the whole form by clicking the **Undock in Parent Container** in the Tasks dialog:

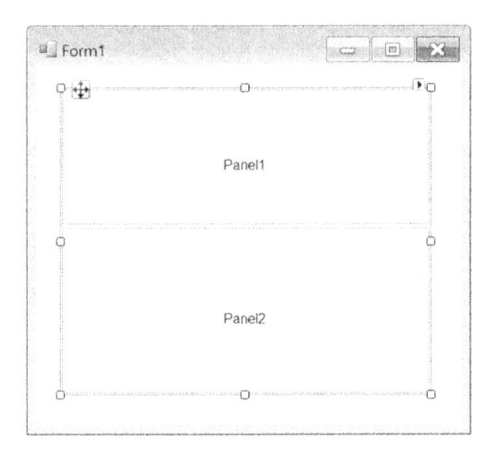

Figure 6.72. The SplitContainer undocked from the form

It is worth noting that we can also resize the panels of the SplitContainers by dragging and dropping the dividing line.

6.3.6. FlowLayoutPanel

This is another container type used in Windows forms applications. FlowLayoutPanel automatically lays out its contents. Its main properties are as follows:

- **FlowDirection**: This property sets the direction of laying out the contents. It may take the values of **LeftToRight**, **TopDown**, **RightToLeft** and **BottomUp**.
- **AutoScroll**: Sets if the scrollbars of the FlowLayoutPanel will be available by default.

We will use the FlowLayoutPanel in an example where we will add several buttons inside the FlowLayout and let it lay out these controls automatically when we click respective buttons.

1. Create a VB.NET project.
2. Add a FlowLayoutPanel on the form. Set the Name property of the FlowLayoutPanel as **changeFlowLayoutPanel**. Set the **BorderStyle** of the FlowLayoutPanel as **FixedSingle** so that we can see borders of the FlowLayoutPanel on the form.
3. Add four Buttons inside the FlowLayoutPanel as follows:

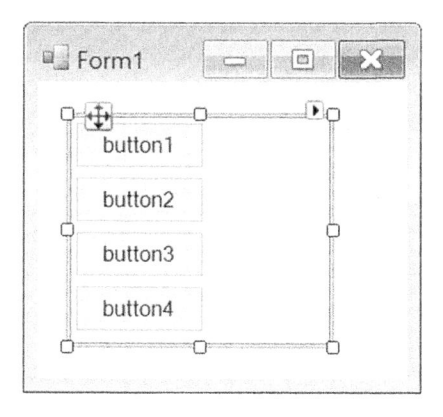

Figure 6.73. The FlowLayoutPanel containing three Buttons

4. Set the Name properties of these Buttons as **lrButton**, **tdButton**, **rlButton** and **buButton** from top to down, respectively.

5. Set the Text properties of these Buttons as **LeftToRight**, **TopDown**, **RightToLeft** and **BottomUp**, respectively.
6. Create the default Click events of these Buttons by double-clicking each of them as follows:

```
Private Sub LrButton_Click(sender As Object, e As
EventArgs) Handles lrButton.Click

End Sub

Private Sub TdButton_Click(sender As Object, e As
EventArgs) Handles tdButton.Click

End Sub

Private Sub RlButton_Click(sender As Object, e As
EventArgs) Handles rlButton.Click

End Sub

Private Sub BuButton_Click(sender As Object, e As
EventArgs) Handles buButton.Click

End Sub
```
Code 6.19

7. When the **LeftToRight** button is clicked, the **FlowDirection** property of the **changeFlowLayoutPanel** will be set as **LeftToRight** with the code line: changeFlowLayoutPanel.FlowDirection = FlowDirection.LeftToRight. For the other three Buttons, we set the FlowDirection property of the FlowLayoutPanel with similar lines. Inserting the respective code lines, the event handlers of the Buttons are obtained as follows:

```
Private Sub LrButton_Click(sender As Object, e As
EventArgs) Handles lrButton.Click

changeFlowLayoutPanel.FlowDirection = FlowDirection.LeftToRight

End Sub

Private Sub TdButton_Click(sender As Object, e As
EventArgs) Handles tdButton.Click
```

CHAPTER 6. MENUS, DIALOGS AND CONTAINERS

```
changeFlowLayoutPanel.FlowDirection = FlowDirection.TopDown

End Sub

Private Sub RlButton_Click(sender As Object, e As
EventArgs) Handles rlButton.Click

changeFlowLayoutPanel.FlowDirection = FlowDirection.RightToLeft

End Sub

Private Sub BuButton_Click(sender As Object, e As
EventArgs) Handles buButton.Click

changeFlowLayoutPanel.FlowDirection = FlowDirection.BottomUp

End Sub
```

Code 6.20 (cont'd)

8. Build and run the project. The following program window will appear with the FlowLayoutPanel having the default FlowDirection of LeftToRight:

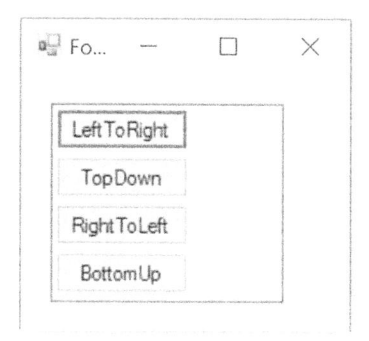

Figure 6.74. The default layout of the form

When the RightToLeft, TopDown and BottomUp buttons are clicked, the contents of the FlowLayoutPanel are automatically laid out as shown in Figures 6.75, 6.76 and 6.77, respectively.

189

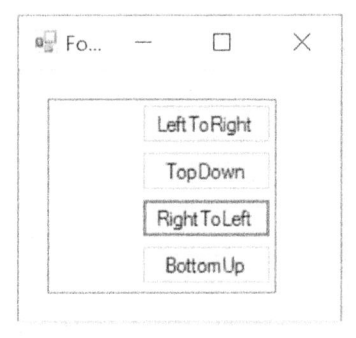

Figure 6.75. The layout after RightToLeft button is clicked

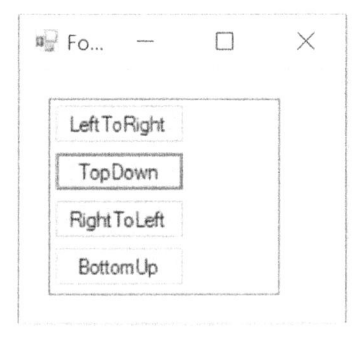

Figure 6.76. The layout after TopDown button is clicked

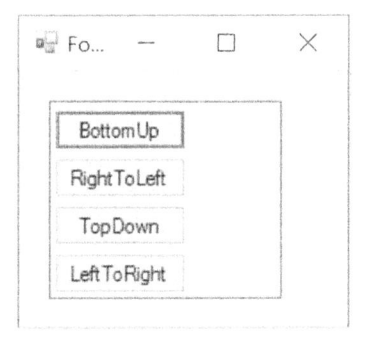

Figure 6.77. The form after BottomUp button is clicked

We have completed the chapter by this example.

Until this point, we learned using Windows forms and controls to design graphical interfaces for our programs. We used each control in an example for creating a solid background in GUI design. We incorporated

VB.NET code snippets for controlling the behaviours of form elements as much as we needed. However, we haven't studied VB.NET programming language in detail. Starting from the next chapter, we will learn VB.NET in a systematic way by the help of hands-on projects.

Chapter 7

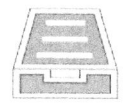

VARIABLES AND CONSTANTS

We will start studying Visual Basic.NET programming language systematically in this chapter. Our first subject is a basic concept in programming: variables and constants.

7.1. Variables

Variables are used for holding data temporarily during the program execution. We can think variables as the addresses (or pointers) of temporary data stored in the random access memory (RAM). In some programming languages, the compiler understands the type of the variable and allocates the required space in the RAM for it. These are called dynamically typed languages. On the other hand, in statically typed languages like VB.NET, the type of the variable should explicitly be defined before being able to store data in it. In VB.NET, when the type of the variable is declared, the VB.NET compiler assigns the required space to that variable in the memory.

7.1.1. Declaring Variables

Variables are declared (dimensioned) with their types and names in the following form:

`Dim name_of_the_variable As variable_data_type`

There are several variable types in VB.NET each having a specific length. When a variable is declared as shown above, the memory space for the variable is allocated but not filled yet. It is because the variable hasn't been assigned a value. Here's an integer type variable definition:

```
Dim a As Integer
```
Code 7.1

In this code line, we request the VB.NET compiler to "allocate space in the memory where an integer number will be stored and this number will be referred as a in the program later". The compiler allocates the space with this line, in other words **the variable a is created**. However it is still empty. If we try to use this variable in our program, the program will shout at us, sorry it will give an error saying that the variable a **is declared but not assigned a value**. The values of variables are assigned using the = operator. Yes, it is the usual equal sign but having a stylish name in VB.NET: assignment operator. We can assign the number 3 to the variable a as follows:

```
a=3
```
Code 7.2

A value can also be assigned during the declaration. This is called as the initialization of the variable:

```
Dim a As Integer = 3
```
Code 7.3

Therefore, this code line does the same job as the combination of Code 7.1 and 7.2: declaring an integer variable a and assigning 3 to this variable.

We can declare multiple variables of the same type in a single line as follows:

```
Dim a, b, c As Integer
```
Code 7.4

We have declared three integer variables a, b and c using commas between them. Similarly, we can also initialize these variables in a single line:

```
Dim d=4, e=5
```
Code 7.5

There are several variable types other than Integer as we will see in a short while. But before that, let's study the rules we need to follow about variable names.

7.1.2. Rules about Variable Naming

Here are the basic rules on variable naming:

- Variable names cannot include space(s). For example, the declaration:

```
Dim my integer As Integer
```
Code 7.6

is illegal since there is a space between the characters y and i in the variable name. If we want to use such a name, we may use an underscore (_) for this aim as follows:

```
Dim my_integer As Integer
```
Code 7.7

- Variable names cannot start with numbers or special characters. They have to start with a letter. The declaration:

```
Dim 8segment As Integer
```
Code 7.8

is wrong. However we may include numbers or special characters after the first character of the variable name as follows:

```
Dim int_segment8to2_a As Integer
```
Code 7.9

- Variable names in VB.NET are case-insensitive. The variable my_integer and My_integer refer to the same variables. However, when you declare the variable my_integer in Visual Studio and then write My_integer, the IDE will correct it to my_integer to avoid confusion.
- Variable names cannot be selected from VB.NET keywords. For example, the keyword Dim cannot be used as a variable name. VB.NET has about 100 keywords. Therefore it is in general unlikely to choose one of them as a variable name. You may refer to the VB.NET keywords list from the website https://docs.microsoft.com/en-us/dotnet/visual-basic/language-reference/keywords/ when you are in doubt about this.

- The variable names may consist of 1023 characters at maximum. This is an example 1023 character name:

Lorem_ipsum_dolor_sit_amet,_consectetur_adipiscing_elit._Duis_sagittis_nibh_tortor,_a_v enenatis_eros_egestas_eu._Maecenas_ut_euismod_lacus._Suspendisse_ut_aliquet_enim ,_suscipit_auctor_augue._Donec_tincidunt_accumsan_neque,_sit_amet_bibendum_ligula_ facilisis_at._Nulla_mattis,_dolor_tempor_ultrices_aliquet,_neque_ipsum_ullamcorper_nequ e,_vitae_condimentum_urna_nibh_ut_nibh._Phasellus_rhoncus_purus_est,_at_pulvinar_ju sto_vulputate_nec._Donec_ut_laoreet_elit._Curabitur_mollis_nec_tortor_non_laoreet._Viva mus_aliquet_leo_et_aliquam_venenatis._Fusce_dui_enim,_ullamcorper_ut_luctus_quis,_v olutpat_vel_ligula_Ut_pharetra_nisl_ut_felis_ornare,_vitae_viverra_libero_venenatis._Etia m_augue_augue,_consequat_sit_amet_nisl_non,_laoreet_lobortis_augue._Curabitur_at_a ccumsan_dui,_ut_ultricies_nulla._Proin_eros_ante,_fringilla_quis_fringilla_eu,_porttitor_pre tium_felis._Nunc_pretium_molestie_quam_quis_sodales._Sed_fringilla_lacus_sit_amet_pu rus_consequat_varius._Sed_auctor_sem_eu_pretium_consequat._Sed_molestie_quam_vit ae_sed

Therefore, it is very unlikely to use a 1023 character variable name anyway ☺.

7.1.3. Variable Types

Variable types define the type of variables and the amount of allocated space in memory for these variables. Variable types in VB.NET can be classified in three categories: numeric variable types, character variable types and other variable types. Firstly, let's see these variable groups in three separate tables:

	Data type	Value range	Allocated memory
Integer	Byte	0~255	1 byte (8 bits)
	SByte	-128~127	1 byte (8 bits)
	Short	-32768~32767	2 bytes (16 bits)
	UShort	0~65535	2 bytes (16 bits)
	Integer	-2,147,483,648~ 2,147,483,647	4 bytes (32 bits)
	UInteger	0~4,294,967,295	4 bytes (32 bits)
	Long	+/-9,223,372,036,854,775,808	8 bytes (64 bits)
	ULong	0~18,446,744,073,709,551,615	8 bytes (64 bits)
Decimal	Double	+/-1.79769313486231570E+308	8 bytes (64 bits)
	Decimal	+/-7.9228162514264337593543950335	16 bytes (128 bits)
	Single	+/-3.4028235E+38	4 bytes (32 bits)

Table 7.1. Numeric variable types in VB.NET

CHAPTER 7. VARIABLES AND CONSTANTS

Data type	Value range	Allocated memory
Char	Holds a single Unicode character	2 bytes (16 bits)
String	Holds multiple Unicode characters	Depends on the length of its content

Table 7.2. Character type variables in VB.NET

Data type	Value range	Allocated memory
Boolean	True or False	1 byte (8 bits)
Date	Holds date-time values	2 bytes (16 bits)

Table 7.3. Other variable types

7.1.3.1 Numeric Variable Types

Let's now study the details of these numeric variable types one by one:

- **Byte**: This variable type is used for holding numbers between 0 and 255. One byte (8 bits) of memory space is allocated for each byte type variable. A variable named myNumber of type byte can be defined as follows:

```
Dim myNumber As Byte
```
Code 7.10

- **Sbyte**: This type also uses one byte of memory space and may take one of the 256 different values as the byte type. The difference is that an sbyte type variable can hold both negative and positive numbers in the range of -128 and 127. The **s** letter in sbyte means **signed**. A variable having sbyte type can be defined as below:

```
Dim mySignedNumber As SByte = -125
```
Code 7.11

- **Short**: A short type variable holds integer numbers between -32768 and 32767. 2 byte of space is allocated for each short variable. A variable named myShort can be declared as follows:

```
Dim myShort As Short = 23819
```

197

Code 7.12

- **UShort**: This type has the same size as short but cannot be used to store negative numbers. An ushort type variable is used to store integer numbers between 0 and 65535. myUnsignedShort having ushort type is declared as below:

```
Dim myUnsignedShort As UShort = 40001
```
Code 7.13

- **Integer**: This is a widely used variable type to store integer numbers. 4 byte of memory space is allocated for an int type and it can be used to store integers between -2,147,482,648 and 2,147,482,647. These limits may seem weird at first glance but they are not randomly chosen. They originate from the allocated space amount of 4 byte = 32 bits. In computer science, a 32 bit data may be used to store 2^{32} different values. When this number is divided into 2 and zero is included, the weird looking limits mentioned above are reached. We do not need to memorize these limits anyway! Here's an Integer type variable declaration:

```
Dim population As Integer = 1311000000
```
Code 7.14

- **UInteger**: It has the same data length on the memory as int but cannot hold negative numbers. Therefore, its limits are 0 and 4,294,967,295. An uint variable can be declared as below:

```
Dim totalPopulation As UInteger = 2691000000
```
Code 7.15

- **Long**: It is used to store long numbers ☺. The limits are: -9,223,372,036,854,775,808 and 9,223,372,036,854,775,807. Here's a long type variable declaration sample:

```
Dim totalNumberofInternetSearchesPerYear As Long =
120000000000
```
Code 7.16

CHAPTER 7. VARIABLES AND CONSTANTS

- **ULong**: Long integer numbers without sign. Therefore, the limits are 0 and 18,446,744,073,709,551,615. A long variable declaration is as follows:

```
Dim numberOfAtomsInOneMilliGramOfGold As ULong = 30573183730000000
```
Code 7.17

The types we studied until here are all used for storing integer numbers, i.e. numbers without a decimal point. The following variable types can be used for storing decimal numbers:

- **Double**: This is the default decimal type in VB.NET. Used for storing numbers between about $\pm 5 \times 10^{-324}$ and $\pm 1.7 \times 10^{308}$. Its decimal part has 15 digits of precision. Here's a sample declaration:

```
Dim myDouble As Double = 3.14
```
Code 7.18

- **Single**: This type is used for holding decimal numbers between $\pm 1.5 \times 10^{-45}$ and $\pm 3,4 \times 10^{38}$. 4 byte of memory space is allocated for each Single variable. It has a 7 digits of decimal precision. A sample declaration is as follows:

```
Dim mySingle As Single = 4.5
```
Code 7.19

- **Decimal**: Used for storing decimal numbers in the limits of 0 to 0 through 7.9...E+28. The precision of this decimal type is 28 digits:

```
Dim AvogadrosNumber As Decimal = 6.02E+23
```
Code 7.20

7.1.3.2. Character Variable Types

There are two character types as mentioned before:

- **Char**: This type is used for holding **one of the Unicode characters**. The Unicode system represents most of the characters found in all languages around the World. It is worth emphasizing that a char variable can only store one character at a time as follows:

```
Dim theLetter As Char = "C"
```
Code 7.21

Note that the characters are written inside double quotes when assigning to a Char type variable.

- **String**: This is a character string. Used for storing more than one character. The string type is a **reference type** variable meaning that the variable in fact stores the reference to its content. Contrary to the other variable types which are **value types**, **reference types** may refer to the same content in the memory meaning that a change in a variable may result the change of the other variable too. If this confuses you, don't worry. We'll use these concepts in our projects soon. Here's a string variable declaration:

```
Dim todaysSong As String = "Careless Whisper"
```
Code 7.22

Each character in a string uses 2 bytes of memory. Therefore the string "Careless Whisper" uses 16x2=32 bytes of memory space since it has 16 characters including the space character.

7.1.3.3. Other Variable Types

There are several other types but the following two are widely the used ones:

- **Boolean**: This variable type is used to store only one of the two different values: True or False. We can think them as the answers to a yes-no question. The following is a Boolean type variable declaration:

```
Dim isBackgroundWhite As Boolean = True
```
Code 7.23

- **Date**: This type is used for holding date and time data between 1/1/0001 12:00:00 and 31/12/9999 23:59:59. 8 bytes of memory space is allocated for each Date variable. In the following code line, the date-time data of the moment is assigned to a `DateTime` type variable named `currentDateTime`:

```
Dim currentDateTime As Date = DateTime.Now
```
Code 7.24

7.1.4. General Type Conversions

We sometimes need to convert data types. Type conversion is in fact taking the data contained in a variable and then placing this data to another variable which has a different amount of allocated space on the memory.

A type conversion example: If the user enters some numbers in a TextBox, it is read as a string in VB.NET. If we need to do mathematical operations on this input, **we firstly convert it to a numeric data type** and then perform the required operation. And then again **the result should be converted to a string** before displaying on a Label or a TextBox.

There are two types of conversions in VB.NET: **implicit** and **explicit** conversions:

- **Implicit conversions**: In this type of conversion, the contents of a variable type can be converted to another type which has a bigger amount of allocated space. Assume that we have an `Integer` type variable. It has a 4 bytes of allocated space. This means that we can convert the `Integer` type to any type which has 4 bytes or more allocated space so that we will not lose information. For instance, an `Integer` type variable can be converted to a `Long` type variable. However, we cannot implicitly convert an `Integer` to a `Byte` type variable because `byte` has only 1 byte of allocated space and the contents of an `int` variable cannot be fit into this 1 byte space. If we try to do this, VB.NET compiler will issue an error and will not build the executable file. The permitted implicit conversions are given in Table 7.4. Here's an example of implicit conversion:

```
Dim myInteger As Integer = 4500
Dim newLong As Long = myInteger
```
Code 7.25

In the first line, we declared an Integer type variable called myInteger and initialized it as 4500. In the second line, we declared a Long type variable called myLong and assigned myInteger's value to myLong. Note that myInteger will not be wiped out, both variables will co-exist in the end.

From type	To type
Byte	Short, UShort, Long, ULong, Integer, UInteger, Duble, Decimal, Single
SByte	Integer, Decimal, Short, Long, Double, Single
Short	Integer, Long, Double, Decimal
UShort	Integer, UInteger, Long, ULong, Double, Decimal, Single
Integer	Double, Long, Decimal, Single
UInteger	Double, Long, Decimal, ULong, Single
Long	Decimal, Double, Single
Single	Double
Char	Integer, Single, Double, Long, Decimal, UInteger, ULong

Table 7.4. Permitted implicit conversions

- **Explicit conversions**: Explicit conversions enable us to convert a data type to another type which has a smaller allocated space. Remember that this is not a permitted operation in implicit conversion as stated above. We do explicit conversion by using one of the given *conversion keywords*: CBool (converts an expression to a Boolean), CByte (converts an expression to a Byte), CChar (converts an expression to a Char), CDate (converts an expression to a Date), CDbl (converts an expression to a Double), CDec (converts an expression to a Decimal), CInt (converts an expression to an Integer), CLng (converts an expression to a Long), CShort (converts an expression to a Short), CSng (converts an expression to a Single), CStr (converts an expression to a String), CUInt (converts an expression to an UInteger), CULng (converts an expression to an ULong), CUShort (converts an expression to a UShort). An explicit conversion example is shown below:

```
Dim myNewDouble As Double = 1.25
Dim myNewShort As Short = CShort(myNewDouble)
```
Code 7.26

In the first line, we declared the variable named myNewDouble and initialized it as 1.25. In the second line, we declare a short type variable called myNewShort. Remember that short type variables have 2 bytes of space while double types have 8 bytes of space therefore it is illegal to convert a double type to a short type implicitly. Because of this we informed the compiler that we'll convert the contents of the myDouble to a short type by the keyword CShort. In the end, we converted 1.25 to short and assigned it to the myNewShort variable. However, myNewShort will hold only 1 instead of 1.25 therefore we lose some information with explicit conversion.

7.1.5. String Conversions

We frequently need to convert String type variables to others and vice versa because form controls generally use String type input and output. Examples include TextBox and Label. The data read from them are strings and we need to use strings to update their Text properties. Therefore, we use CStr conversion keyword very frequently. VB.NET is built upon the .NET framework so we can also use the .ToString() method of the .NET layer instead of CStr. They have no difference from the application viewpoint.

7.1.5.1. From String to Other Types

There are two ways for converting string type data to other types: **Parse() and the methods of the Convert class**.

- **Parse()**: This method is used in the following way:

```
variable_type.Parse(String to be converted)
```
Code 7.27

Let's use this method in a small VB.NET project. We'll take two numbers from the user and multiply them and show the product on the form:

1. Create a VB.NET project.
2. Add three TextBoxes on the form. Set their Names as **input1**, **input2** and **output**.
3. Add a Button on the form between the second and the third TextBox. Set its Name and Text as **multiplyButton** and **Multiply**. The form layout will look as in Figure 7.1.
4. Double-click the Button to generate its default event handler **Click** as follows:

```
Private Sub MultiplyButton_Click(sender As Object, e As
EventArgs) Handles multiplyButton.Click

End Sub
```
Code 7.28

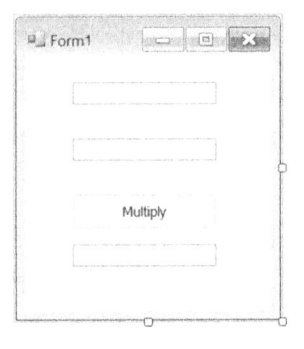

Figure 7.1. The layout of the form

5. The user will input numbers to the first two TextBoxes. These will be the Text properties of these TextBoxes. Let's take them and assign to string type variables called input1String and input2String as follows:

```
Dim input1string As String = input1.Text
Dim input2string As String = input2.Text
```
Code 7.29

6. We cannot directly multiply these strings; we have to convert them to a numeric type first. Considering that the user may enter decimal numbers, let's convert these String types to Double type variables using the Parse() method as follows:

```
Dim input1double As Double = Double.Parse(input1string)
Dim input2double As Double = Double.Parse(input2string)
```
Code 7.30

7. We can now multiply the double type variables input1Double and input1Double. Let's declare a double type variable called product to store the multiplication result:

```
Dim product As Double = input1double * input2double
```
Code 7.31

8. We will display the product on the third TextBox. We will set its Text property as the product. However, we cannot directly assign a double type variable as the Text of a TextBox. We need to convert this double type to string. For this, we will use ToString() method as follows:

```
Dim productString As String = product.ToString()
```
Code 7.32

9. Finally, we need to assign the string type variable productString to the third TextBox:

```
output.Text = productString
```
Code 7.33

The complete Click method of the Button populated by these code lines is also given below:

```
Private Sub MultiplyButton_Click(sender As Object, e As EventArgs) Handles multiplyButton.Click

    Dim input1string As String = input1.Text
    Dim input2string As String = input2.Text

    Dim input1double As Double = Double.Parse(input1string)
```

```
    Dim input2double As Double = Double.Parse(input2string)

    Dim product As Double = input1double * input2double

    Dim productString As String = product.ToString()

    output.Text = productString

End Sub
```
Code 7.34

Note that these operations could be completed by fewer code lines however they are performed explicitly for teaching purposes.

10. Build and run the project. We may enter decimal or integer numbers in the first two input TextBoxes. When the **Multiply** Button is clicked, the result is shown in the third TextBox as shown in Figure 7.2.

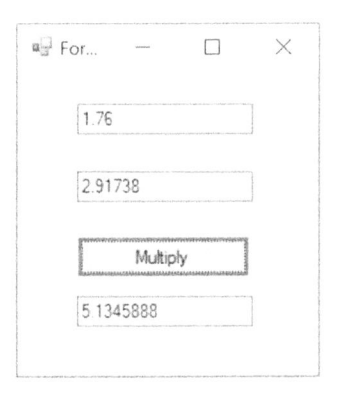

Figure 7.3. Multiplication program in action

If we don't enter any input to one of the TextBoxes, the program will crash because the Parse() method cannot operate on a null (empty) string. For handling these type of errors, a similar method called TryParse() is used. If the string is null, the TryParse() method protects the program from crashing, instead it returns zero as the converted value.

- **Methods of the Convert class**: These methods operates similar to the Parse() method; however they handle null strings automatically. We can convert a string to various data types using the following methods of the Convert class.

Method	Operation
Convert.ToByte(string to be converted)	Converts string to a Byte type variable
Convert.ToSByte(string to be converted)	Converts string to a Signed Byte type variable
Convert.ToInt16(string to be converted)	Converts string to a 16-bit Integer type variable
Convert.ToUInt16(string to be converted)	Converts string to an Unsigned 16-bit Integer type variable
Convert.ToInt32(string to be converted)	Converts string to a 32-bit Integer type variable
Convert.ToUInt32(string to be converted)	Converts string to an Unsigned 32-bit Integer type variable
Convert.ToInt64(string to be converted)	Converts string to a 64-bit Integer type variable
Convert.ToUInt64(string to be converted)	Converts string to an Unsigned 64-bit Integer type variable
Convert.ToSingle(string to be converted)	Converts string to a Single type variable
Convert.ToDouble(string to be converted)	Converts string to a Double type variable
Method	Operation
Convert.ToDecimal(string to be converted)	Converts string to a decimal type variable
Convert.ToChar(string to be converted)	Converts string to a char type variable

Table 7.5. Widely used methods of the **Convert** class

We used Parse() method for string to double conversions in the previous example. We can modify its event handler code using the Convert.toDouble() method as follows:

```
Private Sub MultiplyButton_Click(sender As Object, e As EventArgs) Handles multiplyButton.Click

Dim input1string As String = input1.Text
Dim input2string As String = input2.Text
'Dim input1double As Double = Double.Parse(input1string)
'Dim input2double As Double = Double.Parse(input2string)
Dim input1double As Double = Convert.ToDouble(input1string)
Dim input2double As Double = Convert.ToDouble(input2string)
Dim product As Double = input1double * input2double
Dim productString As String = product.ToString()
output.Text = productString
End Sub
```

Code 7.35

The multiplication program works as expected with these modifications:

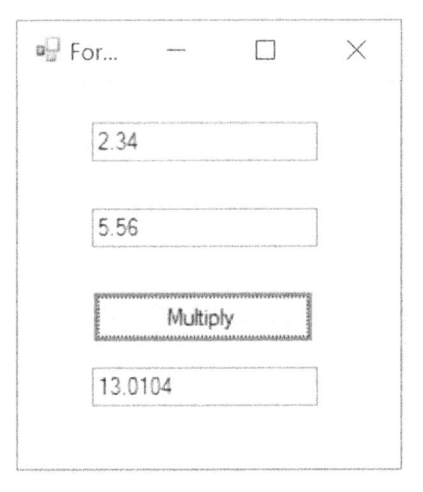

Figure 7.3. Multiplication program utilizing the **Convert.toDouble()** method

7.1.5.2. Other Types to String

As we have used in the multiplication program, the method toString() or the keyword CStr simply converts numeric data types to String easily. We apply this method on the variable to be converted as follows:

```
Dim myInteger As Integer = 3
outputTextBox.Text = myInteger.ToString()
```
Code 7.36

In the first line, we declared an integer variable myInteger and initialized it as 3. In the second line, ToString() method is applied on this variable to convert it to string which is then assigned as the Text of the **outputTextBox**.

7.2. Constants

Constants are the data types which are assigned a value only once. Constants are initialized at the time of their declaration. We can think them as special "non-varying" variables whose values are kept constant through the code. They can be declared by using the Const keyword in front of a variable declaration together with an access specifier (Private or Public) as follows:

CHAPTER 7. VARIABLES AND CONSTANTS

```
Public Const DaysInWeek As Integer = 7
```
Code 7.37

Let's use a constant in a small project where we will calculate the area of a circle. We will define the pi number in the global area as a constant and use it inside a button's event handler:

1. Create a VB.NET project.
2. Add a TextBox on the form where we will enter the radius of the circle. Set its Name and Text as **radiusInput** and **Enter radius here...**, respectively.
3. Add a Button below the radiusInput TextBox. Set its Name and Text as **calculateButton** and **Calculate the area**, respectively.
4. Add another TextBox below the Button where we will display the area. Set its Name and Text as **areaTextBox** and **Area appears here...**. The form will look as in Figure 7.4.

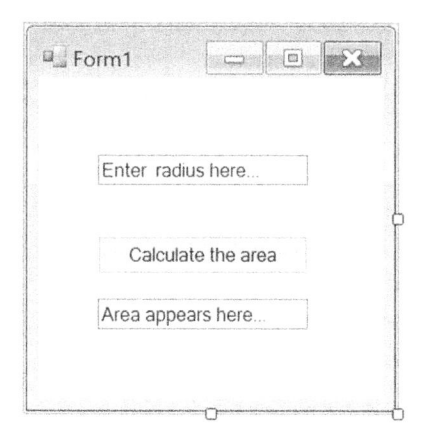

Figure 7.4. The layout of the form

5. Double click the button to create its Click event handler. Form1.vb file will look as follows:

209

Figure 7.5. The global area in the Form1.vb file

6. We generally create and use the variables and constants inside the methods. However, if we are planning to use the same variable or constant inside various methods, we need to define it in the **Global Area** as indicated in Figure 7.5. Since the pi number is a constant, it is good practice to declare it in the global area. Since it will be defined as a constant instead of a variable, there is no risk of altering it accidentally inside a method by a programming error. We may define it as a constant double as follows:

```
Const pi As Double = 3.14
```
Code 7.38

7. Let's implement the formula Area=pi*radius^2 inside the calculateButton_Click handler method:

```
Private Sub CalculateButton_Click(sender As Object, e As
EventArgs) Handles calculateButton.Click

  Dim radius As Double = Convert.ToDouble(radiusInput.Text)
  areaTextBox.Text = (pi * radius * radius).ToString()

End Sub
```
Code 7.39

In the first line, we converted the Text of the **radiusInput** TextBox to Double type and assigned it to a Double type variable named radius. In the second line, the area is calculated according to the formula given above, converted to string and assigned as the Text of the **areaTextBox**.

Please note that the pi number is declared in the global area so that we didn't need to declare the pi number inside this method. The complete Form1.vb file is as follows:

```
Public Class Form1

    Const pi As Double = 3.14
    Private Sub CalculateButton_Click(sender As Object, e As
EventArgs) Handles calculateButton.Click

        Dim radius As Double = Convert.ToDouble(radiusInput.Text)
        areaTextBox.Text = (pi * radius * radius).ToString()

    End Sub
End Class
```
Code 7.40

8. Build and run the project. The program window appears as below:

Figure 7.6. The area calculating program

When we enter a radius value and click the Button, the program successfully calculates the area:

Figure 7.7. Area is calculated successfully

This is all about variables and constants for now. We will study conditional statements in the next chapter, which are used for branching.

Chapter 8

CONDITIONAL STATEMENTS

Conditional statements enable the programs to branch depending on given conditions. Before studying actual conditional statements and keywords, it is better to overview operators which are utilized in conditional statements

8.1. Operators

Operators operate on the operands, which exist at the left and right hand side of the operand. In fact we did use operands before, when we did addition and multiplication in the previous chapters. Those were the arithmetic operators. VB.NET is a flexible language and provides operators in comparison, arithmetic and increment/decrement categories.

8.1.1. Comparison Operators

Logical operators compare its two operands and generate a logical result. Since a logical result can only be true or false, the result of a logical operator is always a Boolean type variable. Comparison operators in VB.NET are shown in the following table:

Operator	Comparison
=	Checks if its operands are equal
< >	Checks if its operands are not equal
>	Checks if the first operand is greater than the second one
<	Checks if the first operand is lower than the second one
>=	Checks if the first operand is greater or equal to the second one
<=	Checks if the first operand is lower or equal to the second one

Table 8.1. Comparison operators

BEGINNER'S GUIDE TO VISUAL BASIC.NET PROGRAMMING

Comparison operators return True if the comparison is correct, and returns False otherwise.

Let's use some of the comparison operators in a sample project:

1. Create a VB.NET project.
2. Add two TextBoxes. Set their Names as **input1TextBox** and **input2TextBox**.
3. Add three Buttons. Set their Names and Texts as **equalsButton**, **greaterButton**, **lowerButton** and **Are they equal?**, **Is the first one greater?** And **Is the first one lower?**, respectively.
4. Add a Label below these controls. Set its Name and Text properties as **resultLabel** and **Click a button for comparison**, respectively. The form may look as follows:

Figure 8.1. The form layout

5. Double-click the buttons to create their default event handler in Form1.cs:

```
Private Sub EqualsButton_Click(sender As Object, e As
EventArgs) Handles equalsButton.Click

End Sub

Private Sub GreaterButton_Click(sender As Object, e As
EventArgs) Handles Button1.Click

End Sub

Private Sub LowerButton_Click(sender As Object, e As
```

CHAPTER 8. CONDITIONAL STATEMENTS

```
EventArgs) Handles lowerButton.Click
End Sub
```
Code 8.1 (cont'd)

6. We'll read inputs from the TextBoxes and convert them to numeric type variables in each of the event handlers created above. Considering that the user may enter decimal numbers, it is better to convert to double type:

```
Dim input1 As Double = Convert.ToDouble(input1TextBox.Text)
Dim input2 As Double = Convert.ToDouble(input2TextBox.Text)
```
Code 8.2

7. We will compare if these numeric values are equal inside the event handler of the **equalsButton** as follows:

```
Dim result As Boolean = (input1 = input2)
```
Code 8.3

We put the comparison result into a Boolean variable called result. Then, we'll write the result on the **resultLabel** as usual:

```
resultLabel.Text = "Are they equal? " + result.ToString()
```
Code 8.4

In this line, we convert the bool type result to string for being able to display on the Label. In addition, we combine **Are they equal?** text with the result string to display the comparison result together with its question.

8. Similarly, the code in the event handler of the **greaterButton** will check if input1 is greater than input2 using the greater operator > as follows:

```
Dim input1 As Double = Convert.ToDouble(input1TextBox.Text)
Dim input2 As Double = Convert.ToDouble(input2TextBox.Text)
Dim result As Boolean = (input1 > input2)
resultLabel.Text = "Is the first one greater? " +
                    result.ToString()
```
Code 8.5

215

9. We apply the same strategy for checking if the first number is lower than the second one with the following code:

```vbnet
Dim input1 As Double = Convert.ToDouble(input1TextBox.Text)
Dim input2 As Double = Convert.ToDouble(input2TextBox.Text)
Dim result As Boolean = (input1 < input2)
resultLabel.Text = "Is the first one lower? " +
                    result.ToString()
```
Code 8.6

The resulting complete event handlers are also given below for your convenience:

```vbnet
Private Sub EqualsButton_Click(sender As Object, e As
EventArgs) Handles equalsButton.Click

Dim input1 As Double = Convert.ToDouble(input1TextBox.Text)
Dim input2 As Double = Convert.ToDouble(input2TextBox.Text)
Dim result As Boolean = (input1 = input2)
resultLabel.Text = "Are they equal? " + result.ToString()

End Sub

Private Sub GreaterButton_Click(sender As Object, e As
EventArgs) Handles greaterButton.Click

Dim input1 As Double = Convert.ToDouble(input1TextBox.Text)
Dim input2 As Double = Convert.ToDouble(input2TextBox.Text)
Dim result As Boolean = (input1 > input2)
resultLabel.Text = "Is the first one greater? " +
result.ToString()

End Sub

Private Sub LowerButton_Click(sender As Object, e As
EventArgs) Handles lowerButton.Click

Dim input1 As Double = Convert.ToDouble(input1TextBox.Text)
Dim input2 As Double = Convert.ToDouble(input2TextBox.Text)
Dim result As Boolean = (input1 < input2)
resultLabel.Text = "Is the first one lower? " +
result.ToString()

End Sub
```
Code 8.7

CHAPTER 8. CONDITIONAL STATEMENTS

10. Build and run the project. I entered the following numbers and when the comparison buttons are clicked, the comparison results are displayed as shown in Figures 8.2, 8.3 and 8.4.

Please note that the equality or inequality comparisons can also be applied on string type variables while the rest of the comparison operators cannot.

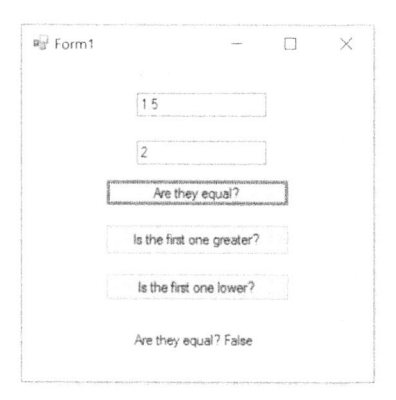

Figure 8.2. Equality comparison result

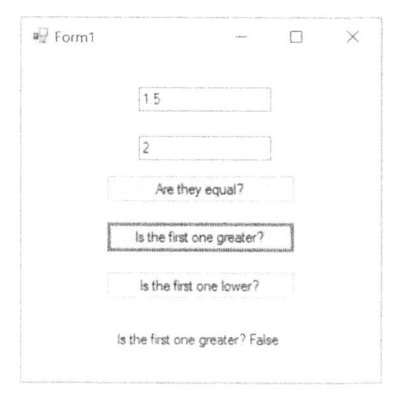

Figure 8.3. First one greater? comparison result

217

Figure 8.4. First one smaller? comparison result

8.1.2. Arithmetic Operators

Arithmetic operators operate on numeric operands and produce numeric results. Below are the frequently used arithmetic operators in VB.NET:

Operator	Operation
+	Adds its operands
-	Subtracts its second operand from the first one
*	Multiplies its operands
/	Divides its first operand to the second one
Mod	The mod operator: gives the remainder when the first operand is divided by the second one

Table 8.2. Arithmetic operators

Usual mathematical operation precedence rules apply: * and / are the first operations to be carried where + and − are the second in order. We can change the operation order using parentheses easily as we do in usual arithmetic operations.

Let's build a simple calculator to show the utilization of these operators in a project:

1. Create a VB.NET project.
2. Add two TextBoxes where the user will enter numbers. Set their Names as **input1TextBox** and **input2TextBox**.
3. Add five buttons which will perform the arithmetic operations when clicked. Set their Text properties as +, -, *, / and **MOD**. Set their Names as **addButton**, **subtractButton**, **multiplyButton**, **divideButton** and **modButton**, respectively.

218

CHAPTER 8. CONDITIONAL STATEMENTS

4. Add another TextBox which will show the result. Set its name as **resultTextBox**. The form layout may look similar to the one shown in Figure 8.5.
5. Double-click the buttons to create their event handlers.
6. We'll firstly write the code for the addButton's Click event handler. First of all, we'll convert the Text inputs of **input1TextBox** and **input2TextBox** to double type variables as we did in the previous example and add these variables to produce the adding result. Then display this result in the **resultTextBox** after converting to string by the ToString() method. These code lines are shown in the event handler shown in Code 8.8.

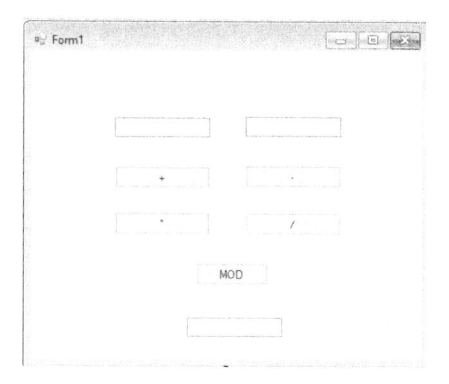

Figure 8.5. The form layout

```
Dim input1 As Double = Convert.ToDouble(input1TextBox.Text)
Dim input2 As Double = Convert.ToDouble(input2TextBox.Text)
Dim result As Double = input1 + input2
resultTextBox.Text = result.ToString()
```
Code 8.8

7. We set the remaining operations with the respective operators in the Click event handlers of their buttons as follows:

```
Private Sub AddButton_Click(sender As Object, e As
EventArgs) Handles addButton.Click

Dim input1 As Double = Convert.ToDouble(input1TextBox.Text)
Dim input2 As Double = Convert.ToDouble(input2TextBox.Text)
Dim result As Double = input1 + input2
resultTextBox.Text = result.ToString()
```

219

```
End Sub

Private Sub SubtractButton_Click(sender As Object, e As
EventArgs) Handles subtractButton.Click

Dim input1 As Double = Convert.ToDouble(input1TextBox.Text)
Dim input2 As Double = Convert.ToDouble(input2TextBox.Text)
Dim result As Double = input1 - input2
resultTextBox.Text = result.ToString()

End Sub

Private Sub MultiplyButton_Click(sender As Object, e As
EventArgs) Handles multiplyButton.Click

Dim input1 As Double = Convert.ToDouble(input1TextBox.Text)
Dim input2 As Double = Convert.ToDouble(input2TextBox.Text)
Dim result As Double = input1 * input2
resultTextBox.Text = result.ToString()

End Sub

Private Sub DivideButton_Click(sender As Object, e As
EventArgs) Handles divideButton.Click

Dim input1 As Double = Convert.ToDouble(input1TextBox.Text)
Dim input2 As Double = Convert.ToDouble(input2TextBox.Text)
Dim result As Double = input1 / input2
resultTextBox.Text = result.ToString()

End Sub

Private Sub ModButton_Click(sender As Object, e As
EventArgs) Handles modButton.Click

Dim input1 As Double = Convert.ToDouble(input1TextBox.Text)
Dim input2 As Double = Convert.ToDouble(input2TextBox.Text)
Dim result As Double = input1 Mod input2
resultTextBox.Text = result.ToString()

End Sub
```

Code 8.9 (cont'd)

Note that the only thing that changes in these event handlers are the arithmetic operators.

CHAPTER 8. CONDITIONAL STATEMENTS

8. Build and run the project. Enter any number you want in the input TextBoxes and click the respective buttons for performing the arithmetic operations. Our calculator operates as expected as shown in the following figures:

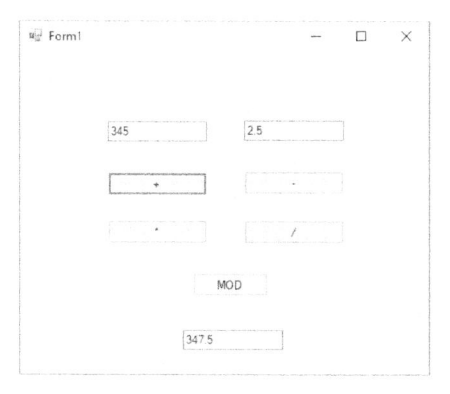

Figure 8.6. Addition operation

- When an arithmetic operation is performed with an int type variable and a float/double type variable, the result will have the double type.
- When an arithmetic operation is performed with a double type variable and a float type variable, the result will have the double type.

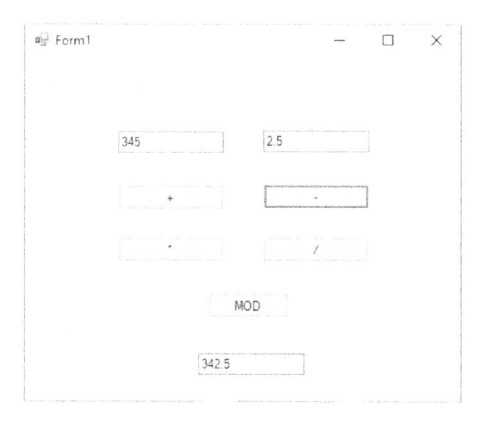

Figure 8.7. Subtraction operation

BEGINNER'S GUIDE TO VISUAL BASIC.NET PROGRAMMING

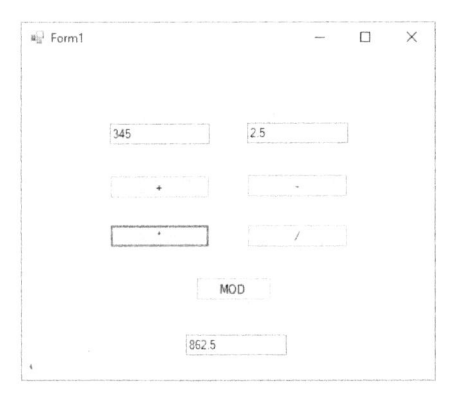

Figure 8.8. Multiplication operation

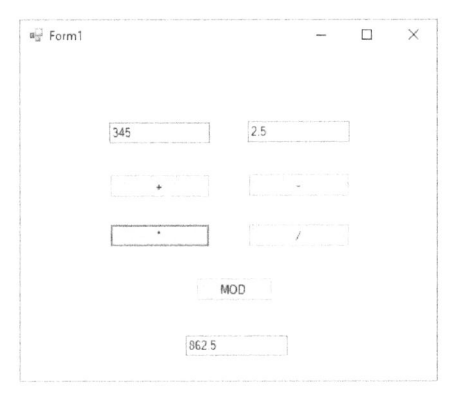

Figure 8.9. Division operation

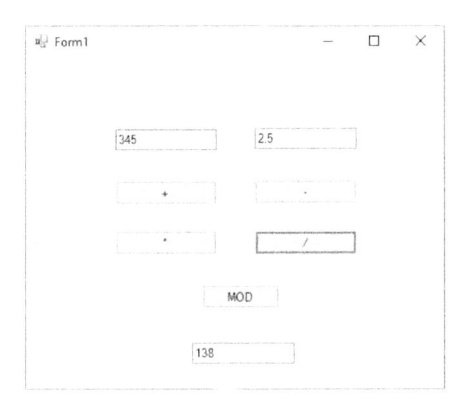

Figure 8.10. Mod operation

8.1.3. Practical Operators

Increment and decrement operators have a wide usage in programming because they enable to sweep in a range in conditional statements or loops. There are basically four increment/decrement operators in VB.NET:

Operator	Operation
+=	Increases its left operand by right operand and stores the result in the left operand
-=	Decreases its left operand by right operand and stores the result in the left operand
*=	Multiplies its left operand by right operand and stores the result in the left operand
/=	Divides its left operand by right operand and stores the result in the left operand

Table 8.3. Increment/decrement operators

Let's use these operators in a project where we will use these operators on operands to observe how they are changed when these operators are applied:

1. Create a VB.NET project.
2. Add two TextBoxes on the form where we will enter numbers. Set their Name properties as **number1TextBox** and **number2TextBox**. Also add Labels to the left of these TextBoxes which display **The first operand**: and **The second operand:**, respectively.
3. Add four buttons for the four increment/decrement operators. Set their Names as **incrementButton, decrementButton, addButton** and **subtractButton**. Set their Text properties as +, −, * and /, respectively.
4. We will not add a Label or TextBox to show the result in this project. Instead, we will update the input TextBoxes with the results. The form layout will look as follows:

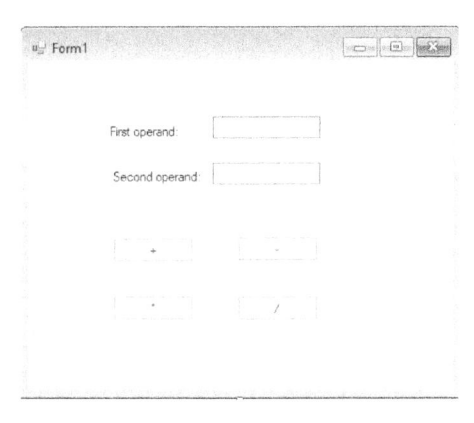

Figure 8.11. Layout of the form

5. Click the Buttons to create their Click event handlers. We will need to read up-to-date values of these TextBoxes in each of these event handlers. We perform this as usual:

```
Dim number1 As Double = Convert.ToDouble(number1TextBox.Text)
Dim number2 As Double = Convert.ToDouble(number2TextBox.Text)
```
Code 8.10

We obtained the numeric values of the inputs by these code lines. For the + Button, let's perform addition operation using the practical addition operator as follows:

```
number1 += number2
```
Code 8.11

Then, update the TextBoxes by the latest values:

```
number1TextBox.Text = number1.ToString()
number2TextBox.Text = number2.ToString()
```
Code 8.12

6. We will do the similar operations for the remaining Buttons. We'll have the following event handler methods as follows after these operations:

CHAPTER 8. CONDITIONAL STATEMENTS

```
Private Sub AddButton_Click(sender As Object, e As
EventArgs) Handles addButton.Click

Dim number1 As Double = Convert.ToDouble(number1TextBox.Text)
Dim number2 As Double = Convert.ToDouble(number2TextBox.Text)
number1 += number2
number1TextBox.Text = number1.ToString()
number2TextBox.Text = number2.ToString()

End Sub

Private Sub SubtractButton_Click(sender As Object, e As
EventArgs) Handles subtractButton.Click

Dim number1 As Double = Convert.ToDouble(number1TextBox.Text)
Dim number2 As Double = Convert.ToDouble(number2TextBox.Text)
number1 -= number2
number1TextBox.Text = number1.ToString()
number2TextBox.Text = number2.ToString()

End Sub

Private Sub MultiplyButton_Click(sender As Object, e As
EventArgs) Handles multiplyButton.Click

Dim number1 As Double = Convert.ToDouble(number1TextBox.Text)
Dim number2 As Double = Convert.ToDouble(number2TextBox.Text)
number1 *= number2
number1TextBox.Text = number1.ToString()
number2TextBox.Text = number2.ToString()

End Sub

Private Sub DivideButton_Click(sender As Object, e As
EventArgs) Handles divideButton.Click

Dim number1 As Double = Convert.ToDouble(number1TextBox.Text)
Dim number2 As Double = Convert.ToDouble(number2TextBox.Text)
number1 /= number2
number1TextBox.Text = number1.ToString()
number2TextBox.Text = number2.ToString()

End Sub
```
Code 8.13

Note that the second operand, number2 in this example, will not change after the practical operators are applied. The result is written to

BEGINNER'S GUIDE TO VISUAL BASIC.NET PROGRAMMING

number1 only. We updated number2's TextBox here for demonstration purposes.

7. Build and run the project. Enter some numbers in the TextBoxes as follows:

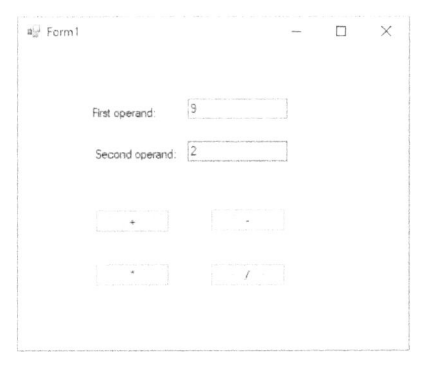

Figure 8.12. Our increment/decrement program

Firstly, when we click the + Button, the first number is incremented as follows:

Figure 8.13. The numbers after the increment operator is applied

Now, click the – button to apply decrement operator. The first number will be decremented after this operation as shown in Figure 8.14.

Now, click the * Button. As you will see, **number1** will be multiplied by **number1** and **number1** will be changed. However, **number2** will not be changed. This is shown in Figure 8.15.

CHAPTER 8. CONDITIONAL STATEMENTS

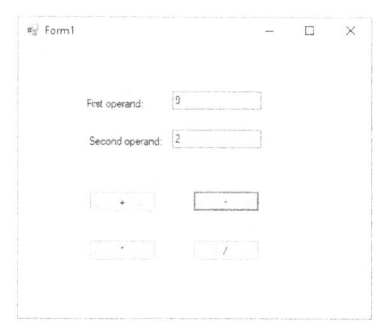

Figure 8.14. The numbers after the − Button is clicked

Figure 8.15. The program after the * Button is clicked

Finally, click the / button. **number2** will be subtracted from **number1** and **number1** will be changed. Again, **number2** will not be changed as shown below:

Figure 8.16. Numbers after the / Button is clicked

227

We now know the utilization of operators and ready to study conditional statements after having a coffee break ☺.

8.2. If-Else Statement Types

Code lines execute from top to down in a VB.NET program. However, it is sometimes needed that the program to skip some code lines or jump to specific lines depending on the states of the variables or inputs. For example, imagine that the user will need to enter a username and a password to access a database in a program. When the user enters his/her username and password and clicks the Login button, the program will compare the entered username/password against the ones in its own records. **If** the username/password combination is correct then it will display the database to the user. **Else**, the program will display an error message and will tell the user to try again. We do these comparison and branching operations using two types of statements in VB.NET: **If-Else** and **Select-Case**.

In this subsection, we will learn how if-else structures are used for condition checking and branching. If-Else statements have three variants: **If**, **If-Else** and **If-ElseIf-Else**.

8.2.1. The If Statement

The If statement is used for checking if a condition is satisfied. If the condition is met, then the code lines inside the **If block** are executed:

```
If(condition) Then

   Here is the if block between the If-End If statements.
   The code written here is executed if the condition is
   satisfied.

End If
```
Code 8.14

Let's use an if statement in an example where the user will enter a username and a password. Our program will check if they are valid:

1. Create a VB.NET project.
2. Add three Labels, two TextBoxes and one Button on the form as in Figure 8.17.

CHAPTER 8. CONDITIONAL STATEMENTS

3. Set the Text of the first Label as **Login window**.
4. Set the Texts of the second and third Labels as **Username:** and **Password:**.

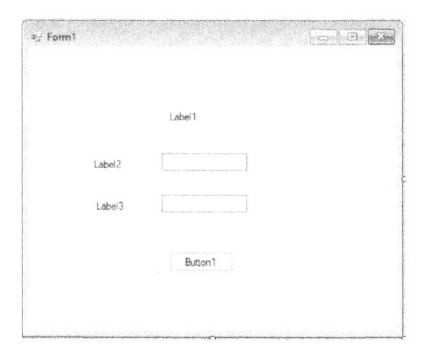

Figure 8.17. Layout of the form

5. Set the Name properties of TextBoxes as **usernameTextBox** and **passwordTextBox**, respectively.
6. Set the Name and Text of the Button as **Login** and **loginButton**.
7. Double-click the Button to create its Click event handler method as usual. We will use the if statement inside this method. We don't have a database yet therefore let's compare the username and password against constant values such as **vbnetprogrammer** and **abc456**, respectively. We do this in the if statement as follows:

```
If (usernameTextBox.Text = "vbnetprogrammer" And
passwordTextBox.Text = "abc456") Then

    MessageBox.Show("Login successful")
```
Code 8.15

Note that the parentheses of the **If structure** is automatically formed in Visual Studio when we write if and then **press the Tab key two times** on the keyboard.

In the first code line, we check if the Texts entered in the usernameTextBox **And** passwordTextBox have the values **vbnetprogrammer** and **abc456** using comparison operators. The only new operator used here is the **And**. It means "And" ☺. Therefore, in this if statement we check the condition: **is the Text entered in the**

usernameTextBox is vbnetprogrammer AND the Text entered in the passwordTextBox is abc456? If this condition is met, then the code line inside the if block, which is `MessageBox.Show("Login successful");` for this example, will be executed. Remember that we need to insert this code inside the Click handler method of the loginButton:

```
Private Sub LoginButton_Click(sender As Object, e As
EventArgs) Handles loginButton.Click

If (usernameTextBox.Text = "vbnetprogrammer" And
passwordTextBox.Text = "abc456") Then
          MessageBox.Show("Login successful")
End If

End Sub
```
Code 8.16

8. Build and run the project, the Login Window will appear as follows:

Figure 8.18. The login program

If we enter random username and password values in the TextBoxes and click the Login button, nothing will happen because the if condition inside the statement will not be satisfied. However, if we enter correct username and password and then click the Login button, then the program will display the corresponding message box:

CHAPTER 8. CONDITIONAL STATEMENTS

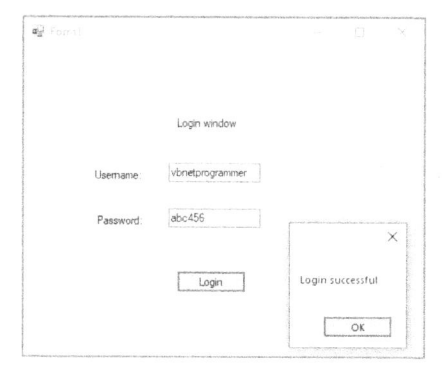

Figure 8.19. Successful login with the correct username and password

Similar to the **And** used for the logical AND, we can use the **Or** for implementing logical OR inside if statements.

By the way, we can hide the password characters as it is a convention for login windows. We do this by setting the **PasswordChar** property of the **passwordTextBox** control to any character we choose. I have set it as the * character as shown below:

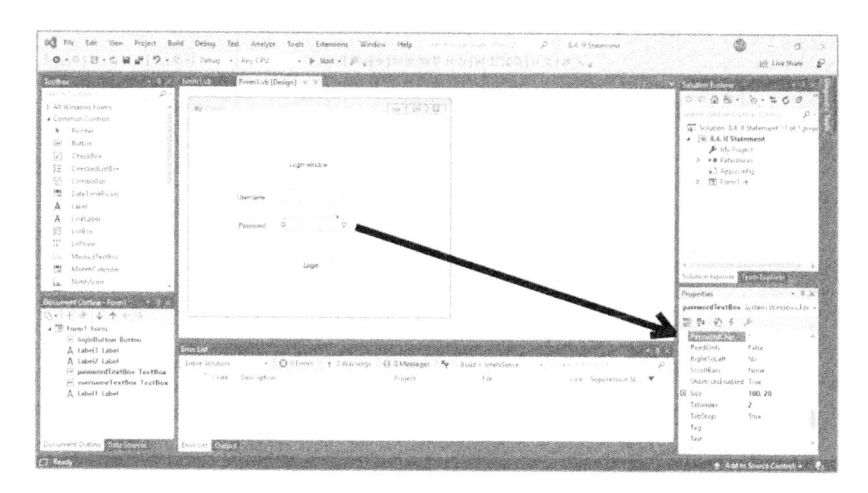

Figure 8.20. Setting the PasswordChar for the password input

After setting the PasswordChar, the password written inside its TextBox will be hidden:

231

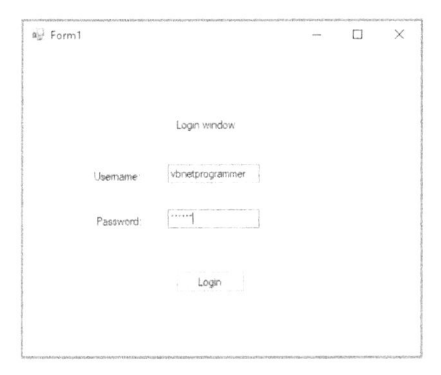

Figure 8.21. Hidden password in the Login window

8.2.2. The If-Else Statement

If-else statements operate the same way as the if statements. However they have the **else block** which is executed when the condition is not satisfied. The template of the if-else statement is given below:

```
If(condition) Then

    Here is the if block between the curly brackets. The code
    written here is executed if the condition is satisfied.

Else

    Here is the else block between the curly brackets. The
    code written here is executed if the condition is NOT
    satisfied.

End If
```
Code 8.17

Let's modify the previous **if** example (remember that you can copy-paste the whole project folder to create a new project for modifying) by adding an **else block** as follows:

```
If (usernameTextBox.Text = "vbnetprogrammer" And
passwordTextBox.Text = "abc456") Then

    MessageBox.Show("Login successful")

Else
    MessageBox.Show("Username/password incorrect")
```

CHAPTER 8. CONDITIONAL STATEMENTS

```
        usernameTextBox.Clear()
        passwordTextBox.Clear()
End If
```

Code 8.18 (cont'd)

When the user enters a wrong username/password combination, the condition of the if statement will be true. **In this case, the else block will be executed.** It will display the message Username/password incorrect and then clear the username and password TextBoxes using the Clear() methods as in Figure 8.22

Note that the else block does not have a separate condition. It is also dependent on the condition of the **if statement**.

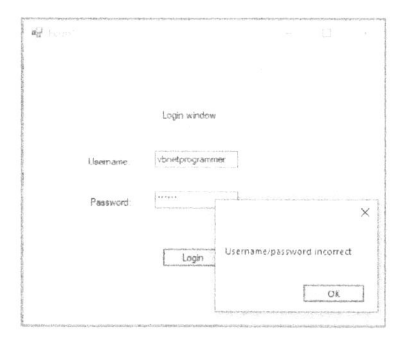

Figure 8.22. The else block is executed when the username/password is incorrect

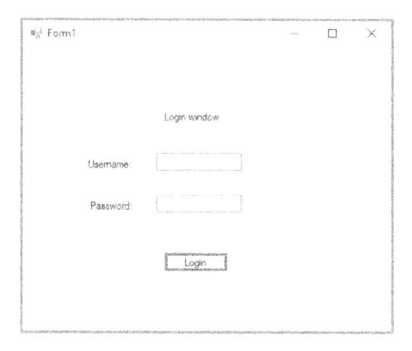

Figure 8.23. The TextBoxes are cleared after the OK button is clicked in the message box

233

8.2.3. The If-ElseIf-Else Statement

We had only one condition to check in **if** and **if-else** structures. In the **if-elseif-else** statements, we can check more than one condition therefore having more flexibility. The template is shown below:

```
If(condition 1) Then

    The code written here is executed if condition 1 is
    satisfied.

ElseIf(condition 2)

    The code written here is executed if condition 2 is
    satisfied.

Else

    The code written here is executed when BOTH condition
    1 AND condition 2 are NOT satisfied.

End If
```
Code 8.19

Let's create a new example where we will check exam results of students and display the corresponding grade as a letter. We may follow the rule shown in the table below:

Exam result	Grade
[90, 100]	A
[75, 89]	B
[60, 74]	C
[45, 59]	D
[0, 44]	E

Table 8.4. Grades vs. exam results

1. Create a new VB.NET project.
2. Add two Labels, a TextBox and a Button on the form as follows:

CHAPTER 8. CONDITIONAL STATEMENTS

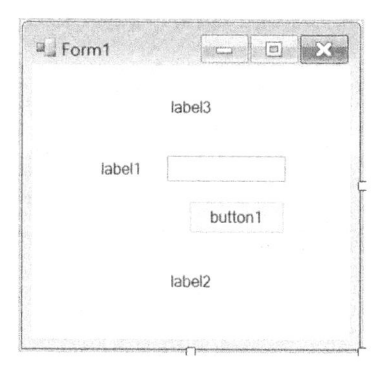

Figure 8.24. Layout of the form

3. Set the top Label's Text as **Grade Mapper**.
4. Set the Text of the middle Label as **Enter the exam result:**.
5. Set the Name of the TextBox as **resultTextBox**.
6. Set the Name and Text of the Button as **gradeButton** and **Show grade**, respectively.
7. Set the Text and Name of the bottom Label as **Grade appears here...** and **gradeLabel**.
8. Double-click the button to create its default event handler named GradeButton_Click(). We will insert our code inside this event handler.
9. Firstly, take the Text of the TextBox and convert it to an integer variable called points as follows:

```
Dim result As Integer = Convert.ToInt32(resultTextBox.Text)
```
Code 8.20

10. We will now employ the if - else if – else chain to check the grade and assign an associated grade to the grade variable:

```
Dim grade As String
If (result >= 90) Then
    grade = "A"
ElseIf (result >= 75) Then
    grade = "B"
ElseIf (result >= 60) Then
    grade = "C"
ElseIf (DialogResult >= 45) Then
    grade = "D"
```

235

```
Else
      grade = "F"
End If
```
Code 8.21 (cont'd)

In this code, we declared a grade variable of string type where we will store the grade information as a letter. Then, we compared the points with the limits given in Table 7.4.

The conditions are checked from top to down in an if - else if - else structure. Note that if any of the conditions is met, the remaining conditions below it are not checked.

11. Finally, we need to update the gradeLabel's Text with the assigned grade. We can do it as follows:

```
gradeLabel.Text = "Grade: " + grade
```
Code 8.22

12. We can now build and run the project as follows:

Figure 8.25. The exam grade program

We can enter an exam point between 0 and 100 and then the program will display the corresponding grade using condition statements as follows:

Figure 8.26. The exam grade is displayed correctly

8.3. The Select-Case Statement

Select-case structures operate similar to if - else if - else statements. The main difference is that we can only check a variable against exact values in a switch-case statement; we cannot use comparison statements as conditions. The template of the switch-case statements is shown below:

```
Select Case(variable)

  Case x To y
    The code written here is executed if the variable is
    Between x and y.
  Case z, t, n
    The code written here is executed if the variable is
    equal to z or t or n.
  .
  .
  .
  Case Else
    The code written here is executed if none of the above
    case conditions are True.

End Select
```
Code 8.23

Let's create a new example where we will switch the string given in a TextBox against two usernames and display a message box if the username is matched:

1. Create a new VB.NET project.
2. Add a Label, a TextBox and a Button to the project.

3. Set the Text of the Label as **Username:**.
4. Set the Name of the TextBox as **usernameTextBox**.
5. Set the Name and Text of the Button as **checkButton** and **Check**, respectively. The form will look as follows:

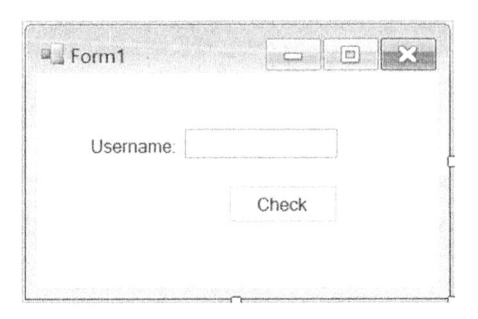

Figure 8.27. The layout of the form

6. Double-click the Button to create its Click event handler method. We will insert our code inside this method as usual. Let's first take the Text of the checkTextBox and then assign it to a String type variable named input as follows:

```
Dim input As String = usernameTextBox.Text
```
Code 8.24

7. We'll switch the input variable against the usernames we decide in this example. Let us use the strings John and James as the reference usernames in the Select-Case statements as follows:

```
Select Case input
    Case "John"
        MessageBox.Show("Successful entry")
    Case "James"
        MessageBox.Show("Successful entry")
    Case Else
        MessageBox.Show("Username not found")
End Select
```
Code 8.25

Note that the **Select-case** structure is automatically formed in Visual Studio when we write **Select** and then **press the Tab key twice** on the keyboard.

CHAPTER 8. CONDITIONAL STATEMENTS

In this code, we compare the `input` variable against two cases. If `input` is `"John"`, then the block inside the `Case "John"` statement is executed. Then the second case `Case "James"` is checked. If none of the cases is satisfied, then the `Case Else` block will be executed. Therefore, if the user enters a username other than John or James, the program will display a message box with the text `"Username not found"`.

8. Let's now build and run the project. The following program window will appear:

Figure 8.28. Program window

When we enter one of the accepted usernames, i.e. John or James, the program will display the successful entry message:

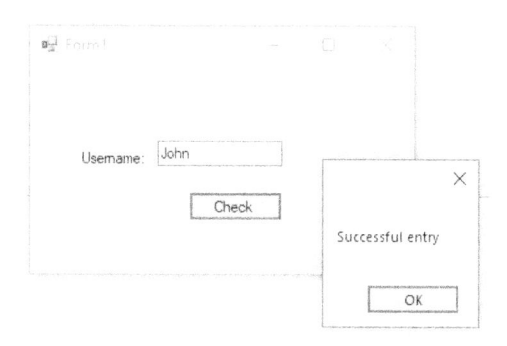

Figure 8.29. A successful entry

If we enter a different username, the program will show the corresponding message box:

239

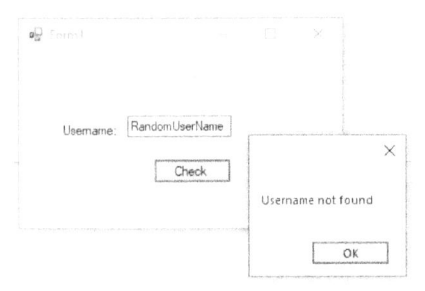

Figure 8.30. An unsuccessful entry attempt

This is all for conditional statements. We will learn the looping structures in the next chapter, which are also frequently needed blocks in VB.NET programming.

Chapter 9

LOOPS

Loops are used when a code line or code block has to be executed multiple times depending on a condition. For example, consider a database with name entries in it. If we want to display all the names one by one, we would do it in the following way:

```
MessageBox.Show(entry 1)
MessageBox.Show(entry 2)
MessageBox.Show(entry 3)
.
MessageBox.Show(entry n-1)
MessageBox.Show(entry n)
```
Code 9.1

In this code, entries refer to the data in the database. As you can see, the number of code lines would be intractable. Instead, we can do the same job using a loop in a more elegant and easier way:

```
For Each(entries in the database)
{
  MessageBox.Show(current entry)
}
```
Code 9.2

There are four types of looping structures in VB.NET: **For-Next**, **For Each-Next**, **While-End While** and **Do-Loop**. We'll study these in this chapter by using them in small projects:

9.1. The For-Next Loop

The general structure of the **For-Next loop** is shown in Code 9.3. Code lines inside the **For block** are executed **as long as** the looping condition written inside the parentheses next to the for keyword is true (satisfied).

241

```
For loop_variable As DataType = initial_value To
final_value

    The code to be repeated is written here.

Next
```
Code 9.3

Let's create a project with a **For-Next loop** to see it in charge:

1. Create a new VB.NET project.
2. Add a Button, a TextBox and a ListBox on the form.
3. Set the Name and Text of the Button as **loopButton** and **Loop!**.
4. Set the Name of the TextBox as **finalValue**.
5. Set the Name of the ListBox as **valuesListBox**. The form will look as follows:

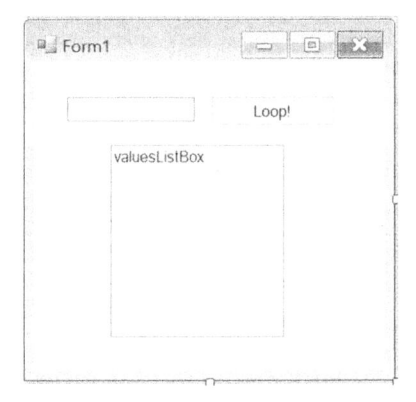

Figure 9.1. Layout of the form

6. Double-click the button to create its Click event handler method. All code will go inside this method as usual. We will take the value entered in the **finalValue** TextBox and loop from 0 to this value. As the loop keeps going, we'll insert the loop variable's current value to the ListBox. Let's take the Text written in the TextBox and convert it to an Integer type variable as follows:

```
Dim finalValueInteger As Integer =
Convert.ToInt32(finalValue.Text)
```
Code 9.4

7. Then, we will write the for loop to do the actual looping. As in the previous code blocks, when we write the keyword (For in this example) and then press the Tab key twice on the keyboard, the structure is automatically formed as follows:

```
For index = 1 To 10

Next
```
Code 9.5

We will now modify this template according to our aim. The loop variable is defined as index and initialized to 1 in the for loop, which is OK. The default final loop value, index = 10, will be modified as index = 1 To finalValueInteger. By this modification, the looping will continue as long as index is equal to finalValueInteger.

In addition, the loop variable has to be increased by 1 in each loop, which is already there as i++. For each loop state, the current value of the loop variable, i, will be inserted to the ListBox. The for loop will be as follows after these modifications:

```
For index = 1 To finalValueInteger
    valuesListBox.Items.Add(index)
Next
```
Code 9.6

Note that we didn't need to convert the integer type variable index to string for adding to the ListBox.

The Click event handler method is also shown below after these code lines are added:

```
Private Sub LoopButton_Click(sender As Object, e As EventArgs) Handles loopButton.Click
Dim finalValueInteger As Integer = Convert.ToInt32(finalValue.Text)
  For index = 1 To finalValueInteger
    valuesListBox.Items.Add(index)
  Next
End Sub
```
Code 9.7

8. Build and run the project. The program will appear as follows:

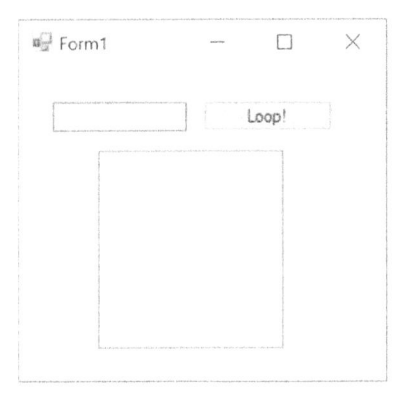

Figure 9.2. The program window

When we enter an integer to the TextBox and click the **Loop!** Button, the for loop will insert the numbers from 0 to the number we entered to the ListBox:

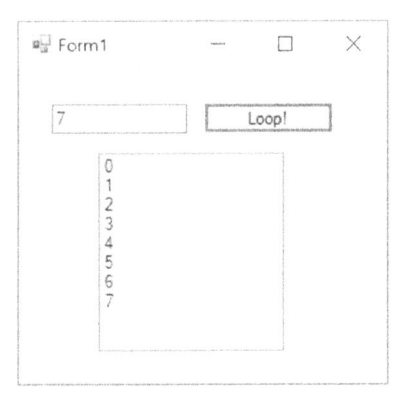

Figure 9.3. The for loop listed numbers from 0 to 7

We should be extra careful about the looping condition. If the looping condition is always satisfied, then the loop never stops and is called an infinite loop, which causes the program to crash.

9.2. The For Each-Next Loop

Foreach loops are similar to for loops. Foreach loops loop over the elements of a collection or an array, which are data structures that contain multiple elements of the same type with an order. The For Each-

CHAPTER 9. LOOPS

Next structure loops over the elements of the collection or array one by one automatically. Its general structure is as follows:

```
For Each (variable As DataType in collection/array)
    The code to be repeated is written here.
Next
```
Code 9.8

We haven't studied collections and arrays yet. However, we can consider a string as a collection sample in our example. Strings are in fact collections of individual characters (chars) as we learned before. Let's develop a project where we will get the Text from a TextBox and use a For Each-Next loop to loop over this strings's characters.

1. Create a new VB.NET project.
2. Add a TextBox, a Button and a ComboBox on the form.
3. Set the Name property of the TextBox as **inputText**.
4. Set the Name and Text of the Button as **splitButton** and **Split**.
5. Set the Name of the ComboBox as **charComboBox**. The layout of the form would look as in Figure 9.4.
6. Double-click the Button to create its Click method. We will insert our code inside this method as usual.
7. Firstly, let's take the Text entered in the TextBox and assign it to a String type variable called inputString as in Code 9.9.

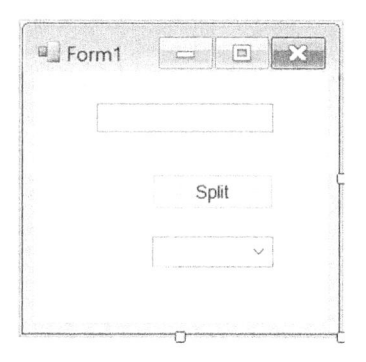

Figure 9.6. Layout of the form

245

```
Dim inputString As String = inputTextBox.Text
```
Code 9.9

8. We'll sweep over the elements, i.e. characters, of the inputString and insert each character as an element to the ComboBox. We do this by the For Each-Next loop. When we write ForEach in the editor and press the Tab key twice, the following For Each-Next template is automatically formed:

```
For Each (Dim item As DataType collection)
    The code to be repeated is written here.
Next
```
Code 9.10

The items (elements) in our string, inputString, are of the char type. Therefore, we will modify the foreach loop as follows:

```
For Each element As Char In inputString
Next
```
Code 9.11

This loop sweeps over all characters (items) it finds in the inputString however, we have to do something for each item. We will insert each item to the ComboBox by the code line charComboBox.Items.Add(element) inside the foreach block:

```
For Each element As Char In inputString
    charComboBox.Items.Add(element)
Next
```
Code 9.12

As we have stated before, all this code will go inside the splitButton_Click() method:

```
Private Sub SplitButton_Click(sender As Object, e As
EventArgs) Handles splitButton.Click

Dim inputString As String = inputTextBox.Text
For Each element As Char In inputString
```

```
        charComboBox.Items.Add(element)
Next

End Sub
```
Code 9.13 (cont'd)

9. Build and run the project. The program window will launch as follows:

Figure 9.5. The program window

Let's enter a string inside the TextBox and click the **Split** Button. The ComboBox will be populated by the characters of the string we entered as shown in Figure 9.6.

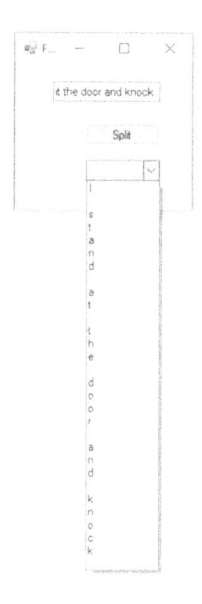

Figure 9.6. The characters of the string added to the ComboBox

9.3. The While-End Loop

The while-end loop is similar to the for loop: the loop cycles as long as the condition of the loop is satisfied. Their difference is that in the while loop, the loop variable and increment/decrement statement of this variable is not written next to the loop condition in the parentheses but before the loop and inside the loop, respectively. Its general structure is as follows:

```
loop variable initialization
While(condition)

    The code that will be repeated will be written here.
    Loop variable is varied here.

End While
```
Code 9.14

As you can see from this template, the loop variable should be declared and initialized before the While-End loop begins. The loop variable is varied inside the while loop so that at some point, the loop condition has to be made False. Otherwise, the loop condition will always be satisfied which will lead to an infinite loop therefore a program crash.

Let's develop our small project which will employ a while loop:

1. Create a new VB.NET project.
2. Add a Button, a TextBox and a ComboBox on the form.
3. Set the Name and Text of the Button as **populateButton** and **Populate**.
4. Set the Name of the TextBox as **stopValue**.
5. Set the Name of the ComboBox as **numbersComboBox**. The form may look as follows:

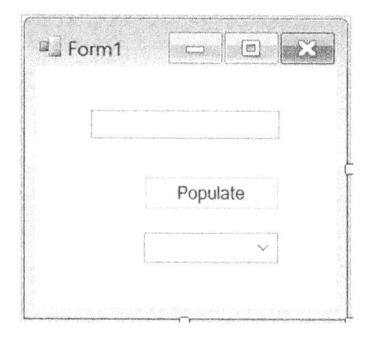

Figure 9.7. The form layout

6. Double-click the Button to create its Click event handler method. Inside this method, we will take the value entered in the **stopValue** TextBox and loop from 0 until this value. Meanwhile, we will insert the loop variable's values to the ComboBox. Let's take the Text written in the TextBox and convert it to an int type variable as follows:

```
Dim stopValueInt As Integer = Convert.ToInt32(stopValue.Text)
```
Code 9.15

7. We have to declare the loop variable before the while loop. Let's declare an integer variable i and initialize it to 0:

```
Dim i As Integer = 0
```
Code 9.16

8. Then comes the While loop. When we write the keyword While and then press the Tab key twice on the keyboard, its template is automatically formed as follows:

```
While True

End While
```
Code 9.17

We will now modify this template. The loop condition will check if the loop variable is smaller or equal to stopValueInt. Therefore the condition will be set as i <= stopValueInt in VB.NET.

- By this modification, the looping will continue as long as i is smaller or equal to stopValueInt.
- Equivalently, when this condition is not satisfied, i.e. when the loop variable i is greater than stopValueInt, the looping will end.

The **while loop** will be as follows after updating the loop condition:

```
While i < stopValueInt

End While
```
Code 9.18

Note the similarity with the For-Next loop example.

9. For each value of the loop state, the loop variable will be added to the ComboBox with the code inside the loop:

```
numbersComboBox.Items.Add(i)
```
Code 9.19

10. Furthermore, the loop variable, i, should be increased by 1 inside the loop with the incrementing operation: i +=1;. Adding all these together, the Click event handler method will be populated as follows:

```
Private Sub PopulateButton_Click(sender As Object, e As EventArgs) Handles populateButton.Click

Dim stopValueInt As Integer = Convert.ToInt32(stopValue.Text)
Dim i As Integer = 0
While i <= stopValueInt
    numbersComboBox.Items.Add(i)
    i += 1
End While

End Sub
```
Code 9.20

11. Build and run the project and the program window will appear as shown below:

Figure 9.8. The program window

When we enter a number inside the TextBox and click the Populate Button, the ComboBox will be populated with the numbers from 0 to this number thanks to the While loop as shown in Figure 9.9.

- We shouldn't forget to declare the loop variable before the loop begins.
- The loop variable should be changed inside the while loop otherwise the loop will be infinite causing the program to crash.

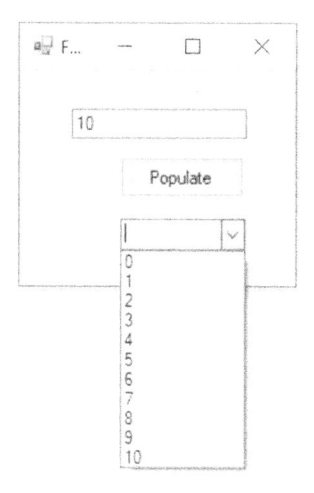

Figure 9.9. ComboBox populated with the numbers from 0 to 10

251

9.4. The Do-Loop Structure

Do-Loop structures are similar to While loops. Their difference is that the loop condition is checked at the end of the loop block in a Do-Loop structure as follows:

```
loop variable initialization
Do
{
   The code that will be repeated will be written here.
   Loop variable change (usually increment/decrement).
}
Loop(loop condition)
```
Code 9.21

As it is seen from this template, when the Do-Loop structure begins, the loop block executes once and then the loop condition is checked. If this condition is satisfied, the loop continues. And as in the While loop, the loop ends when the loop condition is not satisfied. The Do-Loop structure executes at least once as you can see from this code structure.

Let's modify the While loop example for this project:

1. Copy the while loop project folder and rename it as Do-Loop project.
2. Erase the while loop section in the PopulateButton_Click (...) method and set the initial value of the loop variable i as 2:

```
Private Sub PopulateButton_Click(sender As Object, e As EventArgs) Handles populateButton.Click

Dim stopValueInt As Integer = Convert.ToInt32(stopValue.Text)
Dim i As Integer = 2

End Sub
```
Code 9.22

3. Type **Do** and press Enter to form the Do-Loop template as follows:

```
Private Sub PopulateButton_Click(sender As Object, e As EventArgs) Handles populateButton.Click

Dim stopValueInt As Integer = Convert.ToInt32(stopValue.Text)Dim i As Integer = 2
```

CHAPTER 9. LOOPS

```
Do

Loop

End Sub
```
Code 9.23

4. Add the code lines for inserting the loop variable's current value to the ComboBox and increment i by 1 inside the do-while block:

```
Private Sub PopulateButton_Click(sender As Object, e As
EventArgs) Handles populateButton.Click

Dim stopValueInt As Integer =
Convert.ToInt32(stopValue.Text)
Dim i As Integer = 2
Do
    numbersComboBox.Items.Add(i)
    i += 1
Loop

End Sub
```
Code 9.24

5. Finally, set the loop condition as before:

```
Private Sub PopulateButton_Click(sender As Object, e As
EventArgs) Handles populateButton.Click

Dim stopValueInt As Integer =
Convert.ToInt32(stopValue.Text)
Dim i As Integer = 2
Do
   numbersComboBox.Items.Add(i)
   i += 1
Loop While (i <= stopValueInt)

End Sub
```
Code 9.24

6. Build and run the project. The following program window will appear:

253

Figure 9.11. The program window

When we enter a number greater than 2 and click the Populate button, the ComboBox will be populated from 2 to this number:

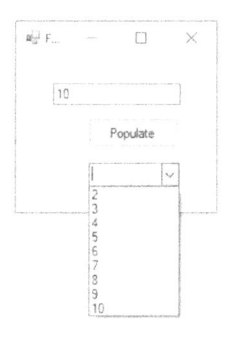

Figure 9.12. ComboBox populated by the values

The operation of the program is the same as the while loop example for the greater or equal to 2 entered in the TextBox. However, if we enter a number lower than 2, e.g. 2, then the difference of the Do-Loop structure comes into play:

Figure 9.13. The output of the program when entered number is 1

According to the loop condition i <= stopValueInt, the loop condition is never satisfied (i=2 and stopValueInt=1 at the beginning). However, since the code lines in the Do-Loop block is executed once before checking this condition, the ComboBox was populated by 2 by the code line numbersComboBox.Items.Add(i) where i=2 for the starting value of the loop variable.

9.5. Continue and Exit Keywords

Continue and Exit keywords let us to control the loop iterations in some cases. When the Exit keyword is executed inside the loop block, the loop immediately ends, i.e. the Exit keyword exits the loop.

There is another keyword used in loops: Continue. It stops the execution of the current iteration and skips to beginning of the loop. Both Continue and Exit keywords are used in conjunction with conditional statements in loops.

Let's use these keywords in our While loop example.

1. Open the While loop project and find the populateButton_Click(...) method as in Code 9.25.

```
Private Sub PopulateButton_Click(sender As Object, e As
EventArgs) Handles populateButton.Click

Dim stopValueInt As Integer =
Convert.ToInt32(stopValue.Text)

Dim i As Integer = 0
While i <= stopValueInt
    numbersComboBox.Items.Add(i)
    i += 1
End While

End Sub
```
Code 9.25

2. Let's skip to the beginning when the loop variable is 3 using the continue keyword:

BEGINNER'S GUIDE TO VISUAL BASIC.NET PROGRAMMING

```
Private Sub PopulateButton_Click(sender As Object, e As 
EventArgs) Handles populateButton.Click

Dim stopValueInt As Integer = 
Convert.ToInt32(stopValue.Text)

Dim i As Integer = 0
While i <= stopValueInt
      If (i = 3) Then
          Continue While
      End If
      numbersComboBox.Items.Add(i)
      i += 1
End While

End Sub
```
Code 9.26

3. Build and run the project. Enter a number greater than 3 such as 10 to the TextBox and click Populate button. You'll notice that the program stops responding because of an infinite loop!:

Figure 9.14. The program in infinite loop

We cannot quit the program by clicking the cross button at its top right because an infinite loop is formed. We can close the program from the Task Manager of Windows or clicking the Stop button in Visual Studio:

CHAPTER 9. LOOPS

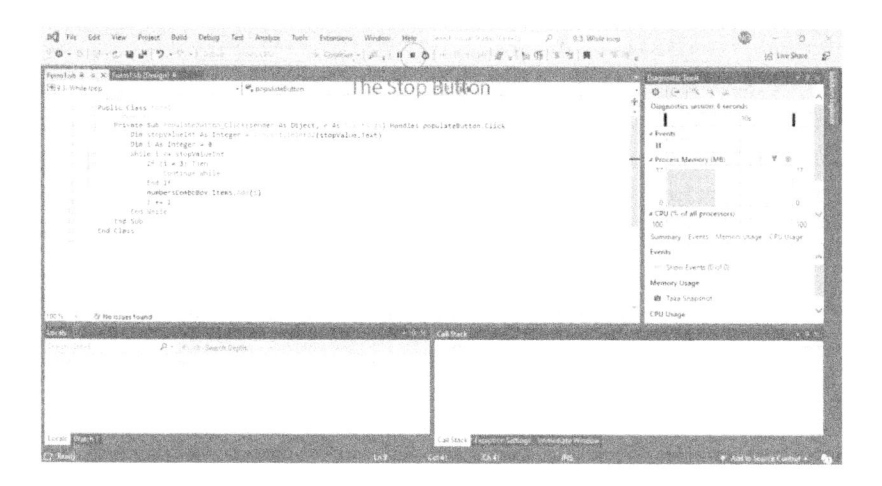

Figure 9.15. Stopping the program in infinite loop

Why does the program go into an infinite loop? At i=3, the if condition is satisfied and the Continue command is executed. The program jumps to the start of the loop with i=3, the if condition is again satisfied with i=3, the continue keyword is executed again jumping the program to the start of the loop with i=3... This procedure repeats over and over causing an infinite loop. We simply need to update the loop variable before the Continue command inside the if block as follows to get rid of this programming error:

```
Private Sub PopulateButton_Click(sender As Object, e As
EventArgs) Handles populateButton.Click

Dim stopValueInt As Integer =
Convert.ToInt32(stopValue.Text)

Dim i As Integer = 0
While i <= stopValueInt
  If (i = 3) Then
    i += 1
    Continue While
  End If
  numbersComboBox.Items.Add(i)
  i += 1
End While

End Sub
```
Code 9.27

257

After this modification, we can run the program and it works fine. When i=3, the condition of the if statement is satisfied, the loop variable is increased to 4 and then the program skips to the beginning of the loop with this new loop variable value. The value 3 is not added to the ComboBox because the program skips to the beginning of the loop at i=3 without executing the code lines below the if statement:

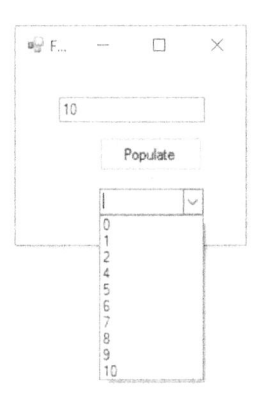

What if we change the Continue keyword to Exit in this program?

```
Private Sub PopulateButton_Click(sender As Object, e As
EventArgs) Handles populateButton.Click

Dim stopValueInt As Integer =
Convert.ToInt32(stopValue.Text)
Dim i As Integer = 0
While i <= stopValueInt
    If (i = 3) Then
        i += 1
        Exit While
    End If
    numbersComboBox.Items.Add(i)
    i += 1
End While

End Sub
```
Code 9.28

In this case, when the loop variable takes the value of 3, i.e. i=3, then the Exit command inside the if block executes causing the loop to exit completely. Therefore, 3 and the numbers greater than 3 will not be added to the ComboBox:

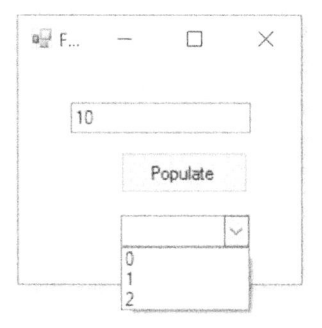

Figure 9.17. The loop is broken at i=3

We now learned variables, conditionals and loops in VB.NET. Before moving to the methods (functions), we will study arrays in the following chapter, which are used for holding multiple values of the same variable type.

Chapter 10

ARRAYS AND COLLECTIONS

Arrays are data structures which are used for holding multiple data of the same type while collections enable to store different type variables together.

10.1. Arrays

Arrays make our lives easier by enabling to save same type data in a list format so that we can access them easily using an index. We can imagine the structure of an array as follows:

Index	0	1	2	3	4	...	n-1
Element	1st element	2nd element	3rd element	4th element	5th element	...	n^{th} element

Table 10.1. Typical array structure

As you can see, each element of an array has an index starting from 0. This is a rule, therefore for an n element array, the indices of its elements will take the values of 0, 1, 2, .., n-1.

10.1.1. Declaring Arrays

An array is easily defined similar to variables. Brackets near the variable type tell the VB.NET compiler that we are declaring an array:

```
Dim new_array() As variable_type
```
Code 10.1

In this code line, we declared an array named new_array however we didn't initialize it or specify its number of elements. In this case, a memory location hasn't yet been allocated for this array. We have to specify the number of elements of the array to actually create it as follows:

```
Dim new_array(5) As variable_type
```
Code 10.2

For example, the following code line creates a four element array having integer type of elements:

```
Dim myIntArray(3) As Integer
```
Code 10.2

We can also initialize an array during its declaration. For example, let's create an integer array with elements 4, 55, 102:

```
Dim myIntArray = New Integer() {4, 55, 102}
```
Code 10.3

Since we initialized the array in this code, we didn't need to specify its number of elements explicitly.

Let's declare an array in a project and display its elements in a ListBox.

1. Create a new VB.NET project.
2. Add a Button and a ListBox on the form.
3. Set the Name and Text of the Button as **showButton** and **Show Elements**, respectively.
4. Set the Name of the ListBox as **showListBox**. The form will look as follows:

Figure 10.1. The layout of the form

5. Double-click the Button to create its event handler ShowButton_Click (...). All our code will go into this method.

CHAPTER 10. ARRAYS AND COLLECTIONS

6. Let's declare and initialize an array called `myIntArray` as follows:

```
Dim myIntArray = New Integer() {3, 5, 7, 8, 10}
```
Code 10.4

This is an integer array holding 5 elements are as follows:

Index	Element
0	3
1	5
2	7
3	8
4	10

Table 10.1. Indices of the elements of the declared array

7. We will display the elements of this array in the showListBox. We need to sweep over all elements of the array. One way of doing this is to take the number of elements of the array and then construct a **for** loop for sweeping. However, **foreach** loop does all this at once. The following foreach loop sweeps over all elements of the array and inserts them into the ListBox:

```
For Each item In myIntArray
    showListBox.Items.Add(item)
Next
```
Code 10.5

In this code, the integer variable item holds the value of the elements of the array one by one in the loop. Then, in each loop this value is inserted to the ListBox. The whole code of the Click event handler method will be as follows:

```
Private Sub ShowButton_Click(sender As Object, e As
EventArgs) Handles showButton.Click
   Dim myIntArray = New Integer() {3, 5, 7, 8, 10}

   For Each item In myIntArray
       showListBox.Items.Add(item)
   Next
End Sub
```
Code 10.6

8. Build and run the code. When the **Show** Button is clicked, the elements of our array will be displayed in the ListBox as shown in Figure 10.2.

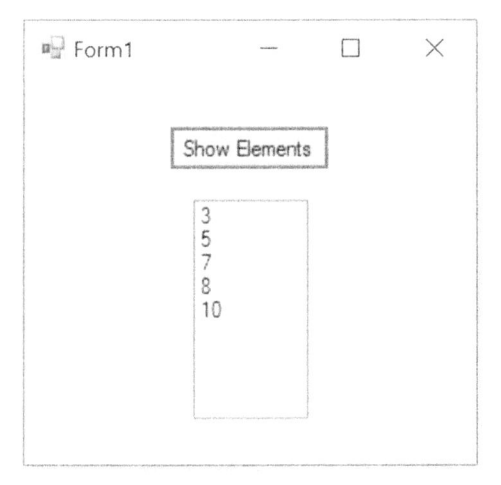

Figure 10.2. Elements of the array inserted to the ListBox using a foreach loop

9. We can modify the array to hold string elements and also the variable type of the foreach loop accordingly as follows:

```
Private Sub ShowButton_Click(sender As Object, e As
EventArgs) Handles showButton.Click
    Dim myStringArray = New String() {"John", "James",
"Joseph"}

    For Each item In myStringArray
        showListBox.Items.Add(item)
    Next

End Sub
```
Code 10.7

The elements of the string array will now be displayed in the ListBox after the project is built and the **Show** Button is clicked:

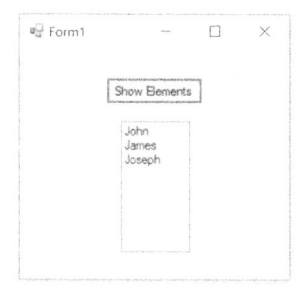

Figure 10.3. The elements of the string array shown in the ListBox

In VB.NET, the **Length** property of an array gives its length as an integer. For the example above, our array named myStringArray has 3 elements therefore myStringArray.Length will return 3. We can use the Length property to access its all elements. Code 10.7 can be modified to utilize for loop instead of foreach loop as follows:

```
Private Sub ShowButton_Click(sender As Object, e As
EventArgs) Handles showButton.Click
    Dim myStringArray = New String() {"John", "James",
"Joseph"}

    For index = 0 To myStringArray.Length - 1
        showListBox.Items.Add(myStringArray(index))
    Next

End Sub
```
Code 10.8

The loop condition is index = 0 To myStringArray.Length - 1 meaning that the loop variable i will take the values of 0, 1 and 2 for this example, which covers all the indices of this array. When the loop variable i takes index values, the corresponding element is added to the ListBox by the code line showListBox.Items.Add(myStringArray(index)). Note that the elements of the array are accessed by the expression myStringArray(i) which takes the values of myStringArray(0), myStringArray(1) and myStringArray(2), respectively as the loop continues. The output of this program is also the same as the one shown in Figure 10.3, as expected.

10.1.2. Multidimensional Arrays

We can also declare and use multidimensional arrays similar to single-dimensional ones. Although VB.NET allows us to define n-dimensional arrays, we rarely need more than 2-dimension. We can visualize 2-dimensional arrays as follows:

	Column 1	Column 2	...	Column n
Row 1	Element [0, 0]	Element [0, 1]	...	Element [0, n-1]
Row 2	Element [1, 0]	Element [1, 1]	...	Element [1, n-1]
...	...	...	...	
Row m	Element [m-1, 0]	Element [m-1, 1]	...	Element [m-1, n-1]

Table 10.2. Structure of a 2-dimensional array

A two dimensional array is declared using the following syntax:

```
Dim array_name(,) As variable_type
```
Code 10.9

Let's declare and initialize a two dimensional string array having 2 rows and 3 columns in a project.

1. Create a VB.NET project.
2. Add a button and a ListBox on the form.
3. Set the Name and Text of the Button as **listButton** and **List elements**, respectively.
4. Set the Name property of the ListBox as **arrayListBox**. The form may look as follows:

CHAPTER 10. ARRAYS AND COLLECTIONS

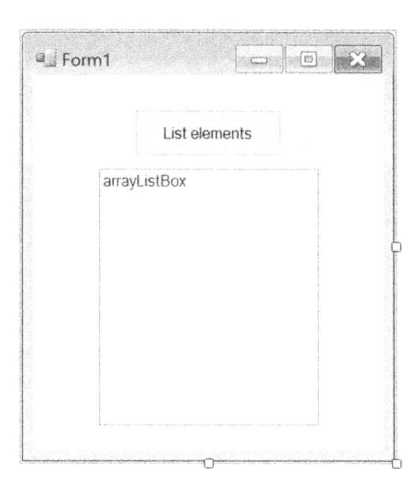

Figure 10.4. The form layout

5. Double-click the Button to create its event handler method ListButton_Click(...). We'll declare the array inside this method.
6. Let's declare a 2 dimensional array called **myStringArray** having 2 rows and 3 columns:

```
Dim myStringArray(2, 3) As String
```
Code 10.10

We'll now assign the elements of this array. We may populate the elements of this array with the strings shown below:

	Column 1	Column 2	Column 3
Row 1	Element 1, 1 "Jim"	Element 1, 2 "John"	Element 1, 3 "James"
Row 2	Element 2, 1 "Paul"	Element 2, 2 "Grace"	Element 2, 3 "Sophia"

Table 10.3. The elements of our array

We will assign these strings to the elements of our array as follows:

```
myStringArray(0, 0) = "Jim"
myStringArray(0, 1) = "John"
myStringArray(0, 2) = "James"
myStringArray(1, 0) = "Paul"
myStringArray(1, 1) = "Grace"
myStringArray(1, 2) = "Sophia"
```
Code 10.11

267

7. Since the array has two dimensions, we will use **nested** for loops to sweep rows first and columns inside it as follows:

```
For i = 0 To myStringArray.GetLength(0) - 1
    For j = 0 To myStringArray.GetLength(1) - 1
        arrayListBox.Items.Add(myStringArray(i, j))
    Next
Next
```
Code 10.12

In this code, the getLength() method gives the number of elements of the array in the specified dimension. Therefore, GetLength(0) returns the number of rows while GetLength(1) gives the number of columns. The associated array element, myStringArray(i, j), is added to the ListBox by the code line arrayListBox.Items.Add(myStringArray(i, j)).

8. Build and run the project. The program window will be shown as in Figure 10.5. When the **List elements** Button is clicked, the elements of the array is written to the ListBox as in Figure 10.6.

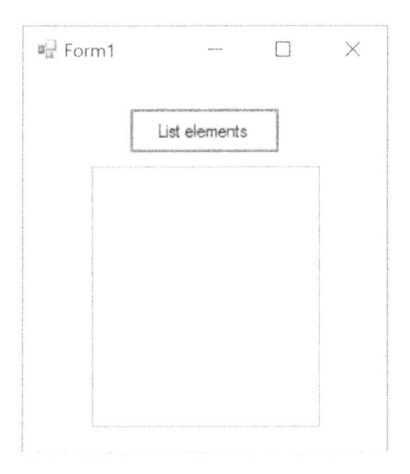

Figure 10.5. The program window

Figure 10.6. Elements of the array listed in the ListBox

Note the order of elements in the ListBox. They are like (0, 0), (0, 1), (0, 2), (1, 0), ..., (1, 2). As it can be seen from this order, i) the first loop executes once, ii) then the inside loop executes and ends, and then iii) the first loop enters the second cycle. This is the general behaviour of nested loops: the inner loop(s) finishes the whole tour until the outer loop takes the next cycle.

10.1.3. Array Operations

There are a lot of methods existing in the System.Array class that can be applied on arrays to modify them. Frequently used array methods are as follows:

10.1.3.1. Resize() Method

This method is used to change the size of an array. For example, if we have an array with 4 elements:

```
Dim myArray = New String() {"Water", "Soda water", "Orange juice", "Lemonade"}
```
Code 10.13

We can make it a 5 element array by the code line:

```
Array.Resize(myArray, 5)
```
Code 10.14

BEGINNER'S GUIDE TO VISUAL BASIC.NET PROGRAMMING

After this resizing, we can assign an element to its 5th element without any problem:

```
myArray(4) = "Tea"
```
Code 10.14

If we tried to do this assignment before resizing the array, VB.NET compiler would issue an error.

Let's create a project to try these code lines:

1. Create a new VB.NET project.
2. Add a Button and a ListBox on the form.
3. Set the Name and Text properties of the Button as **resizeButton** and **Resize**, respectively.
4. Set the Name of the ListBox as **elementsListBox**. The form may look as follows:

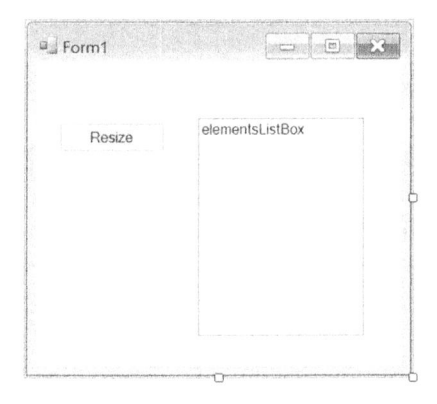

Figure 3.10. The form layout

5. Double-click the Button to create its Click event handler method and then insert the code lines of Code 10.15 inside this method. Let's also use a For Each loop for displaying the array's elements on the ListBox. The event handler method will be as follows after these additions:

```
Private Sub ResizeButton_Click(sender As Object, e As
EventArgs) Handles resizeButton.Click
    Dim myArray = New String() {"Water", "Soda water",
```

270

```
    "Orange juice", "Lemonade"}
    Array.Resize(myArray, 5)
    myArray(4) = "Tea"
    For Each item In myArray
        elementsListBox.Items.Add(item)
    Next
End Sub
```
Code 10.15

Note that we declared and initialized the array before the event handler, which is the global area, so that we can use this array in other event handlers too.

6. Build and run the project. When the **Resize** Button is clicked, the array will be resized and the element `"Tea"` will be appended and shown on the ListBox:

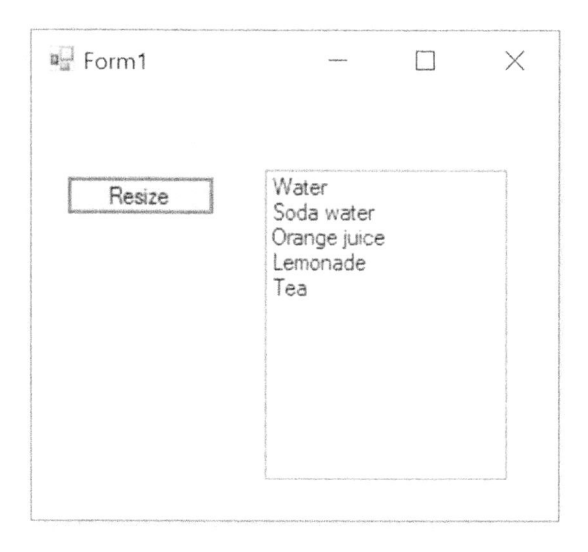

Figure 10.8. Elements of the resized array

10.1.3.2. Copy() Method

This method is used for copying individual elements from one array to another. The Copy() method is used in the following way:

```
Copy(original_array, index, destination_array, index,
                number_of_elements_to_be_copied)z
```
Code 10.16

If we specify the `number_of_elements_to_be_copied` as 1, only one element is copied, otherwise we can copy multiple elements in a single code line. Let's use this method in the recent project we developed for the `Resize()` method:

1. Add a Button on the form below the Resize Button.
2. Set the Name and Text properties of the Button as **copyButton** and **Copy**. The form will look as below:

Figure 10.9. Adding the Copy Button on the form

3. Double-click the **Copy** Button to create its event handler method. Let's define a 2-element string array inside this method as follows:

```
Dim NewArray(1) As String
```
Code 10.17

4. Now, we will copy the first and last element of `myArray` to the first and second elements of `myNewArray`, respectively. We will use the `Copy()` method as follows:

```
Array.Copy(myArray, 0, NewArray, 0, 1)
Array.Copy(myArray, 3, NewArray, 1, 1)
```
Code 10.18

In the first line, we tell the compiler to" start copying the 1st element of `myArray` to the 1st element of `NewArray` and copy 1 element". As you can

CHAPTER 10. ARRAYS AND COLLECTIONS

see, we can copy more than one element from the original array to the destination array if we need to.

5. Let's display the elements of myNewArray on the ListBox using a foreach loop. The whole event handler method will look as below:

```
Private Sub CopyButton_Click(sender As Object, e As
EventArgs) Handles copyButton.Click
    Dim NewArray(1) As String
    Array.Copy(myArray, 0, NewArray, 0, 1)
    Array.Copy(myArray, 3, NewArray, 1, 1)
    For Each item In NewArray
        elementsListBox.Items.Add(item)
    Next
End Sub
```

Code 10.19

6. Build and run the project. When we click the **Copy** Button, we will see the contents of myNewArray as expected:

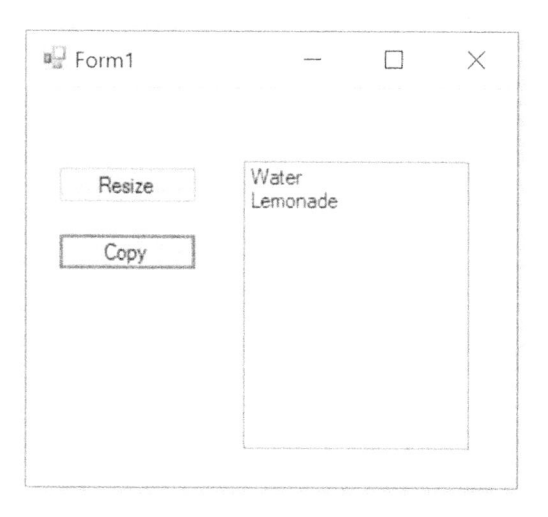

Figure 10.10. The elements of myNewArray shown in the ListBox

10.1.3.3. SetValue() and GetValue() Methods

SetValue() and GetValue() methods are used to set and read the element at the specific address of an array. They are used in the following way:

```
array_name.SetValue(new_element, index)
array_name.GetValue(index)
```
Code 10.20

Let's try these methods in our recent array project.

1. Add a Button on the form below the Copy Button.
2. Set the Name and Text properties of the Button as **setGetButton** and **Set and Get**. The form will look as below:

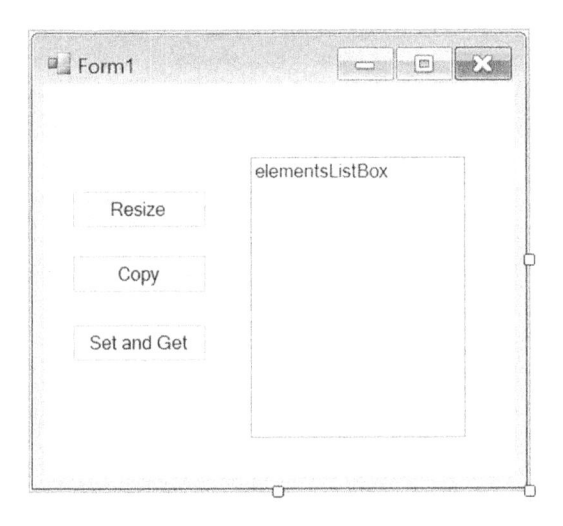

Figure 10.11. The layout of the form

3. Double-click the **Set and Get** Buttons and create their event handler methods. We'll use the setValue() and getValue() methods inside this method.
4. Let's firstly set the 2nd element of myArray as "Coffee" using the setValue() method as follows:

```
myArray.SetValue("Coffee", 1);
```
Code 10.21

5. We can use a for loop for displaying array elements on the ListBox:

```
for (int i = 0; i < myArray.Length; i++)
{
   elementsListBox.Items.Add(myArray.GetValue(i));
}
```

CHAPTER 10. ARRAYS AND COLLECTIONS

Code 10.22

In this code, we read the value at index i using the getValue() method as: myArray.GetValue(i). The whole event handler method will be as follows:

```
Private Sub SetGetButton_Click(sender As Object, e As
EventArgs) Handles setGetButton.Click
   Dim myArray = New String() {"Water", "Soda water",
"Orange juice", "Lemonade"}
   myArray.SetValue("Coffee", 1)
   For Each item In myArray
      elementsListBox.Items.Add(item)
   Next
End Sub
```
Code 10.23

6. Build and run the project. When we click the **Set and Get** Button, the updated contents of myArray are displayed on the ListBox as shown below:

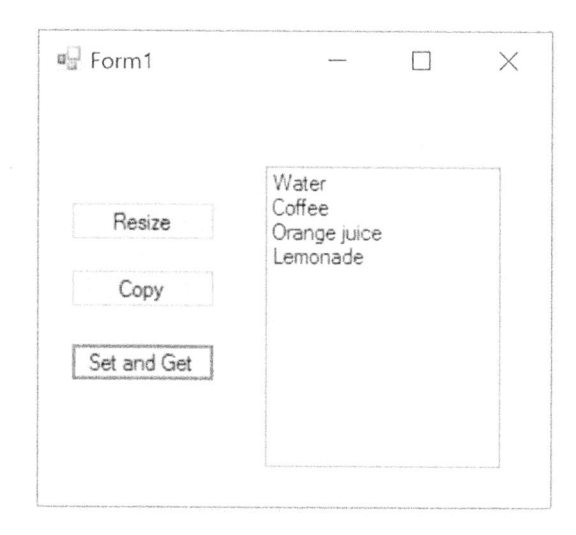

Figure 10.12. The 2nd element of the array set by the setValue() method

10.2. Collections

Collections are data structures that provide a dynamic storage, i.e. the size of collections automatically changes as elements are added or removed from the collection. Furthermore, data types of different types can be held on collections. Frequently used collection types are **HashTable**, **ArrayList**, **SortedList**, **Stack**, **Queue**. We will cover HashTable and ArrayList as these are the popular ones.

10.2.1. Hashtable

Hashtables provide a data structure which is matched as a key-value pair like a dictionary. We set and read the values of the elements of a Hashtable using the keys. A typical Hashtable can be visualised as follows:

Key	Value
Physics	10
Maths	9
Literature	9
History	7

Table 10.4. A key-value pair

In this Hashtable, the keys are lectures and the values denote the exam points of a student. Let's use this Hashtable in an example project.

1. Create a new VB.NET project.
2. Add a Button and a ListBox on the form.
3. Set the Name and Text of the form ask **keyValueButton** and **Show key and value**.
4. Set the Name of the ListBox as **displayListBox**. The form will look as follows:

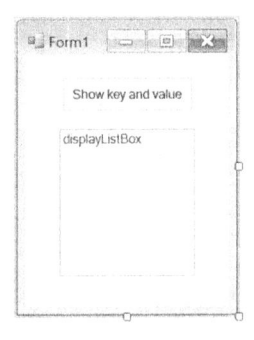

Figure 10.13. The layout of the form

CHAPTER 10. ARRAYS AND COLLECTIONS

5. Double-click the Button to create its event handler method. We'll write our code in this method.
6. Add the collection namespace to our Form1.cs file with `Imports System.Collections` code line.
7. Create a new `Hashtable` by the code line:

```
Dim newHt As Hashtable = New Hashtable()
```
Code 10.24

8. We will add the key-value pairs of the `Hashtable` object `newHt` with the `Add()` method as follows:

```
newHt.Add("Physics", 10)
newHt.Add("Maths", 9)
newHt.Add("Literature", 9)
newHt.Add("History", 7)
```
Code 10.25

9. We will display the key-value pairs in the ListBox. For this, let's firstly take the keys of the Hashtable:

```
Dim keys = newHt.Keys
```
Code 10.26

10. We can now use a `foreach` loop to sweep over these keys:

```
For Each key In keys
    displayListBox.Items.Add(key + "->" + newHt(key).ToString())
Next
```
Code 10.27

As you can see from this code, the values of the Hashtable `newHt` are accessed with the expression `newHt(key)` similar to accessing elements of an array. From this viewpoint, we can consider arrays as Hashtables having the fixed keys of 0, 1, 2, etc. The key-value pairs will be written as key -> value in the ListBox thanks to the string concatenations set by the expression `key + "->" + newHt(key).ToString()`.

The whole event handler method will be populated by these code lines as below:

277

```
Private Sub KeyValueButton_Click(sender As Object, e As
EventArgs) Handles keyValueButton.Click

  Dim newHt As Hashtable = New Hashtable()

  newHt.Add("Physics", 10)
  newHt.Add("Maths", 9)
  newHt.Add("Literature", 9)
  newHt.Add("History", 7)

  Dim keys = newHt.Keys

  For Each key In keys
  displayListBox.Items.Add(key + "->" +
    newHt(key).ToString())
  Next

End Sub
```

Code 10.28

11. Build and run the project. When we click the **Show key and value** Button, the keys and corresponding values will be displayed in the ListBox:

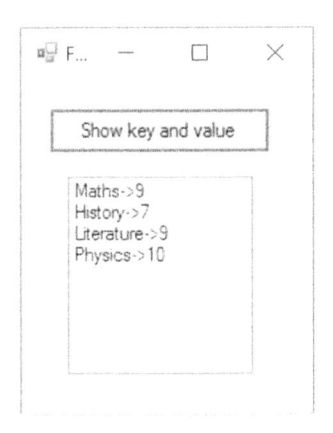

Figure 10.14. The key-value pairs shown on the ListBox

10.2.2. ArrayList

ArrayLists are collection types which are flexible alternatives to usual arrays. ArrayLists have two main advantages: they can hold different data types and they resize automatically as new elements are added or removed. Since the length of an ArrayList is dynamic, their length is not specified during declaration. Another advantage of ArrayLists is that there are various useful methods enabling us to alter the ordering of the structure dynamically.

ArrayLists have integer indices which start from 0 as in usual arrays.

Let's declare and use an ArrayList in a small project.

1. Create a new VB.NET project.
2. Add a TextBox, two Buttons and a ListBox on the form.
3. Set the Name property of the TextBox as **inputTextBox**.
4. Set the Name and Text of the first Button as **addButton** and **Add**.
5. Set the Name and Text of the second Button as **displayButton** and **Display**.
6. Set the Name of the ListBox as **displayListBox**. The form layout may look as follows:

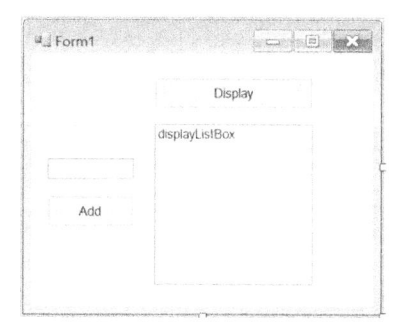

Figure 10.15. Layout of the form

7. Double-click the **Add** Button to create its Click event handler. We will add the value entered to the **inputTextBox** to an ArrayList in this method. However, we will need this ArrayList to be accessible from the **Display** Button also because it will be used to display the elements of the ArrayList. In summary, we will declare the ArrayList in the global area. Firstly, we will add System.Collections namespace to our Form1.cs file:

```
Imports System.Collections
```
Code 10.29

Then, declare an ArrayList named newArrayList in the global area as follows:

```
Dim myArrayList As New ArrayList()
```
Code 10.30

8. We will take the input entered to the **inputTextBox** and then add it as an element in the ArrayList using the Add() method in the Button's event handler method:

```
Private Sub AddButton_Click(sender As Object, e As EventArgs) Handles addButton.Click

    myArrayList.Add(inputTextBox.Text)
    inputTextBox.Clear()

End Sub
```
Code 10.31

Note that we clear the TextBox after the element is added to the ArrayList for making it ready for new entries.

9. Now, double-click the **Display** Button to create its event handler. We will display the elements of myArrayList on the ListBox using a foreach loop as follows:

```
Private Sub DisplayButton_Click(sender As Object, e As EventArgs) Handles displayButton.Click

    displayListBox.Items.Clear()
    For Each item In myArrayList
        displayListBox.Items.Add(item)
    Next

End Sub
```
Code 10.32

In this code snippet, we clear the ListBox before writing the elements of the ArrayList each time. If we haven't done this, the ListBox would be populated with all elements over and over for each click of the **Display** Button.

CHAPTER 10. ARRAYS AND COLLECTIONS

10. Build and run the project. The following program window will appear:

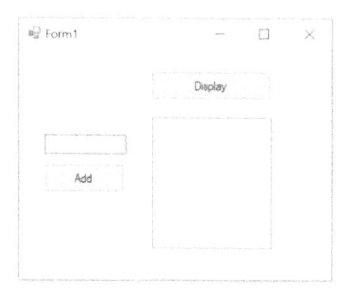

Figure 10.16. The program window

Let's enter some different strings in the **inputTextBox** and click the **Add** Button each time so that these inputs will be added as elements to myArrayList. I entered "Adam", "Joseph", "Peter" and "Benjamin". When I click then **Display** Button, contents of the ArrayList is displayed in the ListBox:

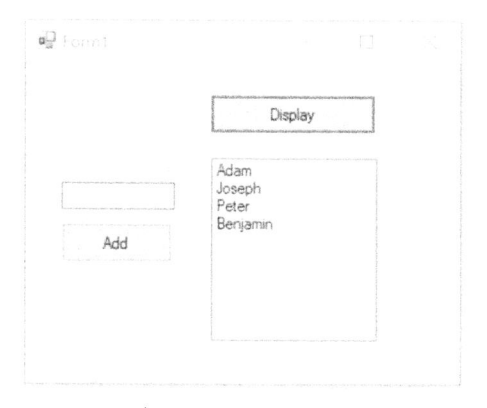

Figure 10.17. The elements of the ArrayList displayed in the ListBox

If we add another string in the inputTextBox and Click **Add**, it will be added to the end of the ArrayList. When we click the **Display** Button, it will be displayed as follows:

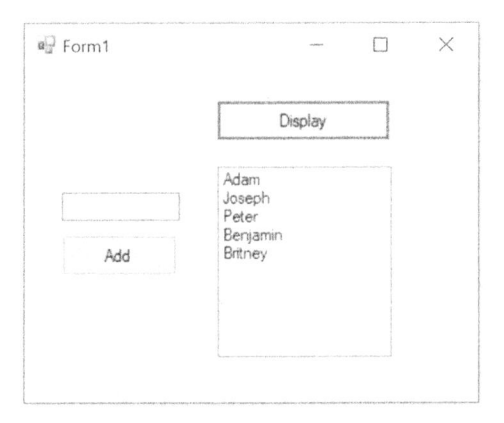

Figure 10.18. A new string "Britney" added to the ArrayList

11. Another advantage of using ArrayLists is that its elements can easily be sorted with `ArrayList.Sort()` method. Let's add another Button which will sort the ArrayList. Add a Button on the form, set its Name and Text properties as **sortButton** and **Sort**:

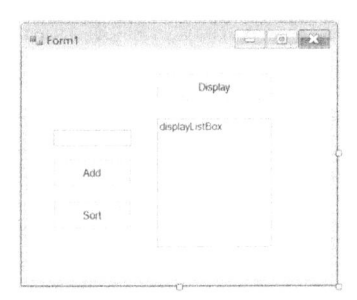

Figure 10.19. The Sort Button added on the form

12. Double-click the **Sort** Button to create its event handler. We'll use the `Sort()` method inside this event handler as follows:

```
Private Sub SortButton_Click(sender As Object, e As EventArgs) Handles sortButton.Click

    myArrayList.Sort()

End Sub
```
Code 10.33

13. Build and run the project again. I entered the same string as before and then clicked the **Sort** Button. When the **Display** Button is clicked, the sorted elements are displayed in the ListBox:

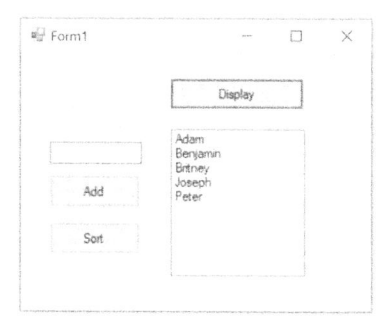

Figure 10.20. The elements of the ArrayList sorted by the Sort() method

That's all about arrays and collections for now; we will use these data structures in our upcoming projects. In the next chapter, we will see how we can shorten our programs by using repeating code in methods.

Chapter 11

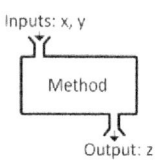

METHODS

In most programs, there exists code blocks which are repeated in several places. Methods enable us to write these code blocks only once and call whenever needed. Methods are declared with a name and a code block. When the method is called, its code block is executed. Code lines inside a method are not executed until the method is called somewhere in the main program.

There are two types of methods in VB.NET: sub procedures and functions. Procedures do not return a value while functions have return values.

11.1. Declaration of Sub Procedures and Functions

The template of a typical method sub procedure declaration is as follows:

```
access_modifier Sub sub_name (parameters)
```
Code 11.1

- The `access_modifier` (sometimes called as access specifier) sets the accessibility level of the method. In other words, it sets the level from where this method can be called. Its possible values are **Private**, **Public**, **Protected** and **Friend**. We'll explain these keywords in a short while.
- The `sub_name` is the name of the sub procedure; we use this name to call the method for execution.
- The `parameters` are the variables we pass to the sub procedure. In other words, they are the inputs to the method.

Similarly, functions in VB.NET are basically procedures having an output value. The template of a function definition is as follows:

```
access_modifier Function function_name (parameters) As
return_type
```
Code 11.2

The declaration template is similar to that of a procedure as it can be seen above with an addition of a return_type specifier:

- The return_type specifies the variable type of the variable the method will return. It can be one of the variable types we learned before.

Let's analyse the components of sub procedure and function declaration syntax:

11.2. Accessibility Modifiers

As we have stated above, the place where a method can be called is specified by its accessibility modifier. An accessibility modifier can take one of the following values:

1. **The Private keyword**: If the method's accessibility modifier is set as private, then this method can only be available for calling from the class it belongs to. For example, if the method is declared inside a Click event handler, it can only be called inside this event handler and cannot be called from another method such as Form's default Load event handler.
2. **The Public keyword**: In this case, the method can be called from anywhere in the program.
3. **The Protected keyword**: If the method's accessibility specifier is Protected, then this method can also be called from the child classes (derived classes, sub classes) of its own class.
4. **The Friend keyword**: In this case, this method can be called from its own assembly, i.e. the .exe or .dll file.

11.3. Function Example

Let's declare a method in a simple project which returns the greater of two given numbers.

1. Create a new VB.NET project.
2. Add three TextBoxes and a Button on the form.

3. Set the Name properties of TextBoxes as **input1**, **input2** and **output**.
4. Set the Name and Text of the Button as **findGreaterButton** and **Find the greater one**, respectively. The form layout will be as follows:

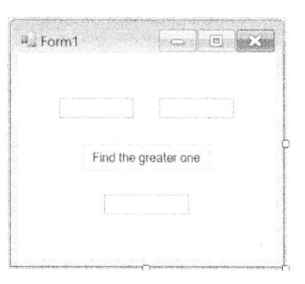

Figure 11.1. Layout of the form

5. Let's declare our method first. Our method will take two integer variables, determine the greater of these variables and return this value as an integer. We can name the method as we like, I named it as FindGreater. The question at this point is: where will we write our method in the Form1.cs code file? There are a few possibilities but the most convenient one is to declare the method inside the Public Class Form1() method which already exists in the code. Right-click somewhere empty on the form and select **View Code** to open the Code view of the Form1.cs file:

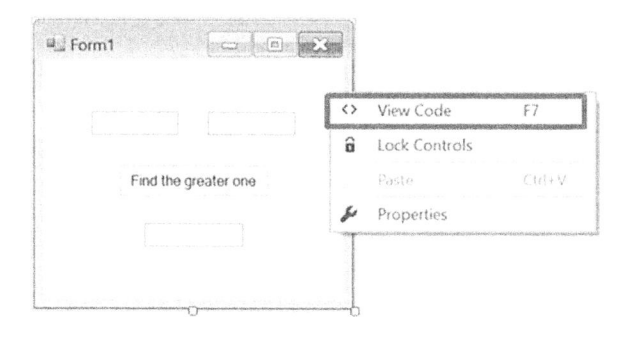

Figure 11.2. Opening the code view

The method will be declared inside the Form1() method as indicated below:

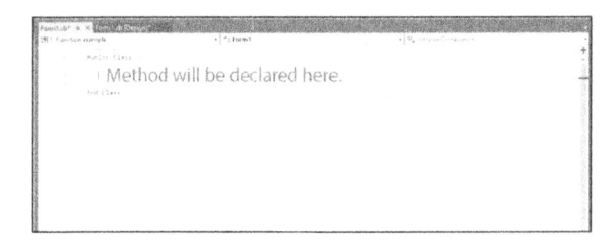

Figure 11.3. The place where our method will be declared

6. We can declare our method as `public` or `private` as this method will be used inside this form only. Let's declare it as `public`:

```
Public Function findGreater(ByVal in1 As Integer, ByVal in2 As Integer) As Integer

End Function
```
Code 11.3

The name of the method is given as `findGreater`. After the name, the parameters (inputs) of the method are declared, `in1` and `in2` which are both integer type variables. The `ByVal` keyword means that the function accepts the inputs by its values and cannot change the values of these input variables. There is an alternative keyword `ByVal` in VB.NET which lets the function to change the value of its parameters. But for the current example we are OK with the `ByVal` keyword as we will not attempt to change the values of input variables.

Since the method will output an integer value, its return type is set as `Integer` at the end. We'll write the contents of the method inside the function body:

```
Public Function findGreater(ByVal in1 As Integer, ByVal in2 As Integer) As Integer
    Dim greater As Integer
    If in1 > in2 Then
        greater = in1
    Else
        greater = in2
    End If
    Return greater
End Function
```
Code 11.4

We declared an integer variable inside the method called `greater` which will hold the value of the greater variable. Then we used a simple if-else structure to determine the greater number and assigned it to the variable `greater`. Finally we returned the `greater` variable with the keyword return in the code line `Return greater`. Note that we use the `Return` keyword to return (output) a value from a function. The complete Form1.vb file will be as follows:

```
Private Sub FindGreaterButton_Click(sender As Object, e As EventArgs) Handles findGreaterButton.Click

End Sub
```
Code 11.5

7. If we build and run the project, nothing happens. Because we declared the method but didn't call it anywhere yet. We need to call the method to make it do its job. **Where will we call this method?** Since we declared this method as public, we can call it anywhere in our code. In our program, we will enter two integer numbers to **input1** and **input2** TextBoxes and when we click the Button, the method will be called to determine the greater one, return the value of the greater one and then this value will be displayed in the **output** TextBox. For these operations, we need to create the default Click event handler method of the Button and then call our `FindGreater()` method from here. Let's double-click the Button and create its Click event handler:

```
Private Sub FindGreaterButton_Click(sender As Object, e As EventArgs) Handles findGreaterButton.Click


End Sub
```
Code 11.6

8. We will take the values entered in **input1** and **input2** TextBoxes and convert them to integers:

```
Dim input1Int = Convert.ToInt32(input1.Text)
Dim input2Int = Convert.ToInt32(input2.Text)
```
Code 11.7

289

BEGINNER'S GUIDE TO VISUAL BASIC.NET PROGRAMMING

9. Let's call our method now. Since the method will output an integer value, we need to assign this value to an integer variable. We declare an integer variable named outputValue for this and then assign the output of our method to this variable as follows:

```
Dim outputValue As Integer = findGreater(input1Int,
input2Int)
```
Code 11.8

Note that we passed our integer numbers to the method as (input1Int, input2Int).

10. Finally, we will display the output value in the output TextBox:

```
output.Text = outputValue.ToString()
```
Code 11.9

The complete code of the Form1.cs file is given follows:

```
Public Class Form1

    Public Function findGreater(ByVal in1 As Integer, ByVal in2 As Integer) As Integer
        Dim greater As Integer
        If in1 > in2 Then
            greater = in1
        Else
            greater = in2
        End If
        Return greater
    End Function

    Private Sub FindGreaterButton_Click(sender As Object, e As EventArgs) Handles findGreaterButton.Click

        Dim input1Int = Convert.ToInt32(input1.Text)
        Dim input2Int = Convert.ToInt32(input2.Text)
        Dim outputValue As Integer = findGreater(input1Int, input2Int)
        output.Text = outputValue.ToString()

    End Sub
End Class
```
Code 11.10

290

11. Build and run the project. When we enter two integers and click the **Find the greater one** Button, our method is called, finds and returns the value of the greater one and the program displays this value in the **output** TextBox as shown in Figure 11.4.

- We may pass as many inputs as we need to a method using commas as separators as we did in this project.
- Similarly, a method may return multiple values separated by commas if needed.

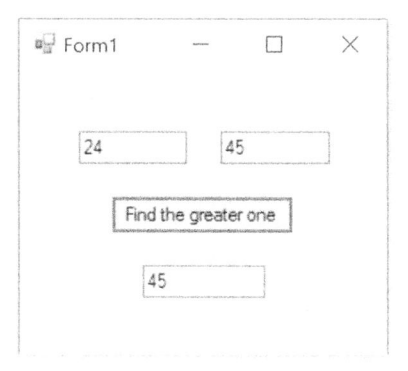

Figure 11.4. Our method works as expected

11.4. Sub Procedure Example

Sometimes we don't need a method to return a value. For example, we may need to change the appearance of the form controls. In this case, the method will not return a value but will change some appearance properties. Let's develop a simple project where our method will switch our GUI to reading mode by making the background of a Label to take a darker colour and its Text a lighter colour.

1. Create a new VB.NET project.
2. Add a Label and a Button on the form.
3. Set the Name of the Label as **readingText** and set its Text property to your favourite quote. I have set it as **Fortitude is the guard and support of the other virtues**.

BEGINNER'S GUIDE TO VISUAL BASIC.NET PROGRAMMING

4. Set the Name and Text properties of the Button as **readingModeButton** and **Reading mode**, respectively. Our form layout will look as follows:

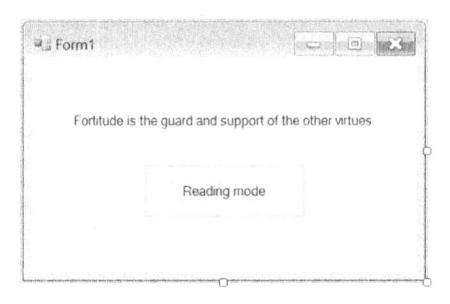

Figure 11.5. Layout of the form

5. We will create our method inside the Form1() method as we did in the previous example. We can name our method as switchToReadingMode(). Since our method will not return a value, its return type keyword will be void as follows:

```
Public Sub switchToReadingMode()

End Sub
```
Code 11.11

Note that we will not input any variable to this method therefore inside of the parentheses of the method is empty. We will change the BackColor and ForeColor properties of the Label which will be better for reading. I've selected Maroon and White colours, respectively:

```
Public Sub switchToReadingMode()

    readingText.BackColor = Color.Maroon
    readingText.ForeColor = Color.White

End Sub
```
Code 11.12

6. We will call our method when the Button is clicked. For this, firstly create the Click event handler of the Button by double-click:

```
Private Sub ReadingModeButton_Click(sender As Object, e As
```

292

```
EventArgs) Handles readingModeButton.Click

End Sub
```
Code 11.13

And then call the method inside this event handler as follows:

```
Private Sub ReadingModeButton_Click(sender As Object, e As
EventArgs) Handles readingModeButton.Click

    switchToReadingMode()

End Sub
```
Code 11.14

The complete Form1.cs file will be as the follows:

```
Public Class Form1

    Public Sub switchToReadingMode()

        readingText.BackColor = Color.Maroon
        readingText.ForeColor = Color.White

    End Sub

    Private Sub ReadingModeButton_Click(sender As Object, e
As EventArgs) Handles readingModeButton.Click

        switchToReadingMode()

    End Sub

End Class
```
Code 11.15

7. Build and run the project. The program window will appear as follows:

Figure 11.6. The initial view of the program

When the **Reading mode** Button is clicked, our method will be executed and change the colours of the Label:

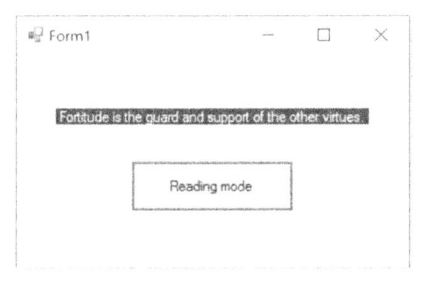

Figure 11.7. Colours of the Label are changed after the method is called

11.5. Passing Parameters to Methods

Parameters (inputs) of methods can be passed (given) in one of the two ways: **call by value** or **call by reference**.

11.5.1. Call by Value

When a variable is passed to a method by value, a copy of this variable is created and sent to the method. We use the ByVal keyword for calling a variable by its value in the parameters list. Consequently, if the method alters this input value, it will in fact alter the copy of the passed variable therefore the value of the passed (original) variable will be protected. Let's see this in a simple example:

1. Create a new VB.NET project.
2. Place a Button on the form.
3. Set the Name and Text of the Button as **showButton** and **Show**, respectively. Our simple form will be as follows:

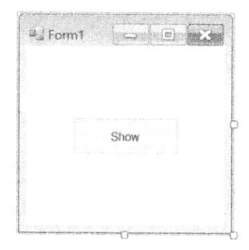

Figure 11.8. The form

5. Let's create our sub procedure inside the automatically created Form1() method as usual. Our sub procedure named CallByValue() will be a void method and have a string type input variable as follows:

```
Public Sub callByValue(ByVal input As String)

End Sub
```
Code 11.16

Let's change the value of the input variable inside the method as follows:

```
Public Sub callByValue(ByVal input As String)

    input = "Modified in this method."

End Sub
```
Code 11.17

As you can see, our method will set the value of the input variable as "Modified in the method." independent of its initial value.

6. Double-click the Button to create its default event handler method. Inside this method declare a string type variable and display the value of this variable in a message box:

```
Private Sub ShowButton_Click(sender As Object, e As EventArgs) Handles showButton.Click

    Dim myString As String = "VB.NET programming"
    MessageBox.Show("Initial value of the string is " + myString)
```

295

```
End Sub
```
Code 11.18

The value of the variable myString will be displayed in the message box as usual. Now, let's call our CallByValue() method and pass myString as the input to this method and then display the value of myString again:

```
Private Sub ShowButton_Click(sender As Object, e As
EventArgs) Handles showButton.Click

    Dim myString As String = "VB.NET programming"
    MessageBox.Show("Initial value of the string is " +
myString)
    callByValue(myString)
    MessageBox.Show("Value of the string after passed to
CallByValue() method: " + myString)

End Sub
```
Code 11.19

The whole Form1.vb file will be as below:

```
Public Class Form1

    Public Sub callByValue(ByVal input As String)

        input = "Modified in this method."

    End Sub

    Private Sub ShowButton_Click(sender As Object, e As
EventArgs) Handles showButton.Click

        Dim myString As String = "VB.NET programming"
        MessageBox.Show("Initial value of the string is " +
myString)
        callByValue(myString)
        MessageBox.Show("Value of the string after passed
to CallByValue() method: " + myString)

    End Sub
End Class
```
Code 11.20

7. Build and run the project. When the **Show** Button is clicked, a message box will appear as follows:

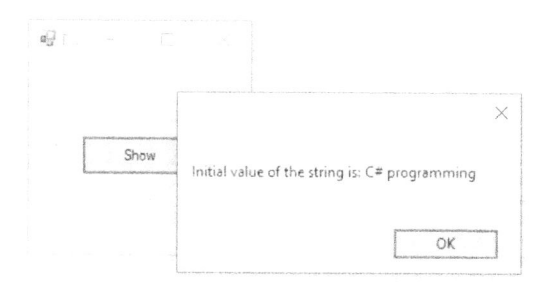

Figure 11.9. The message box displaying the initial value of `myString`

When we click OK in this message box, our `CallByValue()` method will be called and then the current value of `myString` will again be displayed:

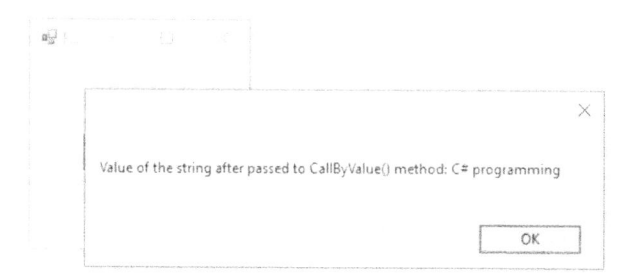

Figure 11.10. The value of `myString` after it is passed to our method

As we can see from these message boxes, the value of `myString` didn't change after it is passed to the method `CallByValue()`. When `myString` is given as the input to this method, its copy is created in the memory. This copy is then changed in the method therefore the value of the original variable is preserved.

11.5.2. Call by Reference

When a variable is passed to a method by reference, the original variable itself (not its copy) is passed to the method. Therefore if it is altered in the method, the value of the original variable will also be affected. We use the `ByRef` keyword for calling a variable by its value in the parameters list. Let's modify our previous example and pass the input of the method by reference as follows to our new method CallByReference():

```
Public Sub callByReference(ByRef input As String)

   input = "Modified in this method."

End Sub
```
Code 11.21

We also have to modify the code line where we call the method in the Button's event handler:

```
callByReference(myString)
```
Code 11.22

The complete Form1.vb is also given as follows:

```
Public Class Form1

    Public Sub callByReference(ByRef input As String)

        input = "Modified in this method."

    End Sub

    Private Sub ShowButton_Click(sender As Object, e As EventArgs) Handles showButton.Click

        Dim myString As String = "VB.NET programming"
        MessageBox.Show("Initial value of the string is " + myString)
        callByReference(myString)
        MessageBox.Show("Value of the string after passed to CallByValue() method: " + myString)

    End Sub
End Class
```
Code 11.23

We can now build and run the project again. When we click the **Show** Button, the initial value of myString will be displayed as before:

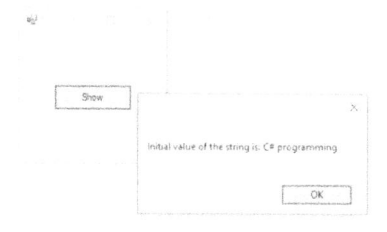

Figure 11.11. Initial value of myString displayed as before

When we click the OK button in the message box, myString variable will be passed to our CallByReference() method by reference and then its current value will be displayed in the message box:

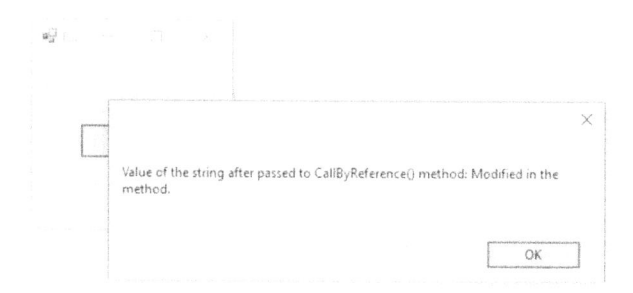

Figure 11.12. The current value of myString

As it is seen in the message box, the value of the original variable myString is altered when callByReference() method called it by reference. Hence, we see the difference of calling by value and calling by reference clearly in these simple examples.

11.6. Passing Arrays to Methods

When the number of parameters (inputs) is unknown at the time of programming, these parameters are passed as arrays. The keyword ParamArray is used for this operation. Let's use this property in a simple project. We'll declare a method which multiplies numbers where it will multiply the any number of inputs entered by the user.

1. Create a new VB.NET project.
2. Add a TextBox and a Button to the project.
3. Set the Name of the TextBox as **inputTextBox**.

4. Set the Name and Text of the Button as **multiplyButton** and **Multiply**. The form may look as below:

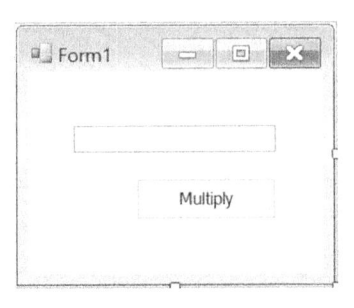

Figure 11.13. The layout of the form

5. We will declare a function named Multiply() inside the Form1() method as usual. Since we don't know the actual number of numbers the user will enter, we will pass an array to our method as follows:

```
Public Function Multiply(ParamArray ByVal inputArray() As
String) As Integer

End Sub
```
Code 11.24

We will employ a For Each loop inside the method to multiply the integer values of the passed string array elements:

```
Public Function Multiply(ParamArray ByVal inputArray() As
String) As Integer

  Dim product As Integer = 1
  For Each item In inputArray
     product = product * Convert.ToInt32(item)
  Next

  Return product

End Function
```
Code 11.25

We do the conversion of each element during the multiplication inside the For Each loop. Finally we return the result of the multiplication stored in the product variable.

CHAPTER 11. METHODS

6. We will multiply the numbers entered in the TextBox. As you can see from the method input above, we should pass a string array. For this, we need to create a string array from the comma separated numbers the user will enter. For this aim create the Click event handler of the Button by double-clicking and then use the `Split()` method of VB.NET to create a string array from the TextBox input as follows:

```
Private Sub MultiplyButton_Click(sender As Object, e As
EventArgs) Handles multiplyButton.Click

    Dim str = inputTextBox.Text.Split(",")

End Sub
```
Code 11.26

The `Split(',')` method splits the Text input according to the separator, which is comma in this example. Then we are ready to pass the `str` array to our `Multiply()` method and then display the multiplication result in a message box:

```
Private Sub MultiplyButton_Click(sender As Object, e As
EventArgs) Handles multiplyButton.Click

    Dim str = inputTextBox.Text.Split(",")
    Dim functionResult As Integer = Multiply(str)
    MessageBox.Show("The multiplicaiton result is: " +
functionResult.ToString())

End Sub
```
Code 11.27

The complete Form1.cs is also given below:

```
Public Class Form1

    Public Function Multiply(ParamArray ByVal inputArray()
As String) As Integer

        Dim product As Integer = 1
        For Each item In inputArray
            product = product * Convert.ToInt32(item)
        Next

        Return product
```

301

```
    End Function

    Private Sub MultiplyButton_Click(sender As Object, e As
EventArgs) Handles multiplyButton.Click

        Dim str = inputTextBox.Text.Split(",")
        Dim functionResult As Integer = Multiply(str)
        MessageBox.Show("The multiplicaiton result is: " +
functionResult.ToString())

    End Sub
End Class
```

Code 11.28 (cont'd)

7. Build and run the project. The program window appears as below:

Figure 11.14. The multiplication program

We can enter any number of inputs to the TextBox for multiplication. Let's input two numbers:

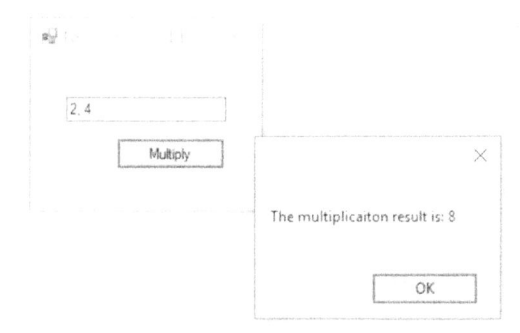

Figure 11.15. Multiplication of two numbers with our Multiply() method

Then let's input one more number and click the Multiply button again. Our method will multiply all of the inputs as expected:

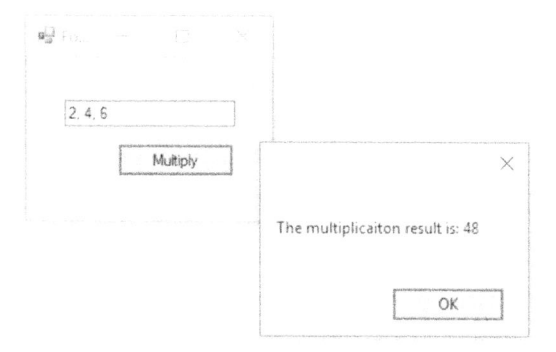

Figure 11.16. Multiplying three numbers with the same method

We have studied creating and using several types of methods in this chapter and this made a basis for learning classes and objects in the following chapter. Class-object concept is the backbone of object-oriented programming therefore better to have a coffee before continuing to the next chapter.

Chapter 12

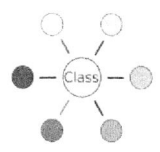

CLASSES AND OBJECTS

12.1. General Information and Template

Classes and objects are bases of the so-called **object-oriented programming**. Classes are used for collecting frequently used variables and methods in a single entity. Then, objects are defined from these classes making a copy of their own methods and variables. We can think classes as templates that have empty properties of the objects created from them. Classes and objects are declared in the following order and relation:

- The **class** containing the required variables and methods are declared first.
- This **class** is then used for the declaration of one or more **objects**.

Let's consider a daily example for understanding classes and objects easily. There exist several different automobile types with specific properties like colour, make, model, production year, etc. The term **automobile** can be thought as a **class** in this case. **Each specific car** (such as make: A, model: B, colour: yellow and year: 2019) will then be an **object** derived from this class. This is shown in the following figure:

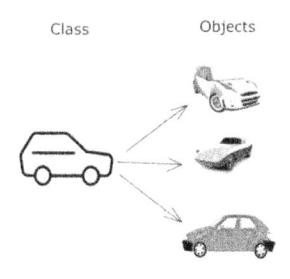

Figure 12.1. Class-object relationship

Classes can be declared and used in VB.NET in one of the following three ways:

- Declaration inside the same source code file of the program such as in Form1.vb
- A separate .vb file can be added to the project. The new class is then declared and coded in this file.
- A completely separate library file can be created in Visual Studio where the class is declared. This library file is then saved as a .dll file available for distribution and use in any VB.NET project.

The general template of a class structure is as follows:

```
access_specifier Class name_of_the_class

    access_specifier field_name_1 As field_type

    access_modifier Sub procedure_1

    End Sub

    access_modifier Function function_1(parameters) As
        return_type

    End Function

End Class
```

Code 12.1

In this template, the class has a class variable (called field) named `field_name_1`, a procedure definition (`procedure_1`) and a function definition (`function_1`).

12.2. Declaring Classes in the Same File

In this example, we will declare a class in the main program which will have a method for performing addition.

1. Create a new VB.NET project
2. Add three TextBoxes and a Button on the form.
3. Set the Names and of the TextBoxes as **input1**, **input2** and **output**.

CHAPTER 12. CLASSES AND OBJECTS

4. Set the Name and Text properties of the Button as **addButton** and **Add**, respectively. The form will look as follows at this stage:

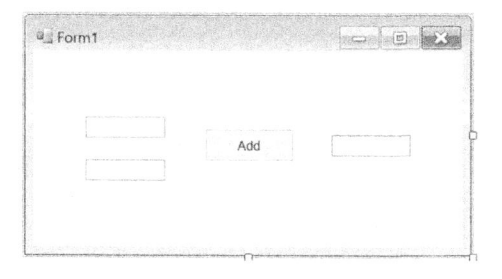

Figure 12.2 Layout of the form

5. Right-click an empty point on the form and select View Code as follows:

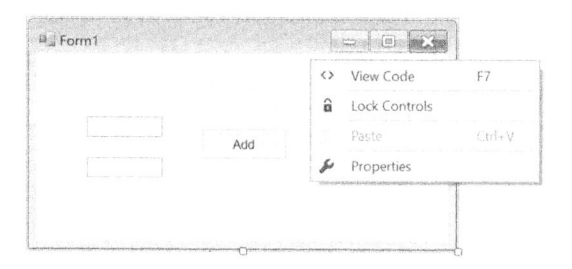

Figure 12.3. Opening the code view of Form1.vb

6. We will add our new class named AddClass() in the Form1.vb file. As it is indicated in Figure 12.4, there is already a class called Form1 in Form1.vb. Therefore, our new class will go just below the end of this class declaration as shown in Figure 12.5.

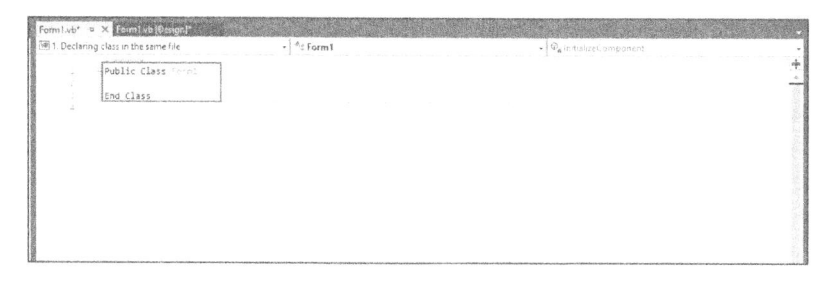

Figure 12.4. Already existing class in Form1.vb

307

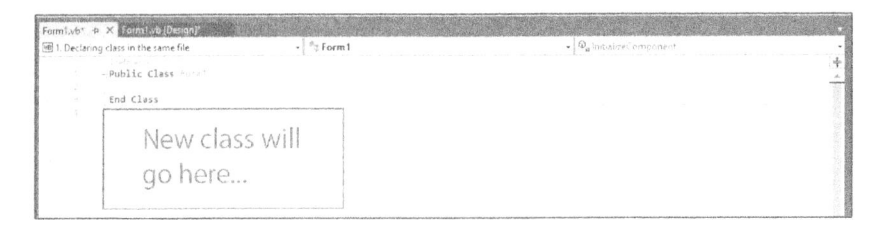

Figure 12.5. The place of our new class

7. Our new class statement will start by specifying its accessibility identifier, declaring it as a class and finally the class name as follows:

```
Public Class AddClass

End Class
```
Code 12.2

8. Let's define two variables (fields) in the class to hold the numbers and a method to actually perform the addition:

```
Public Class AddClass

    Public num1 As Integer
    Public num2 As Integer

    Public Function addFunction()
        Return num1 + num2
    End Function

End Class
```
Code 12.3

Firstly, we declared two integer variables called num1 and num2. Note that Public identifiers are added in front of these integer declarations because the default accessibility level of variables in a class is Friend, which doesn't permit us to access the variables outside the class.

After the variable declarations, a method named addFunction() is declared which returns the sum of num1 and num2 using the expression Return num1 + num2;.

9. We have declared our method. We will now use it in our main program. We will take the numbers entered into the **input1** and **input2** TextBoxes and use our method's variables and method to perform the addition operation. These will take place when the Button is clicked as usual. Therefore, double-click the Button to create its event handler method and take the values entered to the TextBoxes:

```
Private Sub AddButton_Click(sender As Object, e As
EventArgs) Handles addButton.Click

    Dim input1Num = Convert.ToInt32(input1.Text)
    Dim input2Num = Convert.ToInt32(input2.Text)

End Sub
```
Code 12.4

10. **We need to declare <u>an object derived from our class</u>** in order to use the variables and method of this class. We need to give a name to this object, let's say myObject:

```
Private Sub AddButton_Click(sender As Object, e As
EventArgs) Handles addButton.Click

    Dim input1Num = Convert.ToInt32(input1.Text)
    Dim input2Num = Convert.ToInt32(input2.Text)
    Dim myObject As AddClass = New AddClass()

End Sub
```
Code 12.5

11. The object myObject now has a copy of all variables and method the AddClass has. We will pass input1Num and input2Num varibles to the object's variables num1 and num2 **with the dot notation**:

```
Private Sub AddButton_Click(sender As Object, e As
EventArgs) Handles addButton.Click
  Dim input1Num = Convert.ToInt32(input1.Text)
  Dim input2Num = Convert.ToInt32(input2.Text)
  Dim myObject As AddClass = New AddClass()
  myObject.num1 = input1Num
  myObject.num2 = input2Num
End Sub
```
Code 12.6

BEGINNER'S GUIDE TO VISUAL BASIC.NET PROGRAMMING

By these code lines, we set the num1 and num2 fields of myObject as input1Num **and** input2Num, respectively.

12. Finally, we will call AddMethod() of myObject which will return the sum of num1 and num2 of myObject:

```
Private Sub AddButton_Click(sender As Object, e As
EventArgs) Handles addButton.Click

    Dim input1Num = Convert.ToInt32(input1.Text)
    Dim input2Num = Convert.ToInt32(input2.Text)
    Dim myObject As AddClass = New AddClass()
    myObject.num1 = input1Num
    myObject.num2 = input2Num
    output.Text = myObject.addFunction().ToString()

End Sub
```
Code 12.7

The whole Form1.cs is also given below for your convenience:

```
Public Class Form1
    Private Sub AddButton_Click(sender As Object, e As
EventArgs) Handles addButton.Click

        Dim input1Num = Convert.ToInt32(input1.Text)
        Dim input2Num = Convert.ToInt32(input2.Text)
        Dim myObject As AddClass = New AddClass()
        myObject.num1 = input1Num
        myObject.num2 = input2Num
        output.Text = myObject.addFunction().ToString()

    End Sub
End Class

Public Class AddClass

    Public num1 As Integer
    Public num2 As Integer

    Public Function addFunction()
        Return num1 + num2
    End Function

End Class
```
Code 12.8

CHAPTER 12. CLASSES AND OBJECTS

13. Build and run the project. The program window will appear as follows:

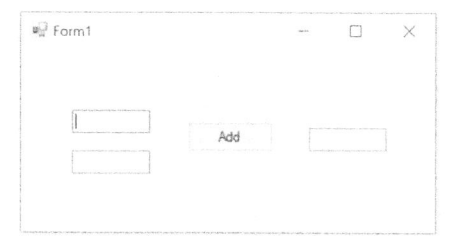

Figure 12.6. The program window

When we enter two numbers and click the **Add** Button, they are added with the function addFunction() of myObject derived from the class AddClass and then the sum is shown in the output TextBox:

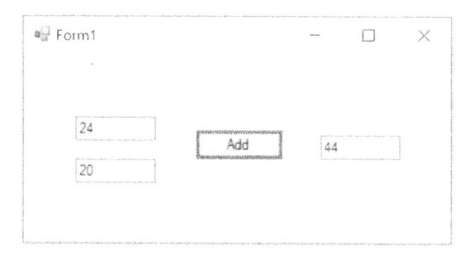

Figure 12.7. Addition is performed properly using the method we declared

12.3. Declaring Classes in a New File

When we have groups of classes, it is better to have them in separate files and add them to a project when needed. It is easy to define a class in a separate file. Let's develop a small project where we will create a class in a new file.

1. Create a new VB.NET project.
2. Add two Buttons and a Label on the form.
3. Set the Names and the Texts of the Buttons as **firstMessageButton**, **secondMessageButton** and **First message** and **Second message**, respectively.

311

BEGINNER'S GUIDE TO VISUAL BASIC.NET PROGRAMMING

4. Set the Name and Text of the Label as **Message will appear here** and **messageLabel**, respectively. The form may look as follows:

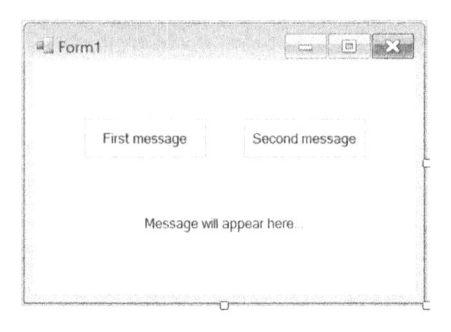

Figure 12.8. Layout of the form

5. When the first Button is clicked, the first message will be written on the Label. Similarly, the second Button will write another message on the Label. We will perform these using a method of a class we will define in a separate file. In order to add a class to a project, click Project → Add Class... as shown below:

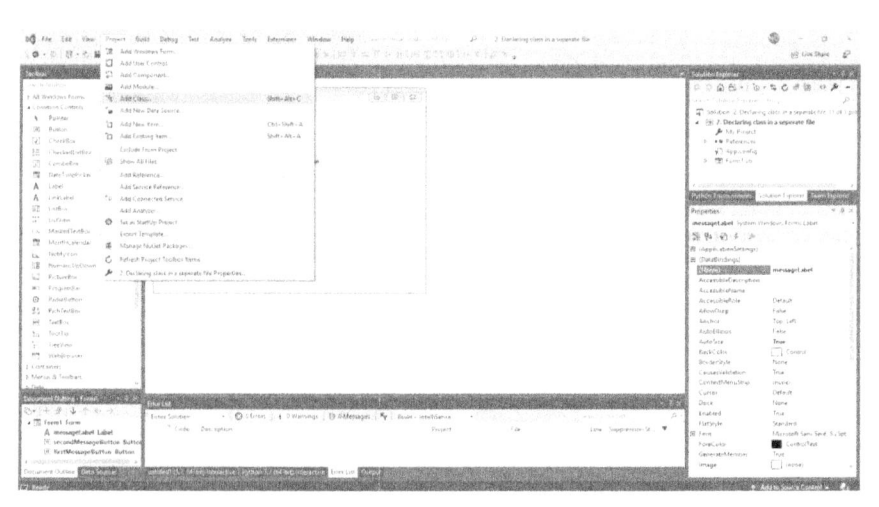

Figure 12.9. Adding a new class to the project

6. Visual Studio will ask for the name of the Class file. I named it as MessageClass.vb:

CHAPTER 12. CLASSES AND OBJECTS

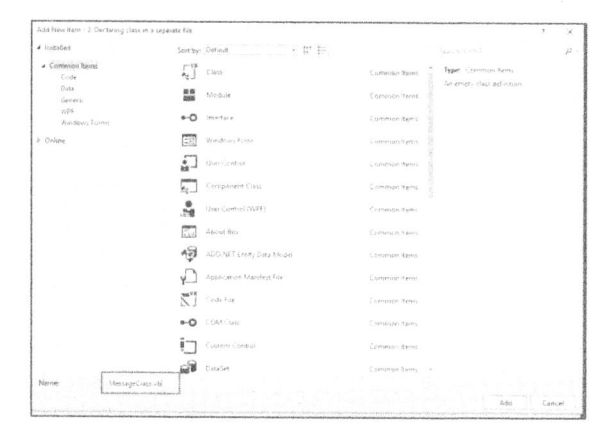

Figure 12.10. Naming the class file

When we click **Add**, the new file will be created and opened in the editor:

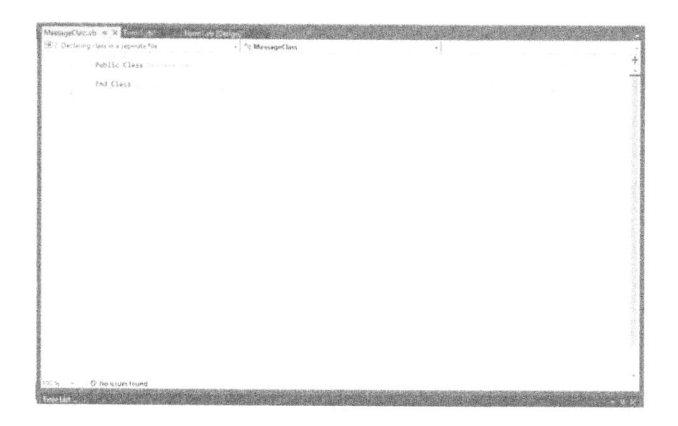

Figure 12.11. The class file opened in the editor

7. Let's analyse this class file:

```
Public Class MessageClass

End Class
```
Code 12.9

We can now add any variable or method to this class and use in the main Form1.vb file of our project since the class is declared as a public class. We want to change the Text of the **outputLabel** according to the clicked

313

Button, therefore let's add two functions to the `MessageClass` which will return two different strings when called:

```
Public Class MessageClass

  Public Function FirstMessage() As String

    Return "This is the first message coming from the " +
            "FirstMessage method of the MessageClass."

  End Function

  Public Function SecondMessage() As String

    Return "This is the second message coming from the " +
            "SecondMessage method of the MessageClass."

  End Function

End Class
```
Code 12.10 (MessageClass.vb file)

8. Now switch to Form1.cs file using the Tabs located at the top of the editor window:

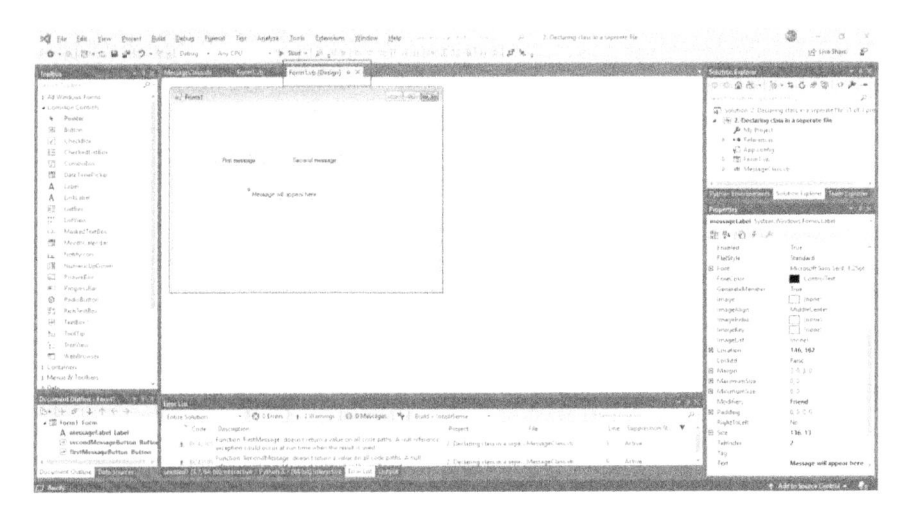

Figure 12.12. Switching back to Form1.vb file

9. We'll now create the event handlers of the Buttons. Double-click the Buttons for this and then create two objects named **firstObject** and **secondObject**, respectively as follows:

```
Public Class Form1
  Private Sub FirstMessageButton_Click(sender As Object, e As EventArgs) Handles firstMessageButton.Click

    Dim firstObject As MessageClass = New MessageClass()

  End Sub

  Private Sub SecondMessageButton_Click(sender As Object, e As EventArgs) Handles secondMessageButton.Click

    Dim secondObject As MessageClass = New MessageClass()

  End Sub
End Class
```
Code 12.11 (Form1.vb file)

Now, we can call FirstMessage() or SecondMessage() method of firstObject and firstObject. We will call FirstMessage() and SecondMessage(), respectively and assign their return values to the Text property of the **messageLabel** as follows:

```
Public Class Form1
  Private Sub FirstMessageButton_Click(sender As Object, e As EventArgs) Handles firstMessageButton.Click

    Dim firstObject As MessageClass = New MessageClass()
        messageLabel.Text = firstObject.FirstMessage()

  End Sub

  Private Sub SecondMessageButton_Click(sender As Object, e As EventArgs) Handles secondMessageButton.Click

     Dim secondObject As MessageClass = New MessageClass()
        messageLabel.Text = secondObject.SecondMessage()

  End Sub

End Class
```
Code 12.12

As it is seen from this code snippet, we declared objects from a class that is written in a different file and then we called the required methods as needed. The whole Form1.vb and MessageClass.vb files are also given below for your convenience:

```vbnet
Public Class Form1
    Private Sub FirstMessageButton_Click(sender As Object, e As EventArgs) Handles firstMessageButton.Click

        Dim firstObject As MessageClass = New MessageClass()
        messageLabel.Text = firstObject.FirstMessage()

    End Sub

    Private Sub SecondMessageButton_Click(sender As Object, e As EventArgs) Handles secondMessageButton.Click

        Dim secondObject As MessageClass = New MessageClass()
        messageLabel.Text = secondObject.SecondMessage()

    End Sub
End Class
```
Code 12.13 – Form1.vb file

```vbnet
Public Class MessageClass

   Public Function FirstMessage() As String

      Return "This is the first message coming from the " +
             "FirstMessage method of the MessageClass."

   End Function

   Public Function SecondMessage() As String

      Return "This is the second message coming from the " +
             "SecondMessage method of the MessageClass."

   End Function

End Class
```
Code 12.14 – MessageClass.vb file

CHAPTER 12. CLASSES AND OBJECTS

10. Build and run the project. The Text of the Label will be changed according to the clicked Button. FirstMessage() or SecondMessage() method will be called which will display the first message or the second message on the Label:

Figure 12.13. The first message is shown on the Label using the string returned from the FirstMessage() method

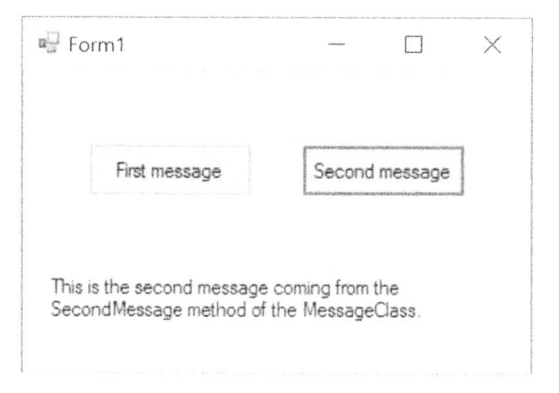

Figure 12.14. The second message is shown on the Label using the string returned from the SecondMessage() method

12.4. Constructor Methods

Constructor methods are special methods which are executed when an instance of a class (i.e. an object) is created. All classes have their own default constructor in the background even if we don't declare one. The constructor method of a class is executed only once when an object is

317

created. The primary duties of constructor classes are the allocation of the memory for member variables and initialization of these variables.

The name of constructor classes should have the same name as the class. Consider how we have created the firstObject object from the MessageClass in the previous example (from Code 12.13):

```
Dim firstObject As MessageClass = New MessageClass()
```
Code 12.15

In this code line, we created an instance of the MessageClass: the object named firstObject. We used the new keyword followed by the constructor method MessageClass() for this aim.

Although all classes have default invisible constructor methods automatically as in this example, we can also explicitly declare a constructor method primarily for passing parameters to member variables.

We can declare constructor methods just like usual method declarations but having the same name as the class.

It is worth noting that a class may have multiple constructor methods which allow different ways of passing parameters to member variables.

Let's develop a small project where we will pass values to member variables using constructor methods.

1. Create a new VB.NET project.
2. Add two TextBoxes and a Button on the form.
3. Set the Names and of the TextBoxes as **input1** and **input2**.
4. Set the Name and Text of the Button as **showButton** and **Show**, respectively. The form will look as follows:

CHAPTER 12. CLASSES AND OBJECTS

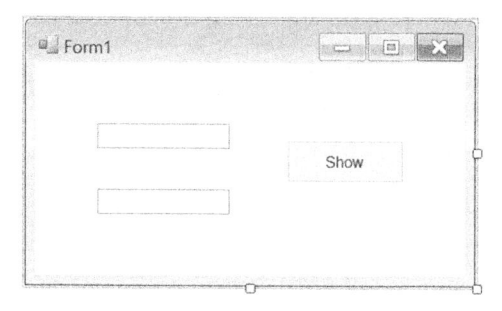

Figure 12.15. Layout of the form

5. Right-click somewhere empty on the form and click View Code as we did before to open Form1.vb in the editor.
6. We will insert our class inside the Form1.cs file as it was done in Subsection 12.2. Declare our custom class named ShowText in Form1.vb file as below:

```
Public Class ShowText

End Class
```
Code 12.16

Remember that we declare classes below the Form1 class in Form1.vb file.

7. **The constructor method(s) of a class is named as** New() **as shown below.** Let's declare two different constructor methods. One of them will take a single string parameter while the other will take two. In the first constructor, we will display a message box showing the passed string while the second constructor class will show the concatenated string made of its parameters in a message box. We can declare these constructor methods as follows:

```
Public Class ShowText

    Public memberString1, memberString2 As String
    Private input1Text As String

    Public Sub New(passedString1 As String)

        memberString1 = passedString1
```

319

```
            MessageBox.Show(memberString1)

    End Sub

    Public Sub New(passedString1 As String, passedString2 As String)
        memberString1 = passedString1
        memberString2 = passedString2
        MessageBox.Show(memberString1 + "-" + memberString2)
    End Sub

End Class
```
Code 12.17

- Our class has two fields named memberString1 and memberString2. These variables are not initialized during declaration.
- In the first constructor method, the passed string is assigned to the first member variable memberString1 and then shown in a message box.
- In the second constructor method, two string variables are passed and then these are assigned to memberString1 and memberString2. Then they are shown in a message box together with a hyphen between them.
- Remember that constructor methods are executed only once when an object is created using them. Therefore either of these message boxes will be displayed when an object is created from this class using one of these constructor methods.
8. Let's return to the form and then double-click the Button to create its click event. We'll take the Texts entered in the TextBoxes and use them in constructor methods for creating two different objects as follows:

```
Private Sub ShowButton_Click(sender As Object, e As EventArgs) Handles showButton.Click
    Dim input1Text As String = input1.Text
    Dim input2Text As String = input2.Text
    Dim object1 As ShowText = New ShowText(input1Text)
    Dim object2 As ShowText = New ShowText(input1Text, input2Text)
    End Sub
```
Code 12.18

CHAPTER 12. CLASSES AND OBJECTS

The constructor method with single parameter is utilized when creating `object1` and the constructor method with double parameter is used for creating `object2`. Therefore, the respective code lines in these constructors (Code 12.17) will be executed one after another.

9. Build and run the project. The program will be shown as follows:

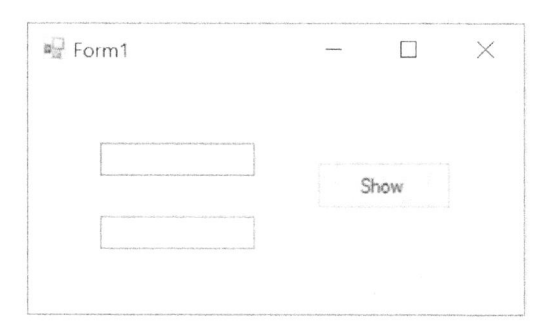

Figure 12.16. The program window

When we enter two strings to the TextBoxes and click the **Show** Button, `object1` and `object2` will be created using the two constructor methods we declared inside the class block. Then, the respective message boxes will be displayed in order during the creation of the objects as shown in Figure 12.17 and 12.18.

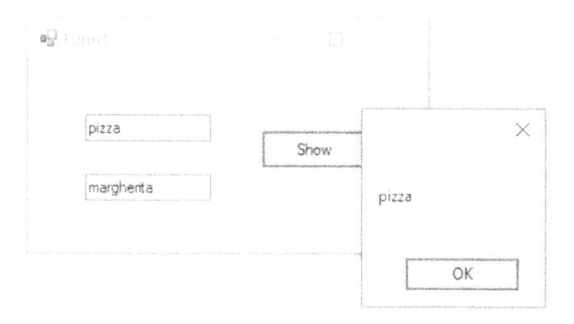

Figure 12.17. The first message box displayed during the creation of `object1`

321

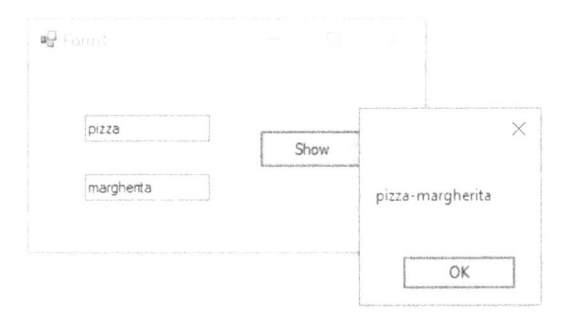

Figure 12.18. The second message box displayed during the creation of object2

It is worth emphasizing that we can declare as many constructor methods as we want provided that they have different number/type of input parameters.

12.5. Property Structures

We can send and read value from a class using **property** structures. There are two blocks in a property structure: **set** and **get**. The set block sets a variable while the get block reads the value of the **same** variable. The template of the typical property structure is as follows:

```
Property property_name As property_type

    Get

        return code; // The value of the property read here
    End Get

    Set

        code = value;   // The value of the property set here

    End Set

End Property
```
Code 12.19

Let's use a property in a small project to learn their functions. We will calculate the factorial of a number entered in the TextBox and display the result in a message box.

CHAPTER 12. CLASSES AND OBJECTS

1. Create a new VB.NET project.
2. Add a TextBox and a Button on the form.
3. Set the Name of the TextBox as **inputNum**.
4. Set the Name and Text of the Button as **calcButton** and **Calculate**. The form layout will look as below:

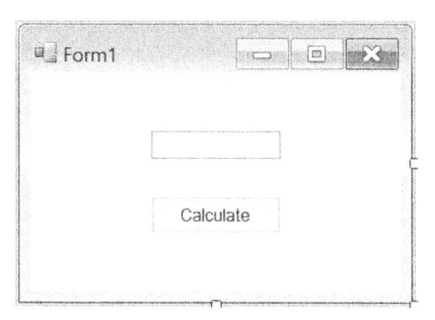

Figure 12.19. Layout of the form

5. Open the code view of Form1.vb as before. We'll create a class named FactCalc where we will do all our operations:

```
Public Class FactCalc

End Class
```
Code 12.20

6. The factorial of a number n is defined as 1.2.3...(n-1).n by the way. We need to hold the number and the factorial value in two variables in the class named n, factorial:

```
Public Class FactCalc

    Dim n, factorial As Integer

End Class
```
Code 12.21

7. We will declare a property in the class now. For this, we can write the Property keyword and press Tab twice as we did for other structures before. The property template will be placed automatically:

```
Public Class FactCalc

    Dim n, factorial As Integer
    Private newPropertyValue As String
    Public Property NewProperty() As String
        Get
            Return newPropertyValue
        End Get
        Set(ByVal value As String)
            newPropertyValue = value
        End Set
    End Property

End Class
```
Code 12.22

We can change the name of the property as we want. I'll name it as prop1. Moreover, since the value we will set (the number n) and get (the factorial) are integers, the type of the property will be changed as int.

```
Public Class FactCalc

    Dim n, factorial As Integer
    Private newPropertyValue As String
    Public Property Prop1() As Integer
        Get
            Return newPropertyValue
        End Get
        Set(ByVal value As Integer)
            newPropertyValue = value
        End Set
    End Property

End Class
```
Code 12.23

We will send the value of the input number to the property. Therefore, **we will set the *sent value to n* inside the set block**:

```
Public Class FactCalc

    Dim n, factorial As Integer
    Private newPropertyValue As String
    Public Property Prop1() As Integer
        Get
```

```
            Return newPropertyValue
        End Get
        Set(ByVal value As Integer)
            n = value
        End Set
    End Property

End Class
```
Code 12.24 (cont'd)

Then, we will make the factorial calculations inside the get block and **get the calculated factorial as the return value**:

```
Public Class FactCalc

    Dim n, factorial As Integer

    Public Property Prop1() As Integer
        Get
            factorial = 1
            For index = 1 To n
                factorial = factorial * index
            Next
            Return factorial
        End Get
        Set(ByVal value As Integer)
            n = value
        End Set
    End Property

End Class
```
Code 12.25

In summary, we when we send a value to a property, we assign this value to a variable in the set structure; when we need to output a value, we return it in the get structure.

8. Now, return to the Design view of Form1 and double-click the Button to create its event handler method. Firstly, take the value of the number entered in the TextBox, convert to integer and assign it to a variable:

BEGINNER'S GUIDE TO VISUAL BASIC.NET PROGRAMMING

```
Private Sub CalcButton_Click(sender As Object, e As
EventArgs) Handles calcButton.Click
        Dim eneterdNum As Integer =
Convert.ToInt32(inputNum.Text)
End Sub
```
Code 12.26

9. We will now create a new object as an instance of our class to use the property:

```
Private Sub CalcButton_Click(sender As Object, e As
EventArgs) Handles calcButton.Click
    Dim eneterdNum As Integer =
Convert.ToInt32(inputNum.Text)
    Dim calculate As FactCalc = New FactCalc()

End Sub
```
Code 12.27

10. We will send the value of enteredNum to the property using the code line **calculate.Prop1 = enteredNum** as follows:

```
Private Sub CalcButton_Click(sender As Object, e As
EventArgs) Handles calcButton.Click
    Dim enterdNum As Integer =
            Convert.ToInt32(inputNum.Text)
    Dim calculate As FactCalc = New FactCalc()
    calculate.Prop1 = enterdNum
End Sub
```
Code 12.28

We sent the entered number value to the Prop1 property by adding this line.

11. We will now read the result of the factorial using to code line
int factorialResult = calculate.prop1;:

```
Private Sub CalcButton_Click(sender As Object, e As
EventArgs) Handles calcButton.Click
    Dim enterdNum As Integer =
            Convert.ToInt32(inputNum.Text)
    Dim calculate As FactCalc = New FactCalc()
    calculate.Prop1 = enterdNum
    Dim factorialResult As Integer = calculate.Prop1
```

```
    End Sub
```
Code 12.29 (cont'd)

Note that we read the return value from the get block of Prop1 and assigned it to a newly created integer variable **factorialResult**.

12. We will now display the factorial result in a message box:

```
Private Sub CalcButton_Click(sender As Object, e As
EventArgs) Handles calcButton.Click
    Dim enterdNum As Integer =
            Convert.ToInt32(inputNum.Text)
    Dim calculate As FactCalc = New FactCalc()
    calculate.Prop1 = enterdNum
    Dim factorialResult As Integer = calculate.Prop1
    MessageBox.Show("Factorial is: " +
                    factorialResult.ToString())
End Sub
```
Code 12.30

The whole Form1.cs is also given as follows:

```
Public Class Form1
    Private Sub CalcButton_Click(sender As Object, e As
EventArgs) Handles calcButton.Click
        Dim enterdNum As Integer =
Convert.ToInt32(inputNum.Text)
        Dim calculate As FactCalc = New FactCalc()
        calculate.Prop1 = enterdNum
        Dim factorialResult As Integer = calculate.Prop1
        MessageBox.Show("Factorial is: " +
                        factorialResult.ToString())
    End Sub
End Class

Public Class FactCalc

    Dim n, factorial As Integer

    Public Property Prop1() As Integer
        Get
            factorial = 1
            For index = 1 To n
                factorial = factorial * index
            Next
            Return factorial
```

```
            End Get
            Set(ByVal value As Integer)
                n = value
            End Set
        End Property

End Class
```
Code 12.31 (cont'd)

13. Build and run the project. The program window will appear as follows:

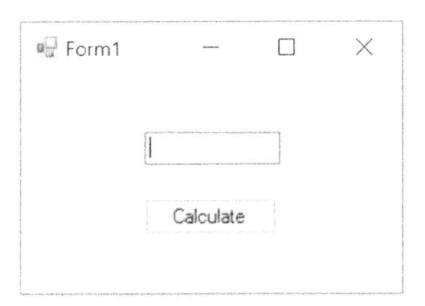

Figure 12.20. The program window

The program calculates the factorial as expected:

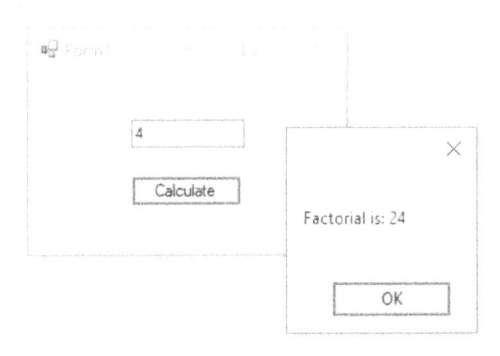

Figure 12.21. The factorial calculation result

We can use as many properties as we need. They are handy when we need to handle large number of variables in a class.

We have learned classes and its properties in this chapter. We are now able to declare and use our own classes providing a better organization of our code. In the next chapter, we will learn and practice frequently used methods of popular built-in classes of VB.NET. Therefore, it is a good time to have a coffee break and relax with a good music for now.

Chapter 13

FREQUENTLY USED CLASSES IN VB.NET

We have been using various methods in our projects since the beginning of this book related to events, variables and operations. We also learned creating our custom methods and classes in previous chapters. In this chapter, we will study frequently used methods of popular built-in classes that are very useful for shortening programming time in VB.NET application development.

13.1. The String Class

As we have learned before, strings are the collections consisting of unicode characters. There are basically two classes that enable us to manipulate strings: the String Class and the StringBuilder class.

The first class we will use for manipulating string objects is the **String** class. String class is located under the System namespace of .NET framework therefore ready for use in our code when we create a new VB.NET project. In other words, we do not need to add a new namespace to use the methods provided by the String class. Frequently used methods of the String class are summarized in Table 13.1:

Method	Template	Explanation
Copy()	new_string=String.Copy(string_to_be_copied)	Copies the string to another one
Empty()	string_to_be_cleared.Empty()	Clears the contents of the string
Join()	string_to _be_populated =String.Join(separator, array)	Copies the elements of the array into the string using the specified separator character

Method	Template	Explanation
Split()	string_to_be_ splitted.Split(separator)	Splits the string according to the separator character
IndexOf()	string_name. IndexOf(searched_character)	Returns the index of the searched character in the string
SubString()	string_name.SubString(start, length)	Returns the substring specified by the start index and length
ToString()	variable_toString()	Converts the variable to string
Concat()	String.Concat(string1, string2)	Combines string1 and string2

Table 13.1. Frequently used methods of the String class (cont'd)

We will now use these methods in an example project.

1. Create a new VB.NET project.
2. Add a three TextBoxes and five Buttons on the form.
3. Set the Names of the TextBoxes as **string1**, **string2** and **output**.
4. Set the Names of the Buttons as **copyButton**, **concatButton**, **substringButton**, **splitButton** and **clearButton**.
5. Set the Text properties of the Buttons as **Copy**, **Concatenate**, **Substring**, **Split** and **Clear**, respectively. The form will look as follows:

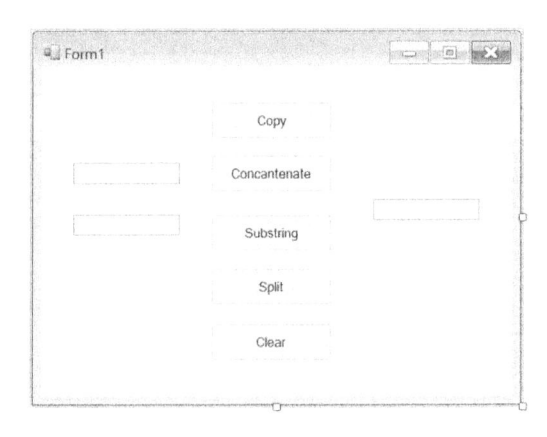

Figure 13.1. The form layout

5. Double-click each of the Buttons to create their event handler methods. We will implement the associated operations in these event handlers.
6. We will use the Copy() method to copy the string entered in the input1 TextBox to a new string and then assign it to the Text of the output TextBox in the first Button's event handler:

```
Private Sub CopyButton_Click(sender As Object, e As
EventArgs) Handles copyButton.Click

    Dim outputString As String = String.Copy(string1.Text)
    output.Text = outputString

End Sub
```
Code 13.1

7. We will concatenate the strings entered in input1 and input2 TextBoxes and show the result in output TextBox in the second Button's event handler:

```
Private Sub ConcatButton_Click(sender As Object, e As
EventArgs) Handles concatButton.Click

    Dim outputString As String =
        String.Concat(string1.Text, string2.Text)
    output.Text = outputString

End Sub
```
Code 13.2

8. In the third Button's event handler method, the first three characters of the Text of the input1 TextBox will be assigned to a new string, which will then be displayed in the output TextBox:

```
Private Sub SubstringButton_Click(sender As Object, e As
EventArgs) Handles substringButton.Click

    Dim outputString As String = string1.Text.Substring(0, 3)
    output.Text = outputString

End Sub
```

Code 13.3

9. The input string will be split by taking the hyphens (if any) as references and the resultant strings will be displayed in message boxes in the fourth function's event handler method:

```
Private Sub SplitButton_Click(sender As Object, e As
EventArgs) Handles splitButton.Click

    Dim outputString() As String = string1.Text.Split("-")
    For Each item In outputString
        MessageBox.Show(item)
    Next

End Sub
```
Code 13.4

Note that the result of the Split() method will be an array of split strings therefore assigned to a string array. Then, the elements of this array are displayed one by one in the message box inside the foreach loop.

10. Finally, the event handler of the **Clear** Button will be implemented. We will empty the string taken from the input1 TextBox and then display it in the output TextBox.

```
Private Sub ClearButton_Click(sender As Object, e As
EventArgs) Handles clearButton.Click

    Dim input1String As String = string1.Text
    input1String = String.Empty

End Sub
```
Code 13.5

11. We implemented the methods of all Buttons and ready to build and run the project. The following program window will appear:

CHAPTER 13. FREQUENTLY USED CLASSES IN VB.NET

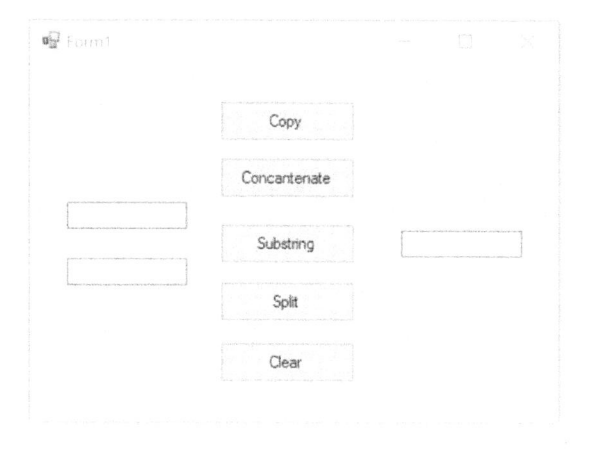

Figure 13.2. The program window

Let's enter two strings in the input TextBoxes and click the Copy Button. The string of input1 TextBox will be copied in a new string and then this will be displayed in the output TextBox:

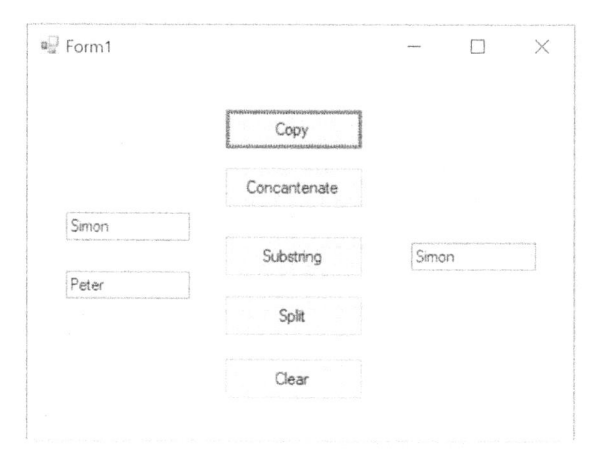

Figure 13.3. The copied string shown in the output TextBox

When we click the Concatenate Button, the two input strings will be concatenated and displayed at the output:

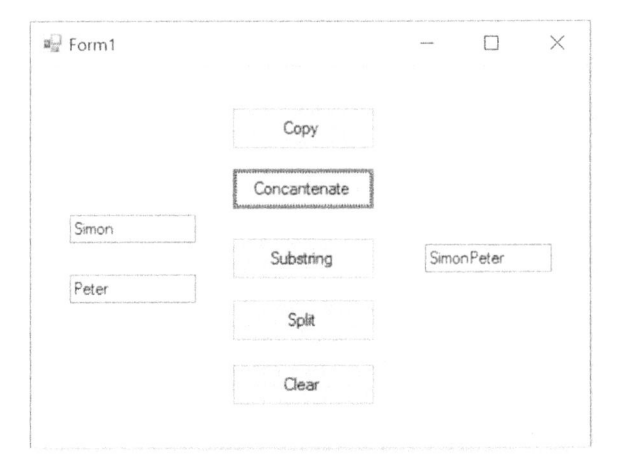

BEGINNER'S GUIDE TO VISUAL BASIC.NET PROGRAMMING

Figure 13.4. Concatenated strings at the output

Then, click the Substring Button to see the substring composed of the first three characters of input1 at the output:

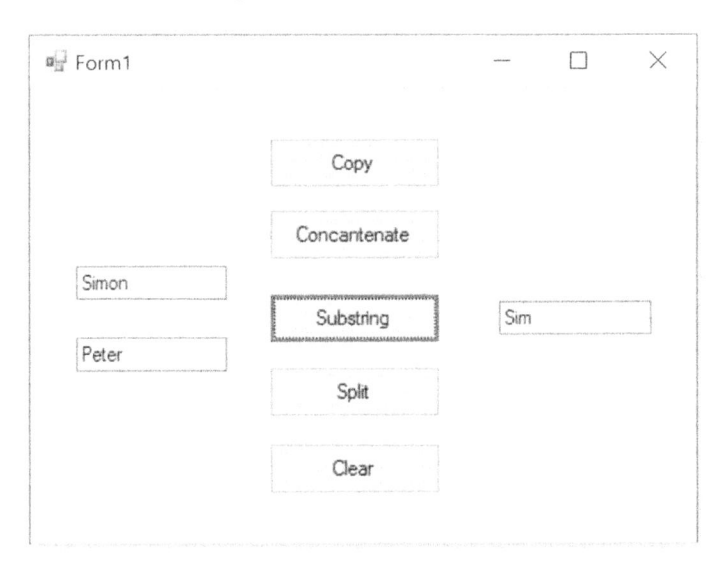

Figure 13.5. The substring displayed at the output

In order to test the Split Button, we need a string with a hyphen in the input1 TextBox. Therefore I modified it as Simon-Peter and then clicked the Split Button. The string is split with the hyphen as the separator and the split parts are displayed in message boxes:

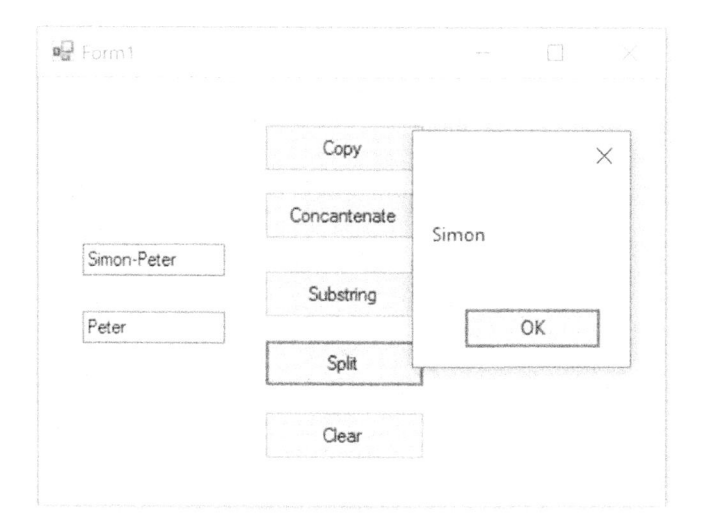

Figure 13.6. The first part of the split string

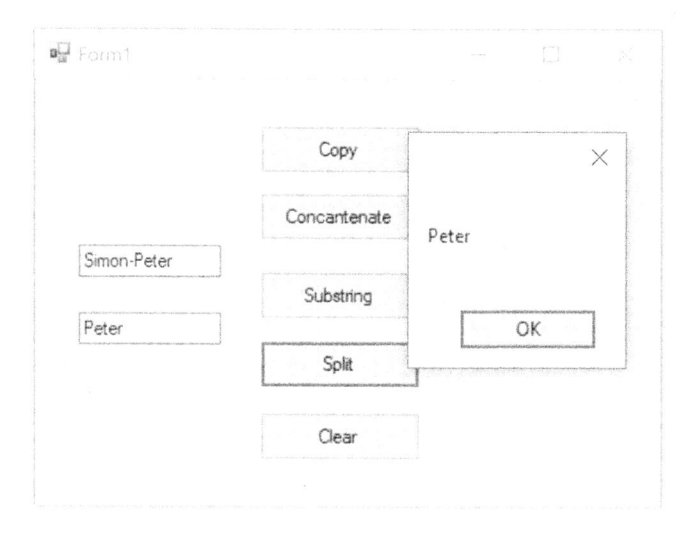

Figure 13.7. The second part of the split string

Finally, when we click the Clear Button, the string will be cleared and assigned to the output TextBox. Since the string is empty, the output TextBox will be empty too:

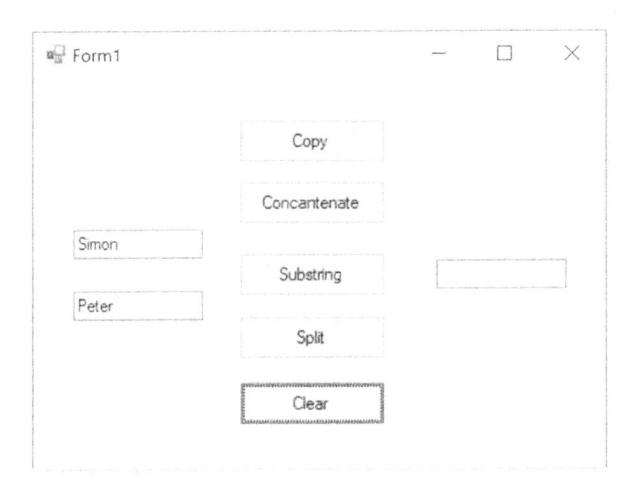

Figure 13.8. Emptied string assigned to the output

13.2. The StringBuilder Class

StringBuilder class also has various methods to operate on strings. However it enables to do these operations faster compared to the usual String class for large number of string elements. We need to add System.Text namespace by the code line `Imports System.Text` in order to use the methods provided by the StringBuilder class in our project.

The popular methods of the StringBuilder class include the following:

Method	Template	Explanation
Insert()	StringBuilder_object.Insert(index, data_to_be_added, number_of_additions)	Adds the data starting from the specified index
Remove()	StringBuilder_object.Remove(index, length)	Removes the specified data from the object
Replace()	StringBuilder_object.Replace(former_data, newer_data, index, number_of_replacements)	Copies the elements of the array into the string using the specified separator character
Clear()	StringBuilder_object.Clear()	Empties the object
Append()	StringBuilder_object.Append(data_to_be_added)	Appends the specified data into the object

Table 13.2. Frequently used methods of the StringBuilder class

We will now use these methods in a small project to have some practice.

1. Create a new VB.NET project.
2. Add four Buttons and a TextBox on the form.
3. Set the Texts of the Buttons as **Create**, **Clear**, **Insert** and **Remove**, respectively.
4. Set the Names of the Buttons as **createButton**, **clearButton**, **insertButton** and **removeButton**, respectively.
5. Set the Name of the TextBox as **displayTextBox**. The layout of the form will look as Figure 13.9.
6. Double-click each Button to create their event handler methods.
7. We will create our StringBuilder object and append a string to it in the Create Button's event handler as follows:

```
Dim sbObject As StringBuilder = New StringBuilder()

Private Sub CreateButton_Click(sender As Object, e As EventArgs) Handles createButton.Click

        sbObject.Append("John")
        displayTextBox.Text = sbObject.ToString()

End Sub
```
Code 13.6

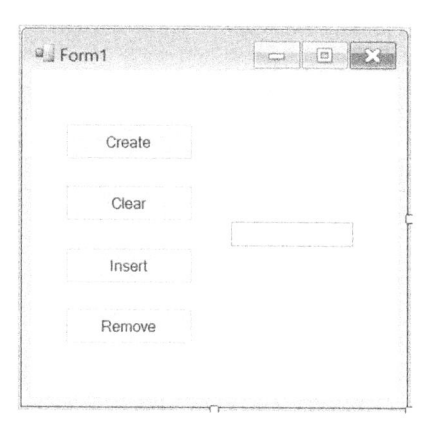

Figure 13.9. The layout of the form

Note that we need to include the code line `using System.Text` in our Form1.vb file for being able to use StringBuilder class.

In the code line just above the handler method, a StringBuilder object named sbObject is created. Note that this code line is in the global area for being able to access sbobject from anywhere in the code. It is created by the StringBuilder() constructor method which means that this object will be empty (i.e. it won't contain any string) at the time of declaration.

In the next code line, we append (add) a string ("John") to this StringBuilder object.

In the last line, the contents of the sbobject are converted to a usual string using the ToString() method for displaying it in the output TextBox.

8. The contents of the event handler method of the Clear Button will utilize the Clear() method to clear the contents of the sbobject:

```
Private Sub ClearButton_Click(sender As Object, e As
EventArgs) Handles clearButton.Click

    sbObject.Clear()
    displayTextBox.Text = sbObject.ToString()

End Sub
```
Code 13.7

The contents of the sbObject is emptied and then displayed in the output TextBox in this event handler method.

9. We will insert a string at the specified index of the sbObject in the Insert Button's event handler method. We'll use the Insert() method for this aim:

```
Private Sub InsertButton_Click(sender As Object, e As
EventArgs) Handles insertButton.Click

    sbObject.Insert(4, "+")
    displayTextBox.Text = sbObject.ToString()

End Sub
```
Code 13.8

CHAPTER 13. FREQUENTLY USED CLASSES IN VB.NET

We add the "+" string at index 4 of the sbobject and then display its contents in the output TextBox.

10. Finally, we will populate the Remove Button's event handler. We will use the Remove() method as follows:

```
Private Sub RemoveButton_Click(sender As Object, e As
EventArgs) Handles removeButton.Click

    sbObject.Remove(1, 1)
    displayTextBox.Text = sbObject.ToString()

End Sub
```
Code 13.9

11. Build and run the project. The program will appear as follows:

Figure 13.10. The program window

Now, click Create Button to create the StringBuilder object, append the given string and then display in the output TextBox:

341

Figure 13.11. The content of the StringBuilder object displayed in the TextBox

Click Clear Button to clear the contents of the sbobject using the Clear() method:

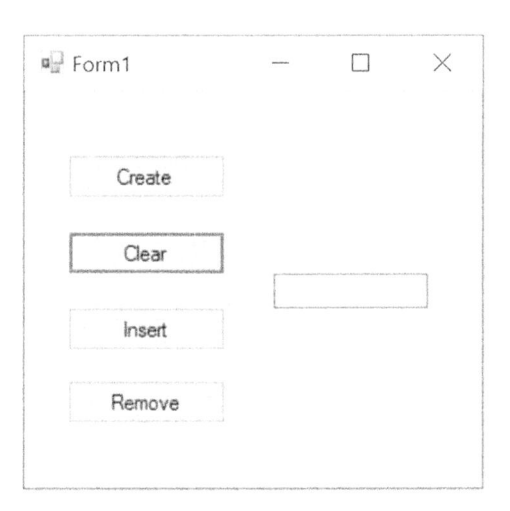

Figure 13.12. Cleared StringBuilder object displayed at the output

Now, let's click the Create Button again to append the string "John" to sbObject. And then click the Insert Button to insert "+" string at its 4th index:

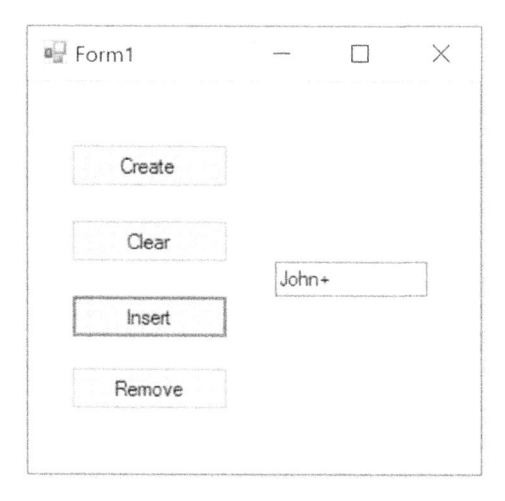

Figure 13.13. The "+" string added at the 4th index

Finally, click the Clear, Create and then Remove Buttons to remove the element with index 1 from the StringBuilder object:

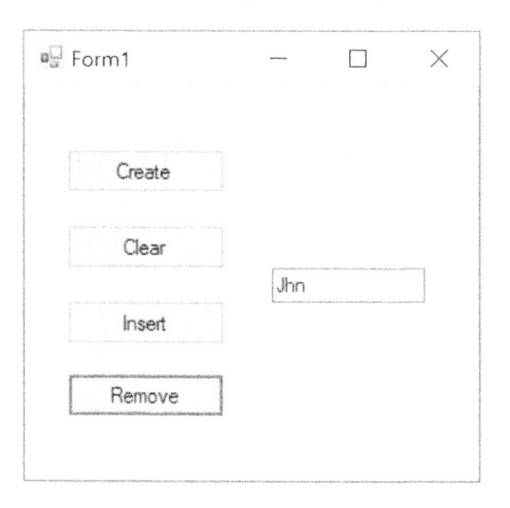

Figure 13.14. The string with length 1 at index 1 (i.e. the "o" character) removed from the StringBuilder object

13.3. The Math Class

The Math class provides necessary methods for performing mathematical operations. Frequently used methods of this class are shown as follows:

Method	Template	Explanation

Abs()	`Math.Abs(number)`	Returns the absolute value of the given number
Ceiling()	`Math.Ceiling(number)`	Returns the smallest integer greater or equal to the given number
Cos()	`Math.Cos(number)`	Returns the cosine of the given number
Exp()	`Math.Exp(number)`	Returns e^{number} where e is the base of the natural logarithm (e=2.71...)
Floor()	`Math.Floor(number)`	Returns the largest integer lower or equal to the given number
Log()	`Math.Log(number)`	Returns the natural logarithm of the given number
Log10()	`Math.Log10(number)`	Returns the base-10 logarithm pf the given number
Max()	`Math.Max(number1, number2)`	Returns the greater of number1 and number2
Min()	`Math.Min(number1, number2)`	Returns the smaller of number1 and number2
Pow()	`Math.Pow(number1, number2)`	Returns $number1^{number2}$
Round()	`Math.Round(number)`	Rounds the given number to the closest integer
Sign()	`Math.Sign(number)`	Returns the sign of the given number
Sin()	`Math.Sin(number)`	Returns the sine of the given number
Sqrt()	`Math.Sqrt(number)`	Returns the square root of the given number
Tan()	`Math.Tan(number)`	Returns the tangent of the number

Table 13.3. Frequently used methods of the Math class

We'll now develop a small project in which we will use some of these methods.

1. Create a new VB.NET project.
2. Add three TextBoxes, three Labels and five Buttons on the form.
3. Set the Names of the TextBoxes as **input1**, **input2**, **output**.
4. Set the Texts of the Labels as **x=**, **y=** and **Output=**.
5. Set the Names of the Buttons as **sinButton**, **ceilingButton**, **maxButton**, **PowButton** and **piButton**.

6. Set the Texts of the Buttons as **Sin(x)**, **Ceiling(x)**, **Max(x,y)**, **x^y** and **Pi number**. Please position these controls so that the form looks as follows:

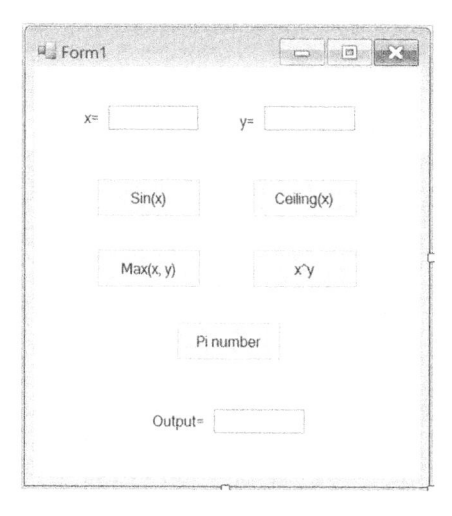

Figure 13.15. The layout of the form

7. Double-click the Buttons to create their default event handler methods.
8. When the user clicks Sin(x), the value of sin(x) will be written to the output TextBox. Therefore we perform the required operation in the Click event handler method as below:

```
Private Sub SinButton_Click(sender As Object, e As EventArgs) Handles sinButton.Click

    Dim x As Double = Convert.ToDouble(input1.Text)
    output.Text = Math.Sin(x).ToString()

End Sub
```
Code 13.10

In this event handler method, we firstly obtain the double type representation of the number entered in the first TextBox and then display the value of sin(x) in the output TextBox by the second code line.

345

BEGINNER'S GUIDE TO VISUAL BASIC.NET PROGRAMMING

9. We obtain the ceiling(x) in a similar way:

```
Private Sub CeilingButton_Click(sender As Object, e As
EventArgs) Handles ceilingButton.Click

    Dim x As Double = Convert.ToDouble(input1.Text)
    output.Text = Math.Ceiling(x).ToString()

End Sub
```
Code 13.11

10. We will use the double type representations of both x and y inputs to calculate the max(x, y) function as follows:

```
Private Sub MaxButton_Click(sender As Object, e As
EventArgs) Handles maxButton.Click

    Dim x As Double = Convert.ToDouble(input1.Text)
    Dim y As Double = Convert.ToDouble(input2.Text)
    output.Text = Math.Max(x, y).ToString()

End Sub
```
Code 13.12

11. Similarly, the x^y, i.e. x^y will be calculated via the pow(x, y) method:

```
Private Sub PowButton_Click(sender As Object, e As
EventArgs) Handles powButton.Click

    Dim x As Double = Convert.ToDouble(input1.Text)
    Dim y As Double = Convert.ToDouble(input2.Text)
    output.Text = Math.Pow(x, y).ToString()

End Sub
```
Code 13.13

12. Finally, we will display the pi (π) number existing in the Math class when the Pi Button is clicked:

```
Private Sub PiButton_Click(sender As Object, e As
EventArgs) Handles piButton.Click
    Dim pi As Double = Math.PI
    output.Text = pi.ToString()
End Sub
```
Code 13.14

CHAPTER 13. FREQUENTLY USED CLASSES IN VB.NET

13. We can now build and run the project. The program window will appear as in Figure 13.16. Let's enter some numbers for x and y TextBoxes. I entered 2 and 4, respectively. Firstly, click the Sin(x) Button to calculate sin(2) as shown in Figure 13.17.

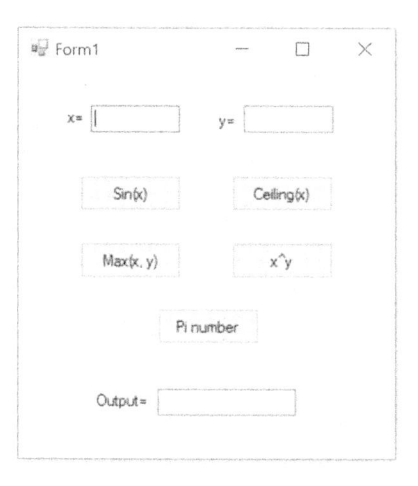

Figure 13.16. The program window

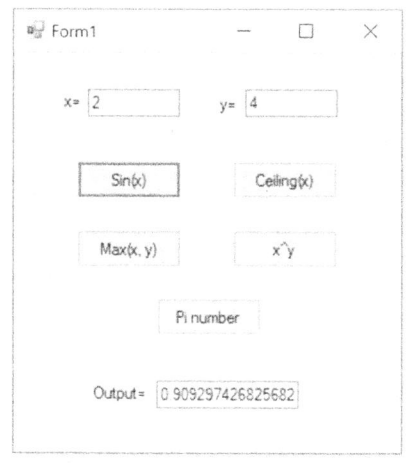

Figure 13.17. The value of sin(2) is calculated and displayed

Then, click the Ceiling(x) Button and then the smallest integer greater or equal to 2 (which is again 2) will be shown in the output TextBox as in Figure 13.18.

347

BEGINNER'S GUIDE TO VISUAL BASIC.NET PROGRAMMING

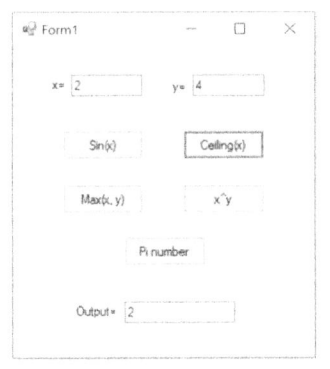

Figure 13.18. The value of ceiling(2) which is 2 is displayed at the output

Then, click the Max(x, y) Button to display the greater of 2 and 4 at the output:

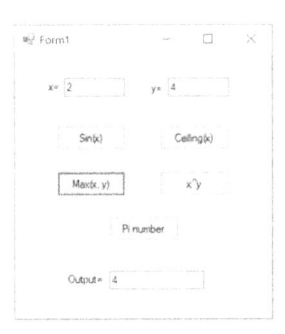

Figure 13.19. Maximum of 2 and 4 is shown at the output TextBox

Pow(2, 4) which is 24 is calculated when the x^y Button is clicked:

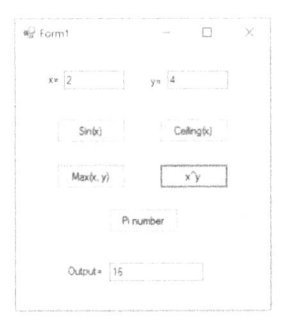

Figure 13.20. The value of 2^4 shown at the output

Finally, click the Pi number Button to display the π number:

CHAPTER 13. FREQUENTLY USED CLASSES IN VB.NET

Figure 13.21. The π number taken from the Math class

We have studied frequently used classes and their methods in this chapter. In the next chapter, we will learn detecting and handling runtime errors.

Chapter 14

HANDLING ERRORS

When an error occurs during runtime, the program stops responding and possibly crashes after a short time. There are various reasons of these errors. For example, imagine that we have a TextBox in which the user is supposed to enter an integer value. Remember how we convert the entered string to an integer variable: we take the Text property of the TextBox, convert to integer and assign it to an integer variable:

```
Dim enteredValue As Integer = Convert.ToInt32(TextBox1.Text)
```
Code 14.1

If the user enters an integer value to the TextBox, all is fine. But what if he/she inputs a floating point value such as 4.35? The method `ToInt32()` will not be able to convert 4.35 to an integer and bingo! The program crashes. This is a typical example of type conversion errors which may occur in most programs. Luckily, we have tools to handle errors to prevent crashes. We will learn about these tools in this chapter which enables us to catch errors and implement required operations to prevent crashes.

14.1. The Try-Catch Structure

The template of this structure is as follows:

```
Try
    //Code with possible error source
Catch ex As Exception
    //Code to be executed when an error occurs above
End Try
```
Code 14.2

We place our main code, which we think may be a source of error, inside the **Try block**. Then the program tries to execute this code. If the code executes without an error, everything is OK and our program exits the try-catch structure. However, if an error occurs during the execution of the code written inside the try block, then the code inside the **Catch block** is executed. We generally display a message box in the catch block to inform the user about the reason of the error.

Let's use the try-catch structure in a simple example.

1. Create a new VB.NET project.
2. Add two TextBoxes and a Button on the form.
3. Set the Name properties of the TextBoxes as **input** and **output**.
4. Set the Name and Text of the Button as **multiplyButton** and **Multiply by 2**. The layout of the form will be as follows:

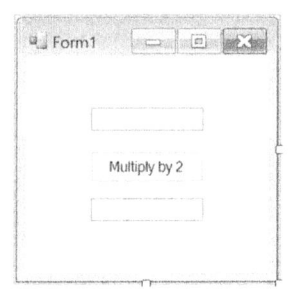

Figure 14.1. Layout of the form

5. Create the Click event handler method of the Button by double-clicking it. And then add the required simple code to take the number from the input TextBox, multiply by 2 and then display the result on the output TextBox as we learned before:

```
Private Sub MultiplyButton_Click(sender As Object, e As
EventArgs) Handles multiplyButton.Click

    Dim inputNum As Integer = Convert.ToInt32(input.Text)
    Dim result As Integer = inputNum * 2
    output.Text = result.ToString()

End Sub
```
Code 14.3

CHAPTER 14. HANDLING ERRORS

6. Build and run the project. When we input an integer and click the Button, the multiplication result will be displayed without a problem as expected:

Figure 14.2. Multiplication of an integer without a problem

7. What if we enter a floating point number to the input TextBox? Let's try it by entering 7.5:

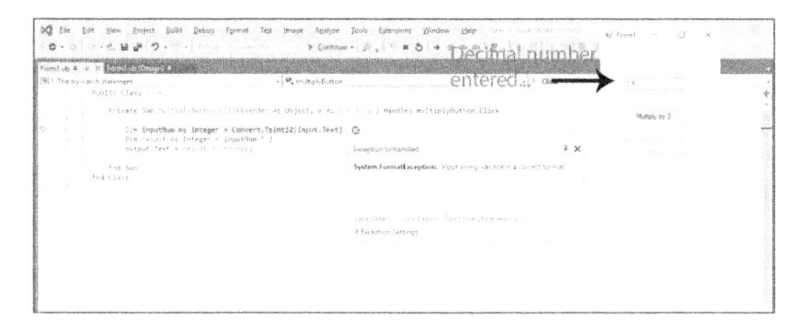

Figure 14.3. Crashed program with a decimal input

The program crashed and Visual Studio has shown the error in the code editor saying that "Input string was not in a correct format". Since the program has crashed, we cannot quit it by clicking the cross button at its top right. Instead, we have to close using the usual stop button in Visual Studio. It is good that Visual Studio shows the error and we can quit the crashed program from it. However if the user runs this program by double-clicking on it outside of Visual Studio, he/she will not have these opportunities. He/she will have to go to the task manager and manually try to close the program. Moreover, the program will not show any clue

353

about the reason of the error. This is where try-catch statement comes into play.

8. We will cover our code lines inside the try-catch block by modifying the event handler method of Code 14.3 as follows:

```
Private Sub MultiplyButton_Click(sender As Object, e As
EventArgs) Handles multiplyButton.Click

  Try
    Dim inputNum As Integer = Convert.ToInt32(input.Text)
    Dim result As Integer = inputNum * 2
    output.Text = result.ToString()

  Catch ex As Exception
    MessageBox.Show(ex.ToString())

  End Try

End Sub
```
Code 14.4

In this code, the program will try to do the required operation. If something fails, the error will be caught in the catch block. The exception object is ex which is an instance of Exception class. The information regarding the error is recorded in this object. Thanks to this, we can display the contents the error by the code line MessageBox.Show(ex.ToString()).

9. Build and run the project again. When we try to process a decimal number again, the program will not crash this time but catch the error and display information regarding the error in a message box as shown in Figure 14.4.

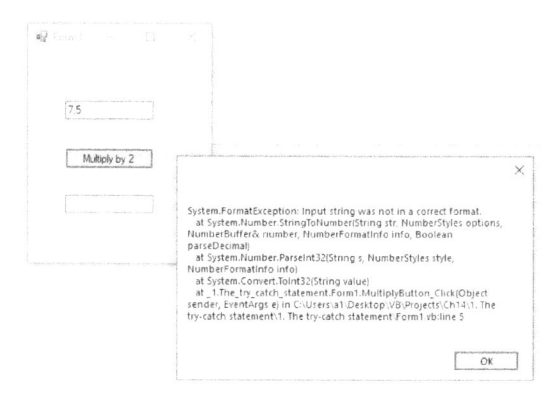

Figure 14.4. The exception (error) caught and displayed

Note that the program continues running normally after an error is caught. New numbers can be entered for multiplication.

14.2. The Try-Catch-Finally Structure

In the Try-Catch-Finally statements, there is a **Finally** block in addition to the Try and Catch blocks. The code inside the Finally block executes regardless of the error. In other words, the code lines in the Finally block runs in both error-free or erroneous execution cases of our main code written inside the Try block. The template of the Try-Catch-Finally block is as follows:

```
Try
    //Code with possible error source
Catch ex As Exception
    //Code to be executed when an error occurs above
Finally
    //Code to be executed regardless of the error
End Try
```

Code 14.5

The **Try-Catch-Finally** statements are used in cases where we have code lines to execute in the end of the program independent of errors. These cases include closing databases or closing opened files.

Let's modify our try-catch example and add the finally statement as follows:

```
Private Sub MultiplyButton_Click(sender As Object, e As
EventArgs) Handles multiplyButton.Click

    Try
      Dim inputNum As Integer = Convert.ToInt32(input.Text)
      Dim result As Integer = inputNum * 2
      output.Text = result.ToString()
    Catch ex As Exception
      MessageBox.Show(ex.ToString())
    Finally
      input.Clear()
      output.Clear()
      MessageBox.Show("TextBoxes are cleared")
    End Try

End Sub
```
Code 14.5

Build and run the project. The TextBoxes will be cleared and the corresponding message will be shown when we try to multiply either an integer or a decimal because the `finally` block will be executed in all cases:

Figure 14.5. The code inside the finally block is executed in both error-free and erroneous cases

The TextBoxes are cleared and the message box is displayed when we enter an integer (error-free case) or a decimal (erroneous case) to the input TextBox for multiplication.

14.3. The Throw Keyword

The `Throw` keyword enables us to throw a planned exception in the program. When an exception is thrown, it is caught by the Catch block as in the usual Try-Catch statements.

Let's try the `Throw` keyword in a sample project.

CHAPTER 14. HANDLING ERRORS

1. Create a new VB.NET project.
2. Add three TextBoxes and a Button on the form
3. Set the Names of TextBoxes as **input1**, **input2** and **output**.
4. Set the Name and Text of the Button as **divideButton** and **Divide**. The form will look as follows:

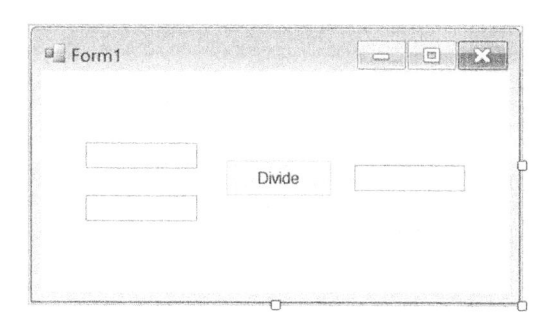

Figure 14.6. The layout of the form

5. Double-click the Button to create its event handler method. We will divide input1 to input2 and display the result in the output TextBox. We will use the try-catch structure for this as follows:

```
Private Sub DivideButton_Click(sender As Object, e As
EventArgs) Handles divideButton.Click

    Try
      Dim input1Num As Double = Convert.ToDouble(input1.Text)
      Dim input2Num As Double = Convert.ToDouble(input2.Text)
      Dim result As Double = input1Num / input2Num
      output.Text = result.ToString()
    Catch ex As Exception

    End Try

End Sub
```
Code 14.6

If input2Num is zero, then the division operation cannot be performed. We will check input2Num for this and throw a corresponding exception as follows:

357

```vbnet
Private Sub DivideButton_Click(sender As Object, e As
EventArgs) Handles divideButton.Click

  Try
    Dim input1Num As Double = Convert.ToDouble(input1.Text)
    Dim input2Num As Double = Convert.ToDouble(input2.Text)

    If input2Num = 0 Then
       Throw New System.Exception()
    End If

    Dim result As Double = input1Num / input2Num
    output.Text = result.ToString()
  Catch ex As Exception
    MessageBox.Show("Division to zero is not permitted")
  End Try

End Sub
```
Code 14.7

If input2Num is not zero, the division will take place as expected as in Figure 14.7. However if input2Num is zero, our exception will be thrown as in Figure 14.8.

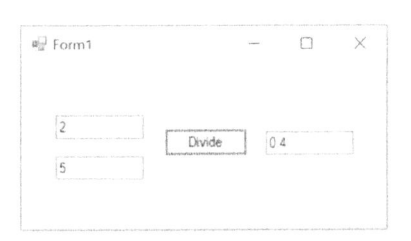

Figure 14.7. Division without an exception

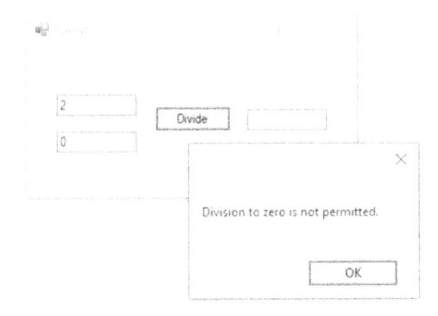

Figure 14.8. Exception thrown due to input2Num being zero

Note that in this way, we can display our custom exception message to the user instead of the default one.

We learned handling errors in this chapter. We are now ready to use databases in our VB.NET programs which will enable us to save data permanently. Let's take a break and have a cup of tea before continuing to the next chapter where we will study database operations.

Chapter 15

DATABASE CONNECTIONS USING ADO.NET

Databases are used for storing data in an organized fashion. We have not saved data in our programs until now. It means losing all the data when our program exits. When we need to store data permanently, we have the possibility to save digital data on the hard disk or a portable drive. If the data is small and unrelated, we can use simple file read/write operations as shown in the OpenFileDialog and SaveFileDialog projects in chapter 6. But if the data contains categorized information, it is better to use databases.

There are various database formats for different aims in the programming world. Databases that can be accessed from VB.NET programs include but not limited to Microsoft Access, Microsoft SQL Server and Oracle Database. We will cover connecting our programs to Access databases in this chapter.

There are various technologies enabling connection to databases from VB.NET such as DAO, ODBC and ADO.NET. Among these, ADO.NET (Activex Data Objects .NET) offers a simple interface for connecting, reading and writing to databases. We will learn utilizing ADO.NET components in this chapter. We need to add System.Data namespace to our project using the code line `Imports System.Data` in order to be able to use ADO.NET components.

15.1. Creating an Access Database

Microsoft Access comes inside the Microsoft Office suite. Access provides a relational database which is basically saved in an Access file. Access files can be read/written using both the Microsoft Access program itself and an external program written in VB.NET or another language which supports Access databases. The performance of Access is great for our application scale.

We must have the Access software installed on our computer to create an Access database for use in our VB.NET program. After the development phase, we will have the standalone program and the database file. We can then use our standalone program and the database file on a computer which doesn't have the Access software.

If you don't have the Access software on your computer at the moment, you can download a time-limited trial version of Microsoft Office from their official website at https://products.office.com/en/try for being able to create Access databases used in this chapter.

Let's now create our first Access database.

1. Select a folder where you want to create your Access database. I created a new folder on my Desktop called **databases**.
2. Open the folder you created and right-click to view the menu. Select **New → Microsoft Access Database** as shown below:

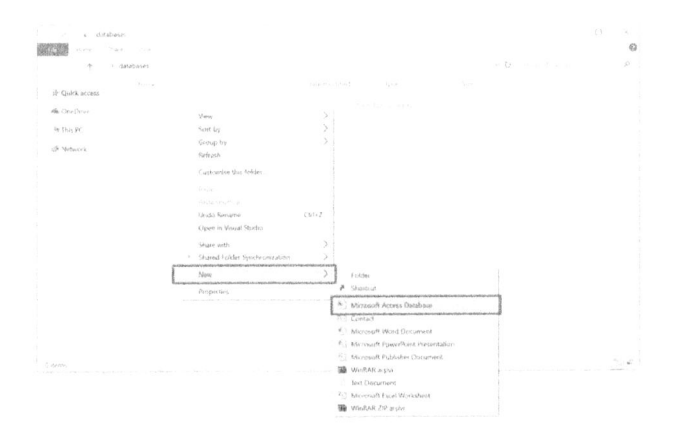

Figure 15.1. Creating a new database

CHAPTER 15. DATABASE CONNECTIONS USING ADO.NET

We will give a name to our database file. I named it as **firstDatabase**. The extension of Access database files are **accdb**. This extension may be displayed depending on your folder viewing options. If it is set to show the extensions, you'll see the database file in your folder as follows:

Figure 15.2. Our database file

3. Now, let's open our database file by double-clicking on it. Access will open the file but will not show its contents issuing a security warning:

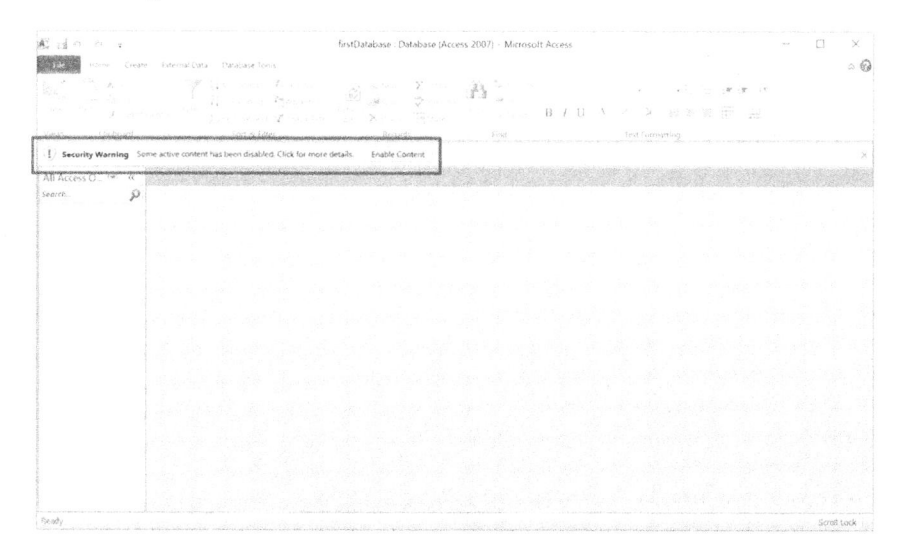

Figure 15.3. The security warning in Access

363

BEGINNER'S GUIDE TO VISUAL BASIC.NET PROGRAMMING

We are sure that this file is OK because we just created it. Therefore, click **Enable Content** to open the file.

4. The file is displayed as empty because we didn't create any tables in it yet:

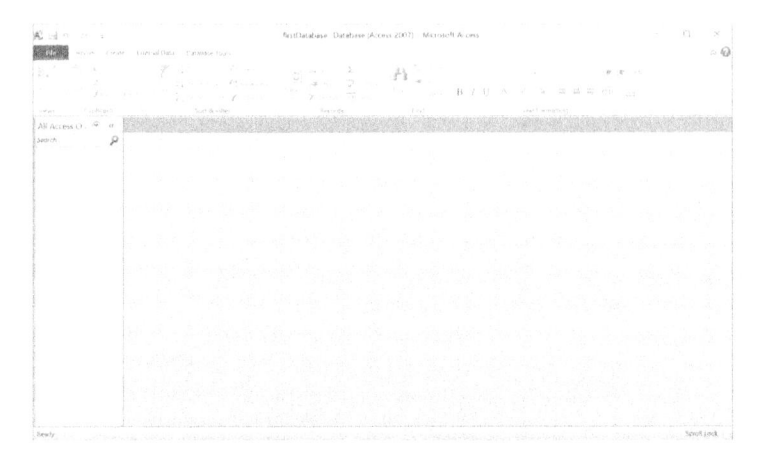

Figure 15.4. The empty database file

Data are stored in related tables in databases. Therefore we will create tables in our database file now. For this, click the **Create** tab and the **Table Design** button:

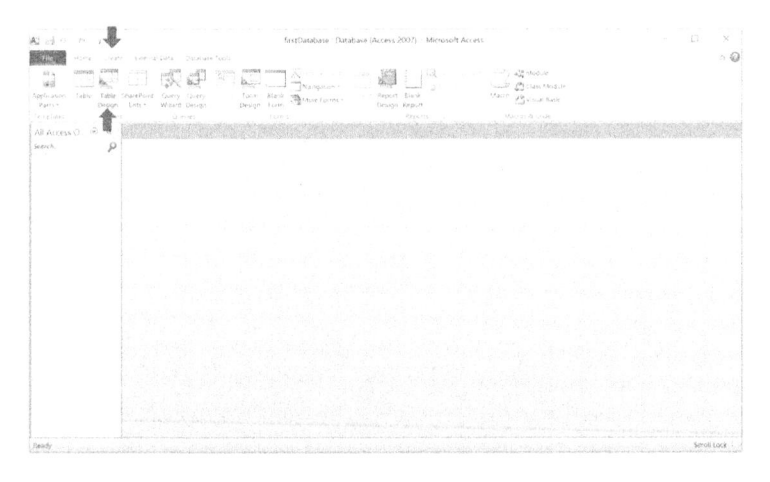

Figure 15.5. Opening Table Design view

364

CHAPTER 15. DATABASE CONNECTIONS USING ADO.NET

5. Tables of databases have two basic properties: field names and data types:

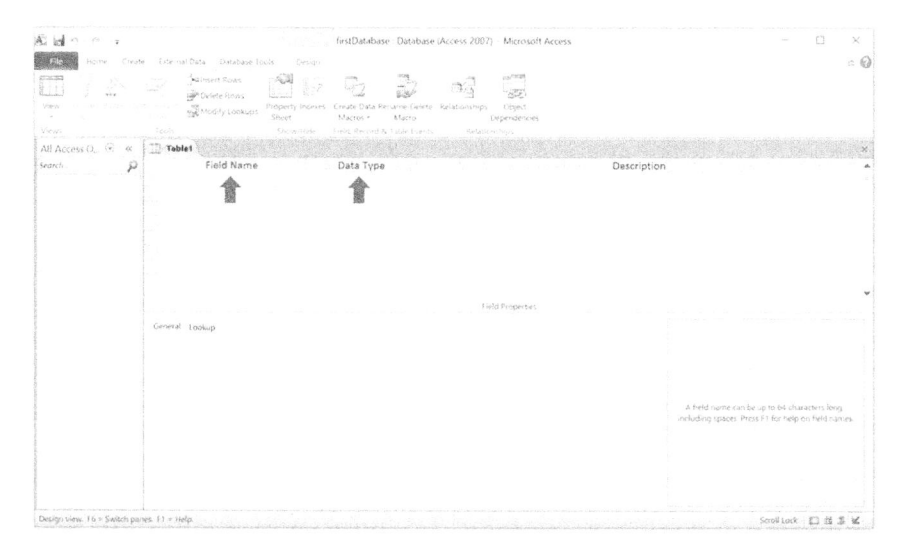

Figure 15.6. Table properties

For example, if we are creating a database that will hold data regarding the staff in a company, the database table will have fields like the id (identification number), name, surname and age of the personnel. The id will be the unique key of each person which typically has an integer value. Name and surname will obviously be character strings and the age will also be an integer value. Note that name, surname or age can be the same for two persons while the id will be different for each one.

Let's create this table in our database. The field names will be the **id_field**, **name_field**, **surname_field** and **age_field**. Data types will be **AutoNumber**, **Text**, **Text** and **Number**, respectively. After defining these fields and types, our database structure will be as in Figure 15.7.

We did set the type of the id_field as AutoNumber meaning that it will increment automatically when new data is inserted into the table. Therefore it is better to set this field as the key to access the data on the table. For this, select the id_field cell and click the **Primary Key** button as shown in Figure 15.8. A small key image will then appear at the left of the field as indicated in Figure 15.9.

BEGINNER'S GUIDE TO VISUAL BASIC.NET PROGRAMMING

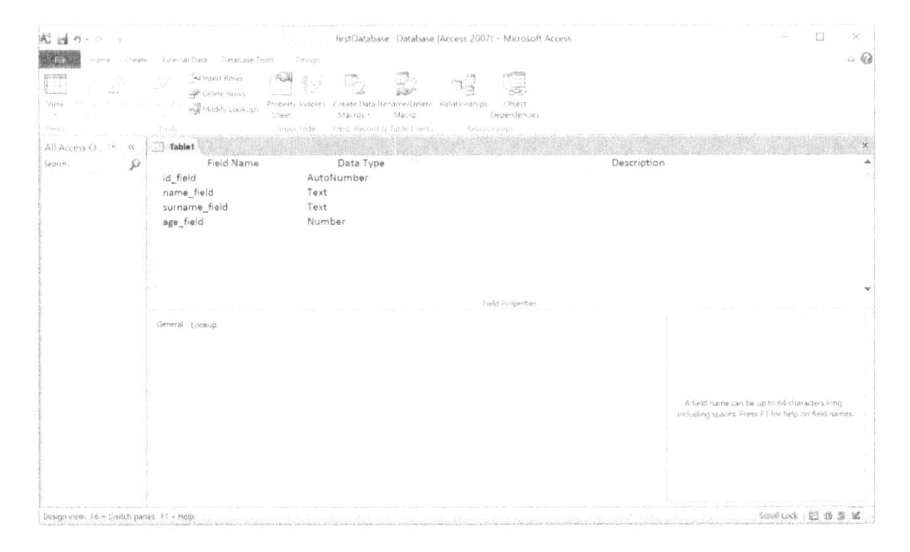

Figure 15.7. Field names and data types of our table

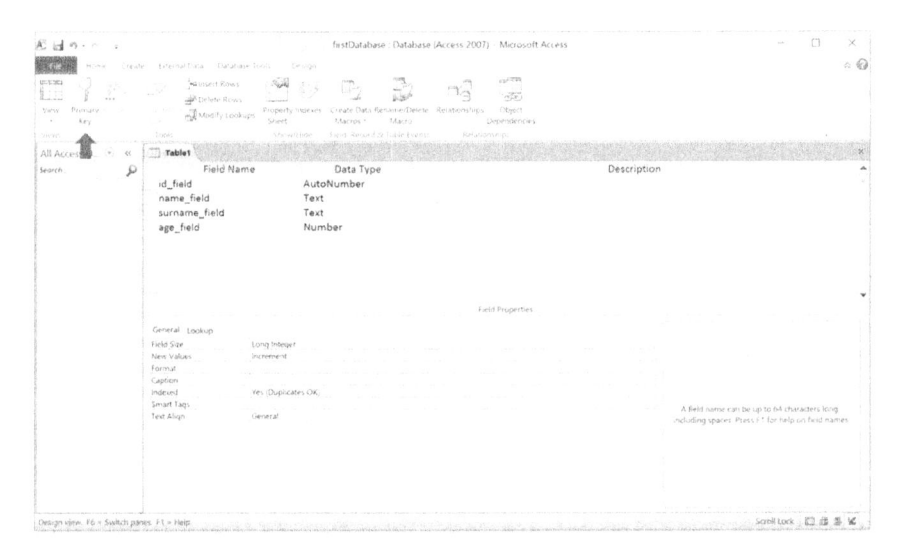

Figure 15.8. Setting the id_field as the primary key

6. Click the usual Save button to save the database file. Access will ask you to give a name to the new table. I kept the default name, Table1. Then right-click the table tab and select Close as in Figure 15.10. You will see that this table will be shown on the left pane as Table1 as given in Figure 15.11.

CHAPTER 15. DATABASE CONNECTIONS USING ADO.NET

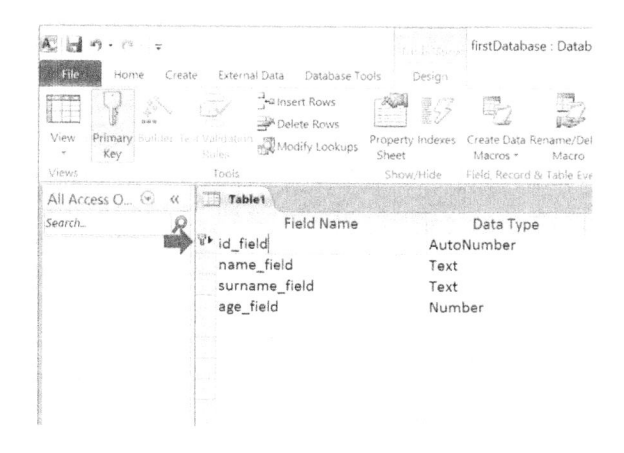

Figure 15.9. id_field set as the primary key

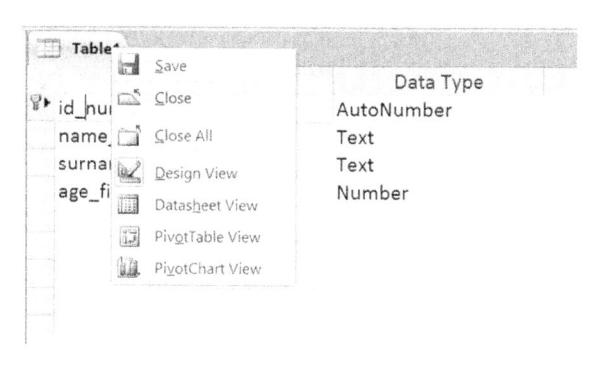

Figure 15.10. Closing the table design view

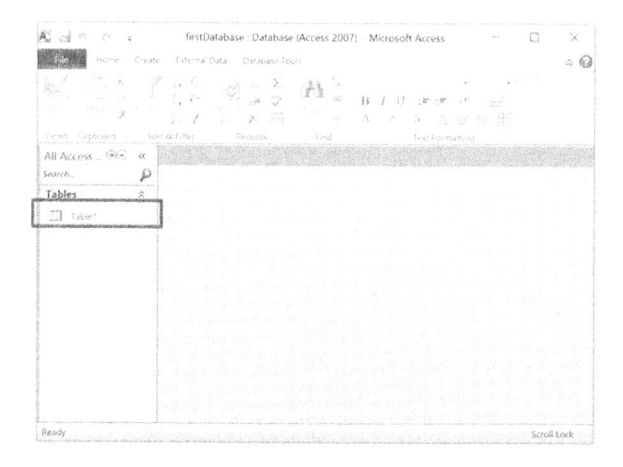

Figure 15.11. Table1 shown on the left pane

367

7. Double-click on Table1 to open its contents. Since we haven't added any data to this table, it will be displayed as empty:

Figure 15.12. The empty table

8. We can add/remove data in the columns of the table as we do in Excel. Let's add some random data to this table:

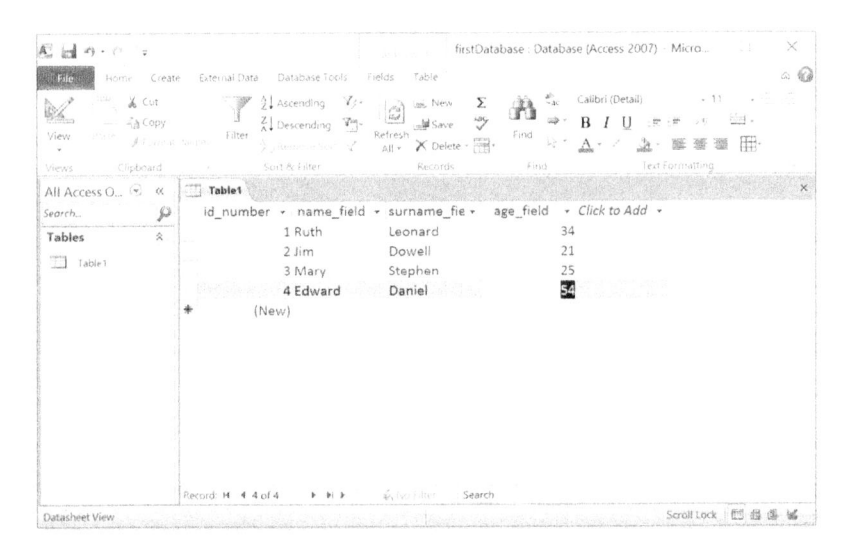

Figure 15.13. Data added to the table in our database

Please click the Save button. We have now created our sample database and added some data into it in Access itself. It is now time to connect to this database from our own VB.NET program.

15.2. Reading Database Entries from our VB.NET Program

Our programs can connect to Access databases via Access Database Engine. If you have an Office suite newer than 2007, Access Database Engine is already installed on your computer. If not, you can download this tool from https://www.microsoft.com/en-us/download/details.aspx?id=13255 (or just search for "Access Database Engine" on the Internet) and install it on your PC.

Databases are accessed using database commands from VB.NET programs. Firstly, a connection to the database is opened. Then, a read or write operation is performed on the database table using database commands. After finishing our job with the database, the connection is closed.

We can use the following objects for accessing and manipulating Access databases:

- **OleDBConnection**: Used for opening or closing a connection to the database. Its constructor method accepts the path to the file and the connection string regarding to the database type.
- **OleDBCommand**: Used for sending queries to the database for selecting and manipulating data.
- **DataReader**: Used for reading data from the database. It is used in conjunction with the OleDBCommand object.
- **OleDBDataAdapter**: Transfers data to a DataSet object.
- **DataSet**: Temporarily stores the data for displaying and manipulating purposes.

Let's see how we can connect to our firstDatabase.accdb using these objects in a typical example.

1. Create a new VB.NET project.
2. Add two Buttons and a ListBox on the form.

BEGINNER'S GUIDE TO VISUAL BASIC.NET PROGRAMMING

3. Set the Names and Texts of the Buttons as **connectDisconnectButton**, **viewEntriesButton**, **Connect-disconnect** and **View Entries**, respectively.
4. Set the Name of the ListBox as **displayListBox**. The form layout will look as follows:

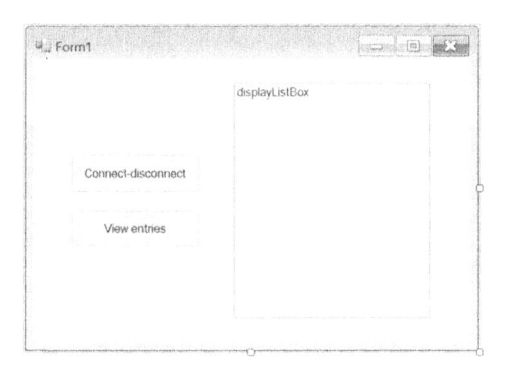

Figure 15.14. Layout of the form

5. Double-click the Connect-disconnect Button to create its Click event handler `ConnectDisconnectButton_Click(...)`. We will open and close database connection in this method for test purposes. Firstly, add the following namespace inclusion code lines at the top section of Form1.cs:

```
Imports System.Data
Imports System.Data.OleDb
```
Code 15.1

We will create an OleDBConnection object inside the `ConnectDisconnectButton_Click(...)` method. An OldeDBConnection object is created with the following constructor template:

```
Dim myConn As OleDbConnection = New
            OleDbConnection(connection string; Data
            Source= full path of the database file)
```
Code 15.2

We need to pass the connection string which specifies the database type and the full path of the database file. How will we specify the full path to our firstDatabase.accdb file? There is a simple trick: place the database file to the folder where our program's .exe file is. As we have learned in the 3rd chapter, the .exe file will be in the /bin/debug folder inside the project folder. Therefore, let's move our firstDatabase.accdb file to this folder as the first step. Then we can use the following code lines to obtain the full path to the database file:

```
Dim path As String = Environment.CurrentDirectory
    Dim databasePath As String = path + 
                                "\\firstDatabase.accdb"
```
Code 15.3

The variable databasePath will hold the full path to the database file. Note that we can move the exe file and the database file together to any other folder (or send them together to anyone) and the databasePath variable will hold the new path automatically.

Each database type will have its own connection string and it is not possible to memorize them. A website at the address www.connectionstrings.com helps us for this. For the Access databases, the connection string is specified as Provider=Microsoft.ACE.OLEDB.12.0 therefore we can create our OleDbConnection named myConn as follows:

```
Dim myConn As OleDbConnection = New 
OleDbConnection(("Provider=Microsoft.ACE.OLEDB.12.0;Data 
Source=" + databasePath)
```
Code 15.4

We can now open and close this connection with the Open() and Close() methods:

```
myConn.Open()
MessageBox.Show("Connection opened successfully.")
myConn.Close()
MessageBox.Show("Connection closed.")
```
Code 15.5

Combining these code snippets, we reach the complete connectDisconnectButton_Click(...) as follows:

```
Private Sub ConnectDisconnectButton_Click(sender As Object,
e As EventArgs) Handles connectDisconnectButton.Click

    Dim path As String = Environment.CurrentDirectory
    Dim databasePath As String = path +
                        "\\firstDatabase.accdb"

    Dim myConn As OleDbConnection = New
            OleDbConnection(("Provider=Microsoft.ACE.OLEDB
                        .12.0;Data Source=" + databasePath)

    myConn.Open()
    MessageBox.Show("Connection opened successfully.")
    myConn.Close()
    MessageBox.Show("Connection closed.")

End Sub
```
Code 15.6

6. Now, double-click the **View entries** Button to create its Click event handler method viewEntriesButton_Click(...). We will connect to the database, read data from Table1 from the database and display these data on the ListBox when this Button is clicked. Therefore, we will open a connection first:

```
Dim path As String = Environment.CurrentDirectory
Dim databasePath As String = path + "\\firstDatabase.accdb"
Dim myConn As OleDbConnection = New
            OleDbConnection(("Provider=Microsoft.ACE.OLEDB.
            12.0;Data Source=" + databasePath)
myConn.Open()
```
Code 15.7

As we have stated before, the command are sent via OleDBCommand objects. Let's create an OleDBCommand object with the required query as the parameter to the constructor method:

```
Dim readCommand As OleDbCommand = New OleDbCommand("SELECT
name_field, surname_field, age_field FROM Table1", myConn)
```
Code 15.8

CHAPTER 15. DATABASE CONNECTIONS USING ADO.NET

The query "SELECT name_field, surname_field, age_field FROM Table1" selects the specified fields from Table1. These data will be temporarily stored in an OleDbDataReader object that will be created via this readCommand object:

```
Dim reader As OleDbDataReader = readCommand.ExecuteReader()
```
Code 15.9

We will display the read data on the ListBox. Let's clear the ListBox first:

```
displayListBox.Items.Clear()
```
Code 15.10

And then use a while loop to insert the read data to the ListBox:

```
While reader.Read()

displayListBox.Items.Add(reader("name_field").ToString() +
" - " + reader("surname_field") + " - " +
reader("age_field"))

End While
```
Code 15.11

The while loop will continue running as long as there is data in the reader object therefore all data of Table1 will be displayed in the ListBox. Finally, don't forget closing the connection:

```
myConn.Close();
```
Code 15.12

The complete viewEntriesButton_Click() method is also given below:

```
Private Sub ViewEntriesButton_Click(sender As Object, e As
EventArgs) Handles viewEntriesButton.Click

    Dim path As String = Environment.CurrentDirectory
    Dim databasePath As String = path +
                              "\firstDatabase.accdb"
    Dim myConn As OleDbConnection = New
            OleDbConnection("Provider=Microsoft.ACE.OLEDB.
            12.0;Data Source=" + databasePath)
```

373

```
myConn.Open()

Dim readCommand As OleDbCommand = New OleDbCommand("SELECT
name_field, surname_field, age_field FROM Table1", myConn)
Dim reader As OleDbDataReader =readCommand.ExecuteReader()
displayListBox.Items.Clear()

While reader.Read()
    displayListBox.Items.Add(reader("name_field").
    ToString() + "-" + reader("surname_field")
    .ToString() + "-" + reader("age_field").ToString())
End While

myConn.Close()

End Sub
```
Code 15.13 (cont'd)

7. Build and run the project. The following program window will appear:

Figure 15.15. The program window

Firstly, click the Connect-disconnect Button. The program will display the message boxes regarding these operations. If your program gives and error, please double-check the connection string and make sure that the database file is in the same folder as the executable file.

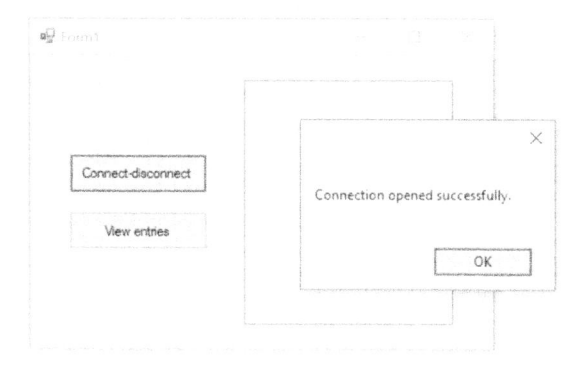

Figure 15.16. Database connection opening message

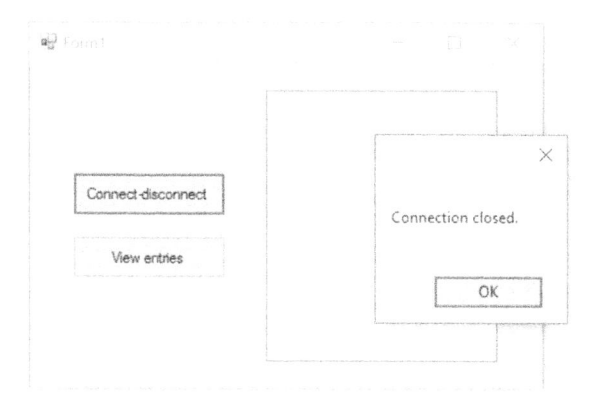

Figure 15.17. Database connection closing message

These messages show that our connection object is being created properly, i.e. the connection string is correct and our database file is at the right place. Now, let's click the View entries Button to read data from the database. The ListBox will be populated by the data we entered in our firstDatabase.accdb file:

Figure 15.18. Data read from database shown in the ListBox

We can update/add/remove entries of our database in Access and then click **View entries** Button again to display the updated data. I have entered new data to Table1 and displayed the updated data in the ListBox as in Figure 15.19.

Figure 15.19. The updated data shown in the ListBox

15.3. Adding/Updating/Deleting Database Entries from our VB.NET Program

We have manipulated data of the database in Access and displayed the updated data in our program. The problem is that the user may not have Access installed on his/her computer or we may need to manipulate entries of our database in a systematic way in our program. Adding new data, removing entries or updating data are all possible in our own program using the corresponding commands for the OleDBCommand object. Let's start developing our example project for learning how we can manipulate database entries.

1. Create a new VB.NET project.
2. Add six TextBoxes, six Labels, four Buttons and a ListBox on the form in the following layout shown in Figure 15.20.
3. Set the Names of the TextBoxes from top to down as insertNameTextBox, insertSurnameTextBox, insertAgeTextBox, updateNameTextBox, updateSurnameTextBox and updateAgeTextBox, respectively (confusing, I know!).
4. Set the Names of the Buttons as insertButton, updateButton, listButton and deleteButton in order.
5. Set the Texts of the Buttons as Insert, Update, List entries and Delete selected, respectively.
6. Set the Texts of the Labels as Name:, Surname:, Age:, Name:, Surname: and Age:, respectively.
7. Finally, set the Name of the ListBox as displayListBox. The form will look as in Figure 15.21 after these modifications.

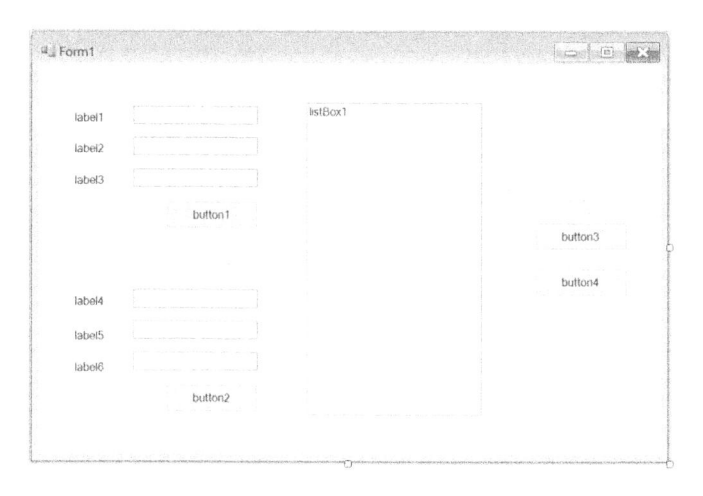

Figure 15.20. Layout of the form

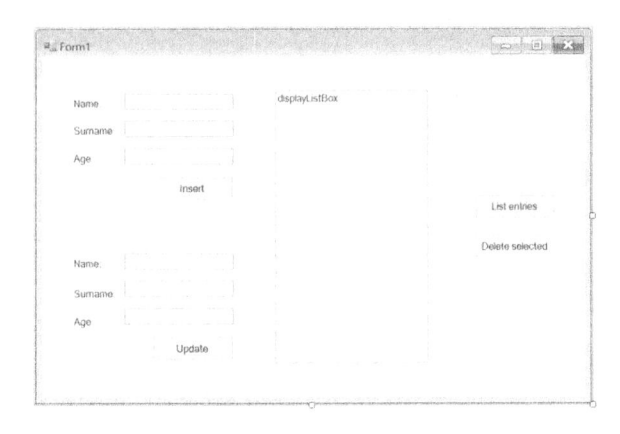

Figure 15.21. The form after setting the Text properties

8. Copy our sample Access database file, firstDatabase.accdb to /bin/debug folder under the project folder.
9. Let's implement the event handler method of the List entries Button borrowing code from the previous example since we have already developed the code for displaying data in the ListBox. Double-click the **List entries** Button to create its event handler method. Copy and paste Code 5.13 to ListButton_Click() for displaying the database entries in the ListBox. But we will have a small modification here. This time we will display the **id_number** too in addition to name, surname and age fields because we will need this information for other operations. We just need to create the readCommand as follows to include the **id_number** too :

```
Dim readCommand As OleDbCommand = New OleDbCommand("SELECT id_field, name_field, surname_field, age_field FROM Table1", myConn)
```
Code 15.14

Also, add the database entries in the while loop using the following Add() method to add **id_number** too:

```
displayListBox.Items.Add(reader("id_field").ToString() + "-" + reader("name_field").ToString() + "-" + reader("surname_field").ToString() + "-" + reader("age_field").ToString())
```
Code 15.15

CHAPTER 15. DATABASE CONNECTIONS USING ADO.NET

Our `ListButton_Click()` method will be as follows after these small modifications:

```
Private Sub ListButton_Click(sender As Object, e As
EventArgs) Handles listButton.Click

    Dim path As String = Environment.CurrentDirectory
    Dim databasePath As String = path +
                                 "\\firstDatabase.accdb"
    Dim myConn As OleDbConnection = New
          OleDbConnection("Provider=Microsoft.ACE.OLEDB
          .12.0;Data Source=" + databasePath)
    myConn.Open()

    Dim readCommand As OleDbCommand = New
                  OleDbCommand("SELECT id_field, name_field,
                  surname_field, age_field FROM Table1",
                  myConn)
    Dim reader As OleDbDataReader =
                                readCommand.ExecuteReader()
    displayListBox.Items.Clear()

    While reader.Read()
displayListBox.Items.Add(reader("id_field").ToString() + "-
" + reader("name_field").ToString() + "-" +
reader("surname_field").ToString() + "-" +
reader("age_field").ToString())
    End While

    myConn.Close()

End Sub
```
Code 15.16

10. Let's build and run the project to see if our **List entries** Button is working properly. The entries should be listed with the **id_number** in the ListBox when **List entries** Button is clicked:

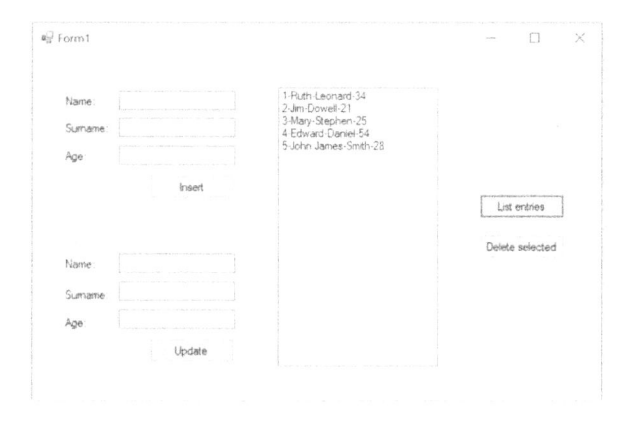

BEGINNER'S GUIDE TO VISUAL BASIC.NET PROGRAMMING

Figure 15.22. Data entries listed in the ListBox

If you cannot see the data or if the program issues an error, please double-check the previous steps before continuing.

11. Let's now develop the code for the **Delete** Button. The user will select a line in the ListBox and then he/she will click this Button to delete the selected entry from the database. Firstly, double-click the Delete Button to create its event handler method DeleteButton_Click(...).
12. Firstly, we will open our connection:

```
Dim path As String = Environment.CurrentDirectory
Dim databasePath As String = path + "\\firstDatabase.accdb"
Dim myConn As OleDbConnection = New
OleDbConnection("Provider=Microsoft.ACE.OLEDB.12.0;Data
                                     Source=" + databasePath)
myConn.Open()
```
Code 15.17

13. Then we will take the selected entry in the ListBox and then get its id_number with the following code lines:

```
Dim selectedEntry As String =
displayListBox.SelectedItem.ToString()
Dim selectedEntry_id_number =
Integer.Parse(selectedEntry.Split("-")(0))
MessageBox.Show("The entry with id_number: " +
selectedEntry_id_number.ToString() + " will now be
deleted."
```
Code 15.18

380

In the first line, we get the whole text of the selected line in the ListBox. And then parse this text to get the first part before the hyphen, which is the id_number. We display a message box informing the user about the entry to be deleted.

14. We will then form the required query that will perform the deletion as follows:

```
Dim deleteCommand As OleDbCommand = New OleDbCommand("DELETE FROM Table1 WHERE id_field=?", myConn)

deleteCommand.Parameters.AddWithValue("?", selectedEntry_id_number)
```
Code 15.19

We constructed a new OleDbCommand object with the query line ("DELETE FROM Table1 WHERE id_field=?" which will operate on myConn. We pass the id_number we obtained before. We use the "?" symbol for passing the id_number by adding it as a parameter to the query.

15. Finally, we execute the cmd object as follows:

```
Dim deleteCommandResult As Integer = deleteCommand.ExecuteNonQuery()

MessageBox.Show("Number of deleted entries: " + deleteCommandResult.ToString())
myConn.Close()
```
Code 15.20

The ExecuteNonQuery() is the method that actually runs the query. It returns the number of entries affected by the query. We store this result in a variable named deleteCommandResult. We then display the information regarding the number of affected entries and then close the connection. The whole DeleteButton_Click(...) is also shown below for completeness:

```
Private Sub DeleteButton_Click(sender As Object, e As EventArgs) Handles deleteButton.Click

    Dim path As String = Environment.CurrentDirectory
    Dim databasePath As String = path +
```

```vbnet
                               "\\firstDatabase.accdb"
  Dim myConn As OleDbConnection = New
OleDbConnection("Provider=Microsoft.ACE.OLEDB.12.0;Data
Source=" + databasePath)
  myConn.Open()

  Dim selectedEntry As String =
                  displayListBox.SelectedItem.ToString()
  Dim selectedEntry_id_number =
               Integer.Parse(selectedEntry.Split("-")(0))
  MessageBox.Show("The entry with id_number: " +
selectedEntry_id_number.ToString() + " will now be
deleted.")

  Dim deleteCommand As OleDbCommand = New
OleDbCommand("DELETE FROM Table1 WHERE id_field=?", myConn)

  deleteCommand.Parameters.AddWithValue("?",
                            selectedEntry_id_number)

  Dim deleteCommandResult As Integer =
                     deleteCommand.ExecuteNonQuery()

  MessageBox.Show("Number of deleted entries: " +
                       deleteCommandResult.ToString())
  myConn.Close()

End Sub
```

Code 15.21 (cont'd)

16. Build and run the project to see if everything is OK for now. Firstly click the **List entries** Button to display the database entries in the ListBox:

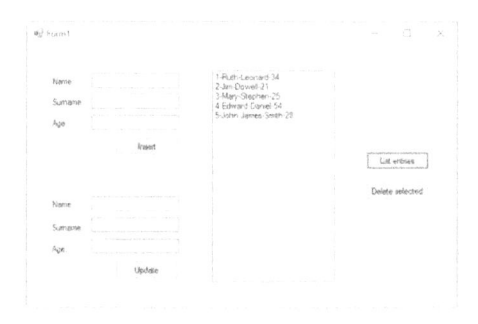

Figure 15.23. Database entries listed in the ListBox

CHAPTER 15. DATABASE CONNECTIONS USING ADO.NET

Click to select an entry in the ListBox. I selected the second one:

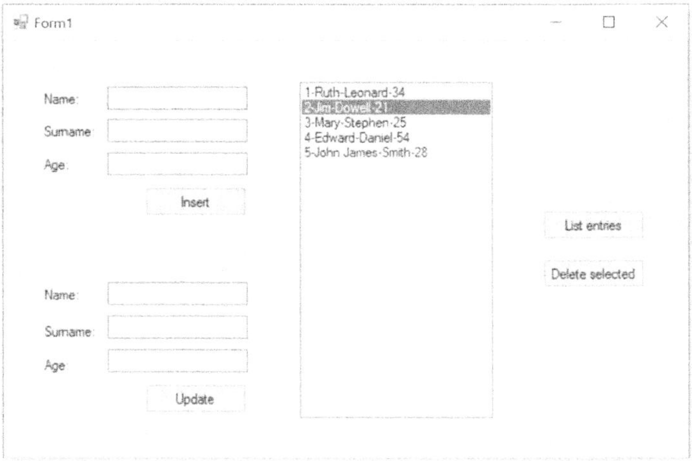

Figure 15.24. The second entry is selected

Now, click the Delete selected Button. The program will issue a message regarding the id_number of the entry to be deleted as in Figure 15.25. Then the entry **will be deleted from the database** and then the information showing the affected entries will be displayed as shown in Figure 15.26.

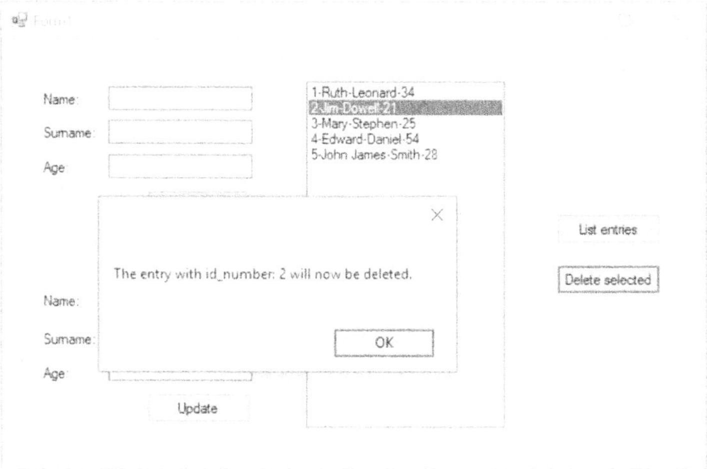

Figure 15.25. The message box displaying deletion information

383

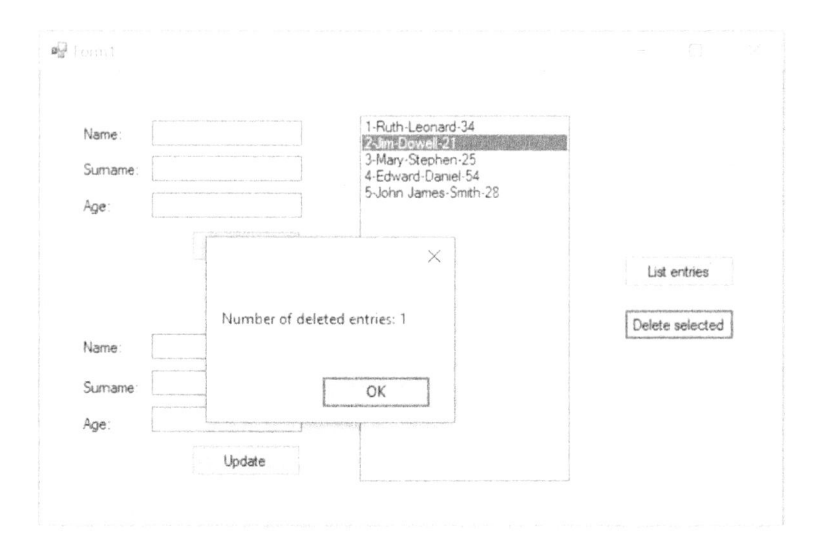

Figure 15.26. Message box showing the number of deleted entries

Click the **List entries** Button to see if the selected entry is actually deleted from the database. It is deleted successfully proving that our **Delete** Button works as expected as shown below:

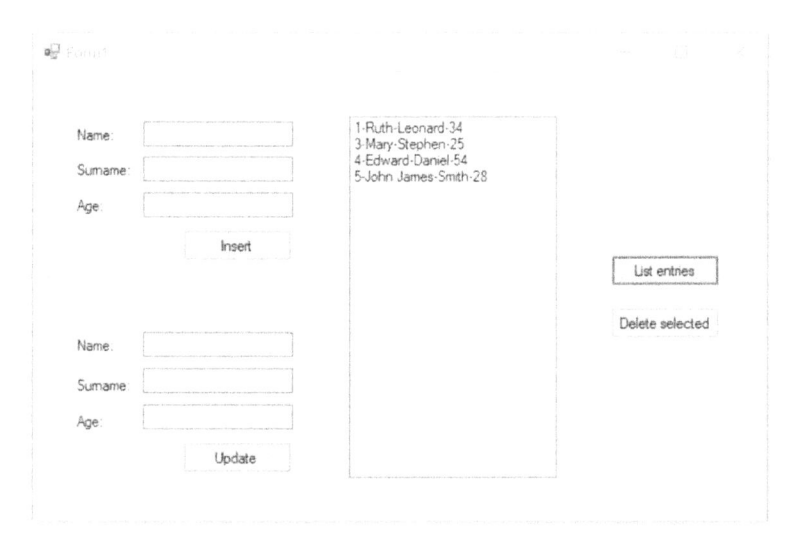

Figure 15.27. The entries of the database displayed after the deletion of the second entry

17. We are now ready to implement the insert operation. We will take the Name, Surname and Age inputs and insert them in a new entry in the database when the **Insert** Button is clicked. Double-click the Insert Button to create its Click event handler InsertButton_Click().

We will write the code of the InsertButton_Click() method. Firstly, copy and paste the standard database connection part as we implemented before:

```
Dim path As String = Environment.CurrentDirectory
Dim databasePath As String = path + "\\firstDatabase.accdb"
Dim myConn As OleDbConnection = New
OleDbConnection("Provider=Microsoft.ACE.OLEDB.12.0;Data
Source=" + databasePath)
myConn.Open()
```
Code 15.22

Now, create an OleDbCommand object which will hold the insertion query as follows:

```
Dim insertCommand As OleDbCommand = New
OleDbCommand("INSERT INTO
Table1(name_field,surname_field,age_field) VALUES (?,?,?)",
myConn)
```
Code 15.23

We will pass the name_field, surname_field and age_field strings from the insertNameTextBox, insertSurnameTextBox and insertAgeTextBox with the utilization of "?" parameters:

```
insertCommand.Parameters.AddWithValue("?",
                              insertNameTextBox.Text)
insertCommand.Parameters.AddWithValue("?",
                              insertSurnameTextBox.Text)
insertCommand.Parameters.AddWithValue("?",
                              insertAgeTextBox.Text)
```
Code 15.24

Finally, execute the query command with the ExecuteNonQuery() method as we did in the Delete Button:

```
Dim insertCommandResult As Integer =
insertCommand.ExecuteNonQuery()
MessageBox.Show("Number of inserted entries: " +
insertCommandResult.ToString())
myConn.Close()
```
Code 15.25

The message will display the number of inserted entries and then the connection will be closed.

The whole `insertButton_Click` event handler method is as follows after these additions:

```
Private Sub InsertButton_Click(sender As Object, e As
EventArgs) Handles insertButton.Click

  Dim path As String = Environment.CurrentDirectory
  Dim databasePath As String = path +
                    "\\firstDatabase.accdb"
  Dim myConn As OleDbConnection = New
          OleDbConnection("Provider=Microsoft.ACE.OLEDB.
          12.0;Data Source=" + databasePath)
  myConn.Open()

  Dim insertCommand As OleDbCommand = New
              OleDbCommand("INSERT INTO
              Table1(name_field,surname_field,age_field)
              VALUES (?,?,?)", myConn)
  insertCommand.Parameters.AddWithValue("?",
                      insertNameTextBox.Text)
  insertCommand.Parameters.AddWithValue("?",
                      insertSurnameTextBox.Text)
  insertCommand.Parameters.AddWithValue("?",
                      insertAgeTextBox.Text)

  Dim insertCommandResult As Integer =
                      insertCommand.ExecuteNonQuery()
  MessageBox.Show("Number of inserted entries: " +
                  insertCommandResult.ToString())
  myConn.Close()

End Sub
```
Code 15.26

CHAPTER 15. DATABASE CONNECTIONS USING ADO.NET

18. Build and run the project to see if the **Insert** Button is working properly. Firstly, click the **List entries** Button to see the current entries of the database:

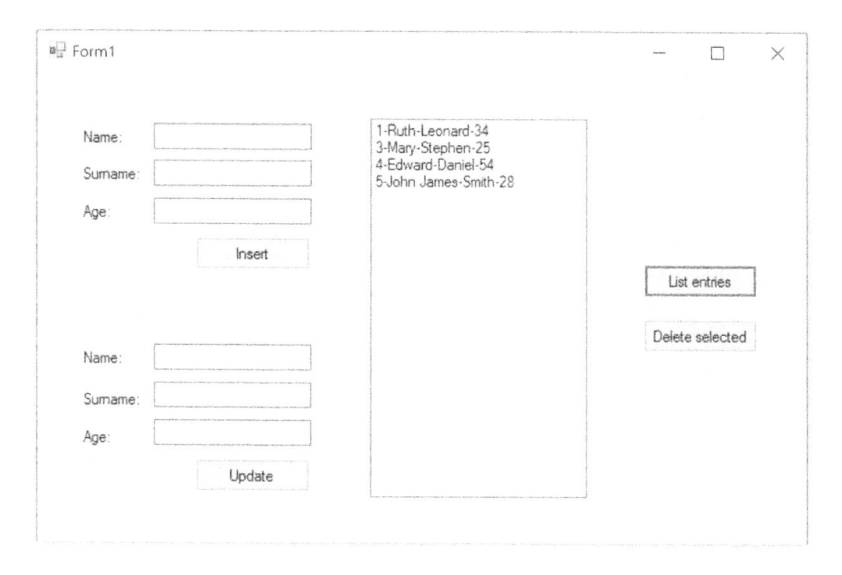

Figure 15.28. Database entries before the insertion

Now, let's enter Name, Surname and Age strings in the insertion TextBoxes and then click the Insert Button. The program will display the number of inserted entries as 1:

387

Figure 15.29. Insertion message

Now, click **List entries** Button to display the current entries in our database:

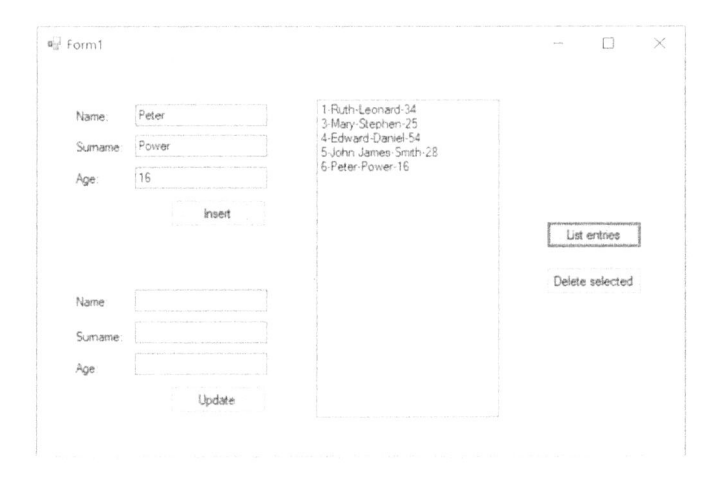

Figure 15.30. Database entries after the insertion

The new entry is inserted into the database successfully as seen from the ListBox.

19. We will finally implement the update operation. The user will select an entry from the ListBox, enter new information in the update TextBoxes and click the **Update** Button. The selected entry will then be updated in the database by the new values. We will start by double-clicking the Update Button to create its UpdateButton_Click() method. We will write our code inside this method as usual.

We will firstly open the connection to the database as before:

```
Dim path As String = Environment.CurrentDirectory
Dim databasePath As String = path + "\\firstDatabase.accdb"
Dim myConn As OleDbConnection = New
OleDbConnection("Provider=Microsoft.ACE.OLEDB.12.0;Data
Source=" + databasePath)
myConn.Open()
```
Code 15.27

CHAPTER 15. DATABASE CONNECTIONS USING ADO.NET

And then take the **id_number** of the selected entry:

```
Dim selectedEntry = displayListBox.SelectedItem.ToString()
Dim selectedEntry_id_number =
                 Integer.Parse(selectedEntry.Split("-")(0))
```
Code 15.28

as we did in the Delete Button's method. We can show an information message regarding the entry being updated:

```
MessageBox.Show("The entry with id_number: " +
selectedEntry_id_number.ToString() + " will now be
updated.")
```
Code 15.29

Now, we will create the OleDbCommand object to perform the update operation. The query with the UPDATE command will be used in the following form:

```
Dim updateCommand As OleDbCommand = New
OleDbCommand("UPDATE Table1 SET name_field =? ,
surname_field =?, age_field=? WHERE id_number =? ", myConn)
```
Code 15.30

Then, pass the required parameters specified by the question marks in order:

```
updateCommand.Parameters.AddWithValue("?",
                          updateNameTextBox.Text)
updateCommand.Parameters.AddWithValue("?",
                          updateSurnameTextBox.Text)
updateCommand.Parameters.AddWithValue("?",
                          updateAgeTextBox.Text)
updateCommand.Parameters.AddWithValue("?",
                          selectedEntry_id_number)
```
Code 15.31

Finally, execute the query with the ExecuteNonQuery() method and display the information message:

```
Dim updateCommandResult As Integer =
updateCommand.ExecuteNonQuery()
MessageBox.Show("Number of updated entries: " +
updateCommandResult.ToString())myConn.Close();
```
Code 15.32

The complete **Update** Button is also shown below:

```
Private Sub UpdateButton_Click(sender As Object, e As
EventArgs) Handles updateButton.Click

  Dim path As String = Environment.CurrentDirectory
  Dim databasePath As String = path +
                               "\\firstDatabase.accdb"
  Dim myConn As OleDbConnection = New
          OleDbConnection("Provider=Microsoft.ACE.OLEDB
          .12.0;Data Source=" + databasePath)
  myConn.Open()
  Dim selectedEntry =
           displayListBox.SelectedItem.ToString()
  Dim selectedEntry_id_number =
          Integer.Parse(selectedEntry.Split("-")(0))
 MessageBox.Show("The entry with id_number: " +
       selectedEntry_id_number.ToString() + " will now be
       updated.")
  Dim updateCommand As OleDbCommand = New
          OleDbCommand("UPDATE Table1 SET
          name_field =? , surname_field =?, age_field=?
          WHERE id_field =? ", myConn)
  updateCommand.Parameters.AddWithValue("?",
         updateNameTextBox.Text)
  updateCommand.Parameters.AddWithValue("?",
         updateSurnameTextBox.Text)
  updateCommand.Parameters.AddWithValue("?",
         updateAgeTextBox.Text)
  updateCommand.Parameters.AddWithValue("?",
         selectedEntry_id_number)
  Dim updateCommandResult As Integer =
          updateCommand.ExecuteNonQuery()
  MessageBox.Show("Number of updated entries: " + u
         pdateCommandResult.ToString())

End Sub
```
Code 15.33

The complete Form1.vb is also given below for your convenience:

```vb
Imports System.Data
Imports System.Data.OleDb

Public Class Form1
Private Sub ListButton_Click(sender As Object, e As
EventArgs) Handles listButton.Click

   Dim path As String = Environment.CurrentDirectory
   Dim databasePath As String = path +
                                "\\firstDatabase.accdb"
   Dim myConn As OleDbConnection = New
           OleDbConnection("Provider=Microsoft.ACE.OLEDB.
           12.0;Data Source=" + databasePath)
   myConn.Open()

   Dim readCommand As OleDbCommand = New
               OleDbCommand("SELECT id_field, name_field,
               surname_field, age_field FROM Table1",
               myConn)
   Dim reader As OleDbDataReader =
               readCommand.ExecuteReader()
   displayListBox.Items.Clear()

   While reader.Read()

displayListBox.Items.Add(reader("id_field").ToString() + "-
" + reader("name_field").ToString() + "-" +
reader("surname_field").ToString() + "-" +
reader("age_field").ToString())

   End While

   myConn.Close()

End Sub

Private Sub DeleteButton_Click(sender As Object, e As
EventArgs) Handles deleteButton.Click

   Dim path As String = Environment.CurrentDirectory
   Dim databasePath As String = path +
                   "\\firstDatabase.accdb"
   Dim myConn As OleDbConnection = New
           OleDbConnection("Provider=Microsoft.ACE.OLEDB.
```

```vbnet
12.0;Data Source=" + databasePath)
  myConn.Open()
  Dim selectedEntry As String =
            displayListBox.SelectedItem.ToString()
  Dim selectedEntry_id_number =
      Integer.Parse(selectedEntry.Split("-")(0))
  MessageBox.Show("The entry with id_number: " +
    selectedEntry_id_number.ToString() + " will now be
    deleted.")
  Dim deleteCommand As OleDbCommand = New
OleDbCommand("DELETE FROM Table1 WHERE id_field=?", myConn)
        deleteCommand.Parameters.AddWithValue("?",
selectedEntry_id_number)
  Dim deleteCommandResult As Integer =
deleteCommand.ExecuteNonQuery()
  MessageBox.Show("Number of deleted entries: " +
deleteCommandResult.ToString())
  myConn.Close()

End Sub

Private Sub InsertButton_Click(sender As Object, e As
EventArgs) Handles insertButton.Click

  Dim path As String = Environment.CurrentDirectory
  Dim databasePath As String = path +
            "\\firstDatabase.accdb"
  Dim myConn As OleDbConnection = New
OleDbConnection("Provider=Microsoft.ACE.OLEDB.12.0;Data
Source=" + databasePath)
  myConn.Open()
  Dim insertCommand As OleDbCommand = New
OleDbCommand("INSERT INTO
Table1(name_field,surname_field,age_field) VALUES (?,?,?)",
myConn)
  insertCommand.Parameters.AddWithValue("?",
        insertNameTextBox.Text)
  insertCommand.Parameters.AddWithValue("?",
        insertSurnameTextBox.Text)
  insertCommand.Parameters.AddWithValue("?",
        insertAgeTextBox.Text)
  Dim insertCommandResult As Integer =
        insertCommand.ExecuteNonQuery()
  MessageBox.Show("Number of inserted entries: " +
        insertCommandResult.ToString())
  myConn.Close()

End Sub
```

CHAPTER 15. DATABASE CONNECTIONS USING ADO.NET

```vb
Private Sub UpdateButton_Click(sender As Object, e As
EventArgs) Handles updateButton.Click

    Dim path As String = Environment.CurrentDirectory
    Dim databasePath As String = path +
        "\\firstDatabase.accdb"
    Dim myConn As OleDbConnection = New
            OleDbConnection("Provider=Microsoft.ACE.OLEDB.
            12.0;Data Source=" + databasePath)
    myConn.Open()
    Dim selectedEntry =
            displayListBox.SelectedItem.ToString()
    Dim selectedEntry_id_number =
            Integer.Parse(selectedEntry.Split("-")(0))
    MessageBox.Show("The entry with id_number: " +
        selectedEntry_id_number.ToString() + " will now be
        updated.")
    Dim updateCommand As OleDbCommand = New
OleDbCommand("UPDATE Table1 SET name_field =? ,
surname_field =?, age_field=? WHERE id_field =? ", myConn)
    updateCommand.Parameters.AddWithValue("?",
            updateNameTextBox.Text)
    updateCommand.Parameters.AddWithValue("?",
            updateSurnameTextBox.Text)
    updateCommand.Parameters.AddWithValue("?",
            updateAgeTextBox.Text)
    updateCommand.Parameters.AddWithValue("?",
            selectedEntry_id_number)
    Dim updateCommandResult As Integer =
            updateCommand.ExecuteNonQuery()
    MessageBox.Show("Number of updated entries: " +
            updateCommandResult.ToString())

    End Sub
End Class
```

Code 15.34 (cont'd)

20. Build and run the project. Click **List entries** Button to see the current entries of the database:

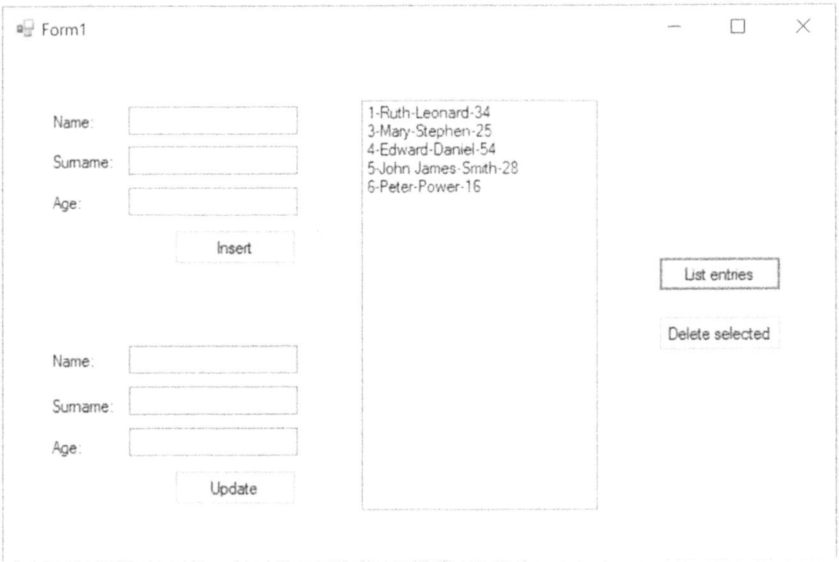

BEGINNER'S GUIDE TO VISUAL BASIC.NET PROGRAMMING

Figure 15.31. Current entries of the database displayed in the ListBox

Now, select an entry such as the first one as in Figure 15.32.

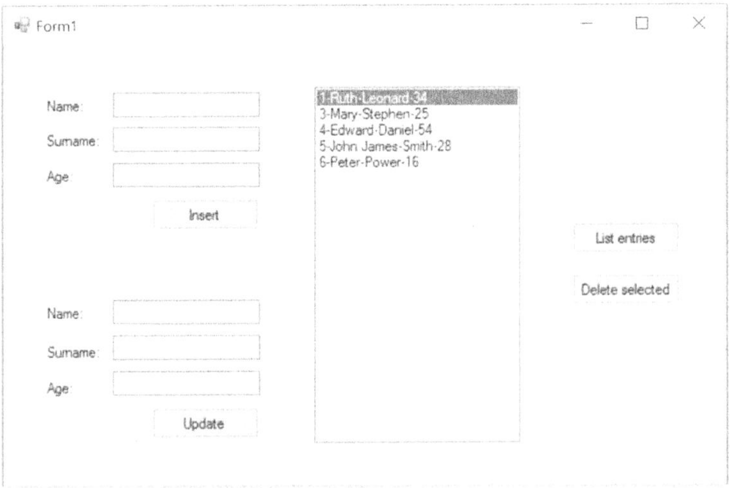

Figure 15.32. The first entry is selected

Now enter new values for this entry in the update TextBoxes and click the **Update** Button. The program will inform us that the entry will be updated:

394

CHAPTER 15. DATABASE CONNECTIONS USING ADO.NET

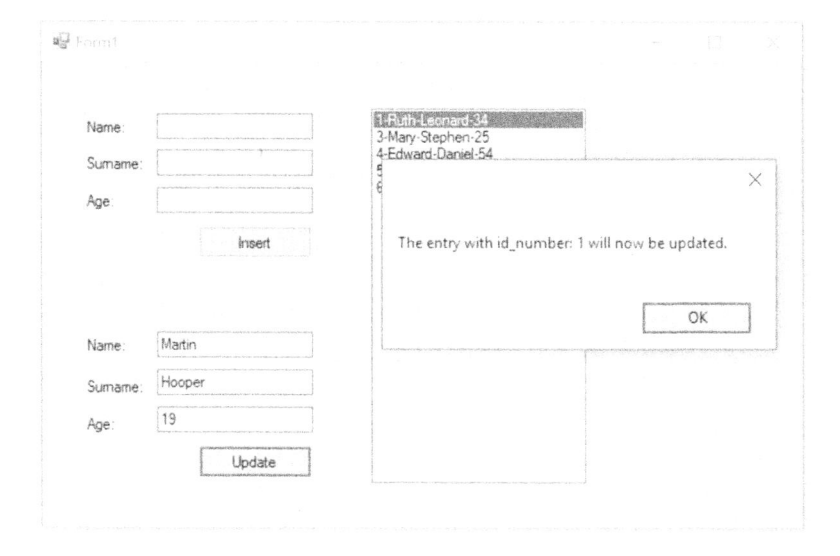

Figure 15.33. Update information

Then, the update will take place and the corresponding message will be shown:

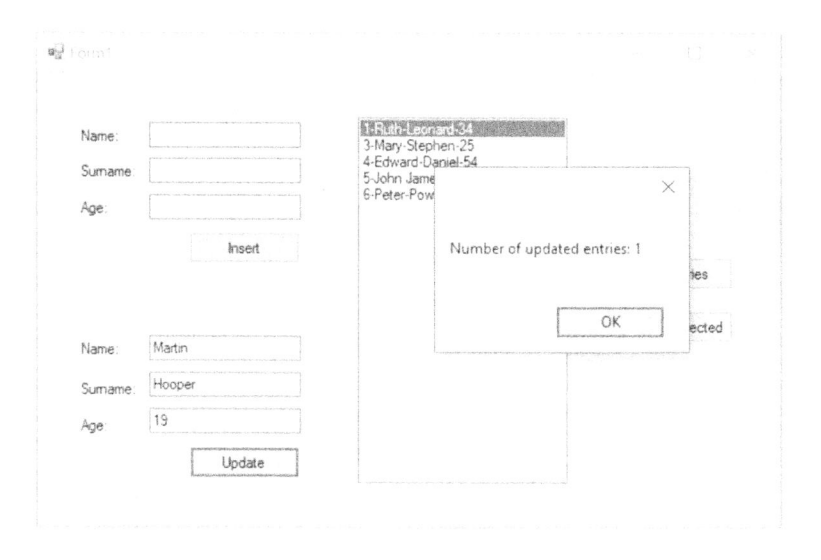

Figure 15.34. The message box after the update operation

Now, click the **List entries** Button to see if the first entry is actually updated in the database file:

395

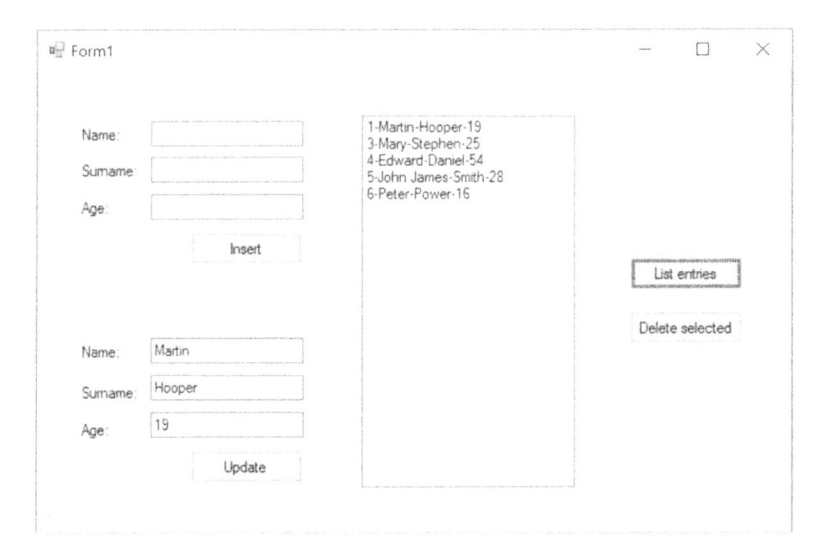

Figure 15.35. Current entries of the database – the first entry is updated

We have learned connecting our VB.NET programs to Access databases for permanent and organized data storage in this chapter. As we have stated before, connecting to other types of databases is also possible. However, Access databases are excellent for our current purposes by providing an optimal performance with ease of use as we have seen in this chapter. In the next chapter (which is also the final chapter), we will use our VB.NET background to develop a 2-dimensional platform game in Unity.

Chapter 16

DEVELOPING A CAR RACING GAME IN VISUAL BASIC.NET

We now have the VB.NET background for developing a wide range of programs. We will put our knowledge and effort to develop a platform game in this chapter.

Games are among the most popular apps. Game developers earn good money once the gamers get addicted to their games. However, developing a game is not a simple task since a good game should have an exciting story, good graphics, realistic physics rules and efficient code to glue all these together. We will develop a simple 2D car racing game in VB.NET in this chapter.

The name of the game we will develop is **Horizontal Racer**. The idea is simple: the user will control a car and will try to avoid colloiding with other cars and stuff on the road. The score of the game will be based on the time the car goes on.

16.1. Creating the Game Project and Preliminary Works

First of all, let's create our usual Windows Forms application in VB.NET:

Figure 16.1. Creating our game project in Visual Studio

Now, we will fix the window size do hat the user will not able to change the game window size by drag-n-drop or using the maximize icon. For this, we will set the maximum and minimum size properties of the Windows form from the Properties as follows:

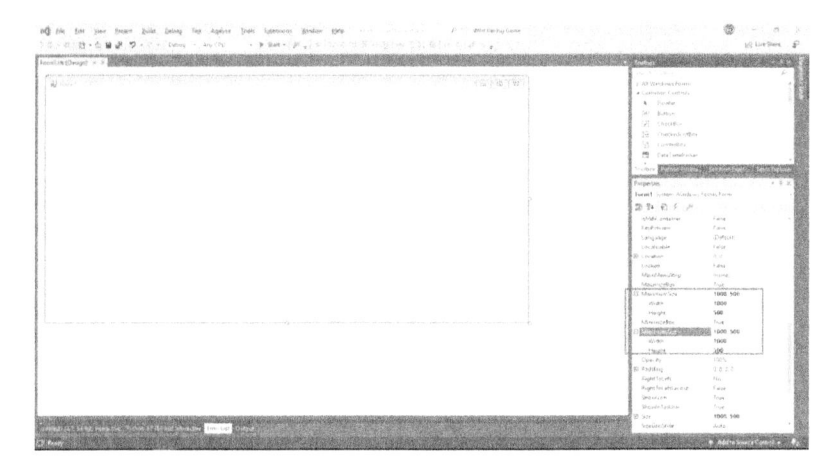

Figure 16.2. Setting a fixed size for the form window

We have set the window size as (width, height) = 1000, 500 but you can set another size if you wish.

CHAPTER 16. DEVELOPING A CAR RACING GAME IN VISUAL BASIC.NET

The roads are generally not white but has an asphalt colour therefore, let's change the road color (i.e. the background colour of the road) to something dark like ControlDarkDark from the Properties window:

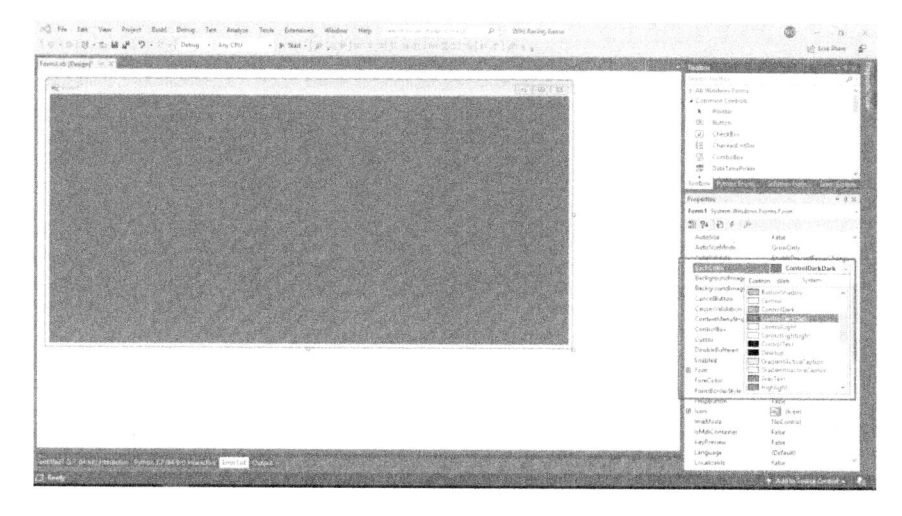

Figure 16.3. Changing the background colour of the window to resemble that of asphalt

We will now add the road lines which will be made of PictureBox items. For this, drag-n-drop a PictureBox from the Toolbox to the Form:

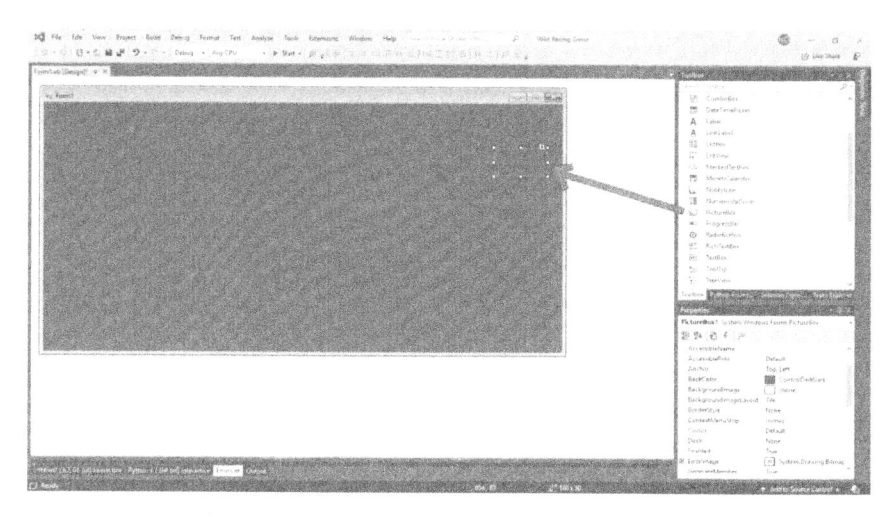

Figure 16.4. Adding a PictureBox to the road, sorry to the form

399

Road lines are usually white therefore we'll change the background colour of the PictureBox to white:

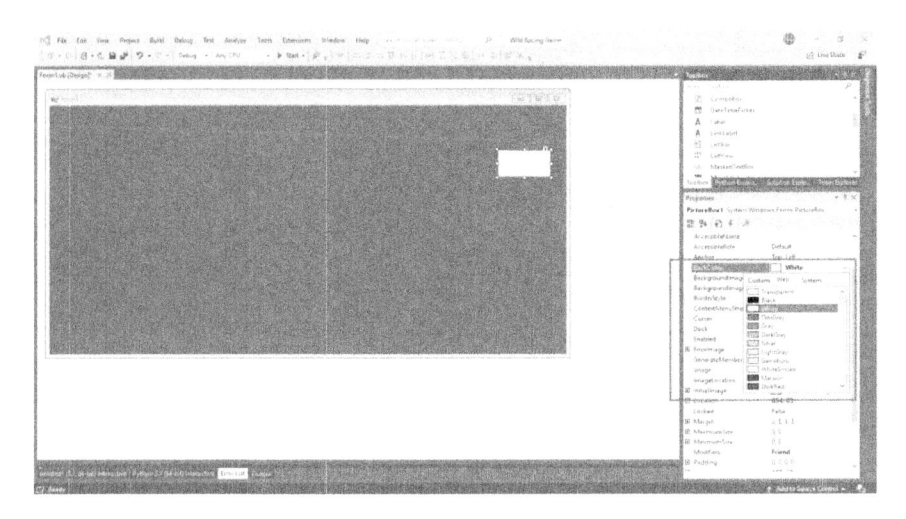

Figure 16.5. Changing the colour of the PictureBox (road line) as white

Road lines are more like thin rectangles therefore we will set the shape of the PictureBox by drag-n-drop one of its corners to make it thinner:

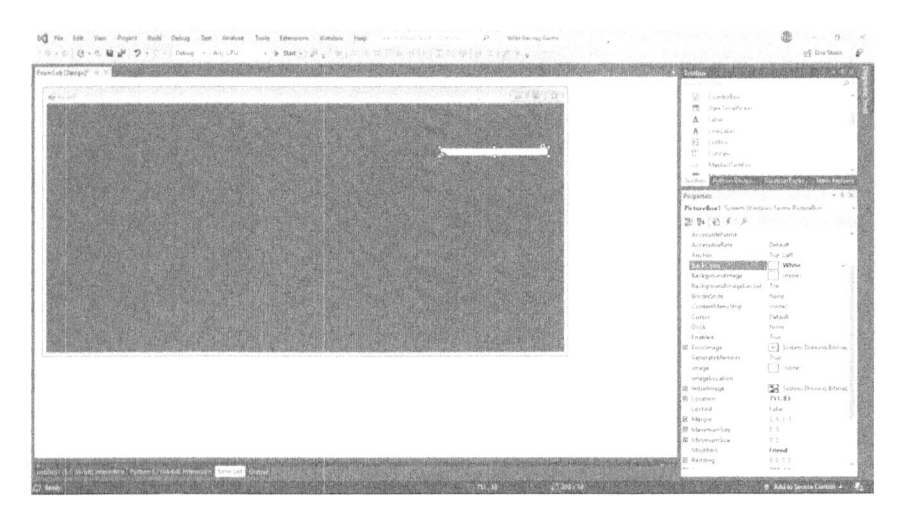

Figure 16.6. Changing the shape of the PictureBox to resemble a road line

CHAPTER 16. DEVELOPING A CAR RACING GAME IN VISUAL BASIC.NET

Now, please copy and paste our road line prototype PictureBox on the form so that there are multiple of them as follows:

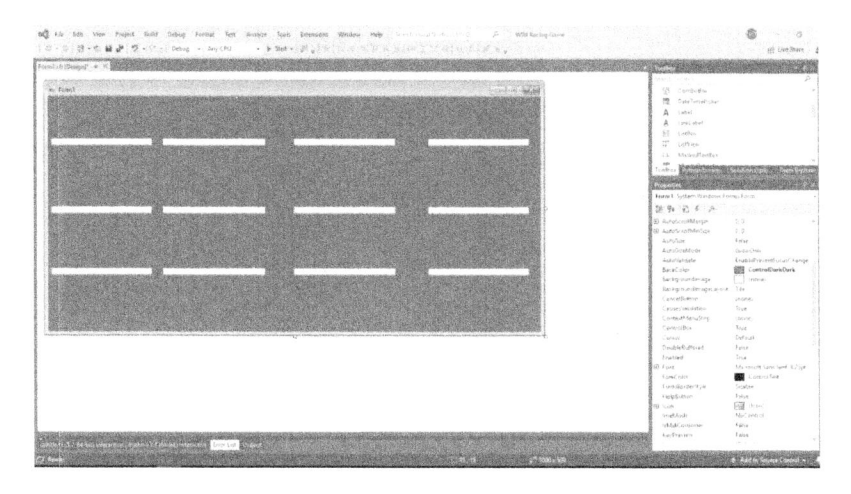

Figure 16.7. Multiple road lines on the form

Please note that Visual Studio automatically numbers the PictureBoxes so we have PictureBox1, PictureBox2,…, PictureBox12 now.

We will move the road lines from right to left to add the moving effect to our game. For this aim, we need to add a Timer item to our Windows form. Timer item is a component which executes its statements in a periodic basis. We can just drag-n-drop a Timer on the form as follows:

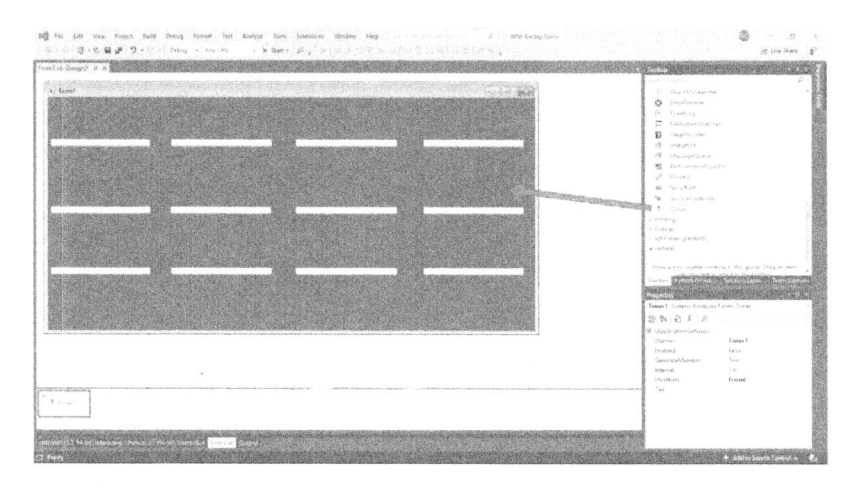

Figure 16.8. Adding a Timer to the project

The Timer component does not appear on the form, it does its job at the background. We can now change the Properties of Timer1 so that it will tick at 30ms (milliseconds) interval and also to enable it as follows:

Figure 16.9. Setting the Timer1's properties

The logic here is that as the Timer1 ticks, the road lines (i.e. PictureBox1...PictureBox12) will move from right to left. Now, please double click Timer 1 to create its tick event handler as follows:

```
Private Sub Timer1_Tick(sender As Object, e As EventArgs) Handles Timer1.Tick


End Sub
```
Code 16.1

The code lines written in this block is executed each time the Timer1 ticks, i.e. each 30 milliseconds in our project. We will move the road lines to the left to make the movement animation as follows:

```
Private Sub Timer1_Tick(sender As Object, e As EventArgs) Handles Timer1.Tick

  PictureBox1.Left -= 10
  PictureBox2.Left -= 10
  PictureBox3.Left -= 10
  PictureBox4.Left -= 10
  PictureBox5.Left -= 10
  PictureBox6.Left -= 10
  PictureBox7.Left -= 10
  PictureBox8.Left -= 10
  PictureBox9.Left -= 10
```

CHAPTER 16. DEVELOPING A CAR RACING GAME IN VISUAL BASIC.NET

```
    PictureBox10.Left -= 10
    PictureBox11.Left -= 10
    PictureBox12.Left -= 10
End Sub
```
Code 16.2

Now, run the project and you will see that the road lines are moving from right to left:

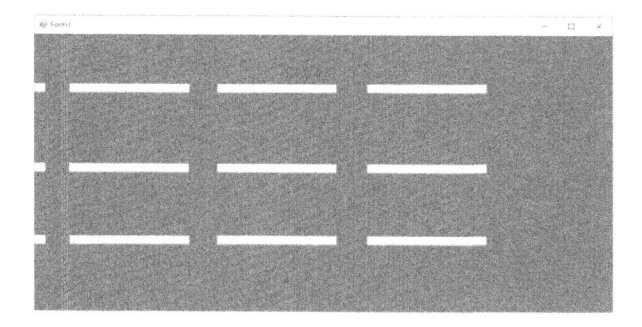

Figure 16.10. Road lines moving from right to left

The problem is that road lines completely disappear after somw time:

Figure 16.11. Road lines disppeared

We obviously need the road lines not to disappear. Therefore, we can repeat the road lines using an if statement inside the Timer1 Ticker method as follows:

```
If PictureBox1.Left + PictureBox1.Width <= 0 Then
    PictureBox1.Left = Me.Width
End If
```
Code 16.3

403

This if statement works as follows: When the left edge position + width of PictureBox1 is less than zero, i.e. leaves the screen, the left edge snapped to the left edge of the screen (Me.Width) therefore the user will see the road lines to continue as an animation. We need to repeat this condition for all road lines:

```
If PictureBox1.Left + PictureBox1.Width <= 0 Then
    PictureBox1.Left = Me.Width
End If
If PictureBox2.Left + PictureBox2.Width <= 0 Then
    PictureBox2.Left = Me.Width
End If
If PictureBox3.Left + PictureBox3.Width <= 0 Then
    PictureBox3.Left = Me.Width
End If
If PictureBox4.Left + PictureBox4.Width <= 0 Then
    PictureBox4.Left = Me.Width
End If
If PictureBox5.Left + PictureBox5.Width <= 0 Then
    PictureBox5.Left = Me.Width
End If
If PictureBox6.Left + PictureBox6.Width <= 0 Then
    PictureBox6.Left = Me.Width
End If
If PictureBox7.Left + PictureBox7.Width <= 0 Then
    PictureBox7.Left = Me.Width
End If
If PictureBox8.Left + PictureBox8.Width <= 0 Then
    PictureBox8.Left = Me.Width
End If
If PictureBox9.Left + PictureBox9.Width <= 0 Then
    PictureBox9.Left = Me.Width
End If
If PictureBox10.Left + PictureBox10.Width <= 0 Then
    PictureBox10.Left = Me.Width
End If
If PictureBox11.Left + PictureBox11.Width <= 0 Then
    PictureBox11.Left = Me.Width
End If
If PictureBox12.Left + PictureBox12.Width <= 0 Then
    PictureBox12.Left = Me.Width
End If
```

Code 16.4

16.2. Adding Cars to the Game

We will now add cars to the project. You can download the car pictures from the book's website at www.yamaclis.com/vbnet. There are two car pictures: white and blue. The user will control the white car while blue cars will be the enemy cars. First of all, please add a new PictureBox to the project and import the white car picture. We can choose the Stretch image selection as follows:

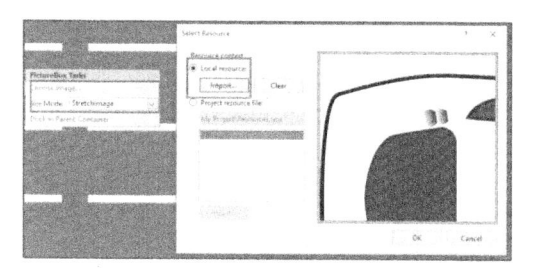

Figure 16.12. Adding the white car

I have renamed the white car's PictureBox as white_car for easier referencing from the code:

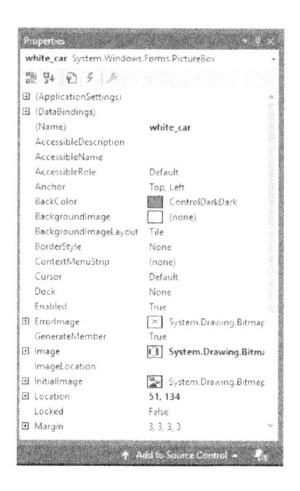

Figure 16.13. Naming the white car

The user will move the car up and down as the road animates hence our game program needs to respond to keyboard strokes. We'll use the

405

KeyDown event of the form for this aim. Let's select the form and then locate the KeyDown event in the Properties window:

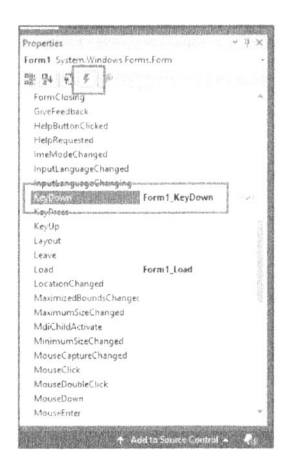

Figure 16.14. Creating the LeyDown event of the form

Double-click the KeyDown event and then we'll have the empty KeyDown event in the code window:

```
Private Sub Form1_KeyDown(sender As Object, e As
KeyEventArgs) Handles MyBase.KeyDown

End Sub
```
Code 16.5

If the key is Up key, the white car will move up a bit and if the key is the Down key, the car will move down a bit. We'll perform this by two If-Then statements as follows:

```
Private Sub Form1_KeyDown(sender As Object, e As
KeyEventArgs) Handles MyBase.KeyDown
    If e.KeyCode = Keys.Up Then
        white_car.Top -= 5
    End If
    If e.KeyCode = Keys.Down Then
        white_car.Top += 5
    End If
End Sub
```
Code 16.5

CHAPTER 16. DEVELOPING A CAR RACING GAME IN VISUAL BASIC.NET

Let's run the project and see how we control the car:

Figure 16.15. Our white car went down a bit after a few clicks to the Down key on the keyboard

The problem is that if we press the Up or Down key a lot, the car goes out off the scene:

Figure 16.16. The car went off the scene!

We will avoid this by adding two conditional statements as follows:

```
Private Sub Form1_KeyDown(sender As Object, e As
KeyEventArgs) Handles MyBase.KeyDown

    If e.KeyCode = Keys.Up Then
      If white_car.Top > 0 Then
         white_car.Top -= 5
      End If
    End If

    If e.KeyCode = Keys.Down Then
      If white_car.Top + white_car.Width < Me.Height Then
         white_car.Top += 5
```

407

```
            End If
        End If
End Sub
```

Code 16.5 (cont'd)

Now, white car is constrained on the scene. Let's add monster cars which will have random positions on the scene. We will again employ PictureBox tools for monster cars. Please download the blue_car.png image from the book's website and then add it to a PictureBox on the form. I have added it three times and named these PictureBoxes as blue_car_1, blue_car_2 and blue_car_3 in the project:

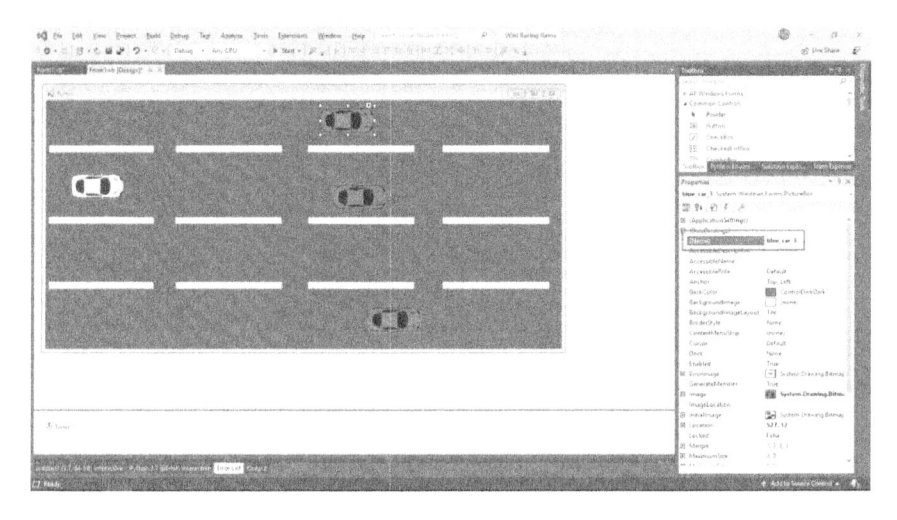

Figure 16.17. Enemy blue cars added to the scene

We will add a new Timer, Timer2, which will move the blue enemy cars to the form. Please enable Timer2, set its interval as 5 milliseconds and then double-click Timer2 to create its default event handler method as follows:

```
Private Sub Timer2_Tick(sender As Object, e As EventArgs) Handles Timer2.Tick

End Sub
```

Code 16.6

CHAPTER 16. DEVELOPING A CAR RACING GAME IN VISUAL BASIC.NET

When a blue car goes out off the scene, we will position it back to a random vertical position using the following code:

```
Private Sub Timer2_Tick(sender As Object, e As EventArgs)
Handles Timer2.Tick

blue_car_1.Left -= 5
If blue_car_1.Left < 0 Then
blue_car_1.Left = Me.Width
Randomize()blue_car_1.Top =
Convert.ToInt32(Math.Ceiling(Rnd() * 300))
End If

blue_car_2.Left -= 5
If blue_car_2.Left < 0 Then
blue_car_2.Left = Me.Width
Randomize()
blue_car_2.Top = Convert.ToInt32(Math.Ceiling(Rnd() * 400))
End If

blue_car_3.Left -= 5
If blue_car_3.Left < 0 Then
blue_car_3.Left = Me.Width
Randomize()
blue_car_3.Top = Convert.ToInt32(Math.Ceiling(Rnd() * 500))
End If

End Sub
```

Code 16.7

Here, the Randomize() function seeds the random number generator of the .NET framework and the Rnd() function generates a number between 0 and 1 randomly. We multiply that random number with a bigger number to obtain a meaningful position on the screen. Here's a snapshot of the scene after blue cars are repositioned:

409

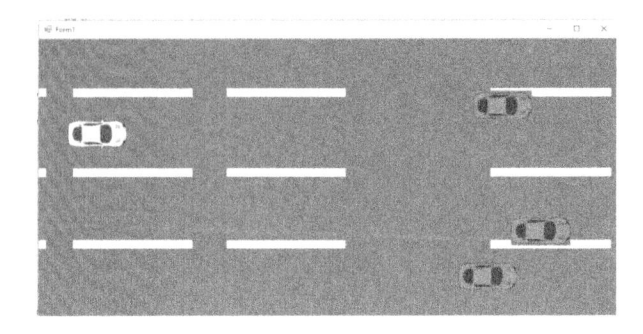

Figure 16.18. Blue cars after random vertical positioning

Let's make our game harder by changing the rate of change of blue car PictureBoxes in the Ticker2_Tick method as follows:

```
Private Sub Timer2_Tick(sender As Object, e As EventArgs) Handles Timer2.Tick

blue_car_1.Left -= 8
If blue_car_1.Left < 0 Then
blue_car_1.Left = Me.Width
Randomize()
blue_car_1.Top = Convert.ToInt32(Math.Ceiling(Rnd() * 300))
End If

blue_car_2.Left -= 5
If blue_car_2.Left < 0 Then
blue_car_2.Left = Me.Width
Randomize()
blue_car_2.Top = Convert.ToInt32(Math.Ceiling(Rnd() * 400))
End If

blue_car_3.Left -= 3
If blue_car_3.Left < 0 Then
blue_car_3.Left = Me.Width
Randomize()
blue_car_3.Top = Convert.ToInt32(Math.Ceiling(Rnd() * 500))
End If

End Sub
```
Code 16.8

All three blue cars will have different speeds now, you can chack this by running the game scene.

16.3. Displaying Score

The score will increase as the user continues to play, in other words, the score will be increasing with the playing time (until the car crashes). Therefore, we will display a score based on the ticks of Timer1 (main timer). Let's add a score TextBox to the scene and then rename it as score_textbox making its text colour red and font size 20 points:

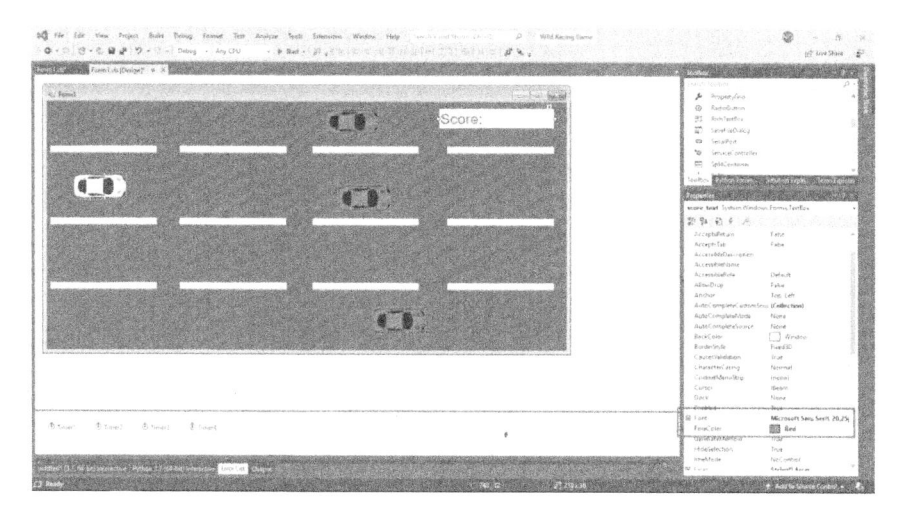

Figure 16.19. Adding a score TextBox

Then, let's change declare a score variable outside Timer1_Tick:

```
Dim score As Integer = 0
```
Code 16.9

And then update the score variable inside Timer1:

```
Private Sub Timer1_Tick(sender As Object, e As EventArgs) Handles Timer1.Tick

        ### PREVIOUS CODE LINES###

        score += 1
        score_text.Text = "Score:" + score.ToString()

    End Sub
```
Code 16.10

BEGINNER'S GUIDE TO VISUAL BASIC.NET PROGRAMMING

Note that we have code lines regarding to the PictureBoxes in Timer1_Tick function that are not shown here. When we run the project now, we will see that the score is continuously increasing:

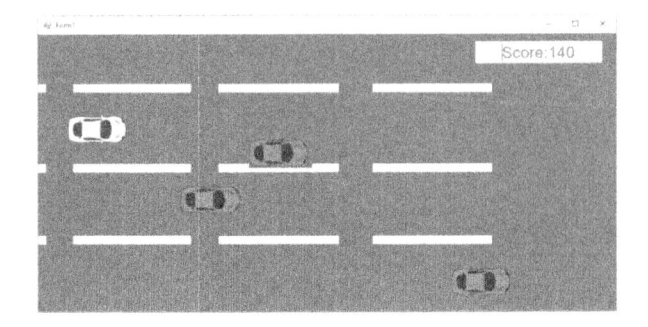

Figure 16.20. Score is displayed in a TextBox

16.4. Detecting Collosions and Ending the Game

VB.NET offers a handy function named IntersectsWith() to control if two controls colloides. We will use this function to check if our white car colloided with any of the blue cars. When the result of this function is True, this means the white car crashed and we will end the game by stopping the Timer1, Timer2 keyboard key controls and displaying a Game Over TextBox in the middle of the screen. Let's first add a game over TextBox in the middle of the screen:

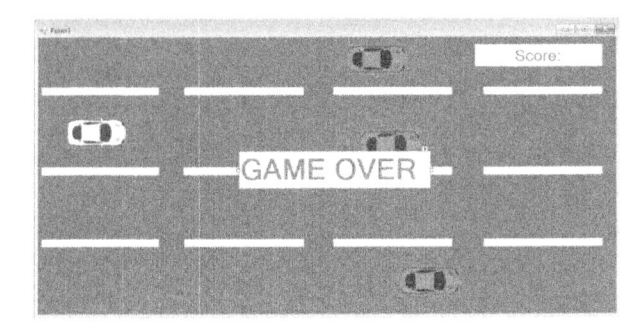

Figure 16.21. Adding the Game Over TextBox

We will set the visible property of this TextBox as False from the Properties window then the user will not see it until it is set as Visible again when the white car crashes:

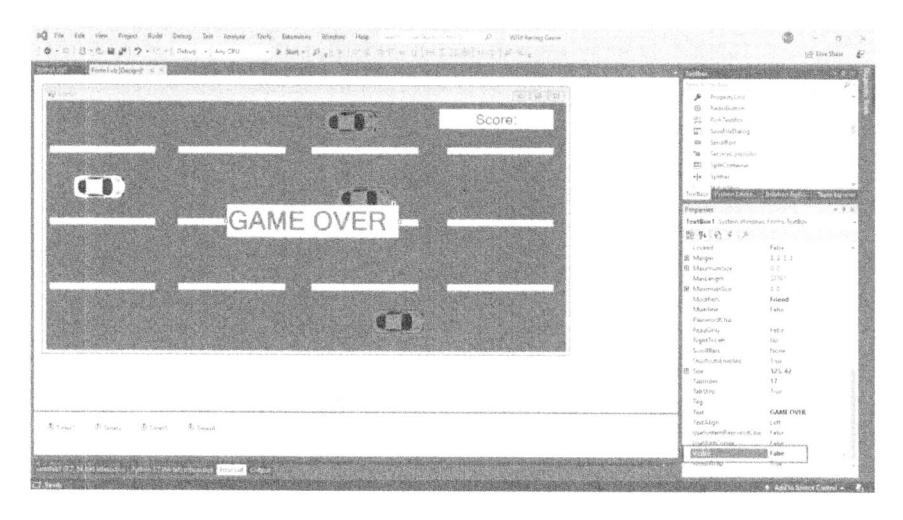

CHAPTER 16. DEVELOPING A CAR RACING GAME IN VISUAL BASIC.NET

Figure 16.22. Setting the Game Over TextBox's Visible property as False

When we run the project now, we will see that the Game Over TextBox is not seen on the scene:

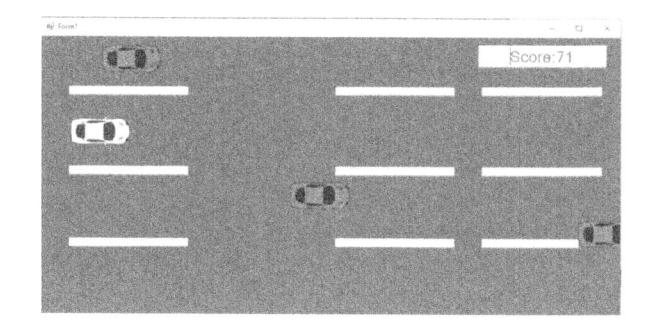

Figure 16.23. The Game Over TextBox not seen on the scene

Let's now turn to detect the collosions. We will check them in Timer2_Tick function as follows:

```
Private Sub Timer2_Tick(sender As Object, e As EventArgs)
Handles Timer2.Tick

    ### PREVIOUS CODE LINES ###

    If white_car.Bounds.IntersectsWith(blue_car_1.Bounds) Then
        gameover_textbox.Visible = True
```

413

```
            Timer1.Enabled = False
            Timer2.Enabled = False
    End If

     If white_car.Bounds.IntersectsWith(blue_car_2.Bounds) Then
        gameover_textbox.Visible = True
        Timer1.Enabled = False
         Timer2.Enabled = False
    End If

    If white_car.Bounds.IntersectsWith(blue_car_3.Bounds) Then
        gameover_textbox.Visible = True
        Timer1.Enabled = False
        Timer2.Enabled = False
    End If

    End Sub
```
Code 16.11

If our white car colloides with any of the blue cars, then the annoying big GAME OVER textbox will be visible and the game will stop. We stop the game by disabling timers as you can see above. The full code listing of our game project is given below for completeness:

```
Public Class Form1
    Dim score As Integer = 0
    Private Sub Timer1_Tick(sender As Object, e As
 EventArgs) Handles Timer1.Tick

            PictureBox1.Left -= 10
            PictureBox2.Left -= 10
            PictureBox3.Left -= 10
            PictureBox4.Left -= 10
            PictureBox5.Left -= 10
            PictureBox6.Left -= 10
            PictureBox7.Left -= 10
            PictureBox8.Left -= 10
            PictureBox9.Left -= 10
            PictureBox10.Left -= 10
            PictureBox11.Left -= 10
            PictureBox12.Left -= 10

            If PictureBox1.Left + PictureBox1.Width <= 0 Then
                PictureBox1.Left = Me.Width
            End If
            If PictureBox2.Left + PictureBox2.Width <= 0 Then
```

CHAPTER 16. DEVELOPING A CAR RACING GAME IN VISUAL BASIC.NET

```vb
            PictureBox2.Left = Me.Width
        End If
        If PictureBox3.Left + PictureBox3.Width <= 0 Then
            PictureBox3.Left = Me.Width
        End If
        If PictureBox4.Left + PictureBox4.Width <= 0 Then
            PictureBox4.Left = Me.Width
        End If
        If PictureBox5.Left + PictureBox5.Width <= 0 Then
            PictureBox5.Left = Me.Width
        End If
        If PictureBox6.Left + PictureBox6.Width <= 0 Then
            PictureBox6.Left = Me.Width
        End If
        If PictureBox7.Left + PictureBox7.Width <= 0 Then
            PictureBox7.Left = Me.Width
        End If
        If PictureBox8.Left + PictureBox8.Width <= 0 Then
            PictureBox8.Left = Me.Width
        End If
        If PictureBox9.Left + PictureBox9.Width <= 0 Then
            PictureBox9.Left = Me.Width
        End If
        If PictureBox10.Left + PictureBox10.Width <= 0 Then
            PictureBox10.Left = Me.Width
        End If
        If PictureBox11.Left + PictureBox11.Width <= 0 Then
            PictureBox11.Left = Me.Width
        End If
        If PictureBox12.Left + PictureBox12.Width <= 0 Then
            PictureBox12.Left = Me.Width
        End If

        score += 1
        score_text.Text = "Score:" + score.ToString()

    End Sub

Private Sub Form1_Load(sender As Object, e As EventArgs) Handles MyBase.Load
        score_text.BackColor = Color.Red
End Sub

Private Sub Form1_KeyDown(sender As Object, e As KeyEventArgs) Handles MyBase.KeyDown
        'MessageBox.Show("Key")
        If e.KeyCode = Keys.Up Then
            If white_car.Top > 0 Then
```

```vb
                    white_car.Top -= 5
                End If
            End If
            
            If e.KeyCode = Keys.Down Then
                If white_car.Top + white_car.Width < Me.Height Then
                    white_car.Top += 5
                End If
            End If
        End Sub
        
    Private Sub Timer2_Tick(sender As Object, e As EventArgs) Handles Timer2.Tick
    
     blue_car_1.Left -= 8
     If blue_car_1.Left < 0 Then
        blue_car_1.Left = Me.Width
        Randomize()
    blue_car_1.Top = Convert.ToInt32(Math.Ceiling(Rnd() * 300))
     End If
     
     blue_car_2.Left -= 5
     If blue_car_2.Left < 0 Then
        blue_car_2.Left = Me.Width
        Randomize()
    blue_car_2.Top = Convert.ToInt32(Math.Ceiling(Rnd() * 400))
     End If
    
    blue_car_3.Left -= 3
    If blue_car_3.Left < 0 Then
       blue_car_3.Left = Me.Width
       Randomize()
    blue_car_3.Top = Convert.ToInt32(Math.Ceiling(Rnd() * 500))
    End If
    
    If white_car.Bounds.IntersectsWith(blue_car_1.Bounds) Then
        gameover_textbox.Visible = True
        Timer1.Enabled = False
        Timer2.Enabled = False
    End If
    
    If white_car.Bounds.IntersectsWith(blue_car_2.Bounds) Then
        gameover_textbox.Visible = True
        Timer1.Enabled = False
        Timer2.Enabled = False
    End If
```

```
    If white_car.Bounds.IntersectsWith(blue_car_3.Bounds) Then
        gameover_textbox.Visible = True
        Timer1.Enabled = False
        Timer2.Enabled = False
    If

    End Sub
End Class
```

Code 16.12

You can now enjoy playing your very own game. Note that I have included a bare minimum for a simple racing game but you can add more properties such as cars with different colours, adding lives for our white car or even adding game sprites such as bushes or buildings to make your game more realistic. Please feel free to send your own game to me at syamacli@gmail.com if you want to challenge me with the most difficuult racing game ever made!

EPILOGUE

Thanks for utilizing my book for beginning your Visual Basic.NET programming journey! I really hope that you enjoyed this book and got some confidence for developing programs in VB.NET. If you would like to share your complaints and suggestions, please feel free to drop me an e-mail at syamacli@gmail.com or alternatively you can share it publicly on the comments section of the book's website www.yamaclis.com/vbnet.

This book is intended to be a beginner's guide. If you have followed this book thoroughly, you should be ready to learn more on VB.NET application development and the first source for this is, of course, the Internet. I recommend the following websites for advanced subjects:

- https://www.tutorialspoint.com/vb.net/index.htm
- https://www.vb-helper.com/
- https://www.vbtutor.net/index.php/visual-basic-net-tutorials/

I'd like to finish this book with the following quotes which I think have deep meanings:

> "Information is the resolution of uncertainty."
>
> Claude Shannon, PhD

> "You need to study other people's work. Their approaches to problem solving and the tools they use give you a fresh way to look at your own work."
>
> Gary Kildall, PhD

——————— References and the password on the next page ———————

REFERENCES

1. https://docs.microsoft.com/en-us/visualstudio/get-started/visual-basic/tutorial-console?view=vs-2019

2. https://www.vbtutor.net

3. http://www.tiobe.com/tiobe-index/

4. Rod Stephens, Stephens' Visual Basic Programming 24-Hour Trainer, Wrox, 2011.

5. Bryan Newsome, Beginning Visual Basic 2015, Wrox, 2015.

6. Alessandro Del Sole, Visual Basic 2015 Unleashed, Sams Publishing, 2015.

You may be interested in my other programming books in the "Yamacli's Beginner's Guide Series" which are also available from Amazon:

1. S. Yamacli, Beginner's Guide to C# Programming: A Practical Approach in Visual Studio, ISBN-13: 978-1548495176, 2017.

2. S. Yamacli, Beginner's Guide to Andoid App Development: A Practical Approach in Android Studio, ISBN-13: 978-1548088163, 2017.

Password for the compressed project files and figures you can download from the book's website www.yamaclis.com/vbnet **is: VBNET2020**

——————— Keep calm because it's the end ☺ ———————

Printed in Great Britain
by Amazon